Explorations
in
Human Potentialities

Explorations in Human Potentialities

Compiled and Edited by

HERBERT A. OTTO, Ph.D.

Associate Professor, the Graduate School of Social Work
Director, The Human Potentialities Research Project
The University of Utah
Salt Lake City, Utah

CHARLES C THOMAS • PUBLISHER
Springfield • Illinois • U.S.A.

Published and Distributed Throughout the World by

CHARLES C THOMAS • PUBLISHER
BANNERSTONE HOUSE
301-327 East Lawrence Avenue, Springfield, Illinois, U.S.A.
NATCHEZ PLANTATION HOUSE
735 North Atlantic Boulevard, Fort Lauderdale, Florida, U.S.A.

Library of Congress Catalog Card Number: 66-18935

With THOMAS BOOKS careful attention is given to all details of manufacturing and design. It is the Publisher's desire to present books that are satisfactory as to their physical qualities and artistic possibilities and appropriate for their particular use. THOMAS BOOKS will be true to those laws of quality that assure a good name and good will.

Printed in the United States of America
C-1

CONTRIBUTORS

BENSMAN, JOSEPH, Ph.D., *Associate Professor at City College of the City University of New York.* Dr. Bensman has written articles for the *American Journal of Sociology, American Sociological Review, Human Organization, Social Research* and *Social Problems.* His books include: *Reflections on the Community* (co-editor with A. J. Vidich and Maurice Stein), Wiley, 1964; *Mass, Class and Bureaucracy,* Prentice-Hall, 1962; *Small Town in a Mass Society,* Princeton University Press, 1958 and Anchor Books, 1960; and *The Human Shape of Work* (co-contributor), Macmillan, 1964.

BERGER, MILTON M., M.D., *Educational Director (and Past President) of Association for Group Psychoanalysis and Process, Inc., New York City; Fellow (and Past President) of American Group Psychotherapy Association; and Group Psychotherapy Consultant to: U.S. Naval Hospital, St. Albans, New York; Veterans' Administration Clinic, New York City; Hillside Hospital, Glen Oaks, New York, and Quaker Committee on Social Rehabilitation.* Dr. Berger's publications include articles in the *International Journal of Group Psychotherapy, American Journal of Psychotherapy, Psychosomatics, International Journal of Social Psychiatry* and *American Journal of Psychiatry.* Dr. Berger has edited two books; one *Group Psychotherapy and Group Function* was co-edited with Max Rosenbaum, Ph.D., New York, Basic Books, 1963. His other book is *The Development of Group Psychotherapy Programs in Various Existing Settings,* Proceedings of the Second Annual Institute of the American Group Psychotherapy Association, edited by Dr. Berger and Maurice E. Linden, M.D., published by A.G.P.A., New York.

BIRDWHISTELL, RAY L., Ph.D., *Professor of Research in Anthropology, Department of Psychiatry, Temple University Medical Center and Senior Research Scientist at Eastern Pennsylvania Psychiatric Institute.* Articles by Dr. Birdwhistell have appeared in *Child Study, American Anthropologist, International Journal of Group Psychotherapy, Human Organization* and *Family Process.* His books include *Introduction to Kinesics,* University of Louisville Press, 1952, and *The Natural History of an Interview,* Grune and Stratton (in press) and contributions in *Expression of the Emotions in Man,* International Universities Press, 1963, and *Teaching of Psychotherapy,* Little, Brown and Company, 1964, and others.

BLOM, GASTON E., M.D., *Professor of Psychiatry and Director of Day Care Center, Child Psychiatry Division, Department of Psychiatry, University of Colorado Medical Center, Denver, Colorado.* Dr. Blom has published extensively in *American Journal of Orthopsychiatry, Pediatrics, American Journal of Psychiatry, Journal of the American Psychoanalytic Association* and *Psychology in the Schools.* He has also written chapters for the following books: *Psychoanalytic Study of the Child,* Volume VII, International Universities Press, 1952; *Dynamic Psychopathology in Childhood,* Grune and Stratton, 1959; *Case Studies of Emotional Disturbances in Children,* American Orthopsychiatric Association, 1953; and *Emotional Problems of Early Childhood,* Basic Books, 1955.

BRANCH, C. H. HARDIN, M.D., *Professor and Head, Department of Psychiatry, College of Medicine, University Medical Center, Salt Lake City, Utah; Psychiatrist-in-Chief of the University Hospital, Salt Lake City; and Consultant in Psychiatry at the Veterans' Administration Hospital since 1952.* Dr. Branch was President of the American Psychiatric Association in 1963. He wrote *Anorexia Nervosa* with Eugene L. Bliss, M.D., published by Paul B. Hoeber, Inc., 1960, and has written extensively in such journals as the *American Journal of Psychiatry, Rocky Mountain Medical Journal, The International Journal of Social Psychiatry, Mental Hygiene* and *Archives of General Psychiatry.*

BROOKS, CHARLES V. W.

BROWN, J. H. U., Ph.D., *Assistant Chief for Operations, Division of Research Facilities and Resources, Department of Health, Education and Welfare, Public Health Service, National Institutes of Health, PHS, DHEW.* His publications include articles in *American Journal of Physiology, Endocrinology, Journal of Laboratory and Clinical Medicine, Journal of Aviation Medicine* and *Journal of Biophysical and Biochemical Cytology.* Dr. Brown has written two books, *Physiology of Man in Space,* Academic Press, New York, 1963, and *Basic Endocrinology,* F. A. Davis Co., Philadelphia, 1962.

BUHLER, CHARLOTTE, Ph.D., *Diplomate in Clinical Psychology and American Board of Examiners in Professional Psychology; Assistant Clinical Professor of Psychiatry, University of Southern California Medical School, Los Angeles, California; and President, American Association for Humanistic Psychology.* Articles by Dr. Buhler have been published in *American Journal of Psychiatry, Journal of Existential Psychiatry, Psychological Reports, American Journal of Psychoanalysis* and *Journal of Humanistic Psychology,* among others. Her books include: *The First Year of Life,* John Day, New York, 1930; *Childhood Problems and the Teacher,* Henry Holt, New York, 1952; *The Human Course of Life as a Psychological Problem,* second revised German edition, *Verlag fur Psychologie,* Gottingen, 1959; and *Values in Psychotherapy,* Free Press of Glencoe, New York, 1962.

DREIKURS, RUDOLPH, M.D., *Director, Alfred Adler Institute, Chicago; and Professor of Psychiatry, Chicago Medical School; Visiting Professor to Southern Illinois University, University of Oregon, BarIlan University and Tel Aviv University in Israel.* Among Dr. Dreikurs' publications are articles in *Journal of Individual Psychology, Group Psychotherapy, Psychiatric Quarterly, School and Society, American Journal of Psychiatry* and *International Journal of Social Psychiatry.* His books include: *Seelische Impotenz,* S. Hirzel, Leipzig, 1931; *Das Nervoese Symptom,* m. Perles, Wien, 1932; *The Challenge of Marriage,* Duell, Sloan & Pearce, 1946; *The Challenge of Parenthood,* Duell, Sloan & Pearce, 1948; *Cultural Upheaval and Modern Family Life,* Community Child Guidance Centers, 1950; *Fundamentals of Adlerian Psychology,* Greenberg, 1950; *Character Education and Spiritual Values in an Anxious Age,* Beacon Press, 1952; *Psychology in the Classroom,* Harper & Brothers, 1957; *Encouraging Children to Learn* (with Don Dinkmeyer), Prentice-Hall, 1963; and *Children: The Challenge* (with Vicki Soltz), Duell, Sloan & Pearce, 1964.

DUNN, HALBERT L., M.D., Ph.D., *Consultant on Aging to the U. S. Office of Education; Chairman, Prince George's County Commission on Aging (Maryland); Consultant and Lecturer in high-level wellness (formerly Chief of the National Office of Vital Statistics for many years); originator of the "High-Level Wellness" Concept.* Dr. Dunn has published widely in *Journal of the National Medical Association, American Journal of Public Health, Canadian Journal of Public Health, Journal of the American Statistical Association* and *Public Health Reports,* among others. He has written *High-Level Wellness,* a collection of twenty-nine short talks on different aspects of the theme "High-Level Wellness for Man and Society" (April, 1961).

ENGLISH, O. SPURGEON, M.D., *Professor of Psychiatry, Temple University Health Sciences Center, Philadelphia, Pennsylvania.* Books by Dr. English include: *Emotional Problems of Living,* W. W. Norton, 1945, revised, 1962; *Psychosomatic Medicine,* W. B. Saunders, 1943, revised, 1949; *Introduction to Psychiatry,* W. W. Norton, 1954; and *Direct Analysis and Schizophrenia,* Grune & Stratton, 1961.

FREYTAG, FREDERICKA F., M.D., *is a practicing psychiatrist and served as Consultant in Psychiatric Research at Wright Patterson Air Force Base from 1961 to 1964.* She has written articles for *American Journal of Clinical Hypnosis* and two books, *The Hypnoanalysis of an Anxiety Hysteria,* The Julian Press, 1959, and *Hypnosis and the Body Image,* The Julian Press, 1961.

GOLEMBIEWSKI, ROBERT T., Ph.D., *Associate Professor of Political Science and Management, University of Georgia.* Dr. Golembiewski has written articles for *Administrative Science Quarterly, American Political*

Science Review, International Review of Administrative Sciences and Personnel and *Public Administration Review*. He is author of: *The Small Group*, University of Chicago Press, 1962; *Behavior and Organization*, Rand McNally, 1962; *Men, Management, and Morality*, McGraw-Hill, 1965; *The Administrator's Many Worlds*, Rand McNally (forthcoming); and *Organizing Men and Power*, Rand McNally (forthcoming).

HALL, PETER M., Ph.D., *Assistant Professor, Department of Sociology, University of California at Santa Barbara, Santa Barbara, California.*

HARMAN, WILLIS W., Ph.D., *Professor, Department of Electrical Engineering, Stanford University, and Associate Director, Institute for Psychedelic Research, San Francisco State College.* His publications include contributions in the *Journal of Humanistic Psychology, Main Currents in Modern Thought, Journal of Neuropsychiatry* and *Psychological Reports.* Dr. Harman is the author of: *Fundamentals of Electronic Motion*, McGraw-Hill, 1952; *Electrical and Mechanical Networks* (with D. W. Lytle), McGraw-Hill, 1962; and *Introduction to Statistical Communication Theory*, McGraw-Hill, 1963.

HEILBRUN, ALFRED B., JR., Ph.D., *Professor of Psychology, Director of Clinical Training and Director of the Psychological Center, Emory University, Atlanta, Georgia.* Articles by Dr. Heilbrun have been published in *Journal of Comparative and Physiological Psychology, Journal of Consulting Psychology, Journal of Abnormal and Social Psychology, Journal of Applied Psychology* and *Child Development.*

HEIST, PAUL A., Ph.D., *Research Psychologist, Center for the Study of Higher Education, University of California, Berkeley, California.* His publications include articles in *Science, Journal of Educational Sociology, Educational Record, Journal of College Student Personnel* and *Review of Educational Research.* He has written chapters for the following books: *The American College*, Wiley and Sons, 1962; *Education for the Professions*, University of Chicago Press, 1962; and *The Superior Student in American Higher Education*, McGraw-Hill, 1965.

JOURARD, SIDNEY M., Ph.D., *Professor of Psychology, University of Florida.* Among Dr. Jourard's publications are articles in *Journal of Abnormal Social Psychology, Journal of Consulting Psychology, Journal of Humanistic Psychology, Journal of Existential Psychiatry, Review of Existential Psychology and Psychiatry*, and two books: *Personal Adjustment: An Approach Through the Study of Healthy Personality*, Macmillan, New York, 1958, second edition, 1963; and *The Transparent Self*, Van Nostrand, Princeton, 1964.

KORNER, IJA N., Ph.D., *Associate Professor of Psychiatry (Psychology), University of Utah College of Medicine.* Dr. Korner has written for *Amer-*

ican Psychologist, Contemporary Psychology, International Journal of Social Psychiatry, Consulting Psychology and *Anthropologica.* A book by Dr. Korner, *Repressive Forgetting,* was published by Teacher's College, Columbia University, 1950.

MARTINDALE, DON, Ph.D., *Professor of Sociology, University of Minnesota.* Dr. Martindale has written the following books: *Elements of Sociology* (with E. D. Monachesi), Harper & Bros., 1951; *The Nature and Types of Sociological Theory,* Houghton Mifflin, 1960; *American Social Structure,* Appleton-Century-Crofts, 1960; *American Society,* D. Van Nostrand, 1960; *Social Life and Cultural Change,* D. Van Nostrand, 1962; *Community, Character and Civilization,* The Free Press of Glencoe, 1963. He is also editor and translator of four books by Max Weber and editor of *Functionalism in the Social Sciences,* Special Monograph No. 5, in a series sponsored by the *American Academy of Political and Social Science,* Philadelphia, 1965.

McDONALD, FREDERICK J., Ph.D., *Associate Professor of Education and Psychology, Stanford University.* Dr. McDonald has written articles for *Business Education Forum, Journal of Educational Research, Child Development, AV Communication Review* and others. His books include *Educational Psychology,* Wadsworth Publishing Company, San Francisco, 1959, second edition, 1965 (Asian edition, Overseas Publications, Ltd., Kaigai Suppan Boeki, K.K., Tokyo; British edition, Prentice-Hall, International, Inc., London, 1961). He wrote chapters for *On Becoming an Educator,* Houghton-Mifflin, New York, 1963, and *Theories of Learning and Instruction,* E. R. Hilgard, Ed., 63rd Yearbook of the National Society for the Study of Education, Part I, Chicago, University of Chicago Press, 1964.

MEAD, MARGARET, Ph.D., *Curator of Ethnology, The American Museum of Natural History, and Adjunct Professor of Anthropology, Columbia University.* Publications by Dr. Mead include articles in *Science, The American Anthropologist, The American Scholar, Journal of Orthopsychiatry* and *Harvard Business Review.* Dr. Mead has written: *Coming of Age in Samoa,* 1928; *Growing up in New Guinea,* 1935; *Sex and Temperament in Three Primitive Societies,* 1935; *and Keep Your Powder Dry,* 1942; and *New Lives for Old,* 1956, all published by William Morrow and Company, New York; and *Continuities in Cultural Evolution,* Yale University Press, New Haven, 1964.

MOGAR, ROBERT EDWARD, Ph.D., *Associate Professor of Psychology, San Francisco State College and Director of Research, International Foundation for Advanced Study.* Dr. Mogar has published articles in the *Journal of Abnormal and Social Psychology, Journal of Consulting Psychology, Psychotherapy: Theory, Research and Practice* and *Journal of Humanistic Psychology.*

MORENO, J. L., M.D., *President, International Council of Group Psychotherapy and the World Center for Psychodrama, Sociometry and Group Psychotherapy; Former President of the American Sociometric Association and Adjunct Professor, New York University, Department of Arts and Science (1951-1964).* Articles by Dr. Moreno have apeared in *Group Psychotherapy* and *International Journal of Sociometry and Sociatry* (of which he is editor), as well as the *American Journal of Psychiatry, L'Evolution, Psychiatrique* and *Mental Health.* His books include *Psychodrama;* Volumes I and II, Beacon House, 1946 and 1958; *Who Shall Survive,* Beacon House, 1934; *Sociometry and the Science of Man,* Beacon House, 1956; *Progress in Psychotherapy,* Volumes I to V, Grune and Stratton, 1956-1961; *The Sociometry Reader,* Free Press of Glencoe, 1959, and *The International Handbook of Group Psychotherapy,* Philosophical Library, 1965.

MURPHY, GARDNER, Ph.D., *holds the Dr. Henry March Pfeiffer Research-Training Chair in Psychiatry and is Director of Research at the Menninger Foundation.* While Chairman of the Department of Psychology at the City College of New York, he collaborated with honors students in a series of studies showing the role of feeling and emotion in perception, memory and other processes and published his chief systematic work, *Personality: A Biosocial Approach to Origins and Structure.* Some of his recent publications are: *Human Potentialities,* Basic Books, 1958; *Development of the Perceptual World* (with Charles M. Solley), Basic Books, 1960; *William James on Psychical Research* (edited with Robert Ballou), Viking, 1960; *Challenge of Psychical Research: A Primer of Parapsychology* (edited with Laura A. Dale), Harper, 1961; *Freeing Intelligence Through Teaching: A Dialectic of the Rational and the Personal,* Harper, 1961.

MURPHY, LOIS BARCLAY, *is Research Psychologist at the Menninger Foundation and Chairman of the Governor's Committee on Preschool Retardation in Kansas.*

OTTO, HERBERT A., Ph.D., *is Associate Professor in the Graduate School of Social Work at the University of Utah, Salt Lake City, Utah, and Director of the Human Potentialities Research Project.* Articles by Dr. Otto have appeared in *Mental Hygiene, Marriage and Family Living, International Journal of Social Psychiatry, Group Psychotherapy* and *Social Casework.* Dr. Otto has written *Your Potentialities: The Undiscovered Self,* University Books, Inc., New Hyde Park, New York, 1966, and co-authored a book with Nina R. Garton entitled *The Development of Theory and Practice in Social Casework,* Charles C Thomas, Springfield, Illinois, 1964.

PEARSON, LEONARD, Ph.D., *Associate Professor of Psychology, Western Reserve University, Cleveland, Ohio.* Dr. Pearson has published articles in the *Archives of Physical Medicine and Rehabilitation* and *The Gerontologist.* He has written a book, *The Use of Written Communication in Psychotherapy,* Charles C Thomas, 1965.

PERLS, FREDERICK, M.D., *Consultant psychiatrist and private practice.* His books include *Ego, Hunger and Aggression,* Allan and Unwin, London, 1947, and *Gestalt Therapy, Excitement and Growth of the Human Personality* (with Ralph Hefferline and Paul Goodman), Julian Press, New York City, 1950.

RHINE, JOSEPH BANKS, Ph.D., *Executive Director, Foundation for Research on the Nature of Man, and Formerly Professor of Psychology, Duke University, and Director of the Parapsychology Laboratory.* His publications include writings in *Scientific Monthly, Science, Proceedings Royal Society of Medicine* and *Journal of Parapsychology.* Books by Dr. Rhine are: *Extrasensory Perception,* Boston, Bruce Humphries, 1934; *Extrasensory Perception After Sixty Years* (jointly with four others), New York, Henry Holt, 1940; *New Frontiers of the Mind,* New York, Farrar and Rinehart, 1937; *New Frontiers of the Mind,* London, Faber & Faber, 1938; *The Reach of the Mind,* New York, Apollo Editions, 1961; *New World of the Mind,* New York, William Sloane, 1953; and *Parapsychology, Frontier Science of the Mind* (with J. G. Pratt), Charles C Thomas, Springfield, Illinois, 1957; and *Extra-Sensory Perception,* Boston, Bruce Humphries, 1964.

ROSENBERG, BERNARD, Ph.D., *Associate Professor at the City College of New York, and Visiting Professor, Graduate Faculty of the New School for Social Research. Currently Senior Investigator: Various Projects for the Lavenburg-Notre Dame Cross-Cultural Studies and Consultant for the President's Committee on Juvenile Delinquency and Youth Crime, Mobilization for Youth, New York University Work Program, and others.* Periodicals which have included articles by Dr. Rosenberg are *Social Problems, American Scholar, American Journal of Economics and Sociology, American Journal of Sociology* and *Social Research.* His books are: *The Values of Veblen,* 1956; *Sociological Theory,* 1957 (second edition, 1964), co-editor and co-author; *Mass Culture,* 1957; *Thorstein Veblen,* 1963; *Mass, Class and Bureaucracy,* 1963; *Mass Society in Crisis,* 1964 (co-author and co-editor); and *The Vanguard Artist,* 1965.

RUDNICK, MARK, Ph.D., *Assistant Professor in the Division of Clinical Psychology and Assistant Director of the Day Care Center, University of Colorado Medical Center, Denver, Colorado.* He has had an article published in *Psychology in the Schools.*

SELVER, CHARLOTTE, *Staff Member of the New School for Social Research.* She has published articles in the *General Semantics Bulletin.*

STOODLEY, BARTLETT H., Ph.D., *Professor of Sociology at Wellesley College.* Articles by Dr. Stoodley have been published in *American Sociological Review, American Journal of Sociology* and *American Anthropologist.* His books include *The Concepts of Sigmund Freud,* Free Press, 1959, and *Society and Self,* editor, Free Press, 1962.

TORRANCE, E. PAUL, Ph.D., *is Professor of Educational Psychology at the University of Minnesota.* He is author of *Guiding Creative Talent,* Prentice-Hall, and *Education and the Creative Potential,* University of Minnesota Press. The Research Awards Committee of the American Personnel and Guidance Association cited *Guiding Creative Talent* as the outstanding contribution to original research in its field in 1962-63, and the book is now being translated into Japanese. The National Education Association selected *Education and the Creative Potential* as one of the three most outstanding education books in the general field of education in 1963-64.

VAN KAAM, ADRIAN, C.S. Sp., Ph.D., *Associate Professor of Psychology and Director of the Institute of Man, Duquesne University, and editor of the Review of Existential Psychology and Psychiatry.* His publications include articles in *Review of Existential Psychology and Psychiatry, Insight, Harvard Educational Review, Journal of Humanistic Psychology* and *Journal of Individual Psychology.* He has written *A Light to the Gentiles,* Bruce Company, 1962, and *Religion and Personality,* Prentice-Hall, Inc., 1964.

VEROFF, JOSEPH, Ph.D., *Senior Study Director, Survey Research Center and Associate Professor of Psychology at the University of Michigan.* Dr. Veroff has written articles for *Journal of Abnormal and Social Psychology* and *American Sociological Review.*

WEIMAN, EDWARD A., B.A., *is teacher at the Day Care Center, Department of Psychiatry, University of Colorado Medical Center, Denver, Colorado.*

WELLS, DONALD A., Ph.D., *Professor and Chairman of the Philosophy Department, Washington State University, Pullman, Washington.* Dr. Wells has had articles published in the *Journal of Philosophy, Crozer Quarterly* and *Crane Review.* He also has written a book entitled *God, Man, and the Thinker: Philosophies of Religion,* Random House, 1962.

INTRODUCTION

THE dimensions of the human potential are only beginning to be understood; yet if man is the instrument of his own evolution and development, knowledge of his potential is indispensable. The subject of human potentialities is emerging as a discrete area of research. It is the purpose and hope of this volume to illuminate the vistas of human potentialities and to "break ground" on avenues of research which can turn these potentialities into actualities. The findings from research in human potentialities have implications not only for the social scientist, social planner and educator, but also for business and industry, the helping professions, psychiatrist, psychologist and social worker as well as the geriatric specialist.

For some, the concept of human potentialities still represents a specie of unorthodox if not wishful thinking. Because of the history and development of the behavioral sciences, trustees and boards of directors of foundations have concentrated much of their enormous funds on the study of illness in an attempt to help man toward wellness. In view of current scientific advances perhaps we are now at the point of realizing that to discover the secret of man's health and optimum functioning, we must turn to the study of healthy man and the unfolding of his potentialities. For those concerned with the investigation of illness and dysfunction this area of research should also hold interest, for the study of health is a requisite to the full understanding of illness.

For the first time professionals from the various behavioral sciences are contributing their ideas on human potentialities in one volume. Certainly this volume is a "straw in the wind" and indicates a readiness for the next step—concentrated research in the area of human potentialities with an emphasis on holistic frameworks and the evaluation of findings and methods *in situs:* in the family; in society; and on the job. As an immediate next step the establishment of an Institute of Human Potentialities suggests itself. It would be the purpose of the Institute to seek out the extensive findings and data from diverse fields which are already available but which have not been adequately related to the uncovering and utilization of latent human powers. An interdisciplinary, imaginative, many-fronted holistic depth approach to man's potential would be undertaken to develop means and methods designed to help the well-functioning person make better use of his huge potential. The Institute would stimulate research, conduct independent studies and establish laboratory groups in business and industry in an effort to effect maximal testing and utilization of findings.

An awakening to the significance of the human potential is not restricted to this country. In an official publication of the USSR dated November, 1964 *(USSR, Soviet Life Today,* "Pedagogical Quests," pp. 42-45), reporting the work by Vasili Davydov of the Moscow Institute of Psychology, we find the following under the heading of "Inexhaustible Brain Potential:"

> The latest findings in anthropology, psychology, logic and physiology show that the potential of the human mind is very great indeed. "As soon as modern science gave us some understanding of the structure and work of the human brain, we were struck by its enormous reserve capacity," writes Yefremov (Ivan Yefremov, eminent Soviet scholar and writer). "Man, under average conditions of work and life, uses only a small part of his thinking equipment. . . .
>
> "If we were able to force our brain to work at only half its capacity, we could, without any difficulty whatever, learn forty languages, memorize the Large Soviet Encyclopedia from cover to cover, and complete the required courses of dozens of colleges."
>
> The statement is hardly an exaggeration. It is the generally accepted theoretical view of man's mental potentialities.
>
> How can we tap this gigantic potential? It is a big and very complex problem with many ramifications.

Research in the USSR might accelerate and complement work conducted in this country and open avenues to cooperative research ventures and increased sharing of information and understanding between scientists of both nations.

It is possible to view the vast concentration of resources and energy bent on the conquest of outer space as but one more manifestation of man's flight from his inner universe which is his cornucopia. Is man afraid of the tremendous powers locked within his organism? In an age which has spawned the first man-made threat to the survival of the species, does man have a *special responsibility to develop his inner self* and bring to flowering his latent possibilities—which include the potential for survival? *Recognition that healthy humanity is operating at 10 to 15 per cent of its potential represents the major challenge and the major promise of this age.*

The close interrelationship between man's social and institutional structures and his potentialities is a theme touched on in many of the papers which make up this volume. Unquestionably, institutional regeneration leading to a healthy society cannot be separated from helping members of society to achieve healthier and more optimal functioning.

Finally, there are now many signs that we have entered the travail of a major revolution: We are undergoing a change in the image of man. The old images are being discarded, and a new image is in the making—*man as the shaper of his own boundless potentialities.* It is an image of HOPE and of BECOMING.

All papers except one in this volume are original contributions. As always in a compilation of contributions from diverse fields, a number of regrettable gaps are demonstrable. These gaps will hopefully be filled by articles in professional and scientific journals.

Sarah M. Otto and Dean Hepworth gave freely of their suggestions and reactions in relation to this volume. Mrs. Nancy Osmond, in her capacity as secretary and editorial assistant, did invaluable work in the preparation of manuscripts. Grateful acknowledgment of their help is hereby extended.

HERBERT A. OTTO

CONTENTS

PART I

HUMAN POTENTIALITIES: SOME BASIC FRAMEWORKS

PART II

SOCIETY AND HUMAN POTENTIALITIES

PART III

THE ROLE OF EDUCATION

PART IV

CONTRIBUTIONS OF THE DISCIPLINES

PART V

CURRENT INVESTIGATIONS IN HUMAN POTENTIALITIES

PART VI

MEANS AND METHODS DESIGNED TO ACTUATE HUMAN POTENTIAL

Explorations
in
Human Potentialities

PART I

HUMAN POTENTIALITIES: SOME BASIC FRAMEWORKS

Chapter 1

HUMAN NATURE AND HUMAN POTENTIALITIES: IMAGINATION AND THE IMAGINARY

GARDNER MURPHY and LOIS BARCLAY MURPHY

WE believe that this volume and the thinking that has gone into it represent a bold attempt to define where American life is going and, better yet, where it *can* go if planfully considered and intelligently implemented through a combination of broad wisdom and specific technical know-how. Our task is simply to map the main areas in which the study of human potentialities can be productive.

From the point of view of one willing to exercise the boldest possible imagination regarding the future of mankind, the only impossible futures are those which involve contradiction in terms. All other trends can be worked out on the drawing board in what Nathan Israeli called a "museum of the future." We can begin immediately with taxonomic groupings of present biological and cultural realities and possibilities, carry their "world-lines" into the future, let them interact and develop into new fantasy worlds and use the feedback from these possible new worlds to throw light on the path we tread today. Mutations, biochemical changes through nutrition and pharmaceuticals, physical, intellectual and social remaking through food, exercise, regimen, child-rearing, schooling and improved adult intercommunication and intercultural relations give us more new worlds than we can adequately assess. If we disagree on the kinds of worlds that are to be wanted, there is the possibility that the reasons for these disagreements may be understood and that we may find a way to utilize the common or basic human realities that we all seek. Even so, there must be a dash of genius leadership here and there to permit us to see more sharply defined areas where there are possible choices. The only trouble with any such schema is that it will fall flat and become insipid in comparison with the actual changes that are opening up before us, just as science fiction, conjured out of the imaginings of fiction writers, regularly fails to equal the cogency and the brilliance of scientific discovery as it actually occurs in the laboratories from the imaginative efforts of great scientists.

Still we must plan our approach, being as systematic as we know how, and peering into the future, even into the perilous abysses, with full awareness that our culture, even our species, may well die within this era of science and technology.

We shall divide our introductory panorama of the human possibilities into a few main themes: the view of human potentialities from the vantage point of evolutionary biology; a cross-cultural and historical view of the modalities in which biological variation, selection and adaptation are occurring and will occur; the problem of drives and growth in bio-social terms with special reference to the ways in which growth potentials are fulfilled or thwarted by bio-social barriers and restraints; the question of limits, how these limits are set, both in qualitative and in quantitative terms, and what the absolute barriers are which prevent transitions in one or another direction; the role of individual human leadership at various levels in the realization of such emerging potentialities; and what can be done by thought and research effort to release through genetics, home environment, education, public communication and public action, the general potentials of mankind and the special gifts through which its specialized fulfillment, its specific human potentials, may be realized.

EVOLUTIONARY VIEWPOINT

The evolutionary viewpoint of today still emphasizes the principle of natural selection. If we plan for a new evolution, we must still plan within the structure of the possible. That survives which is fittest to survive in a particular ecological niche. Those species, those individuals who arise "fortuitously," that is, without specific planning so far as we know, are selected by the environment itself, including the corners in the world where there are favorable temperatures, acid-base balances, foods, absence of predators, opportunities for successful multiplication, etc. There may be, as some geneticists hold, guiding or controlling factors, sometimes called macro-evolutionary factors; but for the moment they are not essential for our present purpose. What is essential is the conception that the environment sets relative or absolute limits. The ceaselessly changing, restless, innovating character of biochemical process, as with viruses and bacteria, creates forms sufficiently unstable to permit variations from among which a few are chosen for persisting existence.

Whether life drifted here from somewhere else or arose solely because of terrestrial conditions, it must at least *meet* such conditions; and it is this ecological note with which we must necessarily begin. No theory of human potentialities is of much use unless it recognizes the physics and chemistry of a rather narrow and coercive system of regulating conditions within which all effective creativity must work, and, at the same time, unless it recognizes the reality of the plant and animal worlds upon which we depend, with which we sometimes compete and in reference to which we constantly remake the terrestrial world in which we ourselves exist. For example, when we get through the present excitement about landing men on the moon, we shall begin to realize that the floor of the ocean, and indeed the whole of the ocean, represents a vast and by no means unconquerable domain for study by oceanographers, biologists and psychologists. It is the physical, chemical and biological limitations alone of the ocean which can determine what human invention may concoct in the field of oceanography. We can say that except within a little self-made capsule built according to his own ecology, man cannot exist outside certain temperature and oxygen pressure conditions; neither can he use the flora and fauna nor even the minerals of the seven seas, except in terms dictated by the physics and biology of this surround.

But it is, of course, the biological evolutionary principle, the principle of the continuity of the germ plasm, the "adaptive radiation" of all forms, including man, into habitats in which they are viable, the kinds of new things which man's mutations will let him do, the rate of development of his brain, the capacity of his autonomic and endocrine systems to adapt to the enormous stresses of changed environmental pressures, that will determine what he will do. Just as his adaptation to outer space will depend ultimately upon what we find out in miniature terrestrial space laboratories, using our animal brethren as pilots and guides in many of these studies, so we shall relentlessly seek ways of stimulating mutational and other evolutionary changes at the same time we are studying the limits which the physical and biological environments may pose.

CROSS-CULTURAL AND HISTORICAL OVERVIEW

To look at our problem from the cross-cultural and historical viewpoints, we may say that our first impression is that human nature is variable, plastic and subtle in its adaptations. The incredible physiological adaptations of the people of the high Andes to reduced oxygen pressure, their capacity to develop a chicken-breasted structure in which the lungs can work adequately and to develop an enormously high red blood count, are paralleled only by the equally exquisite technical adaptation of the Eskimo to the conditions of the Arctic, in which animal fats and skins serve where man's anatomical limitations would otherwise appear to rule him out as a viable member of the world of the great cold. This conception, however, of human plasticity and flexibility seems to us to be very crudely and inadequately developed in most of our contemporary literature. After all, the variations are quite limited compared with those that might be conceived, for the Eskimos and high Andes dwellers all use proteins, fats and carbohydrates. They all show the diurnal rhythm of sleep and waking no matter what the length of the summer day or the Arctic night may be. They all have a human social organization which represents the realities of growth, reproduction, group membership and the quelling of individual combativeness. Indeed, if one looks quite broadly over the face of the earth one does find that "common human nature" which the man in the street sometimes cynically likes to emphasize. There is a general conservatism of human nature.

MANIFESTATIONS OF VARIOUS DRIVES

This general conservatism is true to a point; it is when this point is reached that the interesting questions begin. Is there, for example, a society without fighting? No, not in a strict sense, but observations of various groups of Eskimos make it appear that fighting is very limited indeed; in fact, that the aggressive impulse is in most cases developed only in a rudimentary manner. A number of contemporary societies are said to exhibit very little competitiveness for material gain or for prestige or power, while others are continuously and frantically concerned with these goals. It is easy to conceive human societies in which the prestige motivation could hypertrophy to a far greater degree than we find among ourselves, so that men and women would live almost entirely in terms of the narcissistic delight to which Veblen referred when he used the expression, the degree of "complacency" with which each person may view himself or be viewed by others. Both chemical and educational devices for either reducing or increasing the intensity of sexual feelings have been noted, and the warmth of maternal affection for very small children is apparently highly responsive to both physical and social conditions.

Perhaps most important of all these varying manifestations of drives under different social and historical conditions is the curiosity drive, the excitement and interest in pursuing the novel or the unfamiliar, the fascinating manifestations of the drive to understand and work out the meaning of things, suggested in the writings of Hebb (1) and Harlow (2) and made especially vivid by Berlyne (3). We would, therefore, tentatively offer the hypothesis that, as science and technology go on rapidly developing, an area of a tremendous metamorphosis in human nature is also developing. Scientific information of the last few decades would strongly suggest that at least many, and perhaps all, human beings may begin to recenter their lives more and more in terms of curiosity satisfactions and cognitive satisfactions generally. The imagination can tell something about imagination; indeed, a field day of fresh extrapolation of possibilities regarding the future of cognitive satisfactions appears legitimate. We may expect a rapid diversification of the things to get interested and excited about. Most common things like mushrooms and bugs or even slag and cold have until recently interested mankind only from a practical point of view, while today the biologist and the physicists make a fairyland out of these things.

Actually, the historical and the contemporary cross-cultural data show relatively limited variations in human nature compared with what can be expected as scientific technical changes in the physical environment are affected, as new forms of plant and animal life are exploited and as medical, biological and psychological research show new potentialities for utilizing these not just for immediate purposes but for a deeper understanding of the world. Instead of having to protect ourselves from nature's dangers, we shall be more and more exploiting the physics and the biology of our surrounding world. It is true, to be sure, that political difficulties are enormous; but today there exists the know-how with which to feed, clothe and care for several billion human beings on the face of this earth; and it is the response to this challenge which is the basis for the symposium presented by this book. We shall not digress here into a catalog of opinions about the population explosion or of the real or supposed inadequacy of food, fuel, water, minerals and energy to support an increasing population. Rather, suffice it to say that if our culture is to survive —indeed if man is to survive—facing problems of this sort will have to be accepted as part of the foundation if man's new scientific and artistic potentials are to be free to function.

We have talked too glibly, of course, about things called "cognitive." You may recall how John Stuart Mill, trained by his father to understand and to think, went into a depression until Wordsworth's poetry pulled him out. We plead for a use of intelligence colored, tempered, enriched by the subleties of man's feeling life, his impulse life, his capacity for deep resonance in terms of form color response, as our Rorschach friends might choose to put it.

The term *cognitive* has broader implications also for human values, for rational cultural structures in the realm of justice, generosity, reciprocity, an order of life which enables human beings to exercise sympathy and mercy, to share one another's goals and to build together towards a social structure in which the resonance of feelings combines with the appreciation of other's needs, provided only the social order is rational and mature enough to free man from fear and its twin brother, hate, and ready at all times to push forward into constantly changing opportunities for fulfillment of self and also fulfillment of others. We do not even know much about the craving for justice, the respect for self-control, the charismatic qualities of those to whom we often entrust our destinies. Here is a place for profoundly needed research in human potentialities.

The only thing that seems even *more* important at this juncture is the understanding of the psychosocial structure of human competitiveness, the conditions under which independent self-assertion against the competitive demands of others actually releases the potentials of child and youth and the conditions under which it tenses and strains the creative and imaginative spirit of the competitor and takes joy out of the group task.

This leads us into our question: How are the limits to be set as to what kinds of human development are possible? The answer seems to be that they are set by the very nature of the human; that is, we can imagine all sorts of creatures coming into existence through mutation, selection, surgery, drugs, etc. These could adapt to various conditions, and indeed these new kinds of creatures may well come into existence quite rapidly. The combination of biology and culture mutations may soon bring about among our descendants all sorts of creatures which we may regard as either superhuman or subhuman. Perhaps we would do well not to look too closely now at their gorgon heads. It is right now the *human* potentialities that we are talking about; and if it is the conservation of the human, the raw core of the human potential, that we are discussing, the problem is to select what is distinctly human as compared with physical or animal and to ask what chance there is for it to develop. It would be these cognitive and the related aesthetic and social satisfactions which we would expect to go on developing; and it is the creation of a natural order in which they can function effectively and happily with which we seem to be chiefly concerned. What are the limits upon the satisfactions of this kind of cognitive life? We do not seem to be within a thousand light years of reaching any such limit. Just as it would not have been possible for a nomad in the Arabian desert four thousand years ago to envisage an orchestra playing a Beethoven symphony or education by closed-circuit television, so it is equally impossible for us now to envisage the everyday realities of the world four thousand years in the future.

The limits to human changes lie, in large measure, in the relative fixity of genes and of the biochemical and structural conditions to which they give rise when in a maternal environment and after the time of birth in a given nutritional and socio-cultural environment. In view of the fact that most genes are potentially lethal when disturbed, that is, thrown out of their normal self-reproducing pattern, and that some extreme variations in temperature, acid-base balance, oxidative possibilities, etc. are likewise lethal, we must limit ourselves for a long time to certain structural and functional belts, narrow belts indeed, within which raw human potentials can go on evolving. It is worthwhile, however, to remember that man has always invented little sub-environments within which otherwise impossible changes can be tolerated. We can all wear spectacles even if our eyes get pretty bad; we can all, if necessary, move in the equivalents of iron lungs and space ships, if we want to develop conditions beyond those in which ordinary eyes or ordinary lungs are supposed to work.

The limits, then, while absolute in a sense, are, so to speak, absolutely relative to certain specific environmental fields that are contrived. A good deal depends upon what we want and how far our imaginations are set free by our wants. If we want to spend thirty billion dollars on shooting a man to the moon, we can compare this with sums which can be spent in creating various types of artificial environments in which, for example, man may do scientific or artistic work which in the present environments are difficult for him to do.

Our society has created a bimodality of technological talent *versus* lost creativities. There are worlds of artistic cultivation of individual children which can also be defined and the appropriate change in limits written down, insofar as there is research to show what such special conditions can do to liberate specific capacities.

It seems to us that extraordinary blindness has pervaded our Western liberalism, our lack of bold imagination, relating to the social potentialities of mankind not only in scientific and artistic respects but in relation to ethics. For example, take fellow-feeling, sympathy, justice, moral responsibility. We seem to feel that the ethics of today's liberalism are a sort of absolute or ultimate. But look at the history of ethics: It was a great step forward when the code of Hammurabi went beyond the death penalty meted out by the powerful and set up the relativistic "an eye for an eye and a tooth for a tooth." It was a huge advance, too, when considerations of equity were introduced: "Thou shalt not muzzle the ox that treadeth out the corn," the principle of responsibility as it appeared in the oath of Hippocrates and the principle of mercy and compassion which was destined to play such a large part in the elimination of torture and the slave trade and in present-day social progress. Why do we assume that there are no further ethical conceptions to be discovered and developed? Granted that we do not live up to what we have discovered, there are still long second steps between the pioneers and the mass. The conception of public or community responsibility for the weak and the suffering is still not worked through in a form that brings a clear challenge and points a clear direction. It will be a different humanity when this principle becomes both clear and morally compelling.

BIOLOGICAL LIMITS

So far we have been speaking of broad human capacities as a products of the present human biological and bio-social limits. There is here, however, another problem: the problem of biological individuality, the problem of what may be a potential for some, or indeed for one, while not a potential for others. If sometime you allow yourself the delight of listening to Bruno Walter's rehearsal of Beethoven's Fifth Symphony, you will, we believe, begin to realize what the great conductor releases in the tonal notations of the great genius of one hundred and fifty years ago who left marks on paper and a tradition of devoted disciples and, above all, a way of looking at life which the modern musician and musicologist are still richly exploiting. We recently heard, for example, the brilliant report by the Swedish musicologist, Ingolf Dahl, who worked with the manuscripts of Beethoven and showed how in some instances he literally worked out every musically possible modulation of a theme until he knew exactly what the possibilities were and then selected the one that he really wanted.

There is a problem of human potentialities of a completely

different order if we ask: Under what conditions can particular types of genius appear? There are questions, for example, about sensitivity: how the tonal sensitivity, for example, is to be recognized and cultivated in the earliest years; how it is to be made worthy and lovable even among contemporaries who do not understand or respect it; how it is to receive the reciprocating joyful response of other musically sensitive persons. We know from certain father-son traditions in music, for example, how the capacity can be made most intense and effective in each child who is a member of that musical tradition.

In the same way how can the potential cognitive and creative skills be identified? Some of the work presented in this volume very properly makes use of the conception of supporting and drawing forth, as it were, teasing out assiduously and lovingly, the budding abilities, possibilities for fulfillments at each stage in the development of progressive mastery of an artistic or other creative skill. Here too arises the problem of the cultivation and enrichment of the feeling tone and of the capacity for deep absorption in a task, the willingness, so to speak, to be carried forward by the task and to feel no fear of being engulfed by this type of creative passion.

Side by side with this encouragement of biological individuality is the problem of growth in individual bio-social terms, that is, growth of the individual into a particular niche provided by or created within the ecology, a niche involving similar growth, excitement and creative potential on the part of those surrounding the individual. The individual, we note, may *create* the niche. Desperately needed is research on the potentials, so to speak, of the environment, to help and to make room for growth, a need to view not only the growing individual moving forth into the ecology but to view the potentials of the ecology to move and meet each individual who wishes to lean upon and exploit such ecological potentials. The problem is bio-social, not biological alone, and there will have to be much more study than there is today of individual capacity to respond to particular ecological challenges and possibilities and study of changes needed in the culture to foster individual potentialities. The artistic child, for example, must make the most of a particular type of education and inspiration which his community, family and teacher can provide. We need to discover the types of teacher or school situation which, for this particular child, would give more than the existing teacher or school can give.

In all such matters we shall need vastly more sophistication than we now possess regarding *cross-cultural* issues. Our desire to believe that in the United States we have the most advanced expression of every cultural innovation hurts us everywhere and prevents our learning. Our boys are entitled to the science equipment that Russian children have, but it is hard to get Americans to listen to what the Russian schools are like. It is even harder to get Americans to realize that women in Russia, Poland, even India, are "going places" while American women uneasily wonder about the "feminine mystique." Our schools and colleges hardly discuss political futures at all—we probably would run some risk from a continuing McCarthyism; but a deeper trouble is that imagination regarding all social institutions is just not a part of our way of life, even among intellectuals.

PROBLEM OF CREATIVE LEADERSHIP

This carries us into the problem of creative leadership. It is not enough to assume that those who compete successfully against one another, let us say in a scientific or artistic task, are automatically leaders in the deeper sense of the term. To excel on a scale set by nature or by society is one thing, to give creative stimulus to others working within the same general field is another thing. Our problems in the release of human potentialities are only to a limited degree problems in how to give the best rewards to excite the biggest scientific or artistic efforts. Much more they relate to the problem of identifying early, valuing and cultivating fully the kind of man or woman capable of stimulating, enriching, nourishing, supporting and guiding those with potential passion, possibilities of knowledge, skill or creative achievement. Leadership training is not just training in excelling; it is a special and qualitatively different kind of capacity. So far as we know, there is almost no research on leadership in this sense; but there will certainly have to be much research of this sort if we are to transcend the rat-race theme of contemporary competition and define and train those whose special gift lies not just in surpassing or producing but in leading.

For, if we accept the principle of biological variability with respect to almost every significant characteristic, it is not necessarily the median achievement of the human family that counts, either now or later. It may be that one individual can, under certain conditions, literally pull the whole group forward. Watching a brilliant leader in Nigeria last year reminded us of the way in which Gulliver strode into the water, attached the appropriate cords to the vessels of the Lilliputian fleet and won the war against the Navy of Blefuscu in a few moments. So I visualized our Nigerian friend with his huge gifts and concentrated capacity to give direction lifting the nation forward. Whenever this is true the conditions favoring the unique potentials of leadership are those most important for our theme; and a small experiment with a potentially creative group may be the way to spark the world of the future.

RESEARCH NEEDS AND ACTION PROGRAMS

Our last point relates to the immediate research consequences of this analysis. What we can do must be channeled through research and action programs in three spheres: (a) In the psychology of the family and home, with due attention to the naturalistic or field observation studies of family life in various subcultures as these have been illustrated by modern anthropology and sociology; (b) In psychometric and projective tests, sociometric and spontaneity tests and tests of art and science comprehension and creativity, which are already here, but need belief in the magnitude of the goal to get their temperature red or white hot; and (c) In the studies of public communication through conversation and response to mass media, making possible the rapid evolution of effective mass media teaching techniques such as those of radio and television, the press and the world of magazines and books.

There is need for base lines and control groups and what Albert Mayer in his studies of the Indian village has called the frequent "setting of goals," so that there are always a "before and after" measure, always a capacity to show what has been achieved within a given period and a study of the applicability of the finding to new situations through some sophisticated use of the psychology of transfer of training.

With home, school and public communication defined and their tasks made clear, their tasks can be redefined in terms of research in the development of human potentialities, showing empirically what can be done. Here the methods already used in the teaching of science by television can be pressed into further service; and if proportion is maintained, extrapolation from present science, even by the methods of science fiction, can be utilized, provided we constantly check up objectively on the degree of realism, the degree of genuine creativity, curiosity and imagination liberated by such methods. There is a basic opposition between the spirit of research and the spirit of exploiting a good thing when you find it, and we venture to propose these educational steps only as it is possible by continuous and sensitive research to show the actual changes in actual children which result from the initiation of new methods.

Finally, there is always the invention of new methods appropriate when new discoveries and new applications are available. One of the tragedies of radio and television research is the largely accidental character of most of the discoveries and most of the applications; that is, accidental in the sense that the ultimate meaning for human growth and for human futures was not considered at all. Here is a place, however, in science in its deeper sense and applied science, which, as it comes into technique and into engineering, teaching and other applications, can quickly devise new techniques. For example: new ways of taking photographs; mapping sociometric relationships; sustaining the flagging interest of a child bored in school; or giving that extra pellet of excitement to the potentially creative child who appears once in a blue moon when least expected among any handicapped group. There will always be a place in this world of programming and computers for the special, unexpected case; and whether he is a great genius or just a specially handicapped youngster, we can learn something from him.

We conclude, therefore, on the theme that the techniques, indeed the technology, to effect most of these changes already *exists*. But it is not at the technical level that the problem arises.

The problem arises with our lack of imagination regarding what the new world of scientific and artistic imagination may be. Our difficulty is not that we have no tools but that we are not adequately sensitive to the huge tasks, the basic unfathomed potentials, for which both today's and tomorrow's tools can be worthily applied.

REFERENCES

1. Hebb, D. O.: *The Organization of Behavior.* New York, Wiley, 1949.
2. Harlow, H. F.: Learning and satiation of response in intrinsically motivated complex puzzle performance by monkeys. *J. Comp. Physiol. Psychol., 43*:289-294, 1950.
3. Berlyne, D. E.: *Conflict, Arousal, and Curiosity.* New York, McGraw-Hill, 1960.

Chapter 2

HUMAN LIFE PATTERNS AND POTENTIALITIES

CHARLOTTE BUHLER

THERE is increasing agreement among psychologists that the greatest satisfaction and experience of fulfillment in life is reached by bringing one's best potentials to materialization.

At the same time we have become aware of the coincidence of the many favorable circumstances which this presupposes. By understanding them, we begin to appreciate why fulfillment of life through self-realization is less the rule than the exception.

The conditions that have to be met are threefold. First, the environment must be such that right from the start an individual is given very good chances for his self-development. Second, the individual himself must be able to find and set his own direction. Third, the opportunities available at a certain time and place must be such that the individual can fit himself into them with his given potentials at that point.

Family and cultural environment of a person are very influential in fostering, neglecting or even suppressing a child's initial attempts at developing his potentialities. In many biographies we hear of how the parents' delight in a child's early interests or aptitudes encouraged the child's further pursuit. And, correspondingly, we hear in case histories, how lack or even denial of support made children give up activities and hobbies which actually represented potentials. Only very strong inclinations or determination will sustain a child's or young person's efforts at self-development if the given circumstances are detrimental. An individual with weak determination and interests clearly needs much encouragment and assistance.

Many recent studies (D. C. McClelland [14], F. L. Strodtbeck [17], B. Eiduson [6], Getzels and Jackson [9], Goertzel and Goertzel [10]) have shown how strongly the home, its cultural atmosphere, the parental discipline and the parental ambitions co-determine a child's directedness and self-discipline.

We say *co-determine.* With this we mean to emphasize that the individual himself is not just a passive recipient of these influences, but, beginning quite early in life, he may "choose" varying positions in response to this, depending on his own personality. This early "choosing" of the two- to four-year-old is, of course, not conscious. But the determination or lack of it with which this youngster establishes himself as a person in his own right may be recalled in later years as the beginning of winning or losing the battle for independence. This independence or dependency has been prepared for even earlier in the initial emotional relationships between infant and mother and in the baby's earliest responses to his environment.

As far as the individual's own direction is concerned, this seems to be most pronounced in persons with specific talents. Richly endowed but not specifically talented persons often find it difficult to choose between many directions they could take. As Getzels and Jackson (9) showed in their study of highly intelligent and highly creative high school students, there are remarkable differences in the way in which both groups plan their future. While the highly creative go ahead rather independently on their own chosen way, the highly intelligent are much more apt to fall in with the ideals and goals their families plan for them.

We do not as yet have correspondingly careful studies of average and under-average youngsters' procedures in planning their future. Judging from case histories, we also find two types: the independent individual who looks for adventure or who attempts to find his own opportunity; and the more dependent one who lets himself be guided by his environment.

By and large, the independent one who has enough ego-strength to assert himself may have a better chance to develop himself. But ego-strength and independence as such do not necessarily guarantee that kind of self-determination which brings out an individual's best potentials. If the independence had to be asserted in battles with a highly controlling environment or in self-defense against a rejecting environment, it might result in a course of action that is just oppositional, without realizing any of the individual's potentials. We will later present an example of this.

The third factor of consequence for self-realization includes the opportunities of time and place which may be favorable or detrimental to what a person has to offer. We are thinking here of market opportunities in the widest sense and beyond them, also of those historical conditions and events of which our time is full and which, as we observe daily, can make or break a person.

Before we go into the discussion of various life structures, it might be wise to stop for a moment and ask ourselves how we want to define potentialities.

Gardner Murphy (15) devoted extensive studies to the question of how to conceive of human potentialities. He sees them as emerging out of three kinds of human nature, and he also describes them in terms of fields of developing human potentialities. As for the discovery of individual potentialities, he sees this in three directions: in *Progressive development,* specifically of creativity; in *active effort at self-fulfillment* which would include both the relationships with and understanding of people as well as the mastery of chosen jobs; finally, in what he calls *inner self-realization,* which he defines as a "sensitive, flexible, creative, self-fulfilling deployment of perception, feeling and impulse," with each activity and satisfaction being an "aspect of a larger activity—a phase of a plan, a phase of a life."

All this serves what he calls "Aristotle's *movement toward fulfillment.*"

With this we can readily identify, but for an understanding of the prevailing fulfillment or failure of the development of potentialities in periods or the whole of an individual's life, we need to ask some further questions. We need to conceptualize just how this movement toward fulfillment is implemented. Progressive, creative development, active effort at self-development through enrichment of love and experience—how are they brought to being or how are they failed?

As we said in our introductory paragraphs, we believe that both the person and the environment contribute their share to these results. Already this raises problems, because in this continuous interplay and fusion between individual and environment where is the individual?

Some people are very pessimistic about the individual's chances to determine himself. An example of this point of view is Marion Opler, who states: "The regulatory controls, the styles of expression, the ordained goals, and social role of behavior are defined within the definition of the situation (its meaning and communicated symbols) long before anyone of us is privileged to select and construct a life pattern, or indeed, add personal understanding and interpretation to it" (16).

On the other hand, there is modern observational research on infants where *individuality of behavior* is found to be established right from the start. A recent study of Thomas, Chess, Birch, Hertzig and Corn (18) establishes consistency of infant behavior in a number of defined categories. These findings receive their confirmation in scientifically rigorous studies about the behavior of a given genetic "set-up" in a given environment. Eiduson, Eiduson and Geller (7) state that based upon their comprehensive survey of studies, from the beginning there are individual differences which may be responsible for variability of potentialities and for sensitivity degrees. We might speculate that these data speak for primary activity and selectivity on the individual's side.

We might also say that the genetic set-up that becomes active and the selectivity of its operations represent something which we might call a "core" or a "rudimentary self."

We conceive of this self as having *direction* and *intentionality*. By intentionality is meant purposefulness. As the self emerges it brings out a person's self-determination towards goals which seem to promise fulfillment.

This *self-determination* emerges in its rudimentary beginnings in the form of first choices which we might observe in the eight- to ten-month-old baby. Supported by an ego of which the child becomes aware sometime before he is two, these choices can become very affirmative and usually encounter their first opposition by the environment at this age. This period seems to be the most frequent occasion for a first decision about a child's further *healthy* or *neurotic* self-direction. The child who is too weak or whose environment is too overpowering to sustain his freedom of choice at this time may go on from there forever with what A. Maslow (13) calls *defense motivation* as against *growth motivation.*

The person who keeps his beginning ability for self-determination fairly intact will develop it through various phases all through life in the direction of the envisioned fulfillment. He will utilize his basic tendencies to *need-satisfaction, self-limiting adaptation, creative expansion and to the upholding of his internal order* (Buhler [3]) in whatever degrees they are available to him.

These four tendencies which are always in operation in everyone manifest themselves, however, in individually and developmentally varying degrees. While the infant is primarily need-satisfying, the growing child learns self-limiting adaptation; in adolescence and adulthood creative expansion may become predominant; with climacteric years, self-assessing procedures are more frequent than in the foregoing years. That means the forty-five to sixty-five-year-old individual often feels motivated to ask himself what he did with himself and his life so far and what he is going to do with the rest of it. The aging person may, depending on health, abilities, interests and opportunities, either retire and rest or else go on with creatively expansive pursuits, possibly in different directions than before.

Native disposition, training and education, environment and opportunities may enhance one or the other of these tendencies more in different individuals. In my opinion, if a person wants to develop the greatest human potentialities in the previously defined sense, he can at no time just be need-satisfying and resting. Gardner Murphy in his book, *Human Potentialities* (15), also warns of the fallacy that satisfaction of all needs supposedly leads to fulfillment. What fulfillment we are capable of obtaining can be demonstrated in examples as the result of a proportionate participation of all four basic tendencies. In working toward progressive development, self-fulfillment in relationships and mastery and inner self-realization, we need to be adaptive as well as creative, we need certain needs to be satisfied and we also repeatedly need to make inner order in evaluating ourselves. All this we do, however, to individually varying degrees, and this, together with many other individualizing factors, makes for the differences of life structures.

Human life structures vary with respect to the fulfillment of potentialities from a number of different aspects. Some of the most important may be briefly discussed and exemplified.

A first variable which conditions the degree to which potentialities may be fulfilled is *age*. It is quite evident that at a very young age when aptitudes and knowledge, experience and freedom of movement are very limited, there is only a limited development of potentials possible. As the person grows older through adolescence into adulthood, his potentialities grow, and some of them may reach their peak in middle age.

As Brunswik and Frenkel showed in collaboration with Buhler (2), and as reported by Frenkel in *Studies in Biographical Psychology* (8), certain creative talents reach a very early peak in certain people or else a peak in middle age or even in old age. Also, H. Lehman (12) has examples of these different types, although he finds that on the whole and for the average, the peak of creativity lies in the middle thirties.

This does not imply, however, that with the lessened creativity of later years a person's potentialities are exhausted. Usually, the creative activity of a person has an outgrowth and after-growth in other directions, such as promotion, application, industrialization, teaching and others. Furthermore, there are other potentialities to be developed in the pursuit of other interests, in human relationships and in inner growth and wisdom of understanding. There are people who keep up this process of development into advanced old age and who find that they are never finished with what they want to learn and to understand.

However, this continuous development of new potentialities applies primarily to healthy people who live in an environment that in some measure gives them an adequate chance. Those who are severely handicapped physically and those whose environment robs them, particularly in the early stages, of adequate opportunities to grow are much more limited in what they can do and be.

This brings us to the second important factor which conditions the development of potentialities: *environment* and *opportunities.*

Clinical evidence assembled in the last decades has made us increasingly aware of the fact that, through unfortunate environmental influences, an individual's personality may be warped to such a degree that the development of potentialities is minimized, sometimes from the start.

Let us take the following example of a case observed by M. Marschak.*

> A small baby girl, weighing five and three quarter pounds, but physiologically normal, was born to an unmarried Negro mother, age seventeen, of low intelligence (IQ possibly around 80). While in the hospital the mother had crying spells. She did not look at or touch the baby when it was brought to her for nursing; she did not help the baby to find the nipple although the nurse tried to teach her how to move the child's head, etc. The baby reacted first with angry crying and at later feedings became sleepy when put to the breast and had to be fed in the nursery. Although the hospital and, in particular, the obstetrics department was psychologically-minded, deliveries happened to be at a peak, and the ward was understaffed with nurses. The baby girl was given the bottle by different nurses, and each held her for a minimal time. The baby was hard to awaken, drank very little and soon fell asleep. It lost more weight than is usual during the first days. While alone in her crib, she had periods of persistent, excessive crying.
>
> The mother received psychiatric help during her hospital stay. On the day before she left the hospital and on the last morning, the psychiatrist went with her to the nursery and stayed with her while she held and fed the baby. The nurse tried to teach her how to wash and diaper the baby. During these procedures the mother still had a blank expression on her face; and, when handling the baby, she was hesitant and stiff. When watching mother and child, one could be concerned about the limitations which this child faced. This concern was in no way eased by the appearance of the grandmother, the official guardian for both her daughter and granddaughter, who came to take them home, and who was herself frail and bitter and withdrawn.

---

* I wish to thank Dr. Marschak for making this case available to me.

It is evident that a child like this has everything stacked against a normal development from the start. There is an unmarried mother of low intelligence and very young; she is not only unskillful but seems to reject the child completely. The same attitude prevails with the child's grandmother, who shows her hostility. Besides this rejection, as well as ignorance and low intelligence, there is a most detrimental social position; and there are problems of support. It is a case in which the development of potentialities is completely remote and even survival doubtful.

> If we take the very different case of a little girl born to a young couple who have eagerly awaited this event for some three years, and who, in every way, seem equipped and willing to help their child to a very happy, healthy and full human development, we realize that this represents the opposite end of opportunities. This mother and father, who both are highly educated people, take delight and a never-ending interest in their new baby. Little Sue will have love and understanding, security and education and everything else that a good home can provide for a child.

If all through life the situation in which a person finds himself plays an important role in the development of his potentials, it is of almost decisive significance in those early years in which the foundation of healthy growth depends on the right kind of tending.

In adolescence, another crucial phase of life, the dynamic structure is a little different. If his age-conditioned limitations leave the infant greatly at the mercy of his environment, the potentials of the individual's own personality come to the fore in adolescence. His own ability to make choices and to give himself direction becomes of decisive importance at this stage. With this we come to a third important factor.

While again we must not overlook the predetermining influences of childhood experiences, adolescence is a period in which the feeling of freedom to make decisions prevails. Much of a person's future depends on the directions which his tentative and programmatic *self-determination* takes at this point.

A discussion of the participants of a young adult's psychotherapy group may serve as an example here.

This group had a heated argument one day on the usefulness of further education. All seven are young people in their early twenties; three of them are married, two already have children. Four have had varying degrees of college education; only one has gone as far as a master's degree. They grew up and live in middle class circumstances.

These young people are all at a stage where their decisions about the direction they want to take is of the greatest consequence for the development of their potentialities in later life. None of them has learned about this concept, nor had their attention been called to the fact that the fulfillment of their potentialities would bring them satisfaction. Like most Americans, they have respect for education as being helpful to a person's career; but not all of them take this seriously.

Only two of the girls feel that, to develop fully, they need further education. Sharon interrupted her studies when, after marrying, she had a baby, and now she is quite determined to return to college as soon as her family life will permit this. Patty, a young teacher, is very enthusiastic about her work and wants to further her education, even though she also hopes to marry.

The problem of combining marriage, the raising of a family, continuing one's education and possibly having a job or career is a predominant one in this generation's young women. How does the woman of our time develop her potentialities most adequately? Is there any ideal or are there only individual solutions?

Sharon, who takes time out to read, compares Betty Friedan's book, *The Feminine Mystique,* with Phyllis McGinley's book, *Sixpence in Her Shoe,* and decides Phyllis is dishonest because it is easy to praise household duties when you actually get your real satisfaction from writing books and winning Pulitzer Prizes.

Debby does not agree at all with Sharon. She occupies her time with going to college while trying to find the right man. Marriage, children and an interesting social life are what she looks forward to as what would bring her "happiness." To her all this struggle for education and careers is not meaningful. "I could not care less," she declares.

At this point the other girls get quite excited. While Patty and Sharon feel first you need an education to develop yourself, Lyn's opinion is different. She says she does not feel like a person because she does not have a life and activities of her own, having made herself dependent on a husband and on his sharing his interests with her. This did not work out at all, she finds.

One of the boys, Wayne, sympathizes with her. He also does not think education is the answer. He believes in talents as the means of developing oneself. He tries to help Lyn discover a talent she could cultivate. He himself is a gifted young writer who believes his talent is all that counts. Classes bore him. He thinks he does not need a formal education to develop his talent; but, unfortunately, he is too undisciplined to educate himself, even to keep regular working hours.

Jack despises that approach. He works with determination towards his science degree. Of course he misses out on all the other things in life, as the group repeatedly points out to him. Speaking in terms of fulfillment of potentialities, he neglects all those personal relationships, the early experience of which is practically irreplaceable at a later stage.

Mike is not sure what stand to take. In opposing his domineering, harsh father he neglected his studies all through high school. Then he left home to get himself a job and be on his own. Now he would like to go back to college and become an engineer, as his father always wanted him to be, but now he feels he is "all fouled up." He has no study habits, and he does not want to ask his father for support, and he does not know what to do. The neurotic development of this brilliant boy resulted in considerable initial damage to the development of his potentialities, which, at this point, we can still hope to remedy in psychotherapy.

"Damn it, man," says Jack, "a guy as brilliant as you and not going back to college, you are crazy."

In listening to youngsters like these, one gets a vivid impression of the sometimes fateful decisions they may be making at this stage. With one sometimes irreparable move, with one decision for or against education or participation in the socio-sexual experiments of their peers, they may open up or block their own future development. On the other hand, a therapist may feel that at this present stage a specific individual is not as yet ready to make use of education or the life of his peers, and thus he will want to let this youngster feel free to proceed at his own pace. He will then only indicate, but not pressure, the values he sees (*cf.* C. Buhler [5]).

The young people whose debate we reported briefly are, of course, in psychotherapy and are not necessarily characteristic of all our youth. Reliable data about how our youths generally plan their lives are not as yet available. From all the information I could gather, I conclude that the concept of preparing the use of one's best potentialities is generally more or less unknown.

However, we find that the more thoughtful young adults and also those who have been longer in psychotherapy will get beyond the stage where they debate likes and dislikes, "happiness" and opportunities. They will ask themselves the eternal adolescent questions: Who am I? and What am I here for? And that may take them closer to preparing a life in which they would develop their potentialities.

Discovering and holding on to what one has, what one thinks one can do and be, is, as we mentioned, obviously easier for the creatively expansive person than for the self-limitingly adaptive one. The former is usually more "inner-directed." to use D. Riesman's expression, while the latter is more "outer-directed" and depends more on stimulations and opportunities offered, even on directions given to him. However, even the creative child may often have to overcome tremendous hindrances, as Goertzel and Goertzel (10) showed, before he can develop fully. With the great majority of people not primarily creative, the environment plays a very decisive role all the way through for the development or inhibition of their potentialities.

In the *adult* personality we find the scars of the individual's struggle with the establishing of his own self and of his struggle with circumstances that he had to conquer. If fairly successful, however, this middle period of life, the years from about twenty-five or thirty to forty-five or fifty should show the average individual's potentialities developed to their peak. Whatever he can do in developing and using his given equipment of abilities and basic tendencies and in coping with the given and arising external conditions of his life will consolidate now to a more or less unique individual.

At this time a person's mastery of his "chosen job" and "his relationship with an understanding of people," especially the establishment of a fulfilling marital and family life, should have succeeded. His self-determination should be anchored in definite goals and objectives.

It is hard to estimate how many people actually arrive at this peak at the appropriate time. The constantly increasing divorce rate which is noticeable seems, even more than occupational changes and dissatisfactions, an indication of people's difficulties in finding the right ways towards their fulfillment.

A good example of a successful struggle toward the fulfillment of her potentialities is Linda a social worker, fifty-five, married and the mother of an adolescent daughter. Linda, who offers the picture of an essentially healthy and well-directed development, still had in her thirties and up into her forties considerable difficulties in finding a truly satisfactory solution of the problems that circumstances provided for her.

The daughter of a California ranch manager, she had been a child who knew early what she wanted. While not of exceedingly superior abilities she had always been curious and alert and even in preschool years eager to learn and to know whatever she could make contact with.

In this she was strongly supported by her affectionate mother, whom she loved and with whom she identified. In spite of her father's opposition to intellectual women, she eventually managed to get off to school; and she thought of her future as one in which professional work, marriage and family life would be combined.

However, the man she loved and married in her early twenties, a magazine writer and editor, proved for a while an even greater hindrance to her self-development than her father had started out to be. Hal denied her the child he had promised her for years and depended on her earning an income while securing a spot for himself.

At the end of her twenties Linda was near a divorce, especially since she had met another man who greatly appealed to her. Yet, in working things through for herself and in clarifying things with Hal, she reached the decision to stay. Hal needed her, their sexual and personal relationships were fulfilling and Hal agreed to her having a child.

For several more years Linda's and Hal's struggles persisted and brought her, due to illnesses of her child and her husband's personality difficulties on his jobs, near a breakdown. It was only in the middle of her forties that things began to work out successfully and that she could finish her education and get the long-desired opportunity to combine a career with her marriage and family life. Since this time, she feels she is living fully according to her best potentialities.

The story of this woman is remarkable because of her own consistently clear direction toward a full self-development from early childhood. She kept her creatively expansive direction, even though for long stretches of time she had to adapt herself with self-limitation to circumstances beyond her control. The ability of this well-balanced approach to life had been taught to her first by her mother at the time when she had to find compromises between her own and her father's wishes. This ability stood her in good stead when later she had to cope with the demands of an even more difficult husband.

In contrast to Linda, who could only establish her life in her forties so that she felt she was living now in fulfillment of her best potentialities, there are many others who in this *climacteric phase* (between the forties and the sixties) come to much less satisfying conclusions when they make a self-evaluation. Neurotic approaches to life which up to then might still have seemed interesting and promising emerge now increasingly as futile in both the eyes of the onlooker and the person himself. This may be due to the fact that opportunities actually were missed or also that the person started out with a wrong fantasy image of himself.

The effects of *healthy and neurotic* ways of life seem to become more definite and more distinct as time goes on, and ultimate results show in the individual's personal and occupational life.

In this *period of self-assessment,* breakdowns do occur frequently because of life having been failed. The structures of these unsuccessful lives usually show as their essential feature the possible waste of basic potentialities.

This kind of waste sometimes becomes apparent from its early beginnings. For example, Mike, whom we met in our young adults' group, might easily have taken this course if in psychotherapy he had not been made aware of the fact that the direction he took was conditioned only by opposition to his father and not by any evaluation of his own potentialities. His was the type of negative identification that was unproductive and wasteful.

An example of a life-structure of this type that remained practically wasted up to the end is that of Ben.

Ben, a twice-divorced childless salesman, entered psychotherapy at fifty because of impotence, various psychosomatic complaints and depressions. He explained his depression as due to his empty, meaningless life, about which he felt guilty. He felt he had wasted his life in the pursuit of worthless goals in which he did not believe.

Ben had started this way in opposition to a father he hated because the father had tried to push the gifted boy in a harsh and unloving manner. Ben quit school, left home and got himself a clerical job in order to be independent. Only after his father's death, when he was in his twenties, did he finish high school, go to college and get a degree in law. For some time he practicd law, and he was offered a partnership in a firm, but Ben was restless, and neither in this nor in later managerial jobs was he successful.

At heart Ben was a writer and a scholar, and he grieved forever that he had never gotten beyond haphazard attempts at pursuing his real interests and his true potentialities. Now he was too restless and too disturbed to settle down to anything like that. He did not believe in anything he did.

His bad feelings about himself were confirmed by the failure of two meaningless marriages which ended after short durations.

Psychotherapy enabled Ben to make true progress in at least one area: He became able to love for the first time in his life and developed a happy affair in which his potency was stronger than ever.

But his attempts to write failed tragically. His development had led to a tragic reduction of his original potentialities, which he realized without being able to resign himself to this insight. His early death in an accident was perhaps not quite as accidental as it seemed.

The most difficult and varied, with respect to the availability as well as use of potentialities, is the last phase of life, the years after sixty-five which officially are conceived of as the age of *retirement.* This period, which until recently did not attract too much attention, has suddenly become an important object of study as well as of commercial speculation, because the ever-increasing lifespan keeps enlarging this age group with its human as well as economic potentialities.

Ideally, this last phase of life should be one in which *fulfillment* is experienced, but even the approximation of fulfillment in this stage seems to be the rare blessing of only relatively few human beings.

Those who experience it, as described by me (4) in the case of Bill Roberts, do not necessarily interpret it as the end of their potentialities.

Bill Roberts, after his retirement from his job as traffic employee, showed a rich development of interests and hobbies, some of which he had had no time to pursue before, and some of which were intensified and became important activities.

If many factors beyond one's control may peril or even destroy a young infant's development of potentialities, the same is true of the aged. The greatest of these destructive threats is, as M. Blenkner (1) pointed out, extended severe illness. It can have the effect of reducing a personality and inducing experiences closer to desolation than to fulfillment.

Poverty or completely insecure circumstances may also bring about disintegrating anxiety at this stage, as R. Kuhlen (11) pointed out.

Resignation after a partly failed life or despair that leads to suicide, such as happened in the case of Ben, are other unfortunate patterns of life's last phase.

The more fortunate aging, whose physical ailments are minor

or nil, whose economic conditions are fairly secure and whose lives have been led with a fair amount of satisfaction and success, will enjoy the freedom of more rest and more leisure activities than before.

If sufficiently wise and mentally alert they may embark on the aging's most privileged potentiality: to see in retrospect their life as a whole and to muse or even write on how it all happened and what it was all about.

REFERENCES

1. BLENKNER, M.: Developmental considerations and the older client. In BIRREN, J. D.: Relations of Development and Aging. Springfield, Thomas, 1964.
2. BUHLER, C.: *Der Menschliche Lebenslauf als Psychologisches Problem (The Human Course of Life as a Psychological Problem).* Leipzig, S. Hirzel, 1933.
3. BUHLER, C.: Theoretical observations about life's basic tendencies. *Amer. J. Psychother., 13*:3, 1959.
4. BUHLER, C.: Meaningful living in the mature years. In KLEEMEIER, R. W. (ed.): *Aging and Leisure.* New York, Oxford University Press, 1961.
5. BUHLER, C.: *Values in Psychotherapy.* New York, Free Press of Glencoe, 1962.
6. EIDUSON, B.: *Scientists: Their Psychological World.* New York, Basic Books, Inc., 1962.
7. EIDUSON, B. T., EIDUSON, S., and GELLER, E.: Biochemistry, genetics and the nature-nurture problem. *Amer. J. Orthopsychiat., 119*:342-352, 1962.
8. FRENKEL, E.: Studies in biographical psychology. *Character and Personality, V*:1, 1936.
9. GETZELS, J. W. and JACKSON, P. W.: *Creativity and Intelligence.* New York, Wiley 1962.
10. GOERTZEL, V. and GOERTZEL, M. G.: *Cradles of Eminence.* Boston, Little, Brown, 1962.
11. KUHLEN, R. G.: Developmental changes in motivation during the adult years. In BIRREN, J. E.: *Relations of Development and Aging.* Springfield, Thomas, 1964.
12. LEHMAN, H. C.: *Age and Achievement.* Princeton, Princeton Univ. Press, 1953.
13. MASLOW, A. H.: Defense and growth. *Merrill-Palmer Quarterly, 3*:36-47, 1956.
14. MCCLELLAND, D., ATKINSON, J. W., CLARK, R. A., and LOWELL,

E. L.: *The Achievement Motive.* New York, Appleton-Century-Crofts, 1953.

15. Murphy, G.: *Human Potentialities.* New York, Basic Books, 1958.
16. Opler, M. K.: *Culture, Psychiatry and Human Values.* Springfield, Thomas, 1956, 195.
17. Strodtbeck, F. L.: In McClelland, D., Baldwin, A. L., Bronfenbrenner, L. U., and Strodtbeck, F. L.: *Family Interaction, Values and Achievement.* Princeton, New Jersey, Van Nostrand, 1958.
18. Thomas, A., Chess, S., Birch, H. G., Hertzig, M. D., and Korn, S.: *Behavioral Individuality in Early Childhood.* New York, New York Univ. Press, 1963.

Chapter 3

THE SOCIOLOGY OF MAN'S CREATIVE POTENTIAL

DON MARTINDALE

SO new is the sociological study of man's potential creativity that it is only possible to formulate a few tentative hypotheses as to the ways society simultaneously enormously expands and stringently limits his self-realization.

Biologically, man stands at the terminus of an evolutionary series which finds social life indispensable for survival, but which successively lost the instincts for establishing a particular system of social life.

There is survival value in the instinctive commitment of creative energies, for automatically, without the necessity of previous learning, an appropriate response is evoked by the proper stimulus. Instincts constitute a sort of inherited survival kit. However, the more elegant the adaptation of such a survival kit to a particular environment, the more limited the given creature adapted to the desert to survive in a rain forest or an arctic region. On the other hand, a creature who has retained the energies for survival but who has lost the instinctive commitment of them suffers a loss in the immediate precision and automaticity of behavior but gains an expanded range of adaptability.

Such is the biological peculiarity of man which serves as the starting point for all sociological investigations. Having no substantial heritage of instincts, man must substitute for them survival kits of his own invention. The lack of instinctive commitment of his energies casts him upon the world as its original foundling, for initially he is at home nowhere. He is potentially at home in any habitat his ingenuity can master. The lack of instincts establishes man as a creature with no original nature. Human nature is always and only a most variable second nature of man's own contrivance. Evolutionary development delivered man over to his own self-determination to a degree true of no other creature.

MAN'S SOCIAL DEPENDENCY

Ironically, the very lack of an instinctively predetermined social life carries with it an unusual dependency upon the particular society into which man is born. The lack of appropriate instincts is compensated by an expanded capacity to learn and remember and an extended period of apprenticeship in which he replaces by learning what he lacked by nature. Man has the longest period of dependency of any creature. Even under optimum conditions it is doubtful whether a human individual could survive purely by his own unaided efforts before the age of nine or ten years.

By the time man could potentially survive on his own his behavior has been so completely adapted to the requirements of a particular social group as to make it virtually impossible for him to survive without it. In every society, to be sure, individuals vary in the extent to which they can tolerate isolation from their groups. When an individual *does* survive without the loss of his very sanity, it is usually because he has retained the capacity to remain in psychological communion with his society in the teeth of actual isolation.

Concepts of privacy in a given society are ways in which, in part, various forms and degrees of isolation of the individual from the group are provided for without damage to the group. The toleration of eccentricity is the acknowledgment of forms of privacy which border on behaviors a given community will no longer tolerate. They are the reverse sides of the protection of a social formula from individual challenge.

Every society, in short, may be conceived as a case history in the development of the potentialities of individuals singly and in concert. Any given society crystallizes this potentiality into a relatively fixed form in which more or less clear lines are drawn between what is public and what private in the behavior of the individual. Any given society may be likened to the frozen surface of an uncharted and unplumbed sea. The precondition of the social effectiveness of any single person is that he confine his behavior to this frozen surface. To cut through it is usually to be lost in the unknown depths of social ostracism on the one hand and ineffectiveness on the other.

THE SOCIAL EXPANSION OF HUMAN POTENTIAL

But things are rarely simple, and the very society which limits the potentialities of its members to a restricted range also supplies them with a formula for survival in nature and enjoyment of the richness of human company. And beyond this, human society in general supplied the matrix for inventions that permanently transformed the impersonal and interpersonal environments themselves into spheres of almost inexhaustible possibilities.

Man had two capacities which became peculiarly important as he lost his instincts: the capacity for isolating precise relations in the material environment; and the capacity to fuse the elements of a momentary experience into images. As developed under conditions of a social matrix, these capacities are the foundations of the two accomplishments generally agreed since Darwin to be unique to the human species—tool making and language.

Tools reduce the physical world to precise and controllable relations. They began that analysis and control of the environment which terminated in the scientific management of nature. They started man on that route which would emancipate him from dependence on what nature offered and would permit him to join forces with nature and compel natural laws to his bidding.

Language, on the other hand, by turning the image-making capacity of man into communicable gestures makes possible an inter-individual exchange of experience. By means of language the experience of men dead a thousand years is as accessible as if they were alive. Language annihilates the spatial as well as the time limitations on experience, for by means of it the experience of persons in one part of the globe can be brought effectively into the sphere of the persons in any other. By means of language men may enter into the experience of each other in a most intimate sense. The inter-individual world ceases to be a matter of external contacts but becomes a matter of shared hope and fear, triumph and tragedy, realization and dream.

In the course of his long period of dependency the human individual takes over the linguistically structured experience of his social group. It gives him, potentially, an extraordinary new power over others and puts their experience at his disposal.

> Abhorred slave,
> Which any print of goodness wilt not take,
> Being capable of all ill! I pitied thee,
> Took pains to make thee speak, taught thee each hour
> One thing or other. When thou didst not, savage,
> Know thine own meaning, but wouldst gabble like
> A thing most brutish. I endow'd thy purposes
> With words and made them know.*

But language also gives others an extraordinary new power over the individual.

> You taught me language, and my profit on't
> Is, I know how to curse. The red plague rid you
> For learning me your language!†

Moreover, from his social group the individual acquires an acquaintance with a natural environment transformed by tools. But he also learns to ask from nature many things of which he would never otherwise dream. Enormous quantities of human energy are consumed in the production of all sorts of material things essential to one's society. No one ever formulated better than Thoreau the extent to which one may be enchained by the material accomplishments made possible by man's tools and confirmed in his social order.

> I see young men, my townsmen, whose misfortune it is to have inherited farms, houses, barns, cattle and farming tools; for these are more easily acquired than got rid of. Better if they had been born in the open pasture and suckled by a wolf, that they might have seen with clearer eyes what field they were called to labor in. Who made them serfs of the soil? Why should they eat their sixty acres, when man is condemned to eat only his peck of dirt? Why should they begin digging their graves as soon as they are born? They have got to live a man's life, pushing all these things before them, and get on as well as they can. How many a poor immortal soul have I met well-nigh

---

* Prospero to Caliban in William Shakespeare, *The Tempest* Edited by George Lyman Kittredge (Boston: Ginn and Company, 1936), pp. 10-11.

† Caliban replies, *Ibid.*, p. 11.

crushed and smothered under its load, creeping down the road of life, pushing before it a barn seventy-five feet by forty, its Augean stables never cleansed, and one hundred acres of land, tillage, mowing, pasture and wood lot. The portionless, who struggle with no such inherited encumbrances, find it labor enough to subdue and cultivate a few cubic feet of flesh.*

Through language, restructured experience and its tool-transformed material environment, his society seizes control of the individual and enchains him to one plane in the unmeasured compass of human potentiality.

SOCIAL VARIATION IN CREATIVITY AND CONFORMITY

One effect of the successful survival of any species in a condition of society is the staying of the individual evolutionary process. The mechanisms of natural selection and survival of the fittest no longer operate from case to case on individuals of a social species in a process of slow weeding away which will in the end leave the species quite transformed. Societies protect individuals and tend to conserve the general stock of its properties. In accord with this, and so far as archeological evidence can be interpreted, there seems to have been no fundamental change in Homo sapiens for the last sixty thousand years.

The men of sixty thousand years ago were just as intelligent as men are today. If the social circumstances into which we are born had been present, we can only assume that they would have enjoyed (or suffered) an equivalent condition of society. We differ from them only in the social heritage made possible by the accumulation of language transfigured experience and tool construction.

From the same observations it follows that at any given time in human society the potential number of geniuses is as great as any other. Man's potential creativity must be assumed to be a constant.

If one were to expect from this, however, that human development would show a continuously rising curve of achievement, he

---

* Henry David Thoreau, *Walden* (New York: The New American Library, 1953), p. 8.

would be seriously shocked. In the period of written history the record reveals radical alterations in the rhythm of human creativity. Periods of the dramatic upthrust of creativity contrast with others characterized by powerful forces toward conformity and the stereotyping of cultural achievement.

Since one cannot attribute these differential rates of creative achievement to any changes in human biology nor to racial differences (alterations in creativity appear in all the races, and the general evidence suggests there is no fundamental difference in the creative potential of any), there remains only the possibility that the condition of society releases or encourages creativity as the case may be.

In *Social Life and Cultural Change* some sort of biginning was made in the study of the sociology of creativity on the one hand and the sociology of conformity on the other.* Five major periods of creative efflorescence were brought under analysis. In the ancient world, shortly after 900 B.C., new developments of society and culture got underway with the sweeping away of old cultures and societies in major people's movements. There had been waves of social and cultural creativity before this, but for the first time writing was available to the major high cultural areas of the world, thereby permitting a record of the experience of the participants.

In the four major world areas, China, India, Palestine and Greece, the new waves of socio-cultural development reached a kind of fever pitch around 500 B.C. There is no evidence that these developments in any way influenced one another except in most tangential ways: They were parallel responses to similar types of social circumstances. At the same time the special circumstances and historical peculiarities of the major world areas gave a unique shaping to the respective developments. A distinctive cultural mentality with uniquely located bearers was to be found in the major world areas of the time. China presented a kind of pragmatic traditionalism; India developed a metaphysical salvation consciousness; Palestine brought to an unusual

* Don Martindale, *Social Life and Cultural Change* (Princeton, N.J.: D. Van Nostrand, 1963).

stage of ethical perfection a form of emissary prophecy; and in Greece a form of methodological rationalism dominated all major intellectual and cultural spheres. The bearers of these traditions varied: learned scholar officials and founders of schools in China; house priests and guilds of teachers in India; Yahweh priests and prophets in Palestine; and citizen philosophers in Greece. These contrasts may be summarized in the following table.

TABLE I

CULTURAL MENTALITY AND INTELLECTUALS IN THE MAJOR CULTURAL AREAS OF 500 B.C.*

Area	*Mentality*	*Social Role of Intellectual*
China	Pragmatic Traditionalism	Scholar officials and founders of schools
India	A historical, ascetic, metaphysical otherworldliness	Guru teachers and Purohita house priests
Palestine	Emissary Prophecy and Revolutionary Utopianism	Yahweh priests and prophets
Greece	Methodological Rationalism	Citizen philosophers

* Martindale, *ibid.*, pp. 78, 83.

The world still remembers the brilliant array of men of genius who appeared at this time. In the words of Viktor von Strauss:

> During the centuries when Lao-tse and Confucius were living in China a strange movement of the spirit passed through all civilized peoples. In Israel, Jeremiah, Habakkuk, Daniel and Ezekiel were prophesying and in a renewed generation (521-516) the second temple was erected in Jerusalem. Among the Greeks Thales was still living, Anaximander, Pythagoras, Heraclitus, and Zenophanes appeared and Parmenides was born. In Persia an important reformation of Zarathustra's ancient teaching seems to have been carried through, and India produced Sakyamuni, the founder of Buddhism.*

* Viktor von Strauss's commentary on Lao-tse (1870), quoted by Karl Jaspers in *The Origin and Goal of History* (New Haven: Yale University Press, 1953), pp. 8-9.

Most of the world's great religions were either founded in this period or raised on a foundation of cultural and intellectual traditions created at this time. The world is still drawing major intellectual and cultural sustenance from the traditions. Moreover, the creative energy manifest in persons who have come to be recognized as among the great men of all time seems by no means to have been confined to them alone but was manifest to a lesser degree in many average men of the day.

However, in all cases new times brought quite different milieus. The creative spirit withered, and the new ages canonized the creations of the earlier period and sought to stereotype thought with respect to the canons. The ascendency of the brilliantly equipped individual gave way to the patient conformity of anonymous clerks. In place of prophecy, the law became dominant; in place of the original intellectual speculation on how to found a social order, the cultivation of a traditionalistic style and reverence for the classics was approved; in place of original metaphysical speculation on man's fate, the magical stereotyping of thought and practice was carried through; in place of philosophy, theology was cultivated.

Changes in the social order accompanied these changes in thought and culture that characterized the ages of conformity that followed the great creative periods. In Ancient China and Egypt a world of cities was replaced by imperial orders. In India an age of cities and multiple competing kingdoms was gradually submerged in a system of caste. In Palestine the autonomous city-state was reduced to a status of dependence on foreign conquerors, and the point of socio-religious gravity shifted to an urban-domiciled ethnic minority.

Though the destiny of Western man since the Renaissance has not been worked out, something similar to these ancient developments also characterize our social history. As in the past, a once-dominant ancient culture (Roman) collapsed. A new starting point for social development was made by waves of a new people's movement, which set in motion complex new forms of society formation in which both the institutions of conqueror and conquered were reorganized. The period of community formation was once more a time of the flowering of genius. Here too, human creativity responded to its unique circumstances and produced the humanism and science peculiar to the Western mind. Finally, it has been argued by some persons that Western society and culture have passed their period of greatness and are at present on the threshold of a new era of conformity.

SOME TENTATIVE CONCLUSIONS

One cannot, of course, know whether these dark predictions of a "decline of the West" are correct even though made by such eminent twentieth century men as Oswald Spengler, Arnold Toynbee and Pitirim Sorokin. In any case, in the present context the problem is secondary to the question of the relation between human society and man's realization of his creative potential. Some very broad conclusions may tentatively be formulated: (a) Every society represents a more or less consistent exploration of a range of human potentiality; (b) every society to a greater or lesser degree opposes alternative social formulae; (c) every society hitherto has only explored a small phase of man's potentiality and utilized a limited range of the creative energies of its component members; (d) societies vary to the degree to which they encourage or even permit individuals to exploit their personal resources, and ages of creative genius even in single societies have been followed by periods in which the free expression of individual genius was discouraged; (e) periods of socially encouraged creativity and the flowering of genius have been times of community transition when collectivities have been seeking to find their way to new community formulas with no choice other than to free individuals for the task; (f) periods of conformity have been times in the hardening of community structure when further innovations have assumed the properties of a threat to established social arrangements.

At present it must be emphasized that such formulations are most tentative and in need of modification, extension and proof. The application of the theories and methods of contemporary sociology to the study of man's potential creativity is itself only a potentiality. Some day it will take its place together, perhaps, with the sociology of hope and the sociology of dreams, among the established areas of the field.

REFERENCES

1. Benda, Julien: *The Betrayal of the Intellectuals,* translated by Richard Aldington. Boston, Beacon Press, 1955.
2. Burckhardt, Jacob: *The Civilization of the Renaissance in Italy,* translated by S. G. C. Middlemore. New York, Oxford Univ. Press, 1945.
3. Jaspers, Karl: *Vom Ursprug und Ziel der Geschichte,* translated by Michael Bullock. Munich, R. Piper & Co., 1950. *The Origin and Goal of History.* New Haven, Yale Univ. Press, 1953.
4. Lasaulx, Ernst von: *Neuer Versuch einer alten, auf die Warheit der Tatschen begründeten Philosophie der Geschichte.* Munich, R. Oldenbourg, 1952.
5. Martindale, Don: *Social Life and Cultural Change.* Princeton, New Jersey, Van Nostrand, 1962.
6. Mead, George Herbert: *Mind, Self and Society.* Chicago, Univ. of Chicago Press, 1934.
7. Montagu, Ashley: *Man in Process.* New York, Mentor Books, 1961.
8. Spengler, Oswald: *The Decline of the West,* translated by Charles Atkinson. New York, Knopf, 1926.

Chapter 4

SPONTANEITY, CREATIVITY, AND HUMAN POTENTIALITIES

J. L. MORENO

DEFINITION OF CREATIVITY

IT is not sufficient to define creativity by its semantics, as for instance: "Cause to be or to come into existence; or to make a new form out of pre-existing substance." Creativity can only be defined by its inner dynamics. It requires that we enter into its dialectic opposites so as to make clear what it means. One way of defining creativity is by its maximum condition, maximum creativity—the fullest penetration of the universe by creativity, a world which has been creative from beginning to end and which never ceases to be creative. The opposite condition of creativity would then be zero creativity—a world which is entirely uncreative, automatic, which has no past or future, no evolution or purpose and which is absolutely changeless and meaningless.

SPONTANEITY, CREATIVITY AND THE CULTURAL CONSERVE

Creativity manifests itself in any series of creativity states or creative acts. It belongs to the category of substance; it is the arch substance, the elementary X without any specialized connotation, the X which may be recognized by its acts. Creativity is a sleeping beauty which, in order to become effective, needs a catalyzer. The arch catalyzer of creativity is spontaneity, by definition from the Latin *sua sponte* which means "coming from within." But what is spontaneity? Is it a form of energy? If it is energy it is unconservable. It emerges and is spent in a moment; it must emerge to be spent and must be spent to make way for new emergence, like the life of some animals which are born and die in the love act. It is a truism to say that the universe cannot exist without physical and mental energy which can be conserved. But it is more important to realize that without the other kind of energy, the unconservable one—or spontaneity—the creativity of the universe could not start and could not run; it would come to a standstill. Spontaneity operates in the present, *hic et nunc.* It propels the individual towards an adequate response to a new situation or a new response to an old situation. Thus, while creativity is related to the "act" itself, spontaneity is related to the warming up, to the "readiness" of the act.

The finished product of the creative process is the cultural conserve, which comes from *conservare.* A cultural conserve is anything that preserves the values of a particular culture. It may take the form of a material object, such as a book, film, building or musical composition, or it may appear as a highly set pattern of behavior, such as a religious ceremony, a theatrical performance of a pre-written play, a fraternity initiation or the inaugural ceremonies for the President of the United States. As a repository of the past, cultural conserves preserve and continue man's creative ego. Without them man would be reduced to creating spontaneously the same forms to meet the same situations day after day. For example, a cultural conserve such as the dictionary makes it unnecessary for man to redefine his words every time he wishes to communicate. In addition to providing continuity to the heritage of human existence, *the cultural conserve plays an even more significant role as the springboard for enticing new spontaneity toward creativity.*

However, there lies a danger in the overreliance of mankind on the cultural conserve. This danger is inherent both in the conserve's state of finality and in its abuse by mankind. For spontaneous creativity—however supreme it may be in itself—once conserved is, by definition, no longer spontaneity; it has lost its actuality in the universe. There are two forms of creativity—the freely emerging flowing creativity and conserved creativity. The latter fills the world in the form of cultural conserves which contain creativity in a dormant frozen state. These conserves wait for "Prince Charming Spontaneity" to awaken them from their sleep. Left to themselves, nothing "new" would ever happen. But conserves represent the greatest cultural capital, a form of property and power, a means of expressing superiority when the superiority of immediate spontaneous creativity is not available.

CATEGORIES OF CREATOR

The realization or fullfilment of creativity in man takes many forms. Among them are two outstanding categories of creator: (a) the devotee of the truly perfect; and (b) the devotee of the truly imperfect, the lover of spontaneity.

The devotee of the truly perfect upholds the conserve as the ultimate value and is skeptical of spontaneity. He is a devotee of theory and a master of words. That is why he is compulsive, authoritarian and critical of those who act. He loves to develop magnificent theoretical systems, physical, social and cultural projects. He sponsors theories of religion, of altruism, of love and preferably on the theoretical reflective level. He shrinks from experimenting existentially with religious or theoretical creativity. He does not strive for the embodiment of sainthood in his own life.

The improvising creator, in contrast, is devoted to experimentation of all forms—religious, therapeutic, scientific. He is the improvisor in art, science and religion. Rather than writing books and formulating systems he loves to act and create. Whereas the "truly perfect" is loved by an elite, the improvisor is loved by the multitude. It is a profound contrast between the aristocrat and the people's leader.

Thus, there is a profound contrast between the theoreticians of religion, sainthood and altruism, such as St. John, St. Augustine, Plato, Plotin, Spinoza, Kant, and Hegel, and the experimenters, producers and practitioners of religion and sainthood such as Jesus, Buddha, St. Francis and Baal Schem. These experimenters and lesser luminaries, such as Sabbatai Zwi, Savonarola, Pascal and Kierkegaard often look inadequate, imperfect, overbearing, eccentric, ebullient, stupid, even pathological, but they were trying to live a life of truth and preferred an imperfect existence to a perfect theory.

The future of a culture is finally decided by the creativity of its carriers. If a disease of the creative functions, a creativity neurosis, has afflicted the most primary group, the creative men of the human race, then it is of supreme importance that the principle of creativity be redefined and that its perverted forms be compared with creativity in its original states. There are higher and lower forms of creativity in its original states. There are higher and lower forms of creativity. The highest forms of human creativity are manifest in the lives of prophets, poets, saints and scientists; the lower forms are operating in every humble existence, day by day.

HUMAN POTENTIALITY, MAN AND SPONTANEITY

There is apparently little spontaneity in the universe; or if there is any abundance of it, only a small particle is available to man, hardly enough to keep him surviving. In the past he has done everything to discourage its development. He could not rely upon the instability and insecurity of the moment with an organism which was not ready to deal with it adequately; he encouraged the development of devices such as intelligence, memory, social and cultural conserves which would give him the needed support with the result that he gradually became the slave of his own crutches. If there is a neurological localization of the spontaneity-creativity process, it is the least developed function of man's nervous system. The difficulty is that one cannot store spontaneity; one either is spontaneous at a given moment or one is not. If the spontaneity is such an important factor for man's world, why is it so poorly developed? The answer may be that man *fears* spontaneity and the uncertainty of it just like his ancestor in the jungle feared fire; he feared fire until he learned how to make it. Man will fear spontaneity until he will learn how to unleash it, train and control it. A great deal of man's psycho- and socio-pathology can be ascribed to the insufficient development of spontaneity and therefore the inability to mobilize the potential sources of creativity. Spontaneity "training" is therefore the most auspicious skill to be taught to scientists, educators and therapists in all our institutions of learning, and it is their task to teach students or clients how to be more spontaneous without becoming excessive. To do this we have to first recognize the fact that spontaneity and creativity can operate in our mental universe and evoke levels of organized expression which are not fully traceable to preceding determinants. This fact causes us to recommend the abandonment or reformulation of all current psychological and sociological theories openly or tacitly based upon psychoanalytic doctrine, for example, the theories of frustration, projection, substitution and sublimation. These theories have to be rewritten, retested and based on spontaneity-creativity formulation.

MAN AND THE ROBOT

One can visualize that the course of the universe has been and may continue to move indefinitely in the same principal direction however much the constellation of cultures may change in volume, intensity and depth.

However, if one surveys the long history of human cosmos, this process of unfolding in one direction seems gradually to be called to a temporary halt and uprooted by the phenomenon of the robot, from the Slavic root *robota,* which means to work. It has emerged in manifold varieties, from the book to the high speed electronic computer to the spaceship. It represents forms of existence which are utterly different from the other processes of creativity with which man has identified himself. The robot evolved in many of its applications, not to confirm man's existence and creativity, but to supplant, destroy and deny it. It worked like the dissonance in a symphony which the conductor tries desperately to bring into synchronization with the total composition itself.

What is a robot? It is one of those mysterious paradoxes in the development of man, following the lines of the cultural conserve, emerging out of his greatest loss of spontaneity and creativity. The robot is lifeless. It is neutral. It is the same at every instant; it does not grow, it does not change. A human infant results from the conjugation of a man and a woman. A robot results from the conjugation of man with nature itself. In both cases the offspring takes over some features from both parents. In the robot, for instance, there is some feature of the man-producer and some feature of natural energy modified by him.

Once upon a time we envisioned God as the one who could destroy us anytime he wanted to. This power has been passed over to man; by means of robots he, too, can give a single individual the power to rule and perhaps to destroy the universe instantly. But the robots cannot produce an ounce of spontaneity.

The control of the robot is complicated for two reasons. One, the robot is man's own creation. He does not meet it face to face as he did the beasts of the jungle, measuring his strength, intelligence and spontaneity with theirs. The robot comes from within man's mind; he gives birth to it. He is confounded by it like every parent is towards his own child. Rational and irrational factors are mixed, therefore, in his relationship to robots. In the excitement of creating them, man is unaware of the poison which they carry, threatening to kill their own parent. Second, in using robots, man unleashes forms of energy and perhaps touches on properties which far surpass his own little world and which belong to the larger, unexplored and perhaps uncontrollable universe. His task of becoming a master on such a scale becomes a dubious one as he may well find himself more and more in the position of Goethe's Sorcerer's Apprentice who could unleash the robots but who could not stop them. The apprentice had forgotten the master's formula which stopped the robot. We have the formula to make them but not to stop them.

The fate of man threatens to become that of the dinosaur in reverse. The dinosaur perished because he extended the power of his organism in excess of its usefulness. Man may perish because of reducing the power of his organism by fabricating robots in excess of his control.

Man had to create the robot in order to survive. If there would have been an abundance of spontaneity in man's world, the world of the robot may have never come to being. It may have been a part of the creator rather than separated from him.

The robot may well become the link between the human cosmos and the cosmos at large. It is like the two-faced god, Janus. For if properly manipulated in the hands of creative man, the robot world might be the forerunner of a new kind of universe, one in which man is the propelling and ruling force—creating a new universe which may replace the old one and even replace man himself. But this transformation of himself and the universe may be the greatest expression of his potentialities; for man's creativity may become continuously necessary to feed and propel the robot; thus, the robot, similar to the cultural conserve, becomes the agent to activate, mobilize and constantly stimulate and renew the creative potential of man.

REFERENCES

1. Bischof, Ledford J.: *Interpreting Personality Theories.* New York, Harper & Row, 1964.
2. Moreno, J. L.: *Sociometry and the Science of Man.* Boston, Beacon House, 1956.
3. Moreno, J. L.: The Future of Man's World, *Group Psychotherapy, A Symposium.* Boston, Beacon House, 1945.
4. Moreno, J. L.: Creativity and cultural conserves. *Sociometry, II*:1939.
5. Moreno, J. L.: *The Words of the Father,* 1st German edition. Berlin, Kiepenheuer, 1920.

Chapter 5

MENTAL HEALTH AND THE CONCEPT OF HIGH-LEVEL WELLNESS

HALBERT L. DUNN

IT is the purpose of this chapter to define mental health and high-level wellness as derivative energy concepts and to examine the logistics of inner man in terms of energy characteristics. This is followed by a brief examination of the principal balancing factors and the major directional components which enable man to attain and maintain mental health and high-level wellness and to achieve a higher degree of human potential.

DEFINITIONS

Human Potential

"Growth and learning can lure into being whatever is potential in the inner stuff of humanity but nothing more." This observation by Gardner Murphy (1) is in accord with the modern concept of potential energy, as energy held within the design of matter until it is let loose by some factor that acts as a trigger to release it. With the emergence of the newer knowledge of atomic physics we now know that subatomic, atomic and molecular energy is bound into matter in vast quantities; but it can be released if the proper trigger is found. It would seem, therefore, that these words of Murphy could be modified into a perfectly satisfactory definition of human potential, consistent with energy concepts, i.e.:

> *Human potential is the capacity or potentialities latent within the individual and society which can be released as creative energy when properly triggered or activated.* The creative energy so released implements the imagination which is the structured synthesis of new ideas from elements experienced separately.

Obviously, human potential does not consist solely of physical potential. We expect the athlete, however perfect his body coordination, to use his mind as well. He must be alert and observant and able to analyze problem situations quickly and accurately. He must also have a courageous spirit and hold aspirations for excellence in performance—qualities stemming from the interaction of body, mind and spirit. This state of inter-relationship we call self-integration, and over a period of months or years self-integration becomes synonymous with mental health.

Mental Health

In advancing, below, a definition of mental health, the author is fully aware of the searching examination made in Jahoda's masterly review of various concepts of mental health (2). Yet, the importance of balance, purpose, autonomy, perception of reality and environmental mastery brought out in that review are all implicit in a concept of mental health as a dynamic type of integration.

> *Mental health is balance maintained between the interacting and interrelated energy fields of body-mind-spirit and the environment.*

The terms "balance" and "energy field" in this definition are derivative energy concepts. An *energy field* is the spread of polarized energy over time and space. It is a localized type of force field and is characteristic of all matter. Once created, energy fields come to interlock with one another. Subatomic particles are the smallest energy fields. The subatomic design makes possible the atomic, which in turn creates the molecular structure. Thus, in the crucible of intense heat, chemicals emerge which form the substance of matter, making up the animate and inanimate stuff of which we are made and which we recognize as reality.

These interlocking and interdependent energy systems are ever-changing—sometimes almost static, at other times explosively violent. Stability of energy systems depends upon maintaining an equilibrium between energy systems. Since such systems are in a continual flux of change, this must be a dynamic type of equilibrium. *Balance* is thus the moving axis of equilibrium between interrelated and interacting energy fields.

Necessarily, then, the proposed definition of mental health is a dynamic rather than a static concept. It is geared to a continuum of change.

High-level Wellness

From the above, it is immediately evident that the concept of mental health is closely identified with the concept of high-level wellness.

> *High-level wellness for the individual is an integrated method of functioning which is oriented toward maximizing the potential of which the individual is capable.* It requires that the individual maintain a continuum of balance and purposeful direction within the environment where he is functioning (3).

This definition of high-level wellness is applicable not only to the individual but also to all types of social organizations—to the family, to the community, to groups of individuals, such as business, political or religious institutions, to the nation and to mankind as a whole. For each of these aggregates it implies a forward direction in progress, an open-ended expanding future, interaction of the social aggregate and an integrated method of functioning which recognizes the interdependence of man with other life forms.

THE LOGISTICS OF INNER MAN

The body is an enormous organization of cells which must be understood and operated as a whole. Likewise, the cells of the body are complex worlds, made up of enormous numbers of molecules. All cells are "open" systems, involved with selectivity, self-regulation, maintenance of dynamic, chemical equilibrium and interdependent with other competitive elements.

The life of the individual commences with the fertilization of the ovum. The fertilized ovum contains the inherited components, which are transmitted through cell division to each cell of the growing organism. The growth process uses vast quantities of energy and information. The energy required for growth is taken largely from food and from the oxygen of the air. The amount used is relatively great in early life and relatively small in old age. Information needed by the growing body is of two types: that which comes from the outside world through sensory organs; and that which is stored, assembled, integrated, used and modified and continually reintegrated into the "perceptive form world" by which we run our lives.

In contrast to the body of the individual, which is biologically more or less similar to other life forms, the mind and spirit of man seem to be uniquely human. Are these two components of the individual also manifestations of energy?

The mind, for our purposes here, is defined as "the ability-complex which enables man to use the sum total of the information available to him, for the purpose of solving the problems of living" (3). If our bodies are sound at birth there is reason to conclude that most of us inherit a potentially almost-perfect problem solving mind. If this delicate mechanism is treated with the proper care during the early years, we should be able to enjoy mental health throughout life.

What part does the spirit of man play in mental health? For the purpose of this chapter, "spirit" is used in the sense of vitality and is considered to be the zone of interaction between the energies at the command of the body and those used in the functioning of the mind. As already pointed out, self-integration requires the maintenance of dynamic equilibrium between the energies of mind and body or a continual reintegration of self.

The process of reintegration is carried forward most efficiently when the energy systems of the body are in a state of relative balance. The quiet release of excessive tension requires a balance between the work and struggle of life, on the one hand, and the more relaxing activities of recreation, on the other. Concentration of energy in focused activity does not afford much opportunity for self-adjustment. Likewise, the self-integration process is hampered by maintenance of fixed beliefs mitigating against readjustment and by the existence of frustration, fear and hate which set up concentrated knots of tension.

Since high-level wellness involves a dynamic equilibrium, or self-integration in the midst of change, it must be geared to the realities of the environment in which the individual is living. For instance, it is quite possible that some people might be able to achieve and maintain mental health in certain specific environments and yet not be able to do so under other circumstances.

BALANCE AND DIRECTIONAL FACTORS INVOLVED IN HIGH-LEVEL WELLNESS

Balancing and directional factors are essential in all energy systems. Man and his society are not exceptions. When balance is lost, stresses and strains and tensions occur. What are these? *Stress* is the wear and tear on energy systems due to tension. *Strain* is the distortion in energy systems due to tension. And *tension* is the effect produced by divergent energy flow upon or within energy fields. These energy terms are directly applicable to the individual and to his social groups.

Directional forces help to maintain balance. Forward movement through time and with purpose brings a measure of stability and makes it easier to retain a balanced position. The spinning top, the high-wire performer and the surfboard rider are examples of this principle in the area of mechanics.

The principal balancing factors which are essential to well-being are chemical, physiological and psychological in character and can be little more than mentioned in this limited space.

Chemical Balance

Chemical balance is essential for the proper functioning of body cells. No person can enjoy well-being unless the cells of his body receive what they need and maintain a smooth working relationship with one another. To have cellular wellness involves chemical balance between the fluids inside and outside of the cell, the proper distribution and consistency of body fluid, the presence of hormones in proper amounts and the maintenance of balanced bio-electrical potentials within the body. The entire molecular world of the cell must be maintained in chemical equilibrium, or the cell will die. Threats to the equilibrium come from all sides. Many dangerous forms of energy are constantly being released in the environment. Radiation, for example, and poisons such as those from smog, insecticides and certain drugs injure and frequently destroy the cells which they penetrate.

Each cell has an outer and an inner world of its own. Both contain fluid and soluble salts. Many things can upset the balance of body fluid—the heat of summer, certain foods, various illnesses, loss of blood, etc. The body struggles unceasingly to maintain a proper balance in the body fluid, both to keep it properly distributed and to keep it at the right consistency. For example, the equilibrium between acid and alkali teeter-totters constantly. If the body fluid becomes too acid, the lungs exhale more carbon dioxide than usual in order to restore the balance.

The ductless glands pour their hormones directly into the blood stream. Hormones are chemicals made by the adrenal, pituitary, thyroid, parathyroid, pineal and thymus glands. The sex hormones come from the ovary in the female and from the testis in the male. These hormones take over a considerable amount of the control of the chemical processes within the cells and carry chemical messages. For instance, adrenalin pours into the blood stream whenever the individual is aware that danger threatens and moves the body into high gear to fight or to escape as might be necessary.

Delicate chemical balances are also responsible for the bio-electrical forces which are held in potential by the polarized molecular membranes of body cells. This provides the life force which, when activated by the appropriate enzyme within the cell, brings a discharge of energy and cellular activity. We do not know much about the part that bio-electrical forces play in controlling the cellular commonwealth as a cooperating mechanism, but this probably is a major factor in bringing about self-integration or a state of mental health. Such forces may well be behind the increased effectiveness of the body when it is under the impetus of strong purpose.

Neuromuscular Balance

The neuromuscular system integrates the parts of the body into a functioning whole. It provides the principal channels for inner communication. Motility of the body depends upon it. It redistributes the resources of the body to meet the stresses and strains of each day. It moves the blood and body fluid to parts where the demands for these are greatest. This system plays a part in the problem-solving activities of body and mind.

Balance Between the Inner and Outer Worlds

Each person lives in both an inner and an outer world. The inner world is the cellular commonwealth; the outer, the physical and social environment. Balance between the two requires communication between them. The more open the channels of communication, the greater are the prospects for physical and mental health. Frequently, clogged channels of communication or hate, prejudice and fixed ideas make it almost impossible for the mind to solve problems correctly. Furthermore, as the years go by, the intake ports both for energy and for information begin to close down. The struggle to maintain adequate interchange between the inner and the outer worlds is never-ending.

Balance Between the Individual and His Environment

No person lives in the world alone, insulated from his physical and social environment. High-level wellness and mental health must be sought within the environmental and social conditions in which one lives. In our society it behooves all who value and seek a high potential in life to do their utmost to foster environments favorable to the achievement of this aim.

Many factors in our highly industrialized, urban culture are badly out of balance. To name but a few—

Population density and living space—crowding people too closely together—makes for higher tension with consequent higher incidence of physical and mental illness and social breakdown. Open space needs to be promoted within urban living. Crowded living quarters are a hazard to healthy living.

Materialism, a top value of our times, needs to be balanced with idealism. To possess wealth and to desire material things are not wrong in themselves, but when this becomes the dominant drive in life, it needs to be brought back into balance by idealistic concepts and altruistic effort. The success of the Peace Corps in its appeal to youth is probably symptomatic of the hunger felt by many for idealistic values in a world too oriented towards materialism.

Freedom for the individual is relative. It needs to be balanced by the shouldering of the responsibilities that freedom entails. Otherwise, freedom becomes license.

Urbanization and its demands need to be balanced by considerations focused on keeping the ecological system healthy. The job of planning the growing metropolis calls for sincere dedication on the part of both planners and citizens to recognize the requirements for an ecology that takes its proper supporting place in man's scheme. Social man needs to become responsible toward life in all its forms.

These various types of balances, among many others, are examples of chemical, physiological and psychological factors which can be maintained more easily if there is direction in living. The principal directional components are *time* and *purpose*.

The human race is progressing through time as a relatively minor fraction of the very long life cycle of our planet. The individual is progressing through time as a very small fraction of the relatively long life cycle of the human race. In the short span of the individual's life cycle, direction in the earlier years comes from the biological changes inherent in physical growth. With adolescence and maturity, purpose must take over increasingly, to give direction.

Purpose as a directional component becomes more important with each stage of the life cycle. The infant, in order to grow normally, must establish a secure base in a strange world. The child is the learner, reaching outward toward the rich experience of his parents and teachers. The teenager presses forward eagerly toward the fulfillment of love, a family of his own and job success. As maturity approaches, purpose expressed in social, psychological and religious terms takes on an ever-increasing role. Love ripens, and human relationships broaden. From this emerges ultimately the brotherhood of man, encompassing the human race. Cultural values become increasingly important as the individual strives to contribute something of himself to others before he passes on. Creative expression, if it has been firmly rooted in the earlier years, wells up as a major driving force from within the innermost being of the mature self. Religion becomes the vital, meaningful relationship between the self and the universe —as man reaches outward for something beyond himself.

The directional forces motivating the mature individual and moving him towards self-actualization are a blending of time and purpose until, in the older years as the life cycle nears its end, balance must be largely maintained by having purpose in life sufficient to guide the mind and spirit of man.

Due to the physical limitations of the aging body most older people will need to find their high potential and mental health within the neighborhoods in which they live. This is one reason why a friendly, concerned community is fully as important for the older ages as it is for the rearing of children and the transmittal of values which are conducive to high-level wellness.

SUMMARY

To summarize: Since the entire physical universe is a manifestation of organized energy which is interrelated and interdependent—from the minutest subatomic particles to the farthest galaxies, and since the human body operating as a commonwealth of cells is no exception, the proper functioning of the individual at a high potential depends upon the maintenance of balance between his inner world and the outer world in which he moves.

Through advances in science and technology man has speeded up change and is transforming his physical environment at an ever-accelerated pace. The effects of these changes ripple outward to all parts of the physical environment and the ecology. They penetrate to the deepest recesses of the inner world, changing mental and spiritual patterns in the process. Balance can be maintained only as a dynamic equilibrium. The road to mental health and to high-level wellness, both for the individual and for society, depends largely upon striving to attain and maintain a balanced position within the reality of change, guided by purpose sufficient to light the way.

REFERENCES

1. MURPHY, GARDNER: *Human Potentialities.* New York, Basic Books, 1958, 306.
2. JAHODA, MARIE: *Current Concepts of Positive Mental Health.* Joint Commission on Mental Illness and Health. Monograph Series, No. 1. New York, Basic Books, 1958.
3. DUNN, HALBERT L.: *High-Level Wellness.* A collection of twenty-nine short talks on different aspects of the theme "High-Level Wellness for Man and Society." Arlington, Virginia, P. O. Box 26, R. W. Beatty Co., 1961.

Chapter 6

SOME VALUE CONSIDERATIONS UNDERLYING THE HUMAN POTENTIALITIES CONCEPT

IJA N. KORNER

EVERY field of the sciences has its obnoxious problems; the social and behavioral sciences have an especially generous share of them. One Hydra monster which sociology, cultural anthropology and psychology have inherited from philosophy, more specifically from moral philosophy, is the problem of values. The problem has a Hydra monster quality because it perpetuates itself, coming up again and again in spite of valiant attempts to eliminate it by a variety of methods. It has been ignored, declared unnecessary, unscientific, metaphysical, philosophical; it has been renamed, redefined, reassigned, in the hope that somehow it would go away and cease to plague the fields. Why does the value issue keep reemerging, and why is it so disliked by scientific disciplines?

The concept of *values* has survived all demises because it is based on observations. People will perform certain acts again and again, not because they are useful, economical, rational, intelligent, beautiful, etc., but because they are "important." When the search for an explanation of the importance has led to the end of all possible why's and has terminated in the answer, "I don't know exactly why, simply because it *is* important" (frequently the quality of obviousness is also included), then we call this final statement a statement of values.

This "something," which appears to influence trivial and vital decisions, casual and life-affecting actions, by one or many individuals in a more or less permanent manner, with a greater and smaller degree of "oughtness," finally compelled the reluctant attention of the social science field. Social scientists found the "value" qualities in attitudes, opinions, ideas, creeds, ideals, morals, ethics and others. Although individuals and groups of individuals vary greatly in regard to what appear to be their "values," still the sociologist discerned some common denominator; he felt justified in talking about "group-values." The same phenomenon was observed by the cultural anthropologist in the more uniform conditions of living in primitive societies. The psychologist, most restricted of all social scientists because of his worship of methodology, was the last and the most reluctant to give up his resistance. He suffers considerable methodological discomfort which is inherent in the use of the concept of "value."

The problems confronting scientific students of values are many and obvious. It is rare that an individual can make a concise statement about one of his own values. A value cannot be observed directly but is the result of inferences made from actions and verbal reports. Seldom can these behaviors be compared to each other because they are usually global and elusive in character. Thus, the relationship between a statement and the behavioral correlates from which its value quality is deduced is rarely direct and unambiguous. All the scientific observer can do is to note the verbal statements and/or actions of one or more individuals and observe the qualities of urgency, oughtness and importance. The frequency and regularity with which these qualities occur may lead to the inference that there is a central theme, a mainspring, which in turn is called a value.

Values represent hypothetical constructs; and a link must somehow be forged, reliably and predictably, between the abstraction and the postulated observable behaviors. Once this is successfully accomplished there is need to arrange the postulated values in some form of functional hierarchy. Values increase the understanding of human behavior only when arranged in hierarchical order. Which value is more, which less peripheral; which has more, which less effect on the behavior of one or a group of individuals? But hierarchies and dimensions can only be established after measurements have been taken, and what can one measure when dealing with values? The abstractions cannot be weighed. Only the behaviors to which they refer can be measured.

Thus, the acts of induction required to establish values are fraught with the dangers of inaccurate observations, misconceptions and errors; and the resulting conceptualizations often do not meet the minimum criteria of precision and clarity necessary to satisfy a scientist, intrigued and attracted as he may be by observations.

There can be no better demonstration of the intriguing pull, hesitance, scholarship, and courage than Brewster Smith's recent publication, *Personal Values in the Study of Lives* (5). After discussing his apprehension as well as his attraction to the problem of values, the author reviews some of the pertinent literature and finally arrives at his definition of values: ". . . Such a conception, it seems to me, is that of selective behavior, in which a person chooses, rejects, takes interest in, approves, disapproves —with respect to a physical, social, or ideal object. . . . We employ the terminology of values as a conceptual handle for discerning and dealing with this behavior." Brewster Smith takes as one of his starting points Clyde Kluckhorn's definition: "A value is a conception, explicit or implicit, distinctive of an individual or characteristic of a group, of the desirable, which influences the selection from available modes, means, and ends of action" (2). Smith stresses the importance of the property of "desirable": "The core of Kluckhorn's definition that I would presently stress, then, is the focus on a particular class of personal dispositions: conceptions of the desirable that are relevant to selective behavior." Smith is also impressed by Heider's (1) quality of "oughts"; and he says: "As a first approximation, Heider notes a degree of parallelism between the content of 'I ought to do such and such' and that of 'somebody wants or commands that I do such and such.' "

Smith then proceeds to discuss the social and personal requirements of values. He concludes by developing the notion of (conscious) *self-values,* which he differentiates from the primarily unconscious ones postulated in the Freudian concept of the superego. Brewster Smith's article touches nearly all issues related to the problem of values; his own interpretation and explanation of self-values has all the virtues demanded by psychology. The concept of self-value is broadly inclusive, pertinent and open to research. There is only one thing he does not do, and neither do most others who are concerned with values; and that is to name a value by name.

As long as values are discussed as conceptualizations only, many of the methodological difficulties can be ignored. It is when a specific value is mentioned that disagreements and confusions emerge. Is the specific concept a value, a belief, an attitude? Is the specific value important or very important to the individual, and how can one measure importance? Is it shared by individuals; and if so, how widely? To what degree?

With measurement far away, the discussion of values demands the courage of *speculation*. Values must be assumed to exist, and their hierarchical order must be at least postulated. Only if this is done can the long, tedious process of testing, vertification and rejection commence.

Those interested in value-theory appear to share a vague consensus on some of the basic elements to be included in an eventual definition, but the consensus is small. In the main, each author is asked to state his criteria and to defend his choice of what he postulates values to be. In the following discussion the term "basic values" is used to connote a special category of values with distinct properties. The first and foremost characteristic of the "basic values" is their *must* quality.

Earlier it was noted (Heider) that "oughtness" represents an important quality of values. The "ought" covers a wide span of intensity, from a mild dictate to an imperative and majestic "*must* under all circumstances"; while "ought" grants many degrees of latitude, the "must" permits none. Because of the all-or-none quality of some values, they must be regarded as unique phenomena. They command unique consequences and have a unique position in the psychological system. It is these values which are here assumed to be "basic" to the functioning of the individual and/or the group.

Basic values are held to be properties of individuals or groups of individuals, determining behavior relatively *independent of time and place.* The individual and/or the group are mostly unaware of the existence and rarely aware of the effects of basic values upon behavior. Basic values are highly predictable because they are nearly invariant. They are relatively independent of reward and punishment; they are outside the sphere of good and bad. They are more than "oughts," they have the character of absolute "musts." Basic values are neither rational nor irrational—they are axiomatic. They have the status of basic premises which are not to be and perhaps cannot be questioned. They are not open to proof, discussion and examination. They are beyond the question of "why," to which a rational answer can be given. It is the unconscious—a rational, noncognitive property of basic values—which makes them into quasi-automatic selectors and organizers of perceptions—dictating behaviors and regulating courses of action. Basic values are behavior-motivating, but their function extends beyond that; they serve as stabilizers, as sources of integration for the psychological structure of individuals.

Basic values are but very indirectly related to opinions, attitudes, morals, creeds, beliefs, etc. Verbal communications about the value of life and living, for example, may be expressed as attitudes, creeds or beliefs, all accessible to awareness. On the other hand, the basic values and their impact on action are but rarely recognized with awareness. The superego and self-values postulated by Smith may contain elements and derivatives of the basic values, but these are not of the same order and quality as the basic values. The relationship between basic values and what commonly are regarded as values is one of mutual dependence—neither can exist without the other. The values in the superego as well as the self-values serve among others to protect and sustain the basic values.

All values state that some behaviors are *good,* others less good, others *bad.* Values function as behavior organizers. They carry the implicit promise that "good" behavior will lead to results necessary to *good* living. The good life, on the other hand, is based on the basic tenets of living which are expressed in the basic values.

The value structure with its perspective formulas spells to the individual a sense of internal permanence and predictability which he needs as a shield against the relative unpredictability of his environment.

Analogies to this postulated relationship are hard to find and can be used only within the broadest limits of comparison. Our system of economics, however, can perhaps yield a useful parallel. The gold of Fort Knox has no practical use. It serves an abstract function—its importance consists of people's knowing that the gold is there. As such it provides one of the foundations of the currency system. The currency system must be stable and reliable. Both conditions depend upon the myth-laden assumption of the perpetuity of Fort Knox and its gold. The existence of Fort Knox protects the currency system; the currency system protects Fort Knox. As long as the currency is healthy, it prevents a run on the gold. When it is unhealthy, Fort Knox is depleted; the currency and the total economic system may be destroyed. In an analogous manner, the vast psychological system of values, creeds, beliefs, attitudes and opinions serve to support and protect the basic values.

There remains the most difficult part of the task, to present an example of a basic value and to demonstrate that the assumption of "basic" is warranted.

The first basic value to be postulated is the *life value*. It consists of the individual's axiomatic assumption that the state of being alive is *the* condition of existence and must therefore be maintained under all circumstances. Nearly all people at nearly all times will act in the direction of fostering and protecting what they perceive as their lives. The attempts may be ineffective or detrimental; but the intent is to cope, to continue, to maintain.

Exceptions to this observation will be discussed below. The life value represents an individual's axiomatic assumption that to live and go on living is his most important endeavor. The life value, like any part of the human organism, needs a benign environment for its existence—a climate of moderate freedom from uncertainty, abuse and depletion, on one hand, of modest physical and emotional sustenance and security, on the other; under these conditions the life value will remain strong and active.

Some of the freedom from uncertainty and emotional sustenance is provided by a well-organized and operating value structure. The life value, for example, needs protection from the realistic danger that other individuals can be threatening and dangerous under conditions of deprivation, passion, anger, envy, etc.

The fabric of society and its institutions provide considerable protection—based on the ancient ethical value, "Thou shalt not kill." Thus, the ethical value, "Thou shalt not kill" defends the basic life value; without the life value, "Thou shalt not kill" would make little sense. A series of interrelated, well-integrated and strong values concerned with the sanctity of life and prohibitions against killing—the latter surrounded by clear statements of exceptions to the rule—provide the necessary protection for the life value. The life value itself is to be taken like faith but is, in turn, continuously validated by experiences gained through or as the result of adherence to values.

In our own Western society the life value is transmitted long before the individual can be said to have developed an ego. It is the basic premise of all parental activities and is transmitted in the very act of caring for the infant. It is a totally unconscious message inherent in the absolute dictum that one must care for the infant; it must grow up; it must be protected; it *must* live. A member of Western society who does not care for an infant, who is indifferent as to whether it lives or dies, is an abnormal member of the society and is regarded with horror. The life value surrounds the infant as a totality and therefore is accepted in the very basic structure of his psychological organism. Society in all its organizations mirrors the absolute acceptance of the life value.

This affirmative attitude toward the state of existing must not be confused with the biological concept of life-preservation. Biological assumptions like "survival" cannot be taken into the realm of psychological theory; the biological postulate of survival and the psychological experiences in regard to living must be treated separately. The same behavior may serve both the psychologist and the biologist as the foundation for their respective conceptualizations, but the resulting postulates cannot be equated. They must be dealt with from within their respective systems. Some may postulate that the biological conceptualization of *survival* and the psychological of *life value* are related or equivalent, but the psychologist dealing with psychological phenomena and psychological systems needs a *psychological* explanation of what makes man persist in seeking the condition of living. For the purpose of this discussion, the life value represents a psychological concept unrelated to survival.

The assumption of the life value implicitly states that *nonlife* is feared, negated, turned away from. As long as the individual accepts the life value as his basic premise, he must react to nonlife as being totally unacceptable to him. When the life value is reduced in its power as an axiomatic basic premise, it often corresponds to a greater indifference (reduced fear) to nonliving—it does *not* result in searching for or turning toward nonliving.

There are phenomena and observations which appear to deny the conceptualization of the life value. People do commit suicide, sacrifice their lives for causes and for other people or behave in such a way that their actions can be interpreted as lacking adherence to and acceptance of the life value. Reports from prisoners of war, concentration camp inmates and physicians on acute wards indicate that observers often knew when some individual ceased to care about living. Others in similar physical conditions survived because they wanted to live, because of incredible determination to hang on to life. Dramatic are the reports of prisoners of war in German and Korean camps where living conditions were marginal and physical stress maximal. One observer reports (personal communication): "We always knew in advance when someone would die. The first thing we noted was that he ceased to move, ceased to participate in all activities which were necessary for survival. He would lie on his bunk, stare non-communicatively into space and just be inert. We knew that he would be dead in a few days and invariably that is what happened. One day that happened to the guy who slept above me; he just lay there. I got furious at him and I hauled him out of his bunk which he permitted to happen without any resistance. I then started beating him up really good. After I did it for awhile, he seemed to snap out of it—he went to eat and the whole thing was over after he went to eat."

It appears as if individuals were able to assume psychological attitudes of indifference to living. Psychological indifference to living appears as a condition conducive to physical death.

Mental emotional states as described above have often been mistakenly attributed to and classified as acute, chronic, severe and other forms of pathological depression.

Physical death has two aspects which must be viewed separately. The first is biological death, which is a biological phenomenon and therefore outside the psychological field. Psychology deals with the second aspect, psychological death—man's fear of nonliving, his emotions and feelings about the finality of his existence, his psychological reaction to death. An individual's death fears represent psychological reactions toward biological death. Physical survival in the presence of psychological death can and does happen.

Some individuals may attempt to avoid psychological death by inducing physical death. The latter is often the case in suicide. The action of an individual who is instrumental in terminating his own life can only be discussed within the structure of his psychological functioning. To terminate life, seen only psychologically, may mean protecting basic values from being destroyed, as in an act of self-sacrifice or of heroism. Suicide may represent an attempt to achieve the cessation of psychological pain. In these terms the act of physical termination of life may be regarded not as the denial of the concept of basic value, but rather as a psychological activity designed to achieve a purpose which can only be understood within the context of the psychology of living.

History tells that some Western medieval societies developed cultures and social organizations which stressed the unimportance of physical living. It was held that physical existence was not important, it represented only a postponement of the "true" eternal spiritual existence after death. Yet, in spite of the propagation of this doctrine from the pulpits, the same societies vigorously built houses, raised their children and generally acted in the direction of the life value.

Little is known about societies and their fates when the life value ceased to be adequately transmitted. Data of this nature are hard to establish. Not too many years ago the newspapers reported the death of a member of a slowly dying-out Indian tribe in southern Utah who sat down in the middle of the road and promptly was killed by a passing car. Speculation about irregularities of the life value cannot be avoided. Similarly, the story of civilization and societies who disappeared from the historic scene, not by cultural absorption, starvation, mass murder, etc., but by a quasi-self-induced dwindling of their numbers, warrants the suspicion that something might have occurred which affected adversely the transmission and/or inculcation of the life value.

The individual and the social organization *must* complement and reinforce each other. The strength with which the society represents the life value may well be related to the individual's basic orientation and thereby to his health and well-being.

The life value of an individual, as indicated earlier, may wane and weaken and, in extreme situations, cease. He may continue to be physically alive, but he does so in the absence of psychological activity. He is indifferent to living. He ceases to emote, to cogitate, to choose, to decide, to move toward or away from people. He resembles more a routinized robot than a living person Such instances, often seen as the result of prolonged combat duty, concentration camp inmateship, prolonged exhaustion and stress, seem to occur when the value structure of an individual fails in its basic functions of sustaining and protecting the life value. Dramatically, this may be the case of the soldier in the prisoner of war camp. Faced with living conditions which break the strands of the social matrix, which force upon him the conscious or unconscious awareness that his values are inoperative in the light of the on going events of his life, the value structure may become inoperative. It cannot promote predictability, order, stability or minimal security vis-a-vis the environment. The resulting fear (of non-living), combined with psychological exhaustion, may seriously affect the strength of the life value.

The same process may also be less dramatically demonstrated in the case of adults who live in "ordinary" environments. A man oriented in the direction of humanistic altruism is forced to seek his livelihood in an acute "dog eat dog" business situation; the result may be the progressive erosion of the value structure. The victims of this process frequently appear in the psychoanalyst's office—searching for a new value structure which will harmonize with the basic values.

In this light many of the data emanating from research in psychotherapy are of interest. It was demonstrated that in successful psychotherapy the value structure of the patient becomes more like that of the therapist. In unsuccessful psychotherapy this is not the case. The process of psychotherapy can be described as one in which the psychotherapist transmits values to the patient and helps him to achieve better order among them.

All the qualities characteristic of basic values can be applied to the *socio-value,* which can be expressed by the following statement: "To be related to people, to live with and through contacts with other human beings represents the only condition of living." This basic value is also acquired in the precognitive period, is transmitted by the dynamics and mechanics of human upbringing and is one of the fundamental cornerstones of human personality. The socio-value premise is beyond good or bad, beyond morality; it is a condition *sine qua non.* The absence of the socio-condition (no people to be with) is, usually, feared and dreaded.

The reinforcement and protection of the socio-value is related to the value structure as a whole. When the socio-value is affected adversely, it in turn may threaten the total psychological organization of the individual. Conditions of impairment of the socio-value are considered causal to mental illness. Absence of socio-objects may have similar effects. In extreme instances the reduction or impairment of the socio-value may lead to psychological death. Similarly, infants who in the earliest period of their existence fail to acquire and incorporate the socio-value may develop in a very atypical fashion (child-autism).

The socio-value, its properties and vagaries, can be treated in all respects like the life value. Other values which fall within the definitional scope of basic values are the following: The conscience value (the absolute assumption that to have and act according to one's conscience is a fundamental condition); and the self value (the absolute necessity to act and be determined by self-reflective tenets). There are, undoubtedly, others.

Of all the basic values only two, the life value and the socio-value can be thought of as having validity across the cultures. The first is required to sustain individual life, the second all of social living. The life and the social-value represent psychological concepts which have the same explanatory function as the concept of evolution has for the science of biology. The life value accounts for the individual's *forceful* interaction with his environment, the socio-value for his *unceasing* interaction with other human beings.

The adjectives "forceful" and "unceasing" connote the quality of human beings in contact to the largest extent possible with sources of stimulation in their human and nonhuman environment. Forcefulness and ceaselessness in man's interaction with his environment is taken for granted by members of the Western culture to a greater or smaller extent. The Latin cultures to the south of the United States border hold attraction because of their *mañana* quality, and at the same time they are scorned by the non-Latin American from the north. The Latin South American likes his *mañana* attitude, but he also feels some qualms. He will recall the times when a given locale was bustling with forceful activity as the "good" time. A similar situation has prevailed until recently in Europe, where the Latin countries represented a culture of *dolce fa niente* for the North Europeans, highly desirable for vacationing but conducive to jokes, sarcasm and contempt. Western civilization values forcefulness, ceaselessness and the expending of maximum effort; it scorns a culture of taking life easy.

Man must not be content with using a fraction of his efforts in the pursuit of life and happiness. He must devote a maximum effort to his endeavors. Other cultures have taken an opposite position to the Western in the conceptualization of successful living. They extol the value of withdrawal from contact with the environment, the regression to contemplation and looking inward. Countries in which the religious philosophical system of Buddhism prevails are frequently criticized by Westerners for their "progress obstructing" cultural system. They "ought" to be turning toward wanting progress and development. They "ought" to use their potentialities. The Western value of striving, actively engaging and changing the environment toward the value of maximum use of human potentialities is often met by some oriental philosophers with the questions: Why? For what purpose? For what goal? Westerners hard pressed to admit that they are arguing their value system and unwilling to grant equal validity to the merits of another, often argue in final desperation, "Because it hinders progress, development of . . . ." In turn, they are promptly accused of adhering to the values of materialism and the worship of the material. The value of maximalization and self-maximalization represents statements focal to the total value matrix of Western and more pertinently to American civilization. The value statement contained in the concept of "human potentialities" can be considered part of "maximalization" value.

Western culture avoids statements which cannot be expressed in a system of rationality. There is urgency to provide some rationale for all events and occurrences. Values are no exception to the drive to find reasons and rational explanations. The life and the socio-value can be readily discerned in many a "well-reasoned" social institution and/or social movement, but the basis for the social institution is never acknowledged to have its source in the value structure but is always made to appear deduced from rational premises. The attempts to stress the rational foundations of man's activities and organizations and to avoid the nonrational foundations in the value matrix often lead to curious complication, above all when the future, the goals of Western man's endeavors are contemplated.

All social, economical, moral and ethical reform movements start with the assumption that the human condition is in need of improvement and *can* be improved. When it comes to the discussion of the end product of the improvement—man's assumptions concerning his optimal and desirable achievements—curious confusion exists. Economical movements speak of the man of the future whose physical environment provides him with material abundance, freedom from hunger, want and illness. The social reformer perceives future social organizations which will be regulative without being coercive. Moral and ethical utopianism sees the ideal man as one at peace with himself and his environment. Scientific movements centered around the social and behavioral sciences view man as a remarkably complex and effcient instrument, and they stress that the organism's psychological potentialities have barely been tapped. Of all the promissory notes for the future, the one extended by the behavioral sciences has least form and content.

Common to the statements of goals, and at the same time underlying all calls for development, progress, utilization of human potentialities, is the value of maximalization. It is fully accepted by Western culture but never mentioned explicitly or made reference to.

The notion of human potentialities and their potential development is little supported by facts. It is, in fact, an assumption which has many of the qualities of a value. Doubts that the vast potential for improvement exists are raised by some philosophers, but the scientist and most of society act on the assumption that the potential exists—needs to exist. Without this assumption, without the "human potentialities" value, all undertakings which form the hope of humanity would come to a standstill.

The value "human potential" has many similarities to basic values. It certainly is central in the Western value matrix, especially in the American culture. While the life value is held to be a cross-cultural concept, the human potentiality value is most developed in the Western culture. The combination of the two is the source of the vigor with which Western civilizations turn toward their environment with the purpose to alter, to improve, to conquer it.

The rapid growth in the United States of the social and behavioral sciences can serve as another demonstration of the all-pervasive pressure provided by the "human potentalities value." Psychotherapy (man can be helped to cope better), mental health endeavors (man can have more health and vigor, he can be more stress-resistant), group-sensitivity concepts (man can improve his relationships in groups), interventions by cultural anthropologists (man is made by culture; can he remake his own culture?), sociology-trained planners (man can improve and amend social institutions to better suit his needs)—these and countless other endeavors aim at ever new horizons for man's existence and functioning.

The paramount significance of the human potentialities value for the mental health concept is apparent. The sequence life—human potentialities—mental health value can be seen as a pyramidal structure in which one is causally related to the other, with the life value representing the *conditio-sine-qua-non.* No concept of mental health on the other hand can be postulated which does not contain the other two values and antecedent conditions. A mentally healthy individual must be concerned with the development of his potentialities. The society in which he lives must provide opportunities for growth and development.

It is exactly because of its centrality in the contemporary American culture that the human potentialities value has found few critics. But some words of critical caution need to be said. Human potentialities are finite; individuals have their definite limits; so do social institutions. The zealous pursuit of human potentialities may and sometimes does lead to blindness when the very limits have been reached.

The "oughtness" of maximum use of human potentialities is deeply imbedded in the American culture. It is a dominant feature in American religions, social, political and economic systems. The preoccupation of the behavioral sciences with this subject is of recent origin. As usual the social sciences follow when social demands are strong. As the aftermath to the challenge of American world supremacy, the United States embarked on a course which demanded the marshalling of human in addition to physical resources. The new goal, the mobilization of human resources, joins the older value of optimal utilization of human potentialities. Combined, they account for a vigorous social movement which has swept the country in education, mental health endeavors, the harnessing of human resources in the many new social programs, the Peace Corps and others too numerous to mention.

The social sciences are beginning to enter all these endeavors to an ever-increasing degree, but this is only the beginning. The goals advocated are clearly outlined—the clearance of the physical, emotional and intellectual slum areas of the contemporary American society. What is presently needed are the conceptual, organizational and technical tools to achieve the desired goals. This is a task to which the social scientists can and do lend their fullest support.

Social institutions, governmental agencies, educational organizations and many others actively engage in efforts to eradicate poverty, juvenile delinquency, backwardness of all kinds. It is the social scientist's task to be a participant in, as well as an observer of, the headlong rush into the future. While he contributes his share to the social tasks to be accomplished, at the same time he must look beyond his goals and aims to the value structure underlying social action. He must maintain a social engineer's viewpoint on the parts as well as the whole of the value structure. Atrophied values which have lost their functional significance may have to be removed in carefully conducted educational campaigns in depth. Values exerting considerable effect but not yet sufficiently institutionalized will be in need of clarification, strengthening and integration. The whole value matrix will be subject to constant scrutiny. Social, economic, emotional health in their inextricable interrelationship depend in final analysis on the value structure which must remain to the social scientist an open system with its inputs and outputs tied closely to the need of society.

This task of the behavioral scientist will be difficult to achieve, and he will approach it full of ambivalence and reluctance. He will need to learn more about the nature, the operations, the manipulations of value systems because they underlie the structure of all rational thinking; they are the hidden activators of behavior. Eventually, the behavioral scientist may encounter the *basic values*. It is hoped that he will be able to meet this supreme challenge.

REFERENCES

1. HEIDER, FRITZ: *The Psychology of Interpersonal Relations.* New York, Wiley, 1958, pp. 218-222.
2. KLUCKHORN, CLYDE K. M.: Valves and valve orientation in the theory action. In PARSON, TALCOTT and SHIL, EDWARD A.: *Toward a General Theory of Action.* Cambridge, Harvard Univ. Press, 1951, p. 395.
3. KORNER, I. N.: Of Values, Value Lag, and Mental Health. *The American Psychologist, 11*:10 (Oct.), 1956.
4. MURPHY, GARDNER: *Human Potentialities,* New York, Basic Books, 1958.
5. SMITH, BREWSTER M.: Personal values in the study of lives. In WHITE, R. W.: *The Study of Lives.* New York, Prentice-Hall, 1963, pp. 324-347.

Chapter 7

PHYSIOLOGICAL PARAMETERS OF HUMAN POTENTIAL

J. H. U. BROWN

INTRODUCTION

MAN is a hardy beast. As an individual he has survived extremes of cold, heat and radiation which are far beyond the capabilities of man as a species. Our attention here must be focused upon the race rather than the individual, although, in the ultimate analysis, the race can be studied only in terms of the individual. It is the comparison of the average with the performance of the outstanding which permits some projection of human potential.

There are three major ways in which man may develop his potential. First, he may expand his present armamentarium by training, by development and by synthesis and use of available sources. Second, he may learn to adapt to new situations such as those imposed by space travel which will, in turn, increase the potentialities of some aspects of his being. Finally, he may increase his potential permanently by genetic alteration. The time scales for each of these factors is unpredictable. Some are short term: The development of techniques for space travel with accompanying acclimations has occurred within the last ten years. Others are longer: Man's physical size has changed over the last few hundred years. The rate of alteration of genetic potential is difficult to predict: The opossum has changed little in the past eighty million years; the horse has gone through at least eight distinct genera in sixty million years; man has changed many of his physical characteristics within perhaps a million years, and minor changes have occurred within a few life spans.

Culture is the machine in which man develops his intellectual potentialities. Outside an organized culture, man cannot develop even a major latent talent. Only the individual who develops his potentialities can transcend a culture or make advances in it.

THERMODYNAMIC BALANCE

Man exists in a homeostatic or homeokinetic balance (9). Under normal conditions all living persons exist within a given range of homeokinetic control. Extremes are difficult to tolerate. Increase in man's potential may mean the establishment of new homeokinetic levels at a different intensity of kinetic turnover than in the normal individual.

The principles of thermodynamics have imposed upon mammals severe limitations on spheres of activity (11). The poikilothermic animal has temperature fluctuations which vary with outside temperature. At first glance it would appear that this would relieve these species of thermodynamic restrictions. It must be remembered, however, that such animals are at the mercy of low and high temperatures, particularly because of the restriction of activity at low temperatures. The homeothermic animal, of which man is the prime example, maintains a relatively constant body temperature and therefore a constant state of metabolic activity, of particular importance in the maintenance of a constant brain temperature and therefore a constant level of neural activity, as witness the disordered function which occurs in man with even a few degrees of fever. The rise of human development is tied closely to the homeothermic metabolism of man, and almost all great civilizations have developed in areas where the mean temperature is about 21 degrees C (45). Toynbee (67) has pointed out that development of the highest civilizations has depended upon an environment which is cold enough to provide a stimulus but not cold enough to require that much energy be expended to keep warm.

In many instances it is difficult to predict the range of man's capability. There is no question of the ability of man to adapt to new situations both by the short-term process of acclimation or by the long-term process of genetic alteration. Prosser (53) has pointed out that the processes of adaptation may be short- or long-term, depending on the result to be obtained, and examples of both can readily be found in nature (Table I). So-called "population rule" has been set down (34, 46, 65) demonstrating this principle. For example, Bergman was able to show that the smallest sizes of a given race are located in warmer regions of the world; Allen demonstrated that the protruding members of an organism are smaller in the colder regions to minimize heat loss; Gloger found that the depth of skin color is related to the temperature of the region of dwelling; and Schmidt related optimum temperature of development to skeletal size. Each of these findings suggests the potential of man to modify his external and perhaps internal structure to suit a particular environment.

Short-term adaptation occurs and has been demonstrated by many workers (20, 30, 44, 59) but the potential of long-term adaptation as in the primitives mentioned below has not yet been exploited. Ability to withstand extreme cold (hypothermia) offers interesting possibilities. Although the human cannot survive when the interior of the body is cooled below 25 degrees C, the dog survives at 18 degrees C and the marmot at 0 degrees C (17). Andjus (3) has cooled rats to 1 degree C and kept them at that temperature with no discernible EKG, heart beat or respiration and then obtained survival with apparently normal function. Since the rat is not normally a hibernating animal, the potential of extending such experiments to long-term cooling in man is ex-

TABLE I

THE COURSE OF ADAPTIVE PROCESSES

Process	*Relative Time*	*Result*	*Example*
Direct response	Seconds to minutes	Immediate stress response and neuromuscular activity	Epinephrine Release
Regulation of rate process	Hours to days	Alteration of enzyme concentration or new homeokinetic level	Increase in ability to metabolize
Acclimation	Days to weeks	Steady state at new level of activity	Adaptation to high altitude
Behavior alteration	Many life cycles	Alteration in permanent form in structure or reaction	Tropisms of insects
Genetic selection	Many generations	Permanent genetic transmission	Genetic carry-over of kidney structure in kangaroo rats

citing. Fiction by Leo Szilard (64) has pointed up the moral and political implications of such actions. It is interesting that all homeothermic animals are not completely temperature-regulated. All animals find it difficult to regulate temperature in the immature state, and the development of homeothermia appears to be a function of development. Other animals have learned to adapt to their particular situation. In the evolutionary past the bear, for example, learned to sleep in the winter and burn body fat to maintain a constant temperature. He is not a true hibernator. Man may also learn to adapt.

One sixth of the earth's surface, seven million square miles, is desert. As new technologies and population pressures develop, man must advance into this wasteland and adapt himself to it. By the same token, the decreasing water supply for the ever-increasing population suggests that man must either reclaim large quantities of water from the sea or must adapt himself to arid climates. Probably both will occur.

The homeothermic nature of man means that he functions well at one temperature, about 99 degrees F. His body economy operates satisfactorily only when sufficient water is available. The desert provides neither condition. When the air temperature goes above 92 degrees F, the heat loss from the body can no longer occur through heat transfer, and some means must be found to remove the heat of continued metabolism. The body has adapted to lose heat by vaporization of water. Since continued heat production in the steady resting state is almost 80 cal/hour, about 5 oz of water/hour or about 1½ qts of water/day must be evaporated to dissipate the heat. Under working conditions in the desert such losses may exceed one qt/*hour* (2). The evidence is clear that man can adapt well to increased heat load if water is provided. He cannot adapt to water loss above the normal rate; he must have adequate water sources. An adaptation which appears to offer the possibility of extreme conservation of water is that of the kangaroo rat, which has remarkably long loops of Henle within the kidney and is able to recycle almost all of the water intake. Man who has lived for generations in the desert, as in the nomadic desert tribes, shows no greater tendency to conserve water than does man living in a temperate climate indicating that no such adaptation has yet occurred.

The studies on the African and Australian Bushmen give some idea of the range of human potential to survive adverse climates. Sir Stanton Hicks has reported that the Australian Bushman is able to sleep comfortably on the ground at −8 degrees C with a foot temperature of only 12 degrees C while the investigators were unable to rest because of the cold. The ability to survive and resist cold varies from tribe to tribe and suggests a genetic factor. In contrast, the African Bushman is also able to withstand the cold to much the same degree, but his genetic adaptation has taken a different path towards the same end (68). The adjustment of the Australian Bushman to cold appears to be a physiological one, while that of the Kalahari Bushman appears rather to be intellectual (learning to use fire properly) (73). That some features of the race may enter the picture was demonstrated by Adams and Covino (1), who found that the response to cold of Eskimos, Caucasians and Negroes varied with race, with the greatest response occurring in the Eskimo and the least in the Negro, suggesting that some potential for adaptation to climate does exist.

POTENTIAL OF THE NERVOUS SYSTEM

It is often said that man is great because he has the power to reason. Linton points out that man cannot reason until he has developed the power to *learn* the facts from which he will reason. Learning develops from the stimulus-response mechanisms in lower forms, through the instinctual behavioral patterns, to true learning and then to reasoning. One of the greatest attributes of man, perhaps equal to that of learning, is the development of language and the power of communication. Communications with animals (43) and with beings from other planets may depend upon our expansion of communications and information theory.

A part of the development of human potential must depend upon the drive of the race and the individual which, in turn, depends upon reward and reinforcement of the drive. This has been most aptly demonstrated by Olds (51), who found that certain areas of the brain produce "satisfaction" so that rats run a maze or perform problems in order to obtain electrical stimulation of these areas.

Of particular interest is the suggestion that "reward" or "punishment" are centered in specific cells in the hypothalamus, and the apparatus is a physiological and therefore controllable mechanism. The "imprinting" of the young, learning which occurs without any apparent reward and in which the learning itself is a form of reward, implies a genetic instruction for the good of the race (66). The "goodness" of the result wherein a gosling follows the first moving object whether it is the mother goose or a football, cannot be questioned as a protective measure. The degree of imprinting in the human is unknown; and the possibility of desirable imprinting has not been investigated as a potential good for the race, although Harlow's work on the infant monkey indicates steps in this direction.

Recent demonstrations (5, 22) that chemical or psychological conditioning would produce drastic changes in behavioral patterns of rats or humans, whether induced by the injection of minute quantities of chemicals including sex hormones or by visual stimulation, leads to the interesting supposition that someday it may be possible to condition the population of a country to a desired situation.

Research on "insight," by which a shortcut to problem solution can be developed, has been approached by Deutsch (15) and others, but the methods are still too crude to assess probable future trends. The search for the methods by which the human brain handles information in much the same way as a computer has also not been well developed. It is known, for example, that increasing the complexity of a word list which a subject must read makes little difference in his speed of reaction over a wide range of lists (from four to 256 words) (52). The mechanism by which the human brain accomplishes this feat and the method of further training to enhance it have not been studied.

Another realm of human potential capable of exploitation is memory. Permanent learning becomes consolidated as a result of reverberation or continual neural activity along definite physical pathways (16). McGaugh has discovered that two strains of rats, "dull" and "bright," as measured by performance in maze tests, had equal learning potential if greater time is allowed the "dull" group. Various drugs such as picrotoxin and strychnine improved the learning potential of both groups but increased that of the "dull" group to a greater extent. These experiments suggest that pharmacological investigations may result in formulation of drugs which could increase human potential for learning and point the way to the development of certain techniques of teaching which might particularly improve the lower intelligence group of the race. Recently, new drugs have been introduced but not yet evaluated which appear to have a marked stimulatory effect on learning.

Man has not yet exploited the possibilities inherent in a study of the physiological basis of learning. Learning may be a function of the cellular level. Recent demonstrations (6) that planaria, a very simple organism, can be taught to recognize environmental signals and that, after "learning," dividing of the planaria into two organisms results in both halves "remembering" the previous coaching, together with the demonstration that untrained planaria can be "taught" by eating ground-up portions of previously "taught" animals, points to a serious suggestion that a physical basis for learning exists even in the most primitive organism. These results have not yet been evaluated.

Recent experiments in Cleveland have opened a new vista in the potential of man. The brain has been removed from a Rhesus monkey and kept alive by perfusion for eighteen hours. The viability of the brain was indicated by the EEG, and it appeared to be able to respond to some signals from the periphery. Though the possibilities are enormous, the exploitation of the physical structure in terms of future learning potential of the brain has not been fully accomplished. The cortex is divided into two halves corresponding to right and left cerebral hemispheres of the cerebrum. In general, the right hemisphere is related to motor and sensory activity of the left side of the body and vice versa. Dominance is relative, however; and destruction of one hemisphere may be followed, after a period of relearning, by increased function on the contralateral side.

The brain contains "silent" areas which evoke neither a motor or sensory response upon stimulation. Nerve tracts to them can be cut without affecting intelligence. This physiological and anatomical situation offers the possibility of the use of brain areas not normally in operation and becomes of particular significance when evaluated in conjunction with the work of Myers (49), who found that when the brain was longitudinally sectioned into two halves each half could be taught diametrically opposed actions simultaneously.

An interesting and not well-explored aspect of the human mind is the function of the reticular activating system (RAS). When the nervous system is busy upon one task, the effect of additional extraneous stimuli is lessened (32). Audio analgesia (deadening of pain by distraction with high intensity sound) has been used successfully in dental operations of 5,000 patients, but the operation of this or similar techniques to develop new operant conditioning methods for the human has not been studied.

MAN AND COMPUTER

The nervous system of man is a marvelous instrument. It is estimated that the brain has perhaps 10^4 more memory units, is one third faster and 10^5 times smaller and consumes 10^6 less energy than a large-scale digital computer. At the same time, it is like a computer in many ways; the nerve impulse is all or none, as is a binary system; both the computer and the brain utilize a sequential approach to problem solutions; the brain behaves in many instances like both an analogue (hormonal control of function) and a digital (neural control) computer in combination; both systems require intensive feedback mechanisms; both systems use a form of logic which computer designers try to bring near the human model; both systems require an input, a "black box" operations unit, and an output of data; and both systems "think," although the definition may be at variance.

Von Neumann (72) has estimated that the memory bank of the human brain is about 1×10^{16} bits or 6×10^6 on/off units for each neuron, far beyond the possibilities for any known anatomical structure. However, Woolridge has demonstrated (72) that if most memory is received in "chunks" of twenty-five bits per second, which is all that can be perceived at a time, the memory size is lowered to 5×10^{10} bits, and the off/on elements would number about five per neuron. By further assuming that sensory input is decreased during sleep the above figures may be decreased by 30 per cent. Assumptions of long-term versus short-term memory elements would reduce the ratio still further and bring figures within the realm of physical possibility. This is the largest core memory known, and when we consider the average cross-section of the elements is 10^{-8} sq cm, it must be realized that present technology is far from this biological efficiency.

The human system and that of machines is, in fact, so closely related that the general law of Barcroft states: "Changes undergone by a system are such as will tend to reduce to a minimum perturbances due to the external environment" (41), and it has been applied to chemistry, physics, biology and economics. This concept has been extended and dignified by the science of *cybernetics,* the control and communication of man and machine (69). The principles of cybernetics have been extended to the control of hormone secretion, growth of civilizations and the laws of economics. Man's greatest potential for controlling the factors affecting his daily life may be in the field of cybernetics.

AGING

One of the major burdens which nature imposes upon man is the process of aging. Retardation of this phenomenon offers one of the greatest potentials of man for a greater usefulness. Present knowledge does not permit a judgment that a *general* aging process actually exists (60). Even those factors which can be associated with a definite pathological process, such as decrease in cardiac output and circulatory system dynamics, depend upon genetic and economic factors. Aging may be simply a decrease in the normal reserves upon which the individual calls to meet the stresses of life. Although the physiological and psychological parameters of the aging process have been evaluated (7), we are still not at a stage where prediction of a regime which might delay the process can be outlined.

The many recent surgical experiments in the transplantation of human organs suggest the eventual possibility of replacement of aged or damaged organs. The kidney has been transplanted many times; the heart has been transplanted, as has the liver. The use of organs of animals other than man for transplantation to man has been suggested, and the kidney of the primate has already been used in such a heterotransplant unsuccessfully. Exploitation of this method of survival and increase of man's potential must await better immunological and other techniques.

Singer's experiments (61) have pointed out the possibility of eventual controls of cells and tissues so that regeneration of a damaged organ or limb may be possible. His demonstration that regeneration can be made to occur in animals which do not normally regenerate, by control of nerve supply and other factors, indicates that possibilities exist.

Although life span has increased dramatically in the last one hundred years, it has been due to decreased infant and child mortality. Life span of individuals over forty has scarcely changed (47). Populations are drifting toward old age, and the problem becomes more and more urgent.

The ability of man to control the diseases he is heir to may well be a turning point in history and result in a slowing of the aging process. Here again the adaptability of man is paramount. Before modern communication the North American continent had no smallpox, Europe had no syphilis, the Indian and Eskimo had no tuberculosis, and the introduction of each into new areas was accompanied by ravages unknown in the previous diseased population. It is well known that the Negro is resistant to malaria and that the Chinese may be more resistant to coronary artery disease than Caucasian counterparts. Some groups (Iceland) have a vastly different incidence of caries. Although many of these variations may be due to the environmental factors, a study of each will enable man to reach new potential in the control of diseases (13).

The prospect of man free from disease is often held as one of the great potential benefits of future civilizations, but experiments in gnotobiotic laboratories indicate that in some instances the absence of bacteria produces physiological changes which may be a detriment to the health of the animal.

Other researchers offer different possible solutions to the aging problem. J. E. Davies (14), reporting in Proceedings of the National Academy of Sciences, found that certain antibiotics, streptomycin for one, interfered with the synthesis of protein at specific sites on the ribosomes. This suggests that compounds can be produced which cause a misreading of the genetic code and permit a "wrong" amino acid to be entered into the normal protein pattern in the cell. The possibility of synthesis of desired proteins within the cell is opened by this discovery and might lead to virus-resistant cells, to cells grown with specific inhibitor or stimulator substances or other alterations of the normal genetic pattern.

COMMUNICATION

Man has one of his greatest potentials in the possibility of communication with other species. John Lilly has pointed out (43) the possibility of communication with the dolphin and the realms of new knowledge opened by the possibility of an alien intelligence attacking problems which have baffled man. Despite the fact that the sound production of the dolphin is on a different frequency scale from that of man, it appears that communication is possible. Still further potential development lies in the fact that this intelligent creature is able to hear sounds in the high ultrasonic range at about 140 kilocycles. The possibility of utilizing the remarkable sonar arrangements of these animals to provide an experimental means to study direction finding in living creatures offers exciting vistas.

The eye as a communications organ is one of the most sensitive detectors of energy known. The visual pigments respond to about 100 quanta or 6×10^{-10} ergs in the energy range of the pigments. It has been demonstrated that the requirement of energy for vision is so low that statistical fluctuations in level can be discerned.

If man's eyes were more sensitive, each photon would register, and light would be perceived as flashes (25). The ability of the eye to resolve detail—visual acuity—varies with illumination over a wide range of light intensity. Although nocturnal animals have certain adjustments which permit a greater night vision, man has the greatest visual acuity of all animals (54).

The ability of the ear to distinguish sound is almost as precise as is the ability of the eye to distinguish light. The remarkable ability to distinguish tone is illustrated by the fact that modern conductors have raised the pitch of A from 440 to 444 cycles per second, and this change makes a noticeable difference in the brilliance of the orchestral sound. The threshold of hearing is extremely low. About 10^{-16} watts/cm^2 or 2×10^{-4} dynes/cm can be detected. The ear, however, can distinguish sound 10^{11} times greater than this level without damage. The eardrum responds to such slight intensities of sound vibration that the sound may be heard when the drum moves less than 10^{-9} cm, a length less than the wavelength of light, and the basilar membrane must respond to produce a sensation with movements less than 1 per cent of the diameter of the hydrogen molecule. A greater sensitivity of hearing would result in a continual noise level in the ear due to vibration of molecules from heat. Probably no other animal has a more sensitive ear than man, although several hear over a wider range.

The energy intensity required to produce sensation in the skin is much greater than that required for sight or hearing. It requires about 0.85 gm/mm to produce a pressure sensation. Pain is an interesting problem because it not only has a physical coordinate (0.206 gm-cal/sec/cm^2 threshold), but the psychic coordinates appear to be equally important. Heat has a threshold of 0.00015 gm-cal/sec/cm^2. It has been calculated that an energy input of 10^{-7} of normal hourly loss of heat by radiation can be detected when applied to a single area. The kinesthetic senses which measure the change in position of joints are also very sensitive. Displacements of 0.22 degrees can be discerned at the shoulder. The "Perpetuum Mobile" of Mendelssohn requires playing 5,995 notes in four minutes and three seconds of seventy-two distinct motor actions per second, in the hands alone, each timed exactly, indicating the remarkably sensitive control of this mechanism (62). The vestibular apparatus can respond to accelerations on the order of 0.1 degree/sec^2. The remarkable sensitivity of the sensory apparatus of man does not suggest any improvement by physical alteration.

Although some animals are presumed to have a more acute sense of smell than does man, it is difficult to imagine a situation of greater sensitivity than the olfactory organ of man, where calculations indicate that for mercaptans only one molecule is necessary to stimulate a single cell. However, in man about forty cells may have to respond in order to produce a sensation. It is possible that animals with an acute sense of smell have fewer cells responding for any given olfactory sensation, or a better mechanism exists for passing air over the sensory cells. By contrast, many more molecules are required for production of taste. Conservative figures indicate that about 10^{10} molecules may be required to elicit a sensation (55).

The very fact that the eye is at the threshold of individual quanta, the nose at the limit of one molecule per cell and the ear at the threshold of molecular vibration argue against physical improvement. On the other hand, the remarkable adaptation of these organs offers great possibilities for future exploration. Patients lacking a tympanic membrane have been able to perceive tones from stimulating electrodes placed inside the middle ear cavity (57). Observations suggest that it may be possible to provide a converter to change conversation or music into electrical signals which can then be used to stimulate the auditory nerve or some other location to provide "electrical" hearing. Hearing of "loudness" is affected by the strength of the current used thus providing control of both frequency and loudness. The vibratory sense has been tested but not exploited. Some small amount of research indicates that visual or auditory signals may be transduced into vibrations of either air or solid columns and used to transmit information to sensory areas of the skin.

It should be stressed, however, that study of the sensory apparatus of man and animals may lead to the development of prosthetic devices for the deaf and the blind and to an understanding of mechanisms for the control of balance and the kinesthetic sense. The possibility of artificial limbs or muscles which can respond in a normal fashion to sensory input offer tremendous advantages to the lame. Such devices are under study.

GRAVITATIONAL FORCES

Gravity is a universal force. The development of man's muscles, many of his senses and his skeleton are designed to counteract gravity or to notify him of the responses of it. In addition to the obvious elements (balance and weight) concerned with resistance to gravitational force, an interesting additional factor is that of sleep. It has been noted in investigations in which subjects are placed in a low gravity field, as when suspended in water, sleep occurred rarely and about four hours of sleep per day appeared to be more than adequate. On return to solid terrain, the subjects immediately resumed the usual seven to eight hour sleep pattern. Graveline (27) has summed up these observations by stating: "The biofunction of sleep may be to provide a period with minimal requirements for counteracting gravity so that recovery from the neuromuscular debt accumulating in the active man can take place."

In addition to the possibilities for space flight suggested by the above observations, the possibility of placing earth-bound man in an anti-gravity field or in a null-gravity simulator offers great possibilities of increasing the efficiency of muscular work. The investigations simply point up the fact that we know little about man's potential for long periods of work.

A major problem exists in the attempt to place man in space. Here his potentials must be developed to the fullest because he will be placed in an unfamiliar environment which is hostile to every action and which may require development of powers not now apparent. The loss of muscle tone which occurs in individuals placed in a water tank or in orbit is due to the loss of any need to use anti-gravity muscles. It may be possible to develop hormones or other metabolically important substances which will prevent muscle wasting in these conditions and also develop greater muscle power in men under the influence of gravity (10).

Science fiction writers have pictured man living with little difficulty in space stations placed in orbit and with artificial gravity induced by rotation. Landsberg has pointed out that in such a station the satellist will experience conflicting sensory information from visual, graviceptive and semicircular canal clues, indicating that studies in perception must be extended to develop a new awareness of sensory mechanisms and their control.

Man is accustomed to living in a world where the force of gravity is applied in a downward direction and is always of unit strength. The application of gravitational forces in other directions or in greater magnitude than unity through some method of acceleration causes physical stresses difficult to counteract. Such stresses may be imposed by the demands of space flight or they may be introduced on earth by deceleration in an automobile accident or sudden acceleration in jet flight. The ability of man to survive such changes in gravitational force will depend upon his means of overcoming the force by physical devices or physical conditioning (33).

Although weightlessness is not a problem on the surface of the earth, the possibility of placing men into orbit for long periods of time and the repeated suggestions for the treatment of heart disease by removing the stress imposed by the necessity of pumping blood against a gravitational field, have called attention to problems which may arise. In many cases, the cure might be worse than the disease. Present evidence from Titov's flight, as well as experiments on normal subjects at bed rest (31, 63), indicate that weightlessness may be accompanied by nausea, disorientation and dizziness. Visual after-images may occur. There are problems associated with micturition, feeding, altered neuromuscular patterns and impaired circulation.

As mentioned above, man is essentially an air-breathing, one-gravity-unit creature. Though reduced gravity is of considerable hazard, increased gravity is a major problem due to the acceleration concomitant upon launch in space flights. The problem of increased forces caused by acceleration apply to automobile accidents, high speed aircraft and any other vehicle in which a rapid change in direction or speed is induced. To the present, no means have been devised for protection against increased gravity other than artificial ones which are cumbersome and difficult to maintain and operate. Any development which will increase man's potential to survive high gravity fields will not only take him to the stars but protect him on earth. Man's ability to survive gravitational forces is strictly limited. Although it is possible to endure forces of 3 g for about one hour, greater forces for much shorter periods of time (30 g for .05 sec) may cause serious damage.

OXYGEN TENSION

Man has shown little ability to adapt to increased gravitational forces, to water loss and to other conditions changing environmental conditions. He has, however, demonstrated a remarkable ability to adapt to oxygen tension. Man is an air breathing animal and requires sufficient oxygen to maintain sufficient saturation of the red blood cells to transport oxygen to the tissues. Normal man lives at sea level or slightly above it. At altitudes above 10,000 ft, he is unable to function effectively. On the other hand, the Quechua Indians of Peru have lived at Morochocha in the Andes at altitudes of 14,700 ft for generations; and huts of natives have been found at 17,100 ft (28). Studies in a pressure chamber indicate that man can survive 30,000 ft of stimulated altitude for about two minutes without conditioning. Allowing adaptation, he can survive the same altitude for thirty minutes. Normal man becomes unconscious when exposed to 7 to 8 per cent CO_2, whereas an adapted individual can withstand concentrations of 12 per cent. This ability of man to adapt to changing atmospheric situations may make it possible to support larger populations in the mountains as population pressures increase. For space travel it may prove feasible to investigate the possibility of carrying smaller oxygen supplies into orbit if the astronauts are previously conditioned.

STRESS

Man exists under normal circumstances in a state of homeokinetic equilibrium. Alteration in the rate or level of this equilibrium with attainment of a new balance may be the measure of man's adaptability and the increase in his potentiality. Occasionally, some environmental or other change produces alterations in the homeokinetic equilibrium which cannot be compensated by the attainment of a new equilibrium. This is stress. In this sense, stress may be called a disease of adaptation. The ability of an organism to adapt to stress depends to some extent upon the type of stress—the stressor—which may be of two types, neurotropic or systemic, depending upon the site of action (23). Stress produces definite pathological conditions in man which interfere with normal functioning. In general, the somatic expression of a stress reaction depends upon the susceptibility of the subject (71). Wolf has suggested that an individual may inherit an organ "weakness" which may become apparent only when a stress is imposed. Stress may be imposed by many factors which vary from individual to individual and in degree of stress from person to person. Man, for example, requires a certain amount of sensory input. Deprivation of sensory input results in stressful situations which may lead to nonintegrated outputs and finally to death. There appears to be a hypothalamic involvement due to neuroendocrine demands to maintain homeostatis in the face of stress (55). Zohman (74) came to the conclusion that the stress applied to a subject may be not only a result of sensory deprivation, but in a manner of speaking, of sensory excess when he concluded that emotional stress associated with job responsibility appeared more significant in the development of coronary disease in young adults than many other usually suspected factors. These mechanisms have been discussed (19). Stressful factors are closely linked with hypertensive disease in man (70) with gastrointestinal disorders (ulcers, colitis) (8) and with decrease in the ability of the body to resist infection (40).

Other interesting observations suggest that crowding in overpopulated colonies induces a definite stress characterized by adrenal cortical hypertrophy and other symptoms of a highly stressful situation. The material has been reviewed at length in the Summer, 1964, issue of *Daedalus,* which gives many of the references and other pertinent material.

All of these factors and especially the last suggest that the development of man's potential in a constantly expanding technology and under constantly increasing overcrowding may depend upon some means to pharmacologically or psychologically reduce the stresses to which he is exposed in daily living.

OTHER CONSIDERATIONS

Although we are concerned largely with the ability of man to realize his full potential by adapting to conditions and situations leading to such development, it must not be forgotten that the possibility exists that man will be required to adapt to life on other planets. Dr. Harlow Shapley has estimated that the known universe contains 10^{26} stars which have 10^{17} planets. Of these, some 10^{11} should have suitable conditions of temperature and atmosphere for the support of life, and some 10^{8} planets should have life. It is likely, Shapley concludes, that 10^{5} planets will have life more advanced than our own. Such enormous possibilities should make us look to the stars and consider the potential of man in outer space.

Miller and Urey (48) have produced amino acids from inorganic materials, and Calvin (12) extended the observations by demonstrating that intense radiation would increase the yield of organic molecules from CO_2 and H. Fox (24) has created proteinoid-like material incorporating the eighteen essential amino acids. These observations not only suggest the rise of life on earth but one way to methods by which life might occur on any planet. Man's potential habitat may be other planets, and work (58) has already turned in the direction of suggesting methods by which other planets may be made inhabitable.

Man's past often determines his potential. From the beginning of Homo sapiens, when his pelvic area became bowl-shaped to support the downward thrust of viscera in an erect position, when the articulation of the shoulder loosened for free movement, when his body shortened in proportion to leg length and his hands developed from toes to fingers, and as his stereoscopic vision and nervous coordination developed, the ability of man to survive in a nonarboreal environment increased. These genetic alterations may have been for the good of man; but it is by no means true that all such alterations are for good. Witness the genetic-borne disease of phenylketonuria (PKU) which is now attracting attention because of the hazard to mental health.

For man to achieve his true potentialities he must learn to use the facilities at his command. Huxley (38) has pointed out that to accomplish this end psychophysical reeducation is necessary. The reality of conducting such training for perception of visual images was demonstrated by the tachistoscope, which was used during the war to train thousands of men to recognize objects (planes or ships) on a vastly improved time scale.

THE FUTURE OF MAN

As man looks toward a future of continual overcrowding, ever-increasing genetic defects from preservation of the less likely to survive and a gradually aging population, he must develop the means for controlling these factors. The selection of the fittest to reproduce may be accomplished in the future with present day techniques for sperm preservation; population control may be achieved by newer and more reliable methods of birth control. Population may expand to fill all available areas as we learn to live in the desert, the mountains and under the sea—even, perhaps, on other planets.

The future may not be as bright as it is often pictured. The golden age of technology, of intelligence and of social development and health may not lie in the future. All changes, penal, moral, social, political and financial make some mark on the genetic structure of man. Not all are for the better. The major degenerative diseases which plague mankind do not develop until after the childbearing age, and the possibility of stamping out such diseases is not easily foreseen. Some evidence exists to indicate a slow decline in intelligence in the population (47) rather than the increase predicted by the science fictioneer. Certain inherited characteristics can be stamped out only when the cause, perhaps a disease, which caused the trait is stamped out. For example, sickle cell anemia can be eradicated only when malaria is completely obliterated.

Although man may be at a point close to the limit of his physiological sensory potential, he still has far to go in development of perception, of training and of making maximum use of his environment. Few men are close to the limits of physical endurance, muscular coordination and ability to withstand stress; and here man does have potentialities. Only by development of the maximum ability can man make full use of the future.

REFERENCES

1. Adams, T., and Covino, B. G.: Racial variations in a standardized cold test. *J. Appl. Physiol., 12*:9, 1958.
2. Adolph, E. F.: *Physiology of Man in the Desert.* New York, Interscience, 1947.
3. Andjus, R.: Resuscitation of adult rats cooled close to freezing. *C. R. Acad. Sci. (Paris), 232*:1591.
4. Aschoff, J.: Diurnal rhythms. *Ann. Rev. Physiol., 25*:581, 1963.
5. Berkowitz, L.: Effects of observing violence. *Sci. Amer., 210*:35, 1964.
6. Best, J. B.: Protopsychology. *Sci. Amer., 208*:54, 1963.
7. Birren, J. E., Butler, R. N., Greenhouse, S. W., Sokoloff, L., and Yarrow, R.: Human Aging. *U. S. P. H. S. Bull., 986,* 1963.
8. Brady, J. V.: Ulcers in executive monkeys. *Sci. Amer., 199*:95, 1958.
9. Brown, J. H. U., and Barker, S. B.: *Basic Endocrinology.* Philadelphia, Davis, 1962.
10. Brown, J. H. U.: *Physiology of Man in Space.* New York, Academic Press, 1963.
11. Burton, A. C., and Edholm, O. G.: *Man in a Cold Environment.* London, Arnold, 1955.
12. Calvin, M.: Origin of life on earth and elsewhere. *Proc. Lunar Planet. Exp. Col., 1*:8, 1950.
13. Coon, C. S.: *The Story of Man.* New York, Knopf, 1954.
14. Davies, J. E.: Studies on the ribosomes of streptomycin sensitive and resistant strains of E. coli. *Proc. Nat. Acad. Sci. U.S.A., 51*:659, 1964.
15. Deutsch, J. A.: *Structural Basis of Behavior.* Chicago, Univ. of Chicago Press, 1960.
16. Deutsch, J. A.: Physiological basis of memory. *Ann. Rev. Physiol., 24*:259, 1962.
17. Dill, D. B., and Forbes, W. H.: Respiratory and metabolic effects of hypothermia. *Amer. J. Physiol., 132*:685, 1941.
18. Dock, W.: Stress and the heart. *Heart Bull., 8*:73, 1959.
19. Dreyfuss, F.: Role of emotional stress preceding coronary occlusion. *Amer. J. Cardiol., 3*:590, 1959.
20. Edhol, O. G.: *Polar physiology. Fed. Proc., 19*:3, 1959.
21. Farber, S. M., and Wilson, R. H. L.: *Man and Civilization, Control of the Mind.* New York, McGraw-Hill, 1961. (Comments by Adam Huxley.)
22. Fisher, A. E.: Maternal and sexual behavior induced by intracranial chemical stimulation. *Science, 124*:228, 1956.
23. Fortier, C.: Dual control of ACTH release. *Endocrinology, 49*:782, 1951.
24. Fox, S. W.: How did life begin. *Science, 132*:200, 1960.

25. Geldard, Frank: *The Human Senses.* New York, Wiley, 1953.
26. Glickstein, M., and Sperry, R. W.: Intermanual sonesthetic transfer in split brain Rhesus monkeys. *J. Comp. Physiol. Psychol.*, 53:322, 1960.
27. Graveline, D. E., Balke, B., McKenzie, R. E., and Hartman, B.: *Psychobiological Effects of Water Immersion Induced Hydrodynamics.*
28. Hanrahan, J. S., and Bushnell, D.: *Space Biology.* New York, Basic Books, 1960.
29. Harlow, H.: Love in infant monkeys. *Sci. Amer.*, *200*:68, 1959.
30. Hart, J. S.: Polar physiology. *Fed. Proc.*, *19*:3, 1959.
31. Hawkins, W. R.: *Lectures in Aerospace Medicine.* School of Aerospace Medicine, Randolph Field, 1960.
32. Hernandez-Peron, R., Scherrer, H., and Jouvet, M.: Modification of electrical activity in cochlear nucleus. *Science, 123*:331, 1956.
33. Hershey, R. R.: *Lectures in Aerospace Medicine.* School of Aerospace Medicine, Randolph Field, Texas, 1960.
34. Hess, R., Allee, W. C., and Schmidt, K. P.: *Ecological Animal Geography.*
35. Hessberg, R. R.: *Lectures in Aerospace Medicine.* School of Aerospace Medicine. Randolph Field, 1960.
36. Horridge, G. A.: Integrative action of nervous system. *Ann. Rev. Physiol.*, *25*:523, 1963.
37. Hurtado, A.: *Mechanism of Acclimation.* School of Aviation Medicine, Randolph Field, Texas, 1956.
38. Huxley, A.: *Tomorrow and Tomorrow and Tomorrow.* New York, Harper, 1952.
39. Kalmus, H.: Navigation by animals. *Ann. Rev. Physiol.*, *26*:109, 1964.
40. Kass, E. H.: Hormones and host resistance to infection. *Bacterial Rev.*, *24*:177, 1960.
41. Latil, P.: *Thinking by Machine.* Cambridge, Houghton Mifflin, 1957.
42. Lilijestrand, C., and Zotterman, Y.: Water test in mammals. *Acta Physiol. Scand.*, *32*:291, 1954.
43. Lilly, J. C.: *Man and Dolphin.* New York, Doubleday, 1961.
44. Mackworth, W. H.: Finger numbness in cold winds. *J. Appl. Physiol.*, 5:533, 1952.
45. Markham, S. F.: *Climate and the Energy of Nation.* London, Oxford Univ. Press, 1944.
46. Mayr, E.: Ecological factors in speciation. *Evolution, 1*:263, 1947.
47. Medawar, P. B.: *Future of Man.* New York, Basic Books, 1960.
48. Miller, S. L., and Urey, H. C.: Organic compound synthesis on the primitive earth. *Science, 132*:200, 1960.
49. Myers, R. E.: Function of corpus collosum in interocular transfer. *Brain, 79*:358, 1956.

50. Newman, J. R.: *The World of Mathematics (IV).* New York, Simon and Schuster, 1956.
51. Olds, J.: Self stimulation of the brain. *Science, 127*:215, 1958.
52. Pierce, J. R.: *Symbols, Signals, and Noise.* New York, Harper Bros., 1961.
53. Prosser, C. L.: *Physiological Adaptation.* Washington, D. C., American Physiological Society, 1958.
54. Prosser, C. L.: *Comparative Animal Physiology.* Philadelphia, W. B. Saunders, 1950.
55. Richter, C. P.: *Neurologic Basis of Behavior.* Boston, Little, Brown, 1957.
56. Richter, C. P.: Biological clocks in medicine and psychiatry. *Proc. Nat. Acad. Sci., 46*:1506, 1960.
57. Rosenblith, W. A.: *Sensory Communications.* Cambridge, MIT Press, and New York, Wiley, 1961.
58. Sagan, C.: The planet Venus. *Science, 133*:849, 1961.
59. Scholander, P. F., Walters, V., Hoch, R., and Irving, L.: *Biol. Bull., 99*:225, 1950.
60. Shock, N. W.: Physiological aspects of aging. *Ann. Rev. Physiol., 23*:97, 1961.
61. Singer, M.: Induction of regeneration of the forelimb of the post-metamorphic frog. *J. Exp. Zool., 126*:519, 1954.
62. Smith, H.: *From Fish to Philosophy.* Boston, Little, Brown, 1953.
63. Spencer, W. R.: Personal communication.
64. Szilard, L.: *Voice of the Dolphins.* New York, Simon and Schuster, 1961.
65. Tanning, A. V.: Experimental study of meristic character in fish. *Biol. Rev., 27*:169, 1952.
66. Thorpe, W. H.: *Learning and Instinct in Animals.* London, Methuen, 1956.
67. Toynbee, A. J.: *A Study of History.* London, Oxford Univ. Press, 1946.
68. Ward, J. S., Bredell, G. A., and Werzell, H. G.: Response of Bushmen and Europeans to exposure to winter night temperatures on the Kalahari Desert. *J. Appl. Physiol., 15*:667, 1960.
69. Weiner, N.: *Cybernetics.* New York, Wiley, 1961.
70. Wolf, H. G.: *Headache and Other Pain.* London, Oxford Univ. Press, 1948.
71. Wolf, H. G.: Protective reaction patterns and disease. *Ann. Intern. Med., 27*:944, 1947.
72. Woolridge, D. E.: *Machinery of the Brain.* New York, McGraw-Hill, 1963.
73. Wyndam, C. H., and Morrison, J. F.: Adjustment to cold of Bushmen in the Kalahari Desert. *J. Appl. Physiol., 12*:9, 1958.
74. Zohman, B. L.: Emotional stress and coronary heart disease. *Psychomatics, 1*:18, 1960.

Chapter 8

PARAPSYCHOLOGY AND HUMAN POTENTIALITIES

J. B. RHINE

PARAPSYCHOLOGY, as a new and inadequately recognized branch of science, requires some definition and outlining before discussion of its potentialities for mankind can be profitably undertaken. The brief introduction given here will largely follow the textbook, *Parapsychology, Frontier Science of the Mind* (1).

Defined as the science of *psi* or *parapsychical* phenomena, parapsychology is the branch of psychology dealing with communication or interaction between a person and his environment without reliance on the sensorimotor system. Psi phenomena naturally fall into two classifications broadly describable as "extrasensory" and "extramotor." Long practice has identified the former as *extrasensory perception* or ESP; and for the extramotor responses the term *psychokinesis* or PK has been appropriated.

While PK phenomena have not as yet required subdivision for convenience of study, ESP effects have long been distinguished as *clairvoyance* or ESP of objects or objective states; *telepathy*, ESP of another person's experience; and *precognition* or ESP of a future event.

Having arisen as other natural sciences, out of the study of events spontaneously occurring in nature, parapsychology began with case studies. Collections of reports of puzzling spontaneous occurrences led to the classification of these experiences into the types that represent the branches of the field given above.

An example of a familiar experience of one of the more common of these types will illustrate not only case material but will serve for later reference: Dr. L. of Durham once told me of a dream he had which he believed might have saved his life. In his dream the train on which he was riding was wrecked, and he was injured by the stove (such as was then used for heating the coach) falling on him. He awoke with such fright that he decided to cancel his lecture in Greensboro, scheduled for the next day, and to remain at home. The train on which he was to have traveled to Greensboro was wrecked the next day, and a man was killed by the falling stove.

Fortunately, it was possible to devise test methods specific to the types of psi phenomena suggested by the case material. These methods have been developed to the point of distinguishing one of these types of phenomena from the others while, at the same time, ruling out the possibility of sensorimotor communication and justifying the dismissal of explanation by chance coincidence. A sufficient amount of independent confirmation, too, has long since been obtained from a wide range of investigators and research centers in many lands. Therefore, it is now possible to speak with the confidence of sound experimental verification of psi communication.

Because of the revolutionary character of psi communication, however, and because in our culture new findings of radical nature have still to fight their way against stubborn resistance, a large amount of psi research thus far accumulated has had to be concerned primarily with merely reestablishing over and over again the simple fact of the occurrence of the phenomena. This has led to extreme measures of precaution in experimental procedures not customarily exercised in any other branch of science and to much wearisome detail of outlining of procedures to safeguard against possible errors and alternatives of interpretation. The critical reader approaching the field at this stage will save much time by directing his attention to the most advanced level of experimental controls (1, 2, 3) and from there take up the question of the growing rationale of the body of accumulating evidence of this new field (4). In this way he will see the broader outlines of the achievement of parapsychology as furnishing a rational pattern of lawful relations; this picture should greatly reduce the futile and unreasonable demands for repeatable proof with which the skeptic's approach is sometimes made (5, 6).

It will be seen that parapsychology has established the occurrence of psi phenomena and of their various types, but that it is not claimed that a sufficient understanding of the capacities which produce them has yet been reached to permit a precise formula for controlled demonstration. The first stage of a science has already been reached and passed; namely, that in which the phenomena which characterize the field have been identified and defined and their distinctiveness established (7).

The second stage, the discovery of underlying determinants such as will permit the control of the operations involved, is a far different one—one that has its counterpart in all the natural sciences. It is particularly important for the discussion of human potentialities that this identification of the stage of growth of the science be kept in mind. In a more familiar analogy, psi research has reached a point comparable to medicine at the stage of the reliable diagnosis of a new disease but before the stage of adequate etiology and therapy.

At such a point a question may always be asked as to what assurance there is that control will ever be acquired. One answer would be that according to the logic of natural science understanding always increases control over man's treatment of the principles concerned; and to the scientist everything in nature must be assumed to be subject to the eventual conquest of understanding.

A more specific answer may be had from the mere fact that we can experiment with psi, and the experience of the investigators in parapsychology adds up to a very considerable confidence that the abilities studied, elusive as they seem to be, will progressively be brought under increased control. An example—a very striking one to me at the time it occurred—may be given from my own laboratory observation (8). On this occasion the most thoroughly investigated subject in the work of this laboratory, Mr. H. P., was caught in a particularly happy mood and challenged by an extremely forceful approach to do his utmost in an ESP test. I was the experimenter, holding a pack of cards completely concealed by my hand from the subject's view as he paced back and forth in my office. He succeeded in identifying twenty-five cards (with five types of symbols) correctly in succession as, one by one, I selected a card between the thumb and finger of the other hand and held it still in the pack, without looking at it until he made his call. The point is that in the few minutes in which these twenty-five trials were made, there was a high degree of control exercised over the subject's ability. Control is possible, difficult as it may be to obtain it.

Most of the difficulty over the control of psi is accounted for by the fact that it is unconscious (9). No one knows with dependable confidence just when a psi exchange occurs, whether it is accurate or distorted or whether it concerns a contemporaneous or future event. Sometimes there are traces of introspective awareness, and many spontaneous experiences leave strong, sometimes compulsive, feelings of assurance. Thus far the experimental studies have not broken through to a very marked degree of control over this unconscious function. This, at present, is the limiting condition with regard to control over the exercise of psi ability.

The characteristic of psi communication most significant for its usefulness, especially as it yields to increased control, is its nonphysical status (10). While necessarily regarded as energetic because it produces effects ("does work"), it follows no known relation to the space-time order of the physical world. In fact, psi clearly defies space-time limitations, as, for example, is shown in the precognition experiments. This leaves the way open to the reintroduction of a mental energy theory, oft proposed already in the history of psychology. Psi energy must, of course, be interactive with other forms or states of energy or it would not be observed (1).

THE QUESTION OF RELIABLE USE

In turning now to ask about the value these findings of parapsychology may have for mankind, there are immediately evident two general questions, and both of them are important ones. First, there is the question as to what the value of psi ability may be estimated to be to man and his institutions. The other is the question of the value of parapsychological knowledge itself for the understanding of man and for all those broad social disciplines that depend for their principles of operation on a knowledge of the nature of man. I propose to take up these two broad questions in the order stated, recognizing at the same time that the questions are not entirely independent of each other and that no one today could possibly provide final answers to either one. It will be understood, I am sure, that for an estimate of values such as these questions call for, I cannot claim the objectivity and clinical support that I can for the review thus far given.

Also, in considering the question of the potential value of psi to the human individual or society, it is advisable to consider psi ability as we know it. It would naturally make a very different picture if it were to be supposed that knowledge of this capacity had so greatly increased that a high degree of control over it were possible, even for a few individuals. It seems better to leave to the stage of such developed control the consideration of the use that might then be made. As I have already stated, it is almost taken for granted among experienced workers in parapsychology that control will eventually be achieved. However, such control will not be an isolated fact—there will be qualifications, and it would be idle to speculate on the significance of such control without knowing more about the world of knowledge then existing into which this new development will be thrust. The possibilities are indeed so exciting that they have already aroused a large amount of interest, especially among technologists who need to extend communications across increasingly greater distances.

If we do consider the value to man of the control over psi ability he is *at present* able to exercise, the picture is not a very exciting one. Throughout the ages there have been many practices in every leading culture based on the assumption of psi ability. Some of these have been definitely religious in character; but this in no way dissociates them from their reliance upon the assumption of parapsychical powers, for there is no religion that does not make unqualified assumptions of what is now commonly designated as psi capacity.

Many practices, however, which assume a basis of parapsychical ability, have come down to the present day without religious affiliation. The designation of a suitable place to dig a well, the finding of a lost object, the telling of fortunes and the healing of disease without benefit of medical treatment represent claims, whatever their validity, that assume one type of psi or another. The fact that none of these practices has stood the test of scientific investigation so as to confirm the claims of the practitioner regarding the *extent* of his success is evidence enough that the abilities assumed are unequal to the degree of reliable control necessary for such practices.

Accordingly, even as I must maintain on one page that the abilities underlying these practices do, indeed, exist and to some extent can be exercised and demonstrated, I must add on another that they have not yet been found to be capable of the degree of controlled use which practitioners have claimed. While an adequate statistical check on the practices themselves is not feasible, tests administered to numerous practitioners as to the extent of the assumed ability they can demonstrate under controlled conditions have invariably failed to bear out the magnitude of the claims and the order of dependability taken for granted. This was true even where evidence of some degree of psi ability was registered. So long as the test methods are themselves still capable of improvement there may be ground for question whether they measure *all* of the practitioner's capacity. The answer need not, therefore, be considered final.

This is, however, far from saying that psi, even as it is known and used today, is of no real value to man. Quite the contrary. While it is not possible to say that Dr. L. in the case mentioned actually used precognitive ESP in his dream of the train wreck, it is not unreasonable to think he did, now that precognitive clairvoyance has been demonstrated as a human ability. If we credit his dream to precognition, then precognition probably did save him from tragedy. One can recognize this while at the same time also recognizing that, as is usual in science, it raises many difficult questions.

No one can say what the actual survival value to man and his species the occasional experience of psi might have, but quite evidently it constitutes something. There is no need to speculate as to how much psi experience goes unnoticed and unreported or even to question whether what we have come to recognize as parapsychical experiences may not have a level of functioning that only *occasionally* erupts into a form of conscious experience. It is better on the whole to reserve such interpretations until the explorations advance into this unknown territory. It is enough for the present to know that psi must be of some little value to the individual and to the species.

The fact that the explorations thus far made into the question of psi in animals have led to positive evidence raises another area of questions. No one wants to conclude as yet with finality that the evidence for the occurrence of psi in animals is sufficient. It is already moderately strong and reasonably conclusive (1). If psi occurs in animals, it raises a wide range of questions regarding its evolutionary origin and its probable role in evolution. These questions, too, are sufficiently important to justify in due course the resumption of the research that will answer them.

There are a few investigators of parapsychology who are inclined to think that better methods of utilizing psi (statistical concentration and psychological aid) could lead to a degree of control that would make it practical. The nearest approximation to the controlled identification of concealed targets (comparable to the breaking of a code) makes this exciting possibility worth entertaining but does not guarantee it (11).

One reason for taking a conservative attitude toward these developments is the realization forced upon us that the development of the method does not insure its use. The history of science and invention warns against optimism, especially in the area of the psychological sciences. The long history of the very practical and easily controlled demonstration of hypnosis and the difficulty with which the use of its practice has been advanced into those areas of medicine in which its usefulness has been known for a century or more warns against overoptimism concerning the early application of controlled psi performance, even if it is soon attained.

SIGNIFICANCE FOR THE UNDERSTANDING OF MAN

It is with more confidence and easier optimism that I now turn to the other question as to the value of the findings of parapsychology. This question, restated, is as follows: What significance have the findings of parapsychology today for the understanding of man and his potentialities?

The answer can be given here only in outline. The significance of the simple fact of the existence of psi ability in man touches man deeply in far too many relationships for them all even to be recounted here.

The major point of this large meaning of the facts about psi is due mainly to the nonphysical nature of this function. The fact that psi requires some other explanation than physics can supply puts man in a different philosophical bracket. This one finding alone completely destroys the case for materialism as a philosophy of man. This is to say it is the answer to the philosophical physicalism going back to the times of the Greeks as well as the dialectical or scientific materialsm of communism today. All through the history of human thought, when a scientific fact has confronted a philosophy, it has always brought an end to the speculative system, although the confrontation has usually been a slow and difficult operation. This does not, however, mean that the findings of parapsychology support a contrary philosophy. They do not, for example, constitute a case for a form of dualism; rather, they show first of all that the concept of physics cannot account for the whole of human nature. Thus it is the total *energy* system of nature that is broadened beyond the mere physical determinants (that have been assumed to be all there are). The requirement of a nonphysical energy in the operations which parapsychology has brought to light has caused this radical shift. But merely to have an energetics that includes both physical and nonphysical forms of energy is not to require a metaphysical dualism; it is better to adhere to a cautious, exploratory scientific organization of those findings and relationships.

The psi discoveries do, however, confirm the religious doctrine of the existence in man of a spiritual reality or influence. It has been largely on the basis of intuitive experience that the assumption of a nonphysical or spiritual force in man's nature has been maintained. Now in a limited degree it can be said that the science of parapsychology has, by its proof of an extraphysical operation in man, justified this basic tenet of the world's religions.

Probably the most important of all human problems, if they can in any way be classified, is that identified with the freedom of the will. Again, it has been man's intuitive conception of his nature that he is (in some way completely unknown as yet) able to exercise a degree of volitional independence of the determinism he finds inherent in nature around him and even within him. The conception of an all-governing physical determinism which has progressively infiltrated the modern mind on both sides of the Iron Curtain has almost crowded the discussion of volitional freedom off the stage of respectable intellectual exchange. Yet the whole philosophy of criminal law is said by the lawyers to depend upon it. No such thing as a deterministic morality for mankind has even been offered to supplant it. The other conceptions of freedom, social and political for which men have paid dearly, depend upon it.

Now at last a way appears to have been opened for the discovery of what this intuitive volitional freedom really means. The facts about psi have given to man evidence of another distinction within the unity of his nature; psi has force and properties of its own and with its own powers, its own lawfulness, it offers an instrumentation for controlled interaction with the physically determined world to which man also belongs. By means of this relatively independent system of psi energies the individual may exercise the differential of free interaction that gives man the subjective experience of freedom, a measure (however small) of escape from the remorseless determinism of a sensate mechanistic universe.

To the psychological sciences parapsychology offers a system of nonphysical reality that is distinctively psychical. What other territory has psychology ever been able hitherto with confidence to call its own? Biology, too, now has a new energetic system to consider in its search for the still undiscovered determinants in the evolution of life and mind. No one knows as yet how far back in the great history of life's origins discernible signs of this psi energy can be found. Science has still not learned how to look for new discoveries or how to escape its own artificial barriers against heretical ideas. (Do they not still blind biology students "at birth" against "vitalism"?)

To the field of education the facts of psi have already introduced a new instrument in the research needed as to what goes on in the subtle relation between student and teacher (12). For medicine it should be of interest to know that a new force has been already found to have bearing upon the processes of growth. These new forces cannot fail to be involved in the broad range of problems of health and treatment in the domain of this master discipline.

Physics itself has now for the first time a true frontier. To those increasing numbers of physics students who have thought of the universe and the domain of physics as synonymous, there is now an unanticipated border; and a whole new set of problems arise in the transduction of energies from the parapsychical to the physical and back. What kind of energy form could there be that produces no space-time manifestation? That seems not to follow mass-relations?

The most immediate bearing of the facts of psi upon the world is that of challenge. This revolutionary set of findings is so basically incredible to the organized trained mind of today that it is almost automatically rejected. Indeed, few minds ever are trained to handle a radically new discovery; and the easy test of whether the new is consistent with the old serves most scientists as a sufficient basis for rejection. The facts of psi are not consistent with the physicalistically dominated natural science of today. Most serious of all is the fact that the *accepted* doctrine becomes so closely identified with the natural vanities of those who have acquired it that anything which challenges it offers a personal affront and must be fought to a finish.

My final point then is that parapsychology has the significant but difficult challenge of bringing home to the academic mind of today how far away from the true picture of man it has gotten, how far out on the mechanistic limb it has been forced by the rapidly advancing sciences and technologies centered on the physical world. This small new branch has the opportunity and the responsibility to draw man's attention back to the other side of his own nature—a hidden, difficult side—one he has taken largely on faith and intuition. Can the facts about psi, however reliable, possibly win such a difficult contest?

REFERENCES

1. Rhine, J. B., and Pratt, J. G.: *Parapsychology*. Springfield, Thomas, 1957.
2. Rhine, J. B., Pratt, J. G., Smith, B. M., Woodruff, J. L., and Greenwood, J. A.: *Extrasensory Perception after Sixty Years*. New York, Holt, Rinehart and Winston, 1940.
3. Murphy, G.: *Challenge of Psychical Research*. New York, Harper, 1961.
4. *J. Parapsychol.*, Durham, North Carolina, Parapsychology Press (College Station), 1937.
5. Price, G. R.: Science and the supernatural. *Science, 122*(Aug): 1955.
6. Rhine, J. B.: Comments on "Science and the Supernatural." *Science, 123*(Jan.): 1956.
7. Rhine, J. B.: Some avoidable misconceptions in parapsychology. *J. Parapsychol., 23*:1, 1959.
8. Rhine, J. B.: Special motivation in some exceptional ESP performances. *J. Parapsychol., 28*:1, 1964.
9. Rhine, J. B.: The nature and consequences of the unconsciousness of psi. *J. Parapsychol., 22*:3, 1958.
10. Rhine, J. B.: The science of nonphysical nature. *J. Philosophy, LI*:25, 1954.
11. Ryzl, M.: Assured identification of concealed targets by ESP. *J. Parapsychol., 30*:1, 1966.
12. Anderson, M.: The relationship between level of ESP scoring and student class grade. *J. Parapsychol., 23*:1, 1959.

Chapter 9

AGING PHENOMENA IN THE PERSPECTIVE OF HUMAN POTENTIAL

LEONARD PEARSON

INTRODUCTION

WE are on the brink of a long-brewing revolution in our thinking about people and about their potential. The manifestations range from the publication of this book to the fact that a new small college has been founded at Esalen Institute at Big Sur, California. The curriculum of the new school, which will deal with concepts such as self-awareness, love, increased sensory awareness, etc., is described as dealing with "human growth," because there is no other term extant to describe such a curriculum.

It is likely that all mankind will benefit from the revolution that is erupting, but the aged will benefit the *least!* While there are many unfounded assumptions about human behavior at all ages, those that prevail about the aged are the most pernicious and the most ubiquitous and will be the most difficult to root out, since most of them have existed since antiquity. In one sense a mass delusion has existed in this country and in other Western cultures regarding the aged, and this misconception is only now beginning to show a break with "un-reality."

In this chapter, I will try to examine the myths and fallacies, as well as known findings as they bear on selected aspects of human functioning in the aged. Then I will present the information now available that counters the prevailing stereotyped thinking and suggest needed avenues of reseach to follow up on experimental leads. In some well-worked diggings, e.g., decline of intellectual function in the aged, memory loss in the aged, *ad nauseam,* I will just touch on the "known" facts and point to the newer findings which are indicative of radical changes in scientific thinking about these concepts.

SEXUALITY

In the area of sexual needs and activities of the aged, there exists an unbelievable morass of contradictory statements, inconsistencies, absence of reliable data and even denial of the entire area of human functioning. One indication of the condition of the field is the recent report issued by a prominent group of geriatric specialists entitled "Psychiatry and the Aged: An Introductory Approach." This report, released by the Committee on Aging of the Group for the Advancement of Psychiatry in September, 1965, contains *not one single reference to sexual needs of the aged.* The bulk of the report is concerned with classification of disorders of the aged and descriptions of physiological and psychological changes (18).

The following quotations appearing in recent publications are another indication of the chaos in the field:

> "From a physiological point of view, there is no such thing a a climacteric. Children have been sired by men in their sixties, seventies, and even eighties. A study in Sweden showed that 'men in their nineties were secreting living sperm'" (52).
>
> "As a man enters the years of middle age, a gradual change takes place in his personality. This transformation or change is referred to by the medical profession as the 'climacterium virile' or the 'male menopause'" (8).
>
> " . . . since males do not actually pass through any physiological stage which is truly on a par with female menopause. Still in all, the comparable period in a man's life may have repercussions somewhat akin to female change of life. Suicidal depression, profound withdrawal, compulsive adultery—all of these are extremely common among men in middle age" (38).

Thus, there is little agreement on the intensely important subject of sexuality.

Unfortunately, as pointed out by Shock (56) a number of years ago, "far too much of our knowledge of elderly people is based on residents in institutions." Supplemented by findings from clinical office practice, that observation continues to be true, particularly as it applies to the area of sexuality. Studies of normal functioning of aged men and women are relatively infrequent. Gebhard, Director of the Kinsey Institute in Indiana, recently pointed out *that the alleged male climacteric is a peculiar product of our own Western culture.* He believes that for many men the decline of sexual function is a socio-psychological phenomenon rather than one based on physiological processes (13). The earlier Kinsey report on sexual behavior in American females used the designation "fifty plus" to indicate women over that age, with no further explanation of how far over fifty they were. One can only assume that such a sampling was indeed small.

A recent study by Gagnon and Christenson of the Kinsey Institute staff, included persons in their sixties and seventies. They found a tremendous variation in the degree of sexual activity among such persons, with some in their seventies who would be rated "high" regarding outlet for sexual activity by any standard. Others, however, were rapidly declining in their sexual activities in their fifties and sixties. They found significant correlation between men who maintained a high frequency of sexual activity in their adolescence and adulthood and those maintaining a similar high frequency in their sixties and seventies (13). It may well be that sexual activity is a general indication of good physical condition in the aged and correlates with good health in general.

In Sweden, a recent book entitled *Erotic Minorities* by psychiatrist Lars Ullerstam posed a primary thesis that people require sexual activity "for their mental health" and furthermore that "it should be made available to all." Ullerstam proposed that brothels be established and operated under the supervision of the Swedish Medical Association with prices controlled by the government. He further suggests that a "mobile service be provided for hospitals, mental patients and shut-ins." Ullerstam suggests that a new type of social worker, a "sexual Samaritan" would probably be required to supervise the sex program (22). The *Scandinavian Times* reacted to Ullerstam's book by editorializing, sarcastically, that in the future, if things went as he predicted, " . . . persons past middle age may well hear a rap on the door. They will answer it and be confronted by a smiling young person with a cheery message, 'Good evening. I am your sexual

Samaritan.' If this comes to pass, even a sexually-liberated Swede would probably be shocked to his shoe laces."

While the proposals of Ullerstam are radical, and certainly unlikely to ever be adopted in America, ways of enhancing sexual expression have been described. A number of exercises have been published which are designed specifically to assist in the development of sexual skills. Prudden, a member of the President's Commission on Physical Fitness, has described a series of "sexercises" which she presents as an assist for the "physical expression of genuine love," rather than implying that sex is a type of athletic contest. Prudden uses the analogy that a person being trained for skiing would not be satisfied with just skis, poles, boots and stretch pants. He would also wonder about the muscles required at various points in the skiing act. And again Prudden wryly points out that "a Beethoven sonata will always sound better on a concert piano than on a kazoo." The exercises she recommends include those for the gluteals, pelvic muscles, etc. (48).

The use of endocrine replacement therapy for women has been well documented and has been part of the physicians' armamentarium for some time. The use of hormones with men has been less well established, although the search for aphrodisiacal substances, elixirs, etc. has been described by aging men for centuries.

Turning again to the realities of the large number of noninstitutionalized persons, we may find it helpful to look at the vital statistics concerning marriages of older persons in this country. In 1959, of nearly one and a half million marriages in this country, approximately 2.4 per cent or thirty-five thousand took place in which the bride, the groom or both were sixty-five years of age or older. One can assume a variety of motives were involved, but it seems reasonable that sensual and sexual activities would be involved in a large portion of the over seventy thousand people in these marriages. For the grooms, in the population of sixty-five or over, approximately 48 per cent of the time the bride was ten to twenty years younger than the groom, while in approximately 10 per cent of the cases, the bride was *twenty-five or more years younger* (63). It had earlier been pointed out by Rosow (49) that by the age of sixty-five only 45 per cent of the population is still married and living with their spouse. The implication that there is often no potential "legitimate" outlet for sexual activity among this age population raises other questions about the correlation between sexual activity and physical health among the aged.

Clearly, the total impact of sexual activity, or lack of it, among the aged remains a vast unexplored field of research. Is it possible that increased sexual activities can help fulfill the potential of the aged? Are there any research frameworks which can be established to explore this very hypothesis, or is it necessary to consider anthropological and sociological data based upon studies of other cultures? The entire area of sexual research still remains close to the taboo level with only occasional breakthroughs to clear the murky atmosphere surrounding our impoverished state of knowledge. If the studies carried out at the Kinsey Institute are borne out, it indicates that an active sexual life is to be encouraged by all to facilitate the continued utilization of sexual satisfactions in advanced age. The profound psychological crisis which follows the *apparent* diminution of sexual drive in some middle-aged males is so well documented in the literature as well as in clinical files as to require no further comment. To determine the extent of physical and emotional satisfactions concurrent with sexual activity and its effect on the aged requires intensive research. Further intensive investigation on the individual level is needed as well as broad research to determine the effect of modifying and extending sexual activities among the aged.

STAMINA AND PHYSICAL HEALTH

The time-honored description of the physical status of the aged person usually includes references to his feeble strength, tremulous hands, lack of erect posture and poor gait, etc. A number of salvos are being fired at such encrusted concepts. Recently Swartz (60) presented his beliefs that there were no diseases caused by "the mere passage of time." At an address before the American Academy of General Practice in 1965, Swartz stated:

"The shaky hand and tottering gait are the results of lack of condition and exercise, not the passage of time. The forgetful mind results from lazy habits of study and lack of motivation. The cure for these so-called stigmata of aging is obvious—exercise and study."

The thought of subjecting the ancient body to exercises seems foreign to the usual thinking of most of us. Yet there are a number of indications that this is precisely the direction to consider for future development of potential. The enhancement of physical attitude affects all other aspects of well-being.

In 1966, medical editor and writer Morris Fishbein counseled, "The aged should not give up so easily. Only by exercise can tissues be kept alive—this includes brain cells" (11).

The Royal Canadian Air Force "exercise plans" have, in just a few years, achieved wide popularity in America as well as in Canada. Several million copies of these scientifically developed plans for increasing physical tonus and fitness for all persons, male and female, have been sold. The exercise plans give several levels of exercises and instructions for progression to higher levels. The book includes statements such as "for those fifty to fifty-nine years, at least eight days at each level"; "males over sixty years, at least ten days at each level" (50).

Clearly, it is possible for individuals in their fifties and sixties to follow a graduated program of exercise which will provide increased physical fitness along with the capacity for participating more fully in all aspects of life.

Even for those whose lives are complicated by coronary disease, a frequent concomitant of aging, all hope is not lost. A recent article by Hellerstein and Ford (19) describes the challenge encountered by the physician in treating the persons with coronary disease who have need for comprehensive care. These physicians stress the importance of physical fitness in normal persons as well as those with heart disease. They detail the case of a sixty-four-year-old man who had recovered from heart disease and after training was able to run ten miles in seventy-seven minutes. At a later date, after exercise on a bicycle ergometer, he showed a slower pulse rate than that reported for normal subjects of his own age. It is certainly not indicated for all individuals with heart disease to become long-distance runners, but the point made by Hellerstein and Ford, and others, is that organized programs of physical fitness are important for all individuals, including those who have coronary heart disease.

The need for systematic research of this dimension of aging exists to a marked degree. *We have tolerated stereotyped thinking about the presumed inevitable deterioration and decrepitude of aging without systematically investigating the possibilities of retarding or eliminating this particular dimension from the automatic progression of time.*

At a national level, our policy regarding health for the aged has the unfortunate effect of rewarding those who become ill. Rather than promoting the health potential of the typical aged person, or increasing his reserves, Medicare legislation provides only for dealing with the failure in physical health and stamina. As Bortz (2) makes clear, there is a tragic failure on the part of many to reach their potential because of "preventable human deterioration." Until we can foster a program to develop and maintain sound physical health and stamina, we are likely to see a large portion of our citizens deprived of their potential by the simple virtue of poor physical capacity to realize it. As ironically pointed out by Otto (45) the use of physical exercise, dance, etc. is recognized as beneficial for psychotic patients in mental hospitals, and yet its value for the normally functioning individual as a means of attaining more optimal functioning is largely ignored.

SLEEP AND WAKEFULNESS PATTERNS

Older people are frequently described as taking advantage of periods of "cat-napping," and being able to function after only short periods of evening sleep. The research that has been done on sleep deprivation has tended to focus upon the young healthy male, frequently college students. Kleitman (28) in his epic study entitled *Sleep and Wakefulness* has summarized the pertinent research dealing with sleep deprivation. The question of sleep and wakefulness cycles may become extremely important, especially variations in the usual twenty-four-hour cycle, as man continues his experiments in outer-space or living conditions below the water as in the 1965 Navy experiments off the coast of California.

Kleitman and others (25) have pointed out that the twenty-four hour rhythm is an individually acquired, learned process, and that variations of this routine utilizing longer periods of time are within the reach of man. There have been reports of successful adjustment to eighteen or twenty-eight hour routines of living by subjects in northern Norway, well above the Arctic Circle (29) during a period of months in which the sun does not set.

A puzzling finding was recently reported by the University of Toledo investigators who tested subjects in their twenties after twelve, eighteen, twenty-four, thirty and thirty-six hours of sleeplessness. A number of visual, auditory, as well as physiological tests were given. "In every test the mean thirty and thirty-six hour performances had returned toward or exceeded 'normal' values recorded at zero or twelve hours" (23).

What are the implications of these studies for the aging individual? Additional research needs to be done with the older person in terms of his sleep and wakefulness cycles and ways in which this may be applied to the changing demands of the technology of the future. The aged person may find that altered patterns of sleep and wakefulness allow him to pursue hobbies or work that the traditional pattern precludes. There is no need to assume that long-established patterns cannot be modified. Research is needed to determine what effects follow attempts to change the sleep cycle in older persons. Aged in institutions are fitted into the routines that are established primarily for the convenience of the staff and administration, and research projects should be encouraged to test out the implicit belief that the "early-to-bed, early to rise" ritual *is* most conducive to health and longevity. More knowledge is needed about the absolute amounts of sleep needed by individuals at different ages, separate from cultural and social customs and conveniences.

One of Lawrence Durrell's characters in *The Dark Labyrinth* describes why she no longer sleeps, but engages in deep rest nightly. "There is no more need for sleep than there is for death." She believes that sleep is essentially for tired persons who have a style of body or mind that is cramped. "Now I participate with everything. I feel joined to everything in a new kind of way." She does not anticipate dying until she has really "explored this world to the full. Until I'm used up, and so to speak, emptied out of this world into the next" (9).

As far as we know, sleep is a biological necessity, but new ways of utilizing sleep patterns need to be studied in the aged.

WORK, RETIREMENT, AND LEISURE

Emerging trends in the pattern of work in our society require careful consideration of the role of the aged person. Some writers are predicting that in the near future we can expect a three-day work week with retirement mandatory at age fifty. Others predict that within the next twenty-five to thirty-five years, the average adult male will have to learn three different jobs during his working life because a new technology will rapidly create obsolescence in a number of careers and occupational fields. Sociologists predict that only a small proportion of the total work force will be able to work on a consistent basis, while the majority of adults will be in enforced idleness, supported by the gainful work of the minority who will control complex processes through automation.

Unfortunately, in this field too a number of myths persist. Recently, Kent (26) has criticized the prevalent notion that guilt accompanies leisure activity in the aged. This belief tends to be derived from the middle class value system of those who administer many of the programs for the aged. It has even been pointed out, with piquancy, that the aged have to contend with two sets of problems: first, the result of being old; second, a set of problems that experts in the field *believe* that the aged have.

Yet, despite the increasing emphasis upon early retirement, there are complex factors operating in some careers which seem to favor the aged person and may perhaps contribute to his longevity. London (36) in a recent study of over three hundred and fifty composers and conductors, going back nearly one thousand years, found that social-economic security and emotional catharsis provided by the creative work in music favored a high survival rate. A large number of composers lived into their eighties and nineties and were productive throughout most of their entire adult life. What is more surprising, though, about the creative activities of these men is the indomitable spirit which they displayed in overcoming the debilitating effects of physical disease or injury. The composer Arnold Schoenberg "died" and following cardiac arrest was revived by intra-cardiac injection of epinephrine. He continued working for six more years before dying at the age of seventy-seven. The English composer Frederick Delius died at seventy-one despite a progressive quadriplegia and blindness during the last twenty years of his life. He composed faithfully, even though it meant giving musical dictation to his secretary. Bartok composed all during a two-year course of leukemia. The French composer Darius Milhaud at seventy-one was still active and creative despite a severe degree of rheumatoid arthritis that would have incapacitated the usual person. Looking at a different field of professional endeavor, we find Aldous Huxley described by his brother Julian as dying of a fatal and painful disease yet, "in the last weeks of his life, he was unable to write but dictated a brilliant article on Shakespeare and religion which he signed only two days before his death . . ." (21). It seems that certain types of work are able to free the potential and creativity of the individual to the extent that he is able to ignore physical discomfort and pain that would usually impede a person who was functioning at a lower level of achievement.

There are a number of other professions, all of which involve complex behavior and judgments, where age appears to be an asset, if not a necessity. Statesmen and present rulers of a number of countries in Europe are well in their seventies without evidence of decline or failure. Many top executives in "dynastic" corporations (where the same family maintains control) continue to be gainfully employed throughout most of their lives.

Central to the question of work in later life is the question of retirement. Unfortunately, most retirement programs are grossly inadequate and serve as dispensers of objective information about balancing one's budget, traveling economically, finding a hobby, and similar mundane and sometimes puerile admonitions. Such didactically oriented retirement preparation programs serve a bland diet (44) which is usually rejected by the potential retiree. Retirement planning, in one sense should be planning *for living* and must be done years before reaching the stage where one's sixty-fifth birthday is just thirty days away. Self-realization and development of potential should be conceived as a life-long objective, not one to be considered just before reaching the age of retirement.

There are a number of careers that require skills that depend on the more primitive senses of man—the brewmeister, the whiskey blender, parfumer of scents, the coffee taster, etc., all utilizing highly developed "primitive" senses of smell and taste. Marshall McLuhan, who has been called Canada's new "intellectual comet," has recently described the process of man's alienation from his environment. He laments that modern man is essentially living in an "eye culture" and has failed to sufficiently develop his other senses of touch, taste and smell. He has decried man's over-utilization of his alphabet and other visual stimuli (53).

Related to this are some exciting developments in the use of "other senses." In his address as retiring president of the Division of Experimental Psychology of the American Psychological Association, Frank Geldard dealt with "adventures with tactile literacy" (14).

It may be that the whole dimension of "other senses" remains to be developed and utilized for full enjoyment of life, as well as to increase possibility of careers not usually thought of for the aged person. It matters very little whether an ongoing and growing awareness and in-touchness with the world are gained through employment or through leisure time use of one's total sensorium. However, for the person who is disabled physically or has impaired vision or hearing, the potentials for mastering a new system of communication and relating to the world are paramount. "Training" programs for the development of sensory awareness and openness to a variety of stimuli are indicated for the aged.

The older person has acquired skills in living and working. Jobs which utilize this experience need to be found and more created to give the aged a useful outlet and purpose for living. Society is enriched by their serving as nursery school teachers or aides, assisting in mental hospital programs and acting as psychology and social work assistants, "big brothers," etc. Another less conceptualized role is that of providing an experience which is non-existent for many teenagers. Because of the structure of modern family living, there are millions of teenagers who have no direct contact with an older person. Their attitudes are distorted and based on stereotypes. Formal and informal structures are needed which will allow aged persons to relate on a continuing basis, perhaps for several weeks, with teenagers in order to help enhance their own concept of themselves and their future life. A teenager who was involved with such a program organized at a summer camp was able to express her feelings spontaneously in this manner:

> . . . it was my pleasure to work with these marvelous people, assisting in their activities . . . I worked with and watched them during their stay, and all I have to say is, that they may appear old, but in mind and spirit they are as young as you and me.
>
> If you saw them as I did, dancing, singing, or even just talking to them, you would have the respect and love for them that I have. . . .
>
> They raised our parents, giving them everything they never had, yet many will return to the city and stare at four walls. Thank you so much for letting me get to know you and for everything I've learned during your stay. May you all live long and return here next summer to let other teenagers like me meet you and know you as I have (61).

Doris Twitchell Allen has demonstrated that remarkable results can be obtained by having a group of fourteen-year-olds from various countries and cultures live together in a summer camp. There are even more exciting potentials involved in relationships between the aged American and the teenage American who are severely estranged.

LONGEVITY AND THE AGING PROCESS

After several thousand years of philosophical speculation and several hundred years of scientific theorizing, we are still not close to answering basic questions as to "why" the human organism ages. If we follow the formula described by Bortz based upon mammalia, namely, that the organism expends one sixth of its life span in reaching physical maturation—this would mean that *man should live to be one hundred and twenty-five to one hundred and fifty years* (3)! The explanatory concepts of aging seem to have come full circle. If we ignore the earlier theories that viewed death as a consequence of offending the supernatural powers or deities, we find the emergence of the Hippocratic Theory in the Fourth Century B.C. The essential factor in life was held to be heat (20). As aptly pointed out by Grant in an extensive review of historical concepts, most theories have postulated a finite quantity of "stuff" which is given each person at inception—a substance which was often called innate heat, vital spirit, vital force, etc. (15).

Hippocrates describes the heat in older persons as being feeble and the diminution of this innate heat as leaving the body more vulnerable to diseases. Aristotle, a scant one hundred years later, also used this concept and described a human being as one who could not exist without natural heat. Nearly two thousand years later we find a modern scientist stating:

> "Senescence, then, might be measurable in the production of energy and the failure of that production with time or the aging of the subject. In other words, the older the person the less heat he would produce per hour per square meter, and the decline would be directly related to the amount of time elapsing since birth as he senesces" (7).

While there seems to be general agreement that the aging process is not concomitant *per se* with the diseases of aging, there is a wide range of opinion about the causes of aging.

At one extreme we find the opinion presented that ". . . The ultimate cause of aging . . . may not be found by science at all. The answers available today about various phases of the aging process are given at the phenomenal level only. . . . They do not . . . reveal the ultimate or first cause of aging" (16).

Grant believes that some writers have attempted to extract by rational scientific methods an "understanding of a process which all evidence to date suggests is beyond understanding." He concludes, "it may be that empirical science is not the appropriate medium for its discussion" (17). It is difficult to understand what other medium could be more appropriate, unless one turns to religion with its notorious history for discouraging free inquiry, or one defaults the entire question to philosophy.

The aging process has been described as "fundamentally one of cellular biology" (57). Nevertheless, we have insufficient knowledge of the activities of aging cells. It is, of course, much easier for us to deal with cells which have been organized into tissues or organ systems, and at this level it is possible to discern "old" and "young" structures. Shock, however, has pointed out that there can really be no satisfactory answer to the general question, "When is a man old?" To have any significance, the word "old" needs to be pegged to an additional phrase such as "old—with respect to what performance?"

Some have pointed more specifically to the role of connective tissue and the variety of disorders described as diffuse collagen diseases. Zinsser, for example, has stressed the importance of elasticity of connective tissue and bitterly pointed out, "were the structure of connective tissue of as obvious financial importance as the structure of nylon, I feel sure that we might have many answers now, but which we will be a long time in reaching" (65). There have been a number of provocative statements from scientists in recent years relating to this "ultimate question" about the cause of aging. Sinex has written that "certain hypothesis about aging suggest that preventive therapy is a possibility." Strehler (59) believes that there is no inherent contradiction, no inherent property of cells which *precludes* their organization into perpetually functioning and self-replenishing individuals. Still (40) asserts that we can be "skeptical about the assumption that 'we can't live forever' . . ." The Russian scientist Kuprevich (40) recently asked "Why should man die of old age? I am sure we can find means for switching off the mechanisms which make cells age."

Exciting work in this field comes from the research laboratories of Selye (54, 55). Selye, who developed the concept of "calciphylaxis," on the basis of extensive animal experiments reached the conclusion that changes of aging are related to calcium metabolism. Through biochemical means he has been able to develop in a two month old rat the wrinkled inelastic skin, bad teeth, cataracts, weight loss, calcification of vocal chords and other characteristics of the aged. In addition, through biochemical means Selye has been able to *prevent* manifestations of premature aging. His approach has been a vigorous attack upon the process of senility on a biological level. While he believes it is premature to attribute the same process to prevent natural aging in the human being, his theory offers an original method of approaching this problem.

A large number of studies have been conducted dealing with the consequences of the aging process in man (1, 62). It does not seem fruitful to review or present these extensive studies or the more basic fact that these studies have focused almost exclusively on the pathological concomitants, or sequels, of the aging process. There have recently appeared some breaks in the wall of this pathology-oriented approach to the aging process. Inconsistent findings have emerged, which in some cases, have made it possible to reinterpret those in the light of a phenomenal point of view of the organism itself. These developments may well presage a new way of understanding the aging person in all of his adaptive processes and all of his attempts to realize his potential. I will only refer to a few of these to indicate the tenor of current findings in this area.

Osteo-arthritis ". . . may not be an inexorable concomitant of aging" (58). Usually hypothesized as intrinsic to the aging process are changes in connective tissue, particularly in cartilage, and for years the question of osteoarthritis as a "normal" phenomenon in aging was hardly questioned.

There are a number of psycho-physiological aspects of human functioning which have long been the object of investigation by gerontologists. These include visual motor responses, eye blink reflexes, intellectual functioning and related cognitive factors such as memory, learning, etc. For complete details about this type of work, previous references provide details. However, in this area there are also new findings which break radically with past interpretations and "findings." For example, Luisada, in a study of three hundred and sixty elderly persons found *no incidence of hypertension in persons above age ninety*. Luisada pointed out that the old adage that blood pressure should rise according to age is true only on an individual basis, especially, when an older person has kidney or artery disease (35).

A twelve-year study of ability changes in old age yielded the result that "there is not necessarily a decline in I.Q. scores" in elderly persons who remain healthy, challenging the generally held notion that a decline in intelligence is "normal" for the aging person (27). An adaptation theory has been presented to account for the relative inability of elderly subjects to acquire a conditioned response (eye blink). The report raised the possibility that such a reflex had been "adapted out" and is therefore less susceptible to conditioning (5).

A study on the ability to discriminate differences in lifted weights gave "striking and unexpected results." The speed of response in judging weights *did not decline* as the task became more difficult which was expected in aged subjects (34).

Busse (6) has presented the point of view that there is a need now to focus on eliminating the *diseases* that reduce thinking, feeling, perception, etc., in the aged, implying doubt that the frequently cited changes in those spheres are irrevocably a function of aging. Some perceptual studies have indicated that there is a more efficient response by the aged in situations where their cautiousness may be "motivational" and be done for ego-enhancing reasons.

A therapeutic workshop program for older persons was established at the Jewish Vocational Service in Chicago recently to demonstrate the beneficial effects on the aged of participating in a productive work climate. The assumption was that "a productive work situation will retard, arrest or reverse the negative aspects of psychological aging."

The results of psychological tests often depict "constriction" which is labeled "senile," yet this "constriction" may well be an effective means of adaptation to a negative, stressful environment. Oberleder (41) points out that the effects of "anxiety, motivation, tension and factors related to disuse are so pervasive as to make inconsistency of performance, or even abnormality of performance (in the aged) the rule rather than the exception."

What are some directions for future research in order to deal with this elusive variable of senility, or more precisely, longevity? There are now nearly fifteen thousand people in this country who are centenarians. This incredible pool of potential subjects for research is usually ignored except when one of them reaches his one hundred and first birthday. Then the newspapers, press services or T.V. networks interview the person who has managed to survive in modern society for this length of time. He will be asked the usual inane question about to what does he attribute his long life. The person often replies: "I have never smoked or drunk hard liquor a day in my life."

The next day, in a different part of the country, someone reaches the ripe old age of one hundred and two and is interviewed and asked the same question. His reply is usually: "I always drink a fifth of corn whiskey daily and smoke a dozen good cigars!" We have ignored the potential richness of individuals who have lived past one hundred years and who would probably be delighted to take part in a study which would help others learn how to survive as they have, even though they may not know the precise methods themselves.

Botwinick (4) has pointed out the pressing need to extend the creativity of proven scientists. We do not know why some reach creative fruition early, why some are able to continue to function, and why others are not as productive. Another question which emerges is the question of retraining, or restoring, or providing perceptual reintegration for those who seem to have difficulties in these areas. In other words, we have assumed deterioration, or immutability of the "holy vessel," the cortex, but not enhancement of human cerebral function.

In a pioneering study, utilizing hypnosis to convince people that they had suffered a brain injury in an automobile accident, Fromm and colleagues found that their subjects gave "organic" psychological test responses, both projective and objective, in the absence of organic damage, while under hypnosis (12). The intriguing question raised by this research is that it may be possible to disentangle the effects of functioning which are purely due to physiological damage and those which are due to the emotional responses of the individual. This "somatopsychological" effect can often cloud the functioning as well as the appearance of someone who is responding to an awareness of mild change in his own intellectual functioning. This emotional response can often be modified and yet is frequently overlooked. What is needed now is a series of research projects involving hypnosis which will try to "suggest" that a subject who is in his eighties or nineties and showing signs of senility is now only fifty or sixty, followed by an evaluation of his responses.

Kramer (32), Pearson (46), and others (30) have described psychotherapy with the brain-damaged person; so the precedent is established, and change has been demonstrated.

PERSONALITY, VALUE SYSTEM, AND ATTITUDES TOWARD DEATH

One of the most resistant stereotypes about the aged has been that their personality is not capable of change. Kahn (24), Oberleder (42), Pearson (47), and others (31, 33) have tried to demonstrate that this inaccurate and obsolete notion is one of the factors that prevents the older person from being given the opportunity for psychotherapeutic interaction. The circular reasoning which deprives him of the opportunity for change is often used as a shibboleth to damn him for not being *capable of changing*. It has been shown with sufficient frequency to be pursued on a broad scale that *the older person is capable of changing his personality orientation and value structure*. Unfortunately, most studies about the aged have been concerned with age differences rather than age-related changes. Murphy has made it eminently clear that he believes "we cannot set limits on potentialities of what can or cannot come into existence" (39). Many of our previous observations were based on hospitalized or institutionalized clientele which prevented us from seeing the entire spectrum, including well-functioning aged persons. Otto has suggested that there is a liberating effect on potential when one is able to confront one's value system, including attitudes about death. Until recently, the area of attitudes about death has been one of the taboo areas of modern psychological research (10). The climate seems to be changing, and a number of recent publications have focused on the importance of man's awareness of his own transcience. Existential theory has provided the thrust for man's acceptance of his ultimate destiny and for his own responsibility. However, it is still difficult for this to be verbalized and discussed in a large setting, although beginnings have been made in group psychotherapy in various settings around the country (37). A relevant issue, but more emotionally laden, is the question of suicide and control over one's own death. In the unforgettable *Death of a Man,* Lael Wertenbaker (64) describes how she assisted her husband in committing suicide in the later stages of his terminal cancer. Broad scale investigations and discussions of this issue are vitally needed.

Saunders, an English physician at a hospital for the incurably ill in England, encourages and assists patients in discussing their own imminent death. She feels that during the remaining few days or few weeks a person is able to act more maturely and more fully than ever before (51). Issues of this type, once resolved and brought out from behind culturally determined trappings, may help to free the potential of all individuals, including those who are aged or physically ill. The fear of death is a function of all man, not only the aged.

CONCLUSION: A WORD OF CAUTION

As we progress in our knowledge about "human potential," as we learn more about ways to encourage and facilitate its development, we need to guard against putting it into the familiar matrix of traditional psychological measurement terms, or medical diagnostic nomenclature.

Oppenheimer (43) has warned about the dangers of a psychology that would be influenced to "model itself after a physics which is not there anymore, which has been quite out-dated." He pointed out, at an address before the sixty-third annual convention of the American Psychological Association that the early Babylonians had developed a system of mensuration and had calculated on a mathematical basis lunar cycles, eclipses, etc. The measurements had real value, for without it, the predictions, prophesies, and magic would not work. Oppenheimer questioned the desires of a large group of psychologists for measurement. "It is a real property of the real world that you are measuring, but it is not necessarily the best way to advance true understanding of what is going on; . . ."

We may well need a new language or system of concepts to talk about the essence of "human potential development," a fluid language and one which allows for growth within its own conceptualization. If we try to apply the traditional measures of personal growth and change, we may shackle or even strangle the new process because of our efforts to classify or categorize along a static dimension. At this point, I will argue for broadly defined, qualitative, descriptive terminology which might by some be condemned as being "anecdotal" or "clinical case history." Such a broadly defined, qualitative, descriptive terminology will allow further opportunity for study and for a more detailed grasping of the concepts of the emerging process by which human potentiality is realized.

BIBLIOGRAPHY

1. Birren, James E., Ed.: *Handbook of Aging and the Individual: Psychological and Biological Aspects*. Chicago, Univ. Chicago Press, 1959.
2. Bortz, E. L.: Growth and aging. *Amer. J. Psychiat., 114*:3-17, 1957.
3. Bortz, E. L.: *op. cit.*, p. 8.
4. Botwinick, Jack: Research problems and concepts in the study of aging. *Gerontologist, 4*:121-129, 1964.
5. Braun, H. W., and Geiselhart, R.: Age differences in the acquisition and extinction of the conditioned eyelid response. *J. Exp. Psychol., 57*:386-388, 1959.
6. Busse, E. W.: The aging process and the health of the aged. *Frontiers in Medicine*, Seminar, Duke University, November 15, 1963.
7. Calloway, N. O.: Uncertainties in geriatric data. I. Functional observations. *J. Amer. Geriat. Soc., 12*:731-736, 1964.
8. Caprio, F. S.: *Sex and Love*. New York, Hillman Books, 1960.
9. Durrell, Lawrence: *The Dark Labyrinth*. New York, Dutton, 1962.
10. Farberow, N. L.: *Taboo Topics*. New York, Atherton Press, 1963.
11. Fishbein, Morris: *Chicago Sun-Times*, Monday, January 17, 1966.
12. Fromm, E., Sawyer, J., and Rosenthal, V.: Hypnotic stimulation of organic brain damage. *J. Abnorm. Soc. Psychol., 69*:482-492, 1964.
13. Gebhard, J.: Personal communication, August 30, 1965.
14. Geldard, Frank A.: Adventures in tactile literacy, *Amer. Psychol., 12*:115-124, 1957.

15. GRANT, RICHARD L.: Concepts of aging: an historical review. *Perspect. Biol. Med., 6*:443-478, 1963.
16. GRANT, RICHARD L.: *op. cit.*, p. 475.
17. GRANT, RICHARD L.: *op. cit.*, p. 477.
18. Group for the Advancement of Psychiatry: *Psychiatry and the Aged: An Introductory Approach*. New York, Group for the Advancement of Psychiatry, 1965.
19. HELLERSTEIN, HERMAN K., and FORD, AMASA B.: Comprehensive care of the coronary patient. *Circulation, 22*:1166-1178, 1960.
20. HIPPOCRATES. F. ADAMS (trans.): *The Genuine Works of Hippocrates*. New York, Wood, 1929.
21. HUXLEY, JULIAN: My brother Aldous. *Humanist, 25*:25, 1965.
22. *Jet Magazine,* September 9, 1965. Review of *The Erotic Minorities* by Lars Ullerstam. New York Grove Press, English Translation, 1966.
23. JOHNSON, P. B., LAFFERTY, R., and UPDIKE, W. F.: Physiologic effects of sleeplessness. American College of Sports Medicine Annual Meeting, Minneapolis, 1965.
24. KAHN, ROBERT L.: Emotional needs of older people. American Psychological Association Convention, Chicago, Illinois, September 4, 1965.
25. KATZ, S. E., and LANDIS, C.: Psychologic and physiologic phenomena during a prolonged vigil. *Arch. Neurol. Psychiat., 34*:307-60, 1935.
26. KENT, DONALD P.: *Aging—Fact and Fancy*. U. S. Department of Health, Education and Welfare, Office of Aging. Washington, D. C., U. S. Government Printing Office, 1965.
27. KLEEMEIER, ROBERT W.: Mentioned in: Current activities and events in the field of aging. *Gerontologist, 3*:18, 1963.
28. KLEITMAN, N.: *Sleep and Wakefulness*. Chicago, Univ. Chicago Press, 1963.
29. KLEITMAN, N., and KLEITMAN, E.: Effect of non-24-hour routines of living on oral temperature and heart rate, *J. Appl. Physiol., 6*:283-91, 1953.
30. KLOPFER, WALTER G.: Influence of the changing social role of the aged on psychotherapeutic procedures. American Psychological Association Convention, Philadelphia, 1963.
31. KRAMER, CHARLES H.: Individual and family therapy with the aged—some similarities and differences. Workshop on *Aging in the Affluent Society,* American Orthopsychiatric Association Convention, New York, March, 1965.
32. KRAMER, CHARLES H., and JOHNSTON, GRACE F.: Correcting confusion in the brain-damaged. *Prof. Home Nurs.,* May, 1965.
33. KRASNER, JACK D.: Combined individual and group psychotherapy of the elder person. American Psychological Association Convention, Philadelphia, 1963.

34. LANDAHL, H. D., and BIRREN, J. E.: Effects of age on the discrimination of lifted weights. *J. Geront.*, *14*:48-55, 1959.
35. LANDOWNE, M., LUISADA, A. A., BLAND, J. H., and HARRIS, R.: Panel discussion on problems in the diagnosis and management of cardiovascular disease. *J. Amer. Geriat. Soc.*, 1959.
36. LONDON, S. J.: The ecology of aging in musicians. *Gerontologist*, *3*:160-165, 1963.
37. MARDIS, G. L., MANASTER, A., BONNICI, P., and PEARSON, L.: Crisis group psychotherapy in a physical rehabilitation setting. American Psychological Association Convention, Chicago, Illinois, September 7, 1965.
38. MORSE, B.: *A Modern Marriage Manual.* New York, Lancer Books, 1963.
39. MURPHY, GARDNER: *Human Potentialities.* New York, Basic Books, 1961.
40. NORDEN, E.: Bring 'em back alive. *Fact*, *2*:49-55, 1965.
41. OBERLEDER, MURIEL: Effects of psycho-social factors on test results of the aging, *Psychol. Rep.*, *14*:383-387, 1964.
42. OBERLEDER, MURIEL: Psychotherapy with the aged: an art of the possible? American Psychological Association Convention, Chicago, Illinois, September 4, 1965.
43. OPPENHEIMER, ROBERT: Analogy in science. American Psychological Association Convention, San Francisco, California, September 4, 1955.
44. OTTO, HERBERT A.: Research on human potentialities: application to geriatric programs. *J. Amer. Geriat. Soc.*, *12*:677-686, 1964.
45. OTTO, HERBERT A.: The personal and family strength research projects: Some implications for the therapist. *Ment. Hyg.*, *48*:439-450, 1964.
46. PEARSON, LEONARD: Senility, brain damage, and psychotherapy. American Psychological Association Convention, Philadelphia, 1963.
47. PEARSON, LEONARD: Psychotherapy with the aged. American Psychological Association Convention, Chicago, 1965.
48. PRUDDEN, BONNIE: *How to Keep Slender and Fit after Thirty.* New York, Bernard Geis Assoc., 1961.
49. ROSOW, I.: Old age: One moral dilemma of an affluent society. *Gerontology*, *2*:182-191, 1962.
50. *Royal Canadian Air Force Exercise Plans for Physical Fitness.* New York, Pocket Books, 1962.
51. SAUNDERS, C.: The last stages of life. *Amer. J. Nurs.*, *65*: No. 3, 1965.
52. SAXE, L. P., and GERSON, N.: *Sex and the Mature Male.* New York, Gilbert Press, 1964.
53. SCHICKEL, R.: Marshall McLuhan: Canada's intellectual comet. *Harper's Magazine*, *231*:62-68, 1965.
54. SELYE, HANS: Stress, calciphylaxis, and aging. *J. Amer. Geriat. Soc.*, *11*:1158-59, 1963.

55. Selye, Hans: *Calciphylaxis.* Chicago, Univ. Chicago Press, 1965.
56. Shock, Nathan W.: The contribution of psychology. *The Aged and Society.* Washington, D. C., Industrial Relations Research Association, 1951.
57. Shock, Nathan W.: The age problem in research workers: physiological viewpoint. *Sci. Amer., 62*:353-355, 1951.
58. Sokoloff, L.: The biology of degenerative joint disease. *Perspect. Biol. Med.,* 7:94-108, 1963.
59. Strehler, B. L.: *Time, Cells and Aging.* New York, Acad. Press, 1962.
60. Swartz, Frederick C.: *Salt Lake Times.* Salt Lake City, April 13, 1965.
61. U. S. Dept. of Health, Education, and Welfare: *Aging,* No. 129. Washington, U. S. Government Printing Office, 1965.
62. U. S. Dept. of Health, Education and Welfare: U. S. National Institute of Mental Health: *Human Aging, A Biological and Behavioral Study.* Washington, D. C., U. S. Government Printing Office, 1963.
63. U. S. Dept. of Health, Education, and Welfare, Office of Aging: *Facts on Aging.* No. 2, Washington, U. S. Government Printing Office, January, 1963.
64. Wertenbaker, L. T.: *Death of a Man.* New York, Random, 1957.
65. Zinsser, H. H.: Elastic implications of aging. *Gerontologist, 3*:18-21, 1963.

PART II

SOCIETY AND HUMAN POTENTIALITIES

Chapter 10

CULTURE AND PERSONALITY DEVELOPMENT: HUMAN CAPACITIES*

MARGARET MEAD

EVERY time men are confronted with tremendous change in their own society, every time they have the experience, in an important situation, of meeting other men who are different from themselves, this precipitates a crisis which leads them to wonder about human capacities. A crisis of this kind takes many different forms, but the wondering almost always has to do with the capacities to deal with the state things are in, whatever that state may be. Or does it?

This process has been going on for a very long time, possibly more than a million years. As far back as we can go, we can imagine small wandering groups of "human" creatures going their own way, each group convinced at least of their own "humanity" (1). So far as we know, no group has ever doubted its own humanity, but many groups have defined themselves as *the* human beings and have given various other names to other peoples. If another group appeared to be inferior, they treated them in one way. But if the other group seemed exceedingly superior, they explained the superiority not by denigrating themselves but by putting the others in the position of gods. They themselves were still the only human beings. This kind of thing has happened fairly frequently. Sometimes, when the first Europeans landed on a South Sea island, sailing in on a ship that was larger than anything the islanders had ever seen and magnificently

* This article is reprinted by permission from *The Semi-centennial Lectures at Rice University*. (Chicago, Illinois: The University of Chicago Press, 1963), pp. 241-254. This lecture was given extemporaneously in the Grand Hall, Rice Memorial Center, at 3:30 P.M., October 12, 1962. The transcription was subsequently edited by Dr. Mead.

equipped, they were taken for gods—an impression that vanished quite rapidly on closer contact.

And we can imagine such a group of very early human beings, wandering around, looking over to another hill and seeing some other creatures, and not being sure whether they were humans or animals or creatures that could be turned into prey—wondering whether they were creatures to be fled from or appeased or merely avoided or whether they could be treated as people like themselves. This has been going on right through human history, this worrying as to whether some other people, who look like human beings, really are human beings. Each time new groups of people have been discovered, it has precipitated a crisis. In the period of the great European explorations, when Africa and the New World and the South Seas were opening up, Europeans raised the question as to whether the newly discovered peoples had souls and were to be included in the Divine Atonement. After a great deal of discussion, the Roman Catholic church decided that they were human beings who could become Christians, too, and who, once they were baptized, could not be enslaved. Some Protestant denominations were slower in working out this position. Even today there are denominations which have not quite coped with the theological implications.

Today we are faced by another of these crises, one which has been brought about by two concurrent, related sets of events.

Now, for the first time, we are having to share political action with peoples of exceedingly varied levels of civilization, whose historic past differs one from another and from our own. We have to include in one forum, one world forum, many peoples who, a generation ago, had cultures without a written language and without any knowledge of the wider world; we have also to include other peoples whose ancient civilizations we have thought to be effete or decadent or mystical, but who are coming into the modern world with quite alarming speed and efficiency. All of us, especially those of us who are very conscious of what is happening in the world, are faced with the problem of reevaluating our judgments about these other peoples—not necessarily in genetic terms, but in terms of their experience. As always, we worry. But this time many of our worries are phrased in questions about time: Will the peoples of the new countries—the new countries of Africa, the new countries of southeast Asia—learn the kinds of technology and the kinds of political behavior we think desirable quickly enough? Given their historic past, so different from our own, can they take hold of the modern world quickly enough?

At the same time, in our own society, we are facing a related crisis which has been precipitated by rapid and revolutionary technological change. One of our speakers in the last three days said that man has made more progress in the past fifty years than was made in the whole previous history of the human race. But of course one's interpretation depends on just what one means by "more." I am not at all certain that it is as difficult for us to move from one generation of computers to another as it was for man to take the steps involved in picking up a stone and using it as a tool and then getting the idea of making a tool and then getting the idea of a tool-making object: inventing a tool to make a tool. We have no way of measuring the difficulty of steps of this kind. Conceivably, we might regard the change involved in moving from an earlier stage to the stage in which human beings had an organized language and an organized set of tools and an organized set of relationships—so that children born into that society were in the fullest sense human beings—as equal to or greater than the change we have lived through in the last fifty years.

But there can be no doubt that the change we are experiencing is the most staggeringly rapid in man's history: that no other generation in human history has had to live through, absorb and deal with greater change within a single lifetime. And, of course, those who have had to make the greatest adaptation are the old people, the oldest generation now living. There is a belief that only the young can cope with all these modern developments; in fact, it is the old who have had to cope with the largest number of them. The very young were born into a changed world, but older people have had to learn, step by step, everything that is new, have had to absorb it and accept it. This has been pretty trying. But at the same time, the very primitive peoples who have had an opportunity to come into this modern world have been asked to skip a thousand years, even two thousand years, in a decade; in some cases they have been able to do so. Nothing like this has ever happened before in human history. It may never happen again. We do not know.

Faced by the problem of this rapid change, we also ask: What are the potentialities of the human mind? Is the mind good enough to cope with this tremendous advance in knowledge? Or has civilization outstripped the ability of its inventors to use it? Phrased in this way, the question may perhaps represent an overvaluation of the state of knowledge in relation to the ability of human beings to use that knowledge.

In the recent past the same question has been phrased in various other ways—often in terms of race. In the nineteenth century and the early twentieth century we had an outburst of beliefs about the innate superiority of the "Nordic" peoples, who were believed by many to be responsible for almost every wonderful accomplishment on earth. Some people phrased their questions in terms of the potentialities of uneducated working-class groups; for a long time, for example, there was a great deal of worry for fear that all the less intelligent stock had sunk to the bottom of society. But this has never been confirmed by any careful research. In our own society a great many similar questions were raised about subordinated groups: ethnic groups who had been kept in socially inferior positions and who then showed less ambition than did other Americans, who were certain that any one of them could be President. The changing ethnic composition of the United States worried us, and we passed immigration laws that favored only a small proportion of the peoples of the world—some of the blond peoples (or peoples we thought of as blond)—over all others. The general theory was that this would improve our originality; so far, it has not.

As recently as 1933, in the midst of the Great Depression, an article appeared with the title, "Are All Men Human?"—an extreme phrasing of the question we have been asking (2). Taking off from other published work, the author asked, half satirically, whether the difference between the most superior and the most inferior human being was not greater than the difference between the most inferior human being and an animal and proposed the conveniences of an affirmative answer. When I read the article I was on the Sepik River in New Guinea (where reports about the closing of the banks in the United States had just reached us); the primitive people with whom I was working, the Tchambuli, showed no difficulty in grasping very rapidly a large number of things they had never heard about before.

But essentially questions of this kind are not new. In some form such questions have been asked by every group in human history. What changes is the form the question takes and the object of scrutiny. Sometimes the questions have to do with women: Do women have a soul? Do women have brains? Sometimes (when constancy is in vogue) they are regarded as too variable; at other times (when variability is good), they are charged with being less capable of change than men. Whatever quality is currently under discussion, the question is raised: Do women have it or not? (Can women acquire scientific objectivity? Can women be great artists?) This is a kind of inquiry which may be expected to recur periodically. I see no reason to believe that the matter will be settled quickly.

What we have to expect is that the basic question will only change its form. With more scientific knowledge, some of the old forms will disappear, but new forms will then emerge. Confronted by some new situation, men will still ask: Are human capacities up to it? Are the human capacities of present-day groups adequate? If they are, will they remain so? Or will they deteriorate, as Muller is convinced they will? And if human capacities do deteriorate in the future, as he believes they will, will men have to depend on new mutations to match the new machines (3)?

Mutation is a familiar science-fiction solution to the problem. As we are, science-fiction writers imply, we can't do much with things—but we can be changed. In one version, *Talents, Inc.*, by Murray Leinster, a set of people with talents that are, by and large, disregarded in the present-day world (a water-dowser, a finder of lost objects, a lightning mental-arithmetic calculator, etc.) have been built up into a team; working together, the members of Talents, Inc., are able to solve the problems of a galactic world (4). A great many other people, phrasing the issue in a less fantastic and spectacular way, nevertheless share the belief that we must somehow have many more of certain kinds of human beings, of whom we do not now have enough, in order to tackle the complicated problems before us.

The belief that available intelligence is inadequate in amount or kind to meet our coming needs has been intensified by the present state of the physical sciences. Increasingly, during the last fifty years, physical scientists have become isolated from the community at large, particularly at the top levels of these sciences. Fifty years ago, almost everyone who went to college studied physics, and teachers of physics had to instruct a great many nonphysicists. In fact, they had to teach a great variety of students—students who cared about poetry, students who cared chiefly about living things, students with very concrete minds, students who were primarily sensorially related to the outer world—all kinds of strange people whom no physicist would want in his laboratory. Even girls. (I am, of course, taking physics only as one example, but it is perhaps the best example of what has happened.) Then, with the development of the elective system of studies, teachers of physics and higher mathematics, and so on, were able to scare off anyone who did not have the kind of mind they themselves wished they had (I think this is a fair definition), the kind of mind they found most congenial to their way of teaching. One result of this has been that natural scientists have spent more and more time talking to one another and have become less and less good at talking with other people; and, in turn, other people have become much less able to listen to (talk with) natural scientists. It is as if, brick by brick, a wall of non-communication has been built up, and now those who are inside feel uncomfortable when they take a walk outside. In *Science and the Common Understanding*, Robert Oppenheimer described the "vast house" of science as an "open house, open to all comers," but immediately afterwards he pointed out that a man "is lucky if he has a bit of familiarity outside the room in which he works" (5). In *The Open Mind* he wrote poignantly of the loneliness of the scientist and the artist in the modern world, especially the scientist who, in working at the frontier of a science, finds himself "a very long way from home" (6). He stressed teaching as the means of keeping communication open. But elsewhere, shifting his stance somewhat, he has spoken of the necessity, the regrettable necessity, of popularization. Up to the present, the general response has not been to attempt to open new doors of communication; instead, we have been putting our main effort into producing more natural scientists (7).

As far as we know, such breaks in communication are not necessary. It is probably possible to teach the public enough about the new ideas in the physical sciences so that people can live in terms of them and use them quite comfortably. Throughout the ages it has been possible to teach people who grew up in one kind of world how to live in a different kind of world, to induct into higher learning whole sectors of a population who came from homes without the slightest grasp of what higher learning was about. The contemporary world is not unique in having a great mass of people who are unfamiliar with new knowledge.

The anxiety about the present state of the world is sometimes expressed in arguments as to whether, eventually, the "computers" are going to take over. This is, of course, one way of arguing about whether the natural scientists are going to take over. Arguments about computers reflect a tremendous fear that somehow science will dehumanize people—turn them into exploited creatures called "human components" and generally degrade the human position of human beings. Feeding into this there is the perfectly genuine fear that, under present conditions, science may destroy the entire world it was designed to protect and advance. I shall come back to this.

But first, it is important to recognize that in considering the whole question of human capacities there is one new element. In the past the question of who was and who was not human was decided by ecclesiastical fiat, by a prophet's vision or by a conqueror who could impose his views. Even now, as the newly released colonial peoples are redefining their position in the world, we are seeing the phenomenon of whole peoples rewriting the history of their past. By and large, up to the present, political and ideological activities have been supported—or opposed—by political and ideological concepts. Now, for the first time, we have a great deal of scientific knowledge to bring to bear on the same problems.

Today we know who the peoples of the world are. This information is recent. Up to, even during, the Second World War, fantastic estimates were made of "lost tribes" living somewhere in the center of New Guinea; these estimates were, of course, built up from explorers' accounts of peoples they had glimpsed but never really seen. But today even this stronghold of mysterious peoples has been breached. And we can say with some assurance that all the peoples on the earth belong to one species, as a species is at present defined. We have little hope of finding anywhere on earth a people who belong to a different species, however much such a discovery would cheer up various groups among us.

And we know enough about the ways in which ideas have diffused in the past and about the ways in which children learn in the present to make a good many responsible propositions about human behavior. We know, for example, that the differences between what an Arapesh native of New Guinea and a Rice undergraduate can learn do not result from differences between their brains. The brightest Arapesh is probably as bright as the brightest Rice undergraduate, and since in Arapesh society no very severely defective individual can survive, as he can in our society, the intelligence average in Arapesh may be a little higher than our own. Nevertheless, even a very brilliant Arapesh—a man who was capable of high-level thinking—got a headache whenever he tried to think for five minutes. When I put questions to the Arapesh that no one had asked them before, when they were made to think about linguistic form or any one of a whole series of things that were inexplicitly and inarticulately present in their badly organized, thin, very thin, poor culture, in which no one counts beyond twenty-four, their heads ached. Yet we have no reason for thinking that they were not born with the same kind of brains that we have. They were unable to think because they lacked the equipment for thinking—the cultural equipment.

If we consider the very simplest people we know anything

about—a people who can count only to two or three, who have no calendar and no sense of the past, whose version of their human lineage includes three generations of people and then a cockatoo; and then if we consider what can be done in any laboratory on this campus or the complexity of the ideas that can be discussed in its classrooms, we have some notion of how far contemporary men have come. The difference between ourselves and any very simple people is the result of culture: The long accumulation of new methods and new knowledge and the development, over a very long time, of ways of transmitting that knowledge to new generations and to members of other cultures, laterally.

Using this scientifically based information, we can take another look at human capacities before we try to answer the questions we have been asking: Has the human race, in all its divisions, the capacities to deal with today's events? Are the calculations we need to make in order to move into the future—the calculations necessary for computer programing or for sending out spaceships—too complicated for our present brains? Would we do better to concentrate on a research design for the future which would make it possible for men to preserve the genes of a very few highly gifted people, so they could be replicated and multiplied for future use (8)? Or are there already present, in the full range of living human beings, the capacities which will be needed in an even more complex world?

On the question of the actual use of the brain, it has been estimated by Lorente de Nó that man is at best using his brain at about a tenth of its full capacity. If this is indeed the case, then we have, even now, only begun to tap the human ability to learn whatever human beings can invent, institutionalize, develop and transmit to other human beings. And as we develop, each new development opens new possibilities, that is, in effect, makes us brighter.

There are, of course, people who think that each new development, in effect, makes us stupider—that each new and more difficult stage of knowledge is potentially available to a smaller number of people who alone are capable of dealing with a higher stage of complexity. The present lamentable state of our schooling leads to results that lend themselves to this interpretation. Measured by school standards, a large proportion of the population is condemned to be "stupid" or "defective"; but the proportion of those in the general population who are "defective" is much smaller. The fact is that when the pupils on whom this judgment has been passed leave school and face the real situations of the real world (for which there is no simulation in the school situation), many of them do quite well. As we concentrate on our narrow school standards, we continue to find more students who seem to be unable to deal with the difficulties, and we continue to apply to the world at large the judgments made within the school situation.

Yet the level of the American IQ has been rising. We do not attribute this rise to a change in the population balance brought about by our immigration laws; instead, we relate it to the fact that contemporary children are exposed to a more complicated world and begin to learn at age five what an earlier generation learned at ten or twenty or perhaps did not learn at all. Observation of a tribal group in the process of moving into the modern world (in, perhaps, one of the new African states) can help us to understand better what is involved. It is much more difficult, initially, to grasp geometrical thinking for a child who lives in a circular hut that is not very circular, with a conical roof that is not very conical and that tips slightly to accommodate the branch of an overhanging tree, than it is for a child who lives in a modern setting. The fact is, we build our increasingly scientific knowledge into our culture at every turn and at every point, and simply by living within the culture people absorb it and find it easier to master. So one must take into account, in every culture, not only explicit efforts to teach but also the inexplicit and inarticulate learning that goes into enculturation. A better understanding of this total process is one contribution that the sciences of anthropology and comparative psychology can make to our estimates of human capacities.

There is, however, another set of problems which may be more immediately germane to the survival of mankind. These problems are concerned with emotional aspects of human life, aspects which are the special province of psychoanalysis. Especially relevant is the question of the extent to which human emotional reactions may be regarded as innate and shared with other living creatures and the extent to which they are survivals from pre-Homo sapiens stages of human development. Psychoanalysis deals with the residues in adult behavior of impulses and emotions that have been imperfectly civilized in the process of reaching adulthood. Every functioning human culture has found ways of channeling the biologically given in human beings so that those born into a specific culture are able to learn and mature and become members of their culture. But no culture has ever done this perfectly. In every culture there are lacunae; in a changing culture these may be considerable, and the number of people for whom the organizing procedures have somehow failed may be relatively large. Particularly relevant here is the mode of thought for which Freudians use the term "primary process," which some people call "artistic thinking," and which some people describe as "irrational"—the kind of thinking that is characteristic of dreams, in which associations are based on emotion and on types of analogy that are not subject to digital thinking. As yet we do not know how intractable these things are. We do not know to what extent the humanity of human beings is dependent on the cultural restructuring of impulse structures that were appropriate to "man" at a precultural stage, when his characteristic modes of behavior were closer to animal behavior than to human behavior, as we now define it.

There are problems on which we shall have to work. Part of our difficulty in working out more appropriate forms of political behavior lies in our lack of knowledge about this aspect of human capacities. For political behavior is very firmly grounded in types of behavior which are basically emotional, not rational.

Dr. Shannon ended his lecture on computers and automation with the hope that if computers become more intelligent than man, we shall also find ways of making them wiser. At present the very speed of change has made it all but impossible for us to make use of the accumulated wisdom of individuals. In other more slowly changing societies individuals have acquired wisdom by living long enough and absorbing enough of their culture so that they have attained a certain objectivity and an ability to sort out alternatives. In our own society we may be able to give computers wisdom, in this sense, by a very rapid build-up of experience. In addition we may be able to build into computers another ability of which we are in great need—the ability to think freshly. Human beings cannot, of course, strip themselves of old solutions in order to find new ones; they have to find ways of building on the past. Nor are we certain, as yet, that it is possible to build an unprejudiced computer. Computers are, after all, built and programed by men, some of whom have a feeling at least some of the time that their creations are alive and should not be too different from themselves. So one must assume that contemporary conceptions are being built into computers and into programing. But possibly we can build into computers the ability to sort out alternatives and to tackle problems freshly, free of presuppositions, earlier hypotheses and older ideas about how things should be done, so as to arrive rapidly at better solutions.

In *The Voice of the Dolphins,* Leo Szilard—who at the time took a very dim view of human capacities for thought—constructed a research institute in which Soviet and American scientists learned to communicate with dolphins, who told them how to behave sensibly. But, as you will remember, the institute eventually broke down, and people began to say that there had been no dolphins. But in the last sentence Szilard commented that "it is difficult to see . . . how the Vienna Institute could have accomplished as much as it did if it hadn't been able to draw on considerably more than the knowledge and wisdom of the Russian and American scientists who composed its staff" (9). This fantasy, conceived of by a scientist, expresses very well the kind of despair, the lack of faith and trust in human potentialities that is bred by our present situation. For we are very far from knowing the solutions. In particular, we are very far from knowing the extent to which human beings can be reeducated emotionally.

We do know that extraordinary transformations can take place at the cognitive level. I myself observed one such transformation among the Manus of the Admiralty Islands (10). In 1928 the Manus were a Stone Age people who had no knowledge of geography or history, whose political organization could hold together a group of no more than about two hundred people, who had no script and whose mnemonic devices consisted of such things as sticking small twigs into a larger twig in order, for example, to add up the number of pigs killed for a ceremony. But only twenty-five years later, in 1953, when I returned to the Admiralties to make a restudy of the Manus, I could say to a man who had been a little houseboy during my earlier stay, "Start the generator and take this informant out and make a bilingual tape on the Magnicorder." In 1953 the Manus were a little critical of our electronic devices because, unlike the earlier machinery which they had seen, the new machinery was inclosed in boxes, and only the start and stop buttons were visible. So it was more difficult to understand. But if we would only let them see the channel charts, they said, they could understand how the machines worked without too much difficulty. And in the same twenty-five years in which they had developed this high degree of sophistication about machines, they had moved from a kind of thinking in which they were unable to conceptualize the world beyond their own island to a kind of thinking in which they could understand their place in a trusteeship under the United Nations and their relationship to Australia, to London and to the entire world.

In these twenty-five years the Manus had experienced a cognitive transformation. Not very many peoples have, but we know that cognitive transformations are possible, because they have taken place. Unfortunately, we know much less about the transformation of men's loyalties from smaller to larger groups, the transformation of their expectations about life—their goals—and of the sacrifices they are willing to make in realizing these expectations. We know much less about the new forms that must be invented, without delay, if we are to get the kind of control of our scientifically based types of warfare that will protect us from catastrophic destruction.

The semicentennial celebration at Rice University is an occasion for optimism, and speakers have expressed their optimism in various ways. Dr. Glennan expressed the belief that man's very selfishness, tempered by wisdom, will lead him to choose understanding, cooperation and human and material advancement over disunity, suspicion, hatred and ultimate destruction. Other speakers have expressed their belief in man's rationality, in his capacity for disinterested behavior and in his goodness. Only by implication have we been reminded of the darker side of the picture—our fears about man's irrationality, our doubts about man's goodness, our pessimistic assessments of man's capacity for destruction.

But we have still not fully confronted our uncertainty about the basic relationship of aggression and warfare. Much of our present research leads to the general conclusion that the greatest danger of war comes not from those of man's instincts which we have defined as "bad," but instead from those we have defined as "good"—from the willingness of men to fight and die for the things they value. Throughout history, forces by which men have been passionately moved, which place an urgent and almost irresistible claim on their lives, have been summated in this willingness to defend women and children, to defend land, to defend the name of a country or a religion or a set of ideals—ideals in the widest possible sense, as they are subsumed under words like "freedom" and "progress." What we have to worry about is not aggression as it is expressed in the will to power, destructiveness and violence. Rather, what we have to worry about is men's age-long willingness to die for the things they value beyond their own lives.

Unquestionably, this willingness to fight and sacrifice one's life goes back a very long way—far beyond the life of our present species. During recent field work in Southern Rhodesia and Kenya, Sherwood Washburn made extraordinary motion pictures of troops of baboons. In one sequence we see a troop which has been disturbed in its feeding by the approach of some predator. Sensing its danger, the troop begins to move, the females and infants running ahead and the mature males drifting toward the rear periphery. As the carnivore approaches, the males turn, open their mouths and bare their teeth in a gesture of bravery fantastic to watch (11).

Throughout the history of our own species men have developed more and more effective tools, weapons and battlements for the protection of larger and larger groups of people against other men. Today, we have reached a stage where almost the whole human race can become involved simultaneously in demands for self-sacrifice, on the one hand, and in the mortal dangers which may ensue, on the other. What we must hope for now is a rapid transformation, through which living human beings, everywhere in the world, will learn that this willingness to defend, as it is expressed in a willingness to die, has ceased to be meaningful. When men fought and died for what they valued, they did so in order that other living human beings—parents, children and grandchildren, brothers and sisters, allies—would continue in possession of what was valued. But today all these others too would die; the values through which men live are no longer served by dying for them.

In 1959, at a rather similar symposium at Brown University which brought together a distinguished group of speakers, Isidor Rabi said that he was not worried: He trusted man's instinct for self-preservation (12). Actually, the belief that human beings who live in a culture, who have learned to care for their children and grandchildren, their relatives and friends, and who have fidelity to the past and hope for the future are motivated by an uncomplicated "instinct for self-preservation" is not borne out in history. Man's instinct for self-preservation has always been capable of transmutation into suicidal self-sacrifice. Acting in terms of this instinct, a man will try to swim if he is thrown into the water; he will try to break out of a burning house—providing his child is not in the next room; he will try to walk across a desert when he is lost and all alone. But in our present situation we cannot trust to this instinct to save us, because it also becomes embodied in overriding kinds of learned behavior that may be expressed in a willingness to die in order to protect the well-being of others. Indeed, we have no reason to believe that human *societies* have any built-in capacity to save themselves. On the contrary, over and over again, societies have pursued a suicidal course in the pursuit of aims they have valued above the measures necessary for survival.

The central problem with which we are faced today is that of devising new political institutions which are founded on man's emotional capacities for loyalty and which will enable us to transmute once more our biologically given capacities for self-sacrifice so that, instead of dying, we will be willing to live and work for what we most highly value. As far as man's capacities are concerned, his capacities to learn and learn enormously, the only question is that of time. Can we learn fast enough?

We know the kind of learning situations through which groups of Stone Age men have moved into the modern world within one generation. If we believe the task itself is possible, we can set up the necessary learning situations. But we must also recognize that the transmutation of age-old loyalties is a formidable task. If we succeed, then the journey ahead of man will be even more magnificent than the journey by which the human race came from the Stone Age into the present.

REFERENCES

1. Although it is now well known that species antecedent to Homo sapiens (not necessarily in the direct line of ascent) were culture-bearers, we have not as yet devised a satisfactory inclusive term by which to refer to *all* those of whom this capacity has been characteristic—Homo sapiens and various predecessors.
2. Nock, A. J.: Are all men human? *Harper's CLXVI*:240-246 (Jan.), 1933.
3. Muller, Herman J.: The guidance of human evolution. In Tax, Sol (ed.): *The Evolution of Man* (Vol. II of *Evolution after Darwin*). Chicago, Univ. of Chicago Press, 1960, pp. 423-62.
4. Leinster, Murray: *Talents, Inc.* New York, Avon Books, n.d. In dealing with this theme, English science fiction—in contrast to American—differentiates between spontaneous mutations (which may be beneficial) and mutations that are deliberately sought after or planned for (which are almost invariably harmful).
5. Oppenheimer, J. Robert: *Science and the Common Understanding.* New York, Simon and Schuster, 1954, pp. 83, 85, 87.
6. Oppenheimer, J. Robert: *The Open Mind.* New York, Simon and Schuster, 1955, p. 138.
7. A further suggestion has been made that another source of difficulty in the communication between natural scientists and others is to be found in the prominent position of Continental European scientists today in the natural sciences; in this matter, there has been a considerable difference in the tradition of participation in learning on the Continent, on the one hand, and in England and the

United States, on the other, and today, with Continental natural science in the ascendancy, the European sense of the scientist as a man apart feeds into our current views of the scientist as a man isolated by his special knowledge (Rhoda Métraux, personal communication).

8. Muller, *op. cit.*
9. Szilard, Leo: The voice of the dolphins. In *The Voice of the Dolphins and Other Stories.* New York, Simon and Schuster, 1961, p. 72.
10. Mead, Margaret: *New Lives for Old: Cultural Transformation—Manus, 1928-1953.* New York, Morrow, 1956.
11. Washburn, S. L., and De Vore, Irven: Social behavior of baboons and early man, in Washburn, S. L. (ed.): *Social Life of Early Man.* Chicago, Aldine, 1961, pp. 91-105. See also Washburn, S. L.: Populations of baboons, and De Vore, Irven: Social relations of baboons. In the symposium *Primate Behavior,* Annual Meeting of the American Anthropological Association, Minneapolis, Nov. 20, 1960.
12. Brown University Convocation: *Man's Contracting World in an Expanding Universe,* Oct., 1959, Providence, Rhode Island. Professor Rabi was a discussant in the symposium *The Physical Universe.*

Chapter 11

SOCIAL FACTORS LIMITING THE DEVELOPMENT OF HUMAN POTENTIALITIES

PETER M. HALL

INTRODUCTION

HISTORICALLY and contemporarily, society has often been perceived as an inherently constraining and destructive force upon the individual. In fact, most discussions of the social limitations on human potentialities pose the problem in terms of society *versus* man. The examples which immediately come to mind are Marx, Rousseau and Freud, who concerned themselves with the means of freeing man from society's domination. However, most contemporary sociologists do not accept this approach. They prefer to view society as made up of interacting individuals who are socially influenced, but with varying degrees of autonomy, rather than as constrained and enslaved prisoners. Therefore this chapter will be an attempt to look at the social limits on human potentialities by examining those interactive networks which limit or facilitate autonomy. Underlying this approach is the idea developed by Nelson Foote, that an autonomous or self-determined identity is the key to motivating individuals to realize their potentialities (1). Those aspects of social life which are poorly organized for the formation of meaningful identities will therefore be presented. The areas of disorganization that will be examined are: the world of work; social stratification; racial, ethnic and sexual discrimination.

When sociology emerged in the nineteenth century, it concerned itself primarily with the problem of restoring social solidarity and rebuilding society. It is not surprising, then, that the individual as a unit was lacking from the work of Auguste Comte, who is generally regarded as the father of sociology (2). Emile

Durkheim's approach was not dissimilar. He felt that social controls were breaking down because of excessive individualism. A state of anomie or normlessness prevailed, and this failed to control the behavior of individuals. This anomie had come about as an outgrowth of the developing economic division of labor and the belief in personality and self-interest. Therefore, it seemed essential to Durkheim to reestablish social solidarity, to recement moral beliefs, to bind the individual into the social structure in order to have a going society. The problem was basically one of control. The individual was to be handled in such a way as to facilitate compliant behavior (3).

With the development of social psychology, the individual became a basic unit of sociology. George Herbert Mead, who, like Durkheim, was concerned with a lack of social integration and excessive individualism, sought to show that the individual was social, that the distinction between individual and society was a false one, and by showing that the self developed through social interaction and reflected the attitudes of others he mediated the conflict between the atomistic individualism characteristic of English thought and the sociologism of Comte and Durkheim (4).

Charles Cooley, as well as Mead, spelled out the point of view that man and society are two sides of the same coin, and that man becomes human through social interaction (5). In this way they went beyond Durkheim and described the socialization process whereby society becomes internalized instead of standing guard outside of the individual to constrain him. Rather than a prisoner, man became, as part of this model, a kind of automaton which was programmed for action. The epitome of this approach is found in Mead's ideas on the relation between social control and self-control. Through socialization the individual learns to adjust his behavior to the expectations of others; and when he does this, social control becomes self-control. As the individual engages in this process and imaginatively makes use of symbols, mind comes to represent society because the symbols are socially derived. Mind, self and society are all part of the same process and should lead without any conflict or difficulty to an ultimate level of progress (6).

With the individual regaining his vital role in the subject matter of sociology, a number of possibilities became evident; namely, the consequences of social interaction upon individuals and the influence on and determination of interaction by individuals. The determinist argument, that social influences or forces cause or bring about individual behavior, is not absent; but other options are available which stress emergent situations and voluntarism in individual behavior (7). While the tools are social and to some extent defined, their use remains flexible depending upon the interest and agreements of the actors.

In view of the above comments it would seem incorrect to conceive of the problem of human potentialities in terms of the Durkheimian model of society. Society is a network of interacting social individuals who, by virtue of their continuing interaction, sustain, reaffirm, change and modify society. There is no society apart from the individuals who make it up and no individuals without society. There are, however, different patterns of interaction, different types of social relationships, different models of social structures which differentially influence the development of human potentialities.

The subject of human potentialities is a diffuse and nebulous one, as difficult to define as creativity and productivity. Human potential is generally defined as being some total within the individual, some things which the individual is capable of achieving if the conditions are not constraining. Thus, a person's internal capabilities should equal his recognized abilities which should equal his "outputs" or productivity. Everything that a person possesses should be expressed and used to achieve desirable goals. However, whatever potentiality may mean, it is not synonymous with creativity. While a great deal of both creativity and potentiality may be stifled for one reason or another, not all people can be creative in the sense of making unique contributions, of establishing new modes of operation or of discovering "leaps of nature." The development of potentiality means that a person can choose his arena of operation, have maximum freedom of self-expression, derive maximum satisfaction from those experiences. In sum, he realizes those unique qualities which he defines as himself, and he sees himself as capable of determining and carrying out his own plans of action.

Since the problem of human potentialities is related to the nature of the interaction network, it is important to dispel certain preconceived notions about the structure of that network. It is often assumed that a warm, comfortable, homogeneous and harmonious environment is best for the protection of the individual. There follows an attempt to create in the family, in organizations, even in whole societies, womb-like conditions so that the individual will feel free to proceed with his work, so that he will not be bothered by distractions or torn by conflict and hostile sentiments.

These efforts are self-defeating if the attempt is to structure interactive settings to maximize development, growth, creativity and progress, because complete agreement is boring; complete comfort is regressive; complete peace is stagnating and complete stability is ultimately destructive. Development and growth require open, not closed, flexible, not rigid systems. Development and growth require thinking and consciousness which depend on diversity, heterogeneity, conflict, alternatives, challenges and change. John Dewey and Mead long ago pointed out that thought and consciousness spring from ambiguity and blockage where an individual must choose between alternatives and then commit his energy to the realization of the goal (8). Habit and routine are the consequences of stability and custom and reflect the opposite of development. An individual, to develop and use his potential must be challenged, must accept ambiguity, must participate in conflict and must seek to grow and develop with the rest of his associates.

On the other hand, too much diversity, conflict and ambiguity is destructive and regressive, for people need foundations, landmarks and frames of reference to hold onto, to depend upon, to structure situations, to define reality and to give meaning to their existence (9). It is obvious, therefore, that what is necessary for the development of human potentialities is an appropriate balance between stability-change, homogeneity-heterogeneity, definiteness-ambiguity, comfort-challenge, closedness-openness.

AN INTERACTIONIST APPROACH TO HUMAN POTENTIALITIES

The problem of human potentialities involves process and activity and can be studied in its interactive context by looking at the concept of role and its relationship to the self. Frank Miyamoto clearly points out the dimensions of the problem by naming the culture maintenance function of role and the social interactional function of role (10). The cultural maintenance view of role specifies it as culturally given and completely defined. It therefore operates as a normative prescription to exert pressure on those holding positions within the system to conform. This position, as originally developed by Ralph Linton, is basically a sociologistic and deterministic argument that completely imposes a course of action upon the individual (11). The social interactional approach of role views it not as a cultural given but as a product of the process of social interaction and as a matter for subjective interpretation and definition (12). The emphasis is placed upon the function of role in facilitating interaction between persons or in offering lines of action in situations when the cultural requirements of behavior are not fully specified. The implications for this model of role as applied to the self is that the individual has some control over the construct of the role, how it is played and what it means.

It is in the context of the latter model that a discussion of realization of human potentialities can be held. To clarify this context the subjective aspect of role, identity, must be brought in as well as the process of motivation. Nelson Foote has made clear the relationship between these three concepts—role, identity and motivation. Motivation is:

> . . . the degree to which a human being, as a participant in the on-going social process in which he necessarily finds himself, defines a problematic situation as calling for performance of a particular act, with more or less anticipated consummations and consequences, and thereby his organism released the energy appropriate to performing it (13).

Thus, broadly speaking, in order for an individual to behave meaningfully to himself and ultimately to others, he must know who he is. And:

> . . . he must know who he is with considerable conviction and clarity, if his behavior is to exhibit definiteness, force, which is to say, degree of motivation (14).

Motivation toward realization of human potentialities becomes synonymous with self-realization. Self-realization develops from a sense of autonomy and self-determination. Thus, an individual must be free to choose the identity he defines as appropriate to the situation, because only when he does this will he be motivated to play the role.

The voluntaristic nature of social man is a major assumption of contemporary social psychology. He chooses, he decides, he selects, he acts—which is to say that he has a *self* to which he compares his role behavior and the behavior "expected" of him by others. He is, to some extent, independent and autonomous. Thus the motivation behind a role-identity will reflect the degree to which it is congruent with the self-conception. If a proposed identity is incongruent with the self, it will either be rejected, played half-heartedly or manipulated. It will not be "embraced" or played with full force. The individual will not put himself (all of himself, totally immersed) into the role. Consequently, a person's potentialities will be realized only when he takes on an identity to which he is completely committed, for which he has a high degree of motivation.

Independence and autonomy vary from man to man according to many factors but not least of all because of cultural definitions and distribution of power. In order for interaction to occur, each participant must define the other as well as himself. He does this by making use of, initially, categories which are "provided" by the culture. It is necessary for any society, particularly a complex one, to classify experience, give labels and categories in order to answer a sufficient number of recurrent questions. And such classification with reference to social objects is, of course, the most vital. Individuals, as they grow up in a society, are taught the appropriate classifications. They learn to respond to their environment, both physical and social, according to social definitions. This is strongly evident upon examination of the formal agencies of socialization, such as the public schools and the channels of national communication, such as the mass media. Rather than opening up areas of discussion, presenting alternatives, stimulating creativity, these institutions serve primarily as fact-givers and reinforcers of standard perspectives. Culture tends to be resistant to change. People have a tendency to maintain social definitions, despite discreditation, by selectively perceiving and rationalizing because they have been taught what is truth. The development of human experience is thereby limited.

This is particularly true with reference to stereotyping and stigmatizing, where a person with many roles is identified as being in only one role; that is, using one social identity to stand for the whole person or extending one social definition of a role to exclude participation in other roles. This can be seen easily with reference to occupational roles of minority groups. The response is simply on the basis of a gross classification, irrespective of individual attributes. Erving Goffman has dramatized the effects of this in *Asylums* and *Stigma* (15). Stanley Elkins has shown the ultimate effects of this process in *Slavery*, whereby the Negro slave comes to accept the identity provided by the slave-owner and comes to behave in the stereotypic fashion (16). The slave comes to see himself as "nigger" to the white "massa."

What leads to this type of situation? What, indeed, is the major variable in terms of social definitions and personal identities? It is, without a question, the *power relationship*. The identities which emerge out of an interaction are clearly a function of which member of the relationship has the power and control of the resources which eventuate in the definition of the situation. Clearly, some groups and some persons in their roles in relationships have power to define the behavior of others and to reward or punish for that behavior. The child takes on the identity that the parents give him or "wham!" The slave behaves as slave or else. The subordinate, in general, is a victim of the superordinate will. But this power to define is an outcome of interaction, and when interaction is recurrent the power becomes stabilized. However, if the balance of power becomes upset and the outcome questionable, then the question of definition becomes problematic and will be solved in further interaction. Self-realization requires an appropriate degree of power in one's interactive world. The individual needs resources to say, "This is what I am" and to withstand pressure to change his identity. He must be self-confident, self-sufficient and from this will flow motivation for realization of his human potentialities.

It has become commonplace to discuss the "identity crisis" and "identity diffusion." This is a self-conscious age, an age of status-anxiety, the age of "mass society." Nelson Foote's formulation of the identity problem can be termed the *paralyzed* identity. The basic premise is that an individual must know who he is to behave meaningfully.

> When doubt of identity creeps in, action is paralyzed. . . . Doubt of identity or confusion, where it does not cause complete disorientation, certainly drains action of its meaning, and thus limits mobilization of the organic correlates of emotion, drive, and energy which constitute the introspectively-sensed "push" of motivated action (17).

This leads to retreat, passivity or continuous searching behavior which never seems to find the right outcome. It can be found in the behavior of college students, middle-class housewives and individuals who have achieved "success" in the occupational world but find it meaningless and unrewarding.

There are other forms of the identity problem. One is the *coerced* identity as described by Goffman in *Stigma* (18). This identity is conferred upon the individual without his agreement. The individual may know full well who he is, but he does not like it. He rejects the identity and manifests opposition, hostility, deviance, alienation and possibly self-hatred but at maximum only a moderate degree of motivation. This is the problem characteristic of members of the working class and of minority groups. When membership in these groups overlap, this problem is doubly compounded.

Another aspect of the identity problem is the *stagnant* identity which is conferred and accepted without felt constraint. It is built out of routine and ritual and leads to passivity, lack of awareness and plodding. These characteristics belong to the Milquetoasts, the Babbitts—the oversocialized men who feel completely free yet actually are slaves. They never make real decisions; they follow cultural prescriptions and thus never feel constrained by their disagreement with others. This is to some extent a problem characteristic of employees of large-scale organizations, both white-collar and blue-collar. It is the problem of the common man—the members of the upper working and lower-middle classes.

SOCIAL DISORGANIZATION AND HUMAN POTENTIALITIES

In order to determine why human potentialities are not more fully realized one has to examine the structure of social relationships which result in identity problems and consequently unmotivated behavior. An appropriate degree of social organization, adequate definitions of goals, norms, roles and identities is necessary for participants in established situations. There must be integration and clarity in order for human potentialities to be realized. Conversely, lack of integration and clarity, that is, social disorganization, leads to situations whereby individuals have difficulty determining appropriate conduct or reasons for performing the conduct desired by others. Under conditions of social disorganization, therefore, playing the role will not provide the individual with the desired rewards, nor will collective goals be achieved.

According to Albert Cohen, social disorganization:

> . . . must arise when one or both of . . . two conditions are not satisfied. First, it arises when the situations that the participants confront cannot be defined as system events or when there is no clear definition of the constitutive possibilities of action. This is a situation of normlessness, anomie, or meaninglessness. Secondly, it arises when the participants are not motivated, when their values, interests, and aims are not integrated with the requirements for the continuity of the interaction system (19).

When individuals try to play their role as prescribed and find it unrewarding, they perceive the situation as being normless and meaningless and will not be motivated to continue the behavior. Thus, as Cohen's analogy of the game so ably demonstrates, social disorganization occurs when people do not "play the game," because they do not know the rules or what positions to play; they do not know how to play the positions or cannot play the positions they want; and even if they play according to the "rules" as specified they cannot win. It just does not pay to play the game. When one or more of these conditions prevail, motivated behavior is impeded. Social disorganization leads to wasted effort, inefficiency, social and personal problems and thus to failure to realize human potentialities because it prevents people from developing meaningful and rewarding identities.

The World of Work

We live in an affluent society noted for very high productivity, excellent know-how and efficient organization. Hence, it is easy to gloss over the inadequacies of that society with reference to the self-realization of its members. But as Robert Weiss and David Reisman point out:

> The social system may function in the sense that people are fed, goods distributed, and work performed, while many of those who participate in the system sense their energies are largely wasted and gain little satisfaction or sense of worth from what they feel forced to do (20).

Problems in the structure and meaning of work derive from the goal of rationality and efficiency which has led to the bureaucratization of social life. We live more and more in an organizational society characterized by specialization, hierarchy of authority, specified system of rules and impersonality (21). Such a structure is apparently necessary to coordinate the effort of large numbers of individuals, but it has a number of consequences which change the meaning of work and decrease the satisfaction to be derived by the individual. "Thus work which is too dull, which involves a man too little, or which places him under demeaning supervision, is damaging to him . . ." (22). Workers seek satisfaction from receiving higher pay, getting more time off, having vacations, buying consumer items, moving up in the firm and having security.

> It turns up not only among blue-collar workers but also in the way in which white-collar workers speak of their jobs as the "rat race" and look forward, not to more challenging or interesting work, but to shorter hours now, and early retirement later (23).

Robert Blauner indicates that:

> Work satisfaction varies greatly by occupation. Higher percentages of satisfied workers are usually found among professionals and businessmen. In a given plant, the proportion satisfied is higher among clerical workers than among factory workers, just as in the general labor force samples, it is higher among middle-class than among manual working class occupations. Within the manual working class, job satisfaction is highest among skilled workers, lowest among unskilled laborers and workers on assembly lines (24).

Later on Blauner adds that four factors account for these differences: occupational prestige; control; integrated work groups; and occupational communities (25). Edward Gross elaborates those aspects which give status to an occupation. They are: (a) importance to society; (b) amount and kind of pay; (c) white-collar over blue-collar; (d) authority; (e) freedom; (f) amount of preparation; and (g) work with symbols (26).

What can be gleaned from these studies is that the most desired occupation and the type with the most potential for realization is a professional job. Only here are individuals strongly committed to their work. The work is satisfying because it provides creative outlets for the individual while he serves society. Professions have the following characteristics: the understandardized product; wide knowledge of a specialized technique; high degree of personality involvement; strong sense of obligation to one's art; strong sense of identity with one's colleagues; and essentiality to the welfare of the society (27). The ideal professional should therefore have a high degree of motivation because of his strong sense of identity and his commitment to his role and thus should realize his potentialities.

In contrast, the identity of many a blue-collar or white-collar worker can be described as coerced. He feels constrained, powerless and is able to extract very little meaning from his work. His options are few and he possesses little self-determination. Consequently, as Robert Dubin has demonstrated, the blue-collar worker does not find work to be a "central life interest" (28). He works to live. When one considers that the work role constitutes his productivity and contribution to society, it is not surprising that he has really denied himself. In reaction to the standardization, routinization and monotony of his work, the worker has organized formally and informally to increase the degree of control over his job and to restrict the power of those in authority. Thus, behavior akin to industrial sabotage can be found in most factories and in large offices. Workers establish routines and practices to protect themselves from the "bosses" and do the minimum amount of work necessary to get by. These workers, though not actively rebelling, are definitely not conforming. They have a well-developed underlife of adaptations, adjustments and manipulations to defeat attempts by those in authority to coerce them.

This is a type of role distance, which indicates that those who possess the coerced identity are rejecting it and thus have no real attachment to a work identity. Their struggle to maintain some freedom of determination, however, does not necessarily lead to realization of potentialities in the sense of productivity. It is probably true that the kind of work in which they are engaged is inherently displeasing. Since standardized and rigidly controlled work cannot be eliminated, these problems of nonrealization of potentialities will persist.

However, with the development of the cybernetic revolution, there is some possibility for progress but, one must also add, for regression. Automation can eliminate many of these dull jobs (euphemistically called semiskilled) and will probably decrease the number of unskilled jobs while increasing the number of professionals. There will be an even greater gap between white-collar and blue-collar workers, and there will be increased problems for those who find themselves in the working class because upward mobility will decrease. These consequences could be mitigated by a radical change in the educational system and the amount of motivation of members of the working class. For the present, the hours in the work week for nonprofessionals are decreasing, and there is a frantic attempt to make leisure an outlet for self-realization, but this is more frantic than practical on the part of those concerned and more passive than active on the part of those with the leisure. This attempt has been unsuccessful in part because of the importance of the work ethic in our society. Therefore, leisure usage will not resolve the failure of contemporary work situation to provide meaningful identities.

Social Stratification

According to Max Weber, class represents a distribution of life chances. This points to the very basic relationship between social stratification and human potentialities.

> Distributions of property and income . . . are . . . important because they underpin the class structure and thus the chances of the various ranks of the people to obtain desired values. Everything from the chance to stay alive during the first year after birth to the chance to view fine art, the chance to remain healthy and grow tall, and if sick to get well again . . . and very crucially, the chance to complete an intermediary or higher educational grade—these are the chances that are crucially influenced by one's position in the class structure of a modern society (29).

Education is a very basic variable in the choice of occupation and in upward mobility (30). And education is, of course, a function of position in the class structure. It is accepted as commonplace that upper-middle and upper class children will go to college. For generations their ancestors have tended to monopolize this all-important means of access to desirable occupations which are noted for providing a great deal of freedom and independence as well as possibilities for creativity, self-realization, status and wealth.

On the other hand, the working class youth is faced with innumerable obstacles to upward mobility via education. According to Kaare Svalastoga:

> Perhaps the most serious defect of socially stratified systems is the low aspirational ceiling they tend to produce in the lower and numerically important strata. Thus, studies of recruitment to universities reveal a consistent underrepresentation of youth of working class origin even when IQ is held constant (31).

Involved in low aspirations are a number of other class-bound variables, among them attitudes towards education, knowledge about different educational resources and family aspirations for social mobility (32). When lack of economic security and a high degree of social instability are added, it is small wonder that the working class youth has low motivation and little chance for self-realization. The values which his parents pass on to him simply do not point him in that direction. This process has been aptly described by Joseph Kahl who has identified the lower class (unskilled workers) as being characterized by apathy and the working class (semiskilled workers) by "getting by" which are passive responses to the environment (33).

When work does not provide self-realization, individuals may turn, as is often the case for the lower middle class person, to seeking their identities through consumption patterns as in conspicuous consumption. It is questionable whether this type of activity helps to achieve self-realization. Another avenue is through voluntary association membership. This is the way chosen by some lower middle class persons but mostly by the upper middle class woman. However, the involvement for most is of a superficial nature and does very little to fill the identity gap.

In summary, it would appear that much of the activity of working and lower middle class America represents passive attachments and stagnant identities. What is sought is a secure impermeable world with the emphasis on consumption and relaxation.

Discrimination

Where racial and ethnic discrimination exist, the most insurmountable obstacles stand in the way of the development of human potentialities. This is particularly true in the area of work. The fact that minority group and lower or working class memberships often overlap serves to compound the problem faced by many Negroes, Puerto Ricans, Mexicans and Indians in this country. Because of the majority group ideology which labels these groups as inferior, opportunities for satisfying and rewarding occupations are severely limited, as are the possibilities for realization of potential. This has been shown by Vander Zanden in regard to Negroes. He states:

> Within employment, Negroes are disproportionately represented in the lower rungs of the job hierarchy and underrepresented in skilled, clerical, business, and professional positions. The years have witnessed a slow erosion of the color line, yet a job ceiling is still prevalent in Negro employment, relegating Negroes chiefly to the less skilled, menial, or unpleasant jobs. . . . But even if this bias could be erased, Negroes as a group tend to be handicapped by lack of education in acquiring the skills that might lead them into new endeavors (34).

The concept of coerced identity would seem to be particularly applicable in the case of the American Negro. His identity of Negro overshadows all of his other identities—husband, worker, Christian, Democrat and so on. Even when he manages to achieve professional and middle class status, his socially defined identity of Negro still binds him; and he is expected to have Negro clients if he happens to be a physician or to study reconstruction if he is a historian. He is being coerced and cannot achieve his potential. It might be noted in passing that the coercion comes from both sides, for the Negro who attempts to be a professional first and a Negro second is accused by his people of self-hatred and irresponsibility. The segregation of the social worlds of Negro and white ensures the maintenance of the social definition of the Negro, the limited opportunities and the lack of motivation. Much of the behavior which occurs in the "Negro community," both positive and negative, is a reaction to and a rejection of the coerced identity. Thus, by constraining the identity, by limiting opportunities, the white majority has successfully limited the development of a tremendous amount of potential. The social costs of racial and ethnic discrimination are fantastic in addition to the psychological damage it does to individuals. Until Negroes and other minority groups are integrated into American society and are given the appropriate opportunity to develop identities apart from racial and ethnic ones, they will remain unmotivated, and the problem will persist.

Women, who represent a minority group in the sociological if not numerical sense, may also develop identity problems as a result of prejudice and discrimination. As Edward Gross states:

> . . . the evidence speaks loudly for the existence of sexual segregation in the United States as in all other cultures. We have then two sets of facts to reconcile: on the one hand is the increasing number of women, of all marital statuses and ages, who are employed; on the other hand, there is a definite conception of men's and women's jobs, so that women find entry into many jobs very difficult or impossible. Does the former trend imply that sex-typing in occupations will disappear or decline greatly in the United States? The answer seems to be a loud NO (35).

And Caplow adds:

> Women are barred from four out of every five occupational functions, not because of incapacity or technical unsuitability, but because the attitudes which govern interpersonal relationships in our culture sanction only a few working relationships between men and women, and prohibit all others on grounds that have nothing to do with technology.

The grounds are, according to Caplow:

> . . . 1) that it is disgraceful for a man to be directly subordinated to a woman, except in family or sexual relationships;

> 2) that intimate groups, except those based on family or sexual ties, should be composed of either sex but never of both (36).

The majority group has made the definitions, and the woman is expected to stick to her housekeeping and reproductive roles. Since the situation is posed in terms of two alternatives, career or home, the woman who has a career feels that she has rejected home; and she is likely to experience tremendous guilt feelings. And bcause many more women are employed and have careers, and because our belief systems are changing, many women in our society have identity problems.

The woman who never even contemplates what alternatives are offered her and who sees herself only as a housewife can be described as having a stagnant identity. She manufactures routine to fill her day and proudly writes in "housewife" when she fills out a form. Those women who by choice or accident or ignorance become mothers at an early age are thereby coerced into an identity which binds them to their biological function. The frustrations and dissatisfactions of this kind of role are felt by husbands and children as well.

According to Gross there is one solution to this problem, and that is for the woman to take on the role of:

> . . . the housewife who works but continues to regard her role as wife and mother as the major one. She is able to accomplish this by limiting herself to a distinct set of occupations (which may, however, change over time) rather than try to enter full scale into direct competition with men, for the latter would force her to give her primary attention to her job rather than to her family (37).

This resolution can be just as problematic because society, in limiting certain occupations to women and failing to allow them equal opportunity, also fails to permit the full realization of potential and puts women into occupations which are notorious for their lack of satisfaction. Low status, low rewards, low utilization of ability provide a good explanation for the fact that many working women cannot find an identity either at home or at work. That there is a vast source of untapped potential here need hardly be said.

SUMMARY AND CONCLUSION

As a result of social disorganization in the world of work, social, racial and ethnic stratification and the nature of the relationships between the sexes, some individuals in American society have difficulty establishing a meaningful identity for themselves. Because of this situation, they are unmotivated in terms of occupational roles and consequently do not realize their potentialities.

However, social disorganization can be lessened to bring about new situations whereby individuals may choose appropriate identities. However, reorganization proceeds through the acts of men and does not occur by fiat. If the interactionist theory presented in the chapter does have some semblance to reality rather than represent only philosophy, many of those individuals caught in these negative identities will eventually oppose and alter the limitations. It is obvious that the civil rights movement constitutes such an attempt. Change is possible when men define relationships as needing modification and then act to alter them. Thus, while some limitations on human potentialities are probably inevitable, men can continue to reduce the amount through concerted action.

REFERENCES

1. FOOTE, N.: Identification as the basis for a theory of motivation. *Amer. Sociol. Rev.*, *16*:14-21, 1951.
2. COMTE, A.: *The Positive Philosophy of Auguste Comte.* London, Chapman, 1853. For a history of sociology, see MARTINDALE, D.: *The Nature and Types of Sociological Theory.* Boston, Houghton Mifflin, 1960.
3. DURKHEIM, E.: *The Division of Labor in Society.* Glencoe, The Free Press, 1960. See also TIRYAKIAN, E. A.: *Sociologism and Existentialism.* Englewood Cliffs, Prentice-Hall, 1962.
4. MEAD, G. H.: *Mind, Self, and Society.* Chicago, Univ. of Chicago, 1934. See also PFUETZE, P. E.: *Self, Society, Existence.* New York, Harper, 1961.
5. COOLEY, C. H.: *Human Nature and the Social Order.* New York, Scribner's, 1902.
6. MEAD, G. H., *op. cit.* See also SHIBUTANI, T.: *Society and Personality.* Englewood Cliffs, Prentice-Hall, 1961.

7. For a discussion of voluntarism in American sociology, see Hinkle, R. and G.: *The Development of Modern Sociology.* New York, Random House, 1954.
8. Dewey, J.: *How We Think.* New York, Heath, 1910. Mead, G. H., *op. cit.*
9. Turner, R., and Killian, L.: *Collective Behavior.* Englewood Cliffs, Prentice-Hall, 1957. Schultz, D. P.: *Panic Behavior.* New York, Random House, 1964.
10. Miyamoto, F.: The impact of different conceptions of role. *Sociol. Inquiry, 33*:2, 1963, pp. 114-123.
11. Linton, R.: *The Study of Man.* New York, Appleton-Century, 1936.
12. Miyamoto, F., *op. cit.*, p. 119.
13. Foote, N., *op. cit.*, p. 15.
14. Foote, N., *op. cit.*, p. 16.
15. Goffman, E.: *Asylums.* Garden City, Doubleday, 1961.
Goffman, E.: *Stigma.* Englewood Cliffs, Prentice-Hall, 1963.
16. Elkins, S.: *Slavery.* Chicago, Univ. of Chicago, 1959.
17. Foote, N., *op. cit.*, p. 18.
18. Goffman, E., *op. cit.*
19. Cohen, A.: The study of social disorganization and deviant behavior. In Merton, R., Broom, L., and Cottrell, L. (eds.): *Sociology Today.* New York, Basic Books, 1959, p. 480.
20. Weiss, R., and Riesman, D.: Social Problems and Disorganization. In the World of Work in Merton, R., and Nisbet, R. (eds.): *Contemporary Social Problems.* New York, Harcourt, Brace and World, 1961, p. 461.
21. Blau, P.: *Bureaucracy in Modern Society.* New York, Random House, 1956, p. 19.
22. Weiss, R., and Riesman, D., *op. cit.*, p. 464.
23. Weiss, R., and Riesman, D., *op. cit.*, p. 483.
24. Blauner, R.: The meaning of work in an industrial society. In Toby, J.: *Contemporary Society.* New York, Wiley, 1964, p. 105.
25. Blauner, R., *op. cit.*, p. 107.
26. Gross, E.: *Work and Society.* New York, Crowell, 1958, pp. 120-126.
27. Gross, E., *op. cit.*, pp. 77-82.
28. Dubin, R.: Industrial workers' worlds: A study of the "central life interests" of industrial workers. In Rose, A.: (ed.): *Human Behavior and Social Processes.* Boston, Houghton Mifflin, 1962.
29. Gerth, H., and Mills, C.: *Character and Social Structure.* New York, Harcourt Brace, 1953, p. 313.
30. Gross, E., *op. cit.*, p. 162.
31. Svalastoga, K.: Social differentiation. In Faris, R. (ed.): *Handbook of Modern Sociology.* Chicago, Rand McNally, 1964, p. 568.
32. Barber, B.: *Social Stratification.* New York, Harcourt Brace, 1957, 401.

33. Kahl, J.: *The American Class Structure.* New York, Holt, Rinehart and Winston, 1961, pp. 184-221.
34. Vander Zanden, J.: *American Minority Relations.* New York, Ronald, 1963, p. 218.
35. Gross, E., *op. cit.*, p. 160.
36. Caplow, T.: *The Sociology of Work.* New York, McGraw-Hill, 1964, p. 237.
37. Gross, E., *op. cit.*, p. 162.

Chapter 12

SOCIAL FACTORS FOSTERING THE DEVELOPMENT OF HUMAN POTENTIALITIES

BARTLETT H. STOODLEY

INTRODUCTION

THIS paper deals with the social factors contributing to human potentialities and *not* with the individual factors contributing to social experience. The writer does not deny the importance of these individual factors, and he will have occasion to refer to them in this paper; but his task is to present as convincing an account as he can of the importance of social factors. The main argument is in the body of this paper, and supporting research will usually be found in the footnotes.

As a society we are committed to an image of individualism that cannot be empirically confirmed. A paper of this sort may help us to bring our vision of the individual into a richer association with those social factors which, while they limit the individual in one sense, also enlarge his prospect and stimulate his individuality.

A society (and social structure) is a certain type of empirical fact that requires its own kind of theoretical consideration, as we shall try to point out. We are going to deal with the *potentials of societies* in general to contribute to human potentials, although unfortunately they do not always make these contributions. Some instances from our own society will establish both propositions.

A paper with the purposes of this one must make its frame of reference clear; indeed, this is half the battle. The elements of perspective discussed below are rather newly emerging among social scientists interested in the relations between the individual and the society, and doubtless we suggest a consensus which is not so much an achieved as an emerging precipitate. It does appear, however, to be a logical development of present thinking and research.

PRELIMINARY PERSPECTIVE

The Freudian Model of Behavior

The Freudian view of individual behavior is complex even when we confine ourselves to Freud's own works and the development of his theory over time (1). When we add to this the views of Freud that have been held by his "disciples," by the legion of neo-Freudians and by those who have sought to impose a major reinterpretation on the Freudian view, together with the popular image of Freud that has much currency, we are in fact dealing with a number of views all making a claim to legitimacy.

For our purposes there are three aspects of Freud's theory that are of utmost importance. First, there is the insistence on a "body ego." The individual is a biological system in action, and this must be held to produce an important input into personality. The nature and boundaries of this input are still problematical; but there is one certain element—the individual is not a product solely of the work done on him by other individuals. Although he has a face toward exteriority, he is not a slave to the outsider. His biology is in a sense his secret, and the somatic satisfactions that attach or fail to attach to external "expectations" are important determinants of action.

Second, Freud insisted on personality as a structured system. The distinctions between the ego, the superego and the id represent his attempts to structure the personality. The specification of these categories and their properties occupied Freud's intellectual life from beginning to end. His commitment to biological reductionism, partly resulting from his desire to work in a scientifically respectable system of biological concepts, resulted in an overemphasis on the role of the id. A legion of ego theorists have been engaged in repairing his error (2). How far they have gone may be seen in this statement from Erikson. "It is in the ego that the equivalence of all truly individualized experience has its organizing center, for the ego is the guardian of the indivisibility of the person" (3). Freud's insistence on the basic defective nature of human personality, resulting from biological "press" running into culturological barriers, is turned by Erikson into a basically indivisible ego system that not only adjusts the individual personality to the contrasting claims of biology and society, but actually draws from both in the formation of a personality that cannot be reduced to either. This emphasis on the ego requires some alterations in all of the Freudian categories and their dynamic relations; but it confirms Freud's insight that the personality is a structured, dynamic system existing at both conscious and unconscious levels and capable of what Talcott Parsons might call extensive boundary-maintaining behavior.

The third important element that Freud contributed to our perspective is the concept of human capacities. These capacities are tools used by the self to work on the material in the mind and to relate the personality to inner and outer forces. What we might term major capacities consist, first, of the ability for dynamic initiative made possible by quanta of mental energy, and second, of the ability to organize the personality in terms of some kind of rationale—the ego function. These major capacities are supplemented by others which specify certain procedures of the mind, such as volition, cognition, ideation, imagery, cathexis and affect (4).

The Durkheimian Model of Behavior

Freud's contributions to a systematic approach to human personality have been supplemented by Emile Durkheim's specifications about the nature of society. Durkheim's views have often seemed to suggest social realism or the "group mind," and they have also been taken at times to indicate unacceptable limitations on human initiative. The animadversions associated with Durkheim's views have so obscured them that they are only now emerging in their basic simplicity.

Durkheim pointedly and even flagrantly disregarded the drive and motivational approach to human behavior. He emphasized a datum that he called the "social fact." The category of social facts, he said, is endowed with "very distinctive characteristics:

it consists of ways of acting, thinking and feeling, external to the individual and endowed with a power of coercion, by reason of which they control him" (5). He warned that social facts should not be confused with psychological phenomena which exists, he said, only in the "individual consciousness and through it." One cannot resort to introspection to learn about social facts but must look outside to the social milieu.

This view attracted a storm of protest on the ground that it reinstated a discredited "group mind" theory. But, in his introduction to the second edition of *The Rules of Sociological Method,* Durkheim was eminently reasonable and tried to reorient his critics from ontological polemic to an important type of empirical datum. Societies consisted of systems of conventions that the individual disregarded at his peril but which he had, in the typical case, no part in creating. *These conventions, social facts or behavior modalities, were not, in their analytical significance, motivational electives but established items for individual orientation.* Durkheim said that the term *social fact* referred to "all the beliefs and all the modes of conduct instituted by a collectivity." Social facts conforming to a certain type were also "institutions" (6). Durkheim had a strong pedagogic interest in using the term *social fact.* He wished to establish the existence of an empirically and theoretically distinct type of human behavior. His demonstration clearly implies that while the Freudian drive model may be adequate to throw light on the *emergence* of a social fact, it is not apposite to the essential nature of the social fact, namely, that the social fact carries a certain external urgency, or constraint. " . . . social beliefs and practices act on us from without . . . " (7).

Durkheim's point of view was derived from a clear, long look at the stability and the dynamism of human institutions. Once the social fact had been isolated as a datum (and Durkheim performed this operation with impressive skill), it was necessary to recognize the consequence—that social institutions have a basic characteristic which is analytically separate from the motivational systems involved in them. Durkheim was not unaware of the problem this posed in reconciling individual behavior and social institutions, and he left a clue to the mode of reconciliation that is possible. Although he had emphasized constraint, he knew perfectly well that most individuals, like Falstaff, do not take kindly to compulsion. In the introduction to the second edition of *The Rules of Sociological Method* he met the problem of how social constraint operates. "The peculiar characteristic of social constraint is that it is due, not to the rigidity of certain molecular arrangements, but to the prestige with which certain representations are invested" (8).

Certainly, with this clue from Durkheim, some rapprochement is possible between the Freudian and the Durkheimian models, both of which have a well-founded claim to empirical support.

An Operational Framework

Harry Stack Sullivan criticized the Freudian model on the ground that the human individual is not really a tension *discharge* system, but rather a tension *buildup* system (9). Social man has incorporated into his self structure elements foreign to "natural" man which redirect and reformulate somatic energy. This view is undoubtedly correct. The explanation of such a state of affairs is often sought in the concept of internalization whereby values and standards, through socialization, become internal commitments of the personality. This view also is true so far as it goes. But the Durkheimian analysis of social facts indicates a more molecular process which is perhaps more fundamental than internalization in the structuring of the self. Durkheim refers to the prestige of social facts. Perhaps, after Weber, it would be preferable to refer to the legitimacy of social facts. This legitimacy is, of course, communicated through socialization. As a result, the individual is disposed to accept the institutional forms of the society and to examine them, consciously or unconsciously, *for what gratification gain they may afford.* Social facts, then, invite adaptation and exploration; they are *not,* in a crucial sense, objects for tension discharge. Acceptance and adaptation to social facts would be the most general basis for the reorganization of the self that Sullivan refers to, and internalization would be one specific form that this adaptation takes. Both the Freudian cathexis orientation to behavior and the Durkheimian legitimacy orientation are hopelessly confounded in actual behavior, but this need not obscure the important theoretical distinction between them.

This preliminary discussion will aid us in making clear some of the social contributions to human potential. The items discussed are illustrative and not exhaustive.

SOCIAL CONTRIBUTIONS

The Irritation of Culture

The human individual emerges to selfhood through the social act. George H. Mead has called attention to the fact that the self is roused to an idea of itself through social interaction (10). The individual and the society are tangent to each other, and at the point of contact there is interaction and interchange.

A culture is a residue of consensus. The consensus has become propriety and is guarded by sanction. But this does not mean that the biological system has been injured. This very consensus is also habit and commitment and is guarded by need. The process of social learning is not so much a forced feeding as a confrontation. The capacities of the self, which have been mentioned above, guarantee that the struggle between culture and the reluctant biological system will be a lively one. Studies of simple, homogeneous societies have shown us that even in such societies there is a wide range of personality types and a wide spectrum of "maladjustment" (11).

What is the secret of society that it sells itself to the little barbarians that invade it every generation? Some of our social science thinking has put more emphasis on the trees than on the forest. Following out the implications of "social facts" we can see society as a world that is *there*—a world to explore, a world of opportunity. It is an invitation to the "drives" for mastery or "competence" (12). It is an invitation to potential. The forms of enticement that social systems employ are real enough, and the mechanisms of socialization together with their hazards are real enough too; but more molar than they is the disposition to be enticed, a fascination with the possibilities of cultural exploration.

Culture, as patterned forms of behavior and norms, forms a prospect for the individual at different levels. But at each level the prospect that it forms is a stimulation to experience. The Maine lobsterman has adapted the plastic Clorox bottle to use as a boat bailer by cutting it in the shape of the old wooden bailer. Its flexibility makes it superior. The old wooden bailer as a cultural artifact attended by a wider cultural complex formed the frame of reference for the newer invention. We see that culture is not only a prospect for experience but an irritation to invention and further experience.

At "higher" levels the cultural prospect is of course more imposing. It defines ways of life, such as the Greek way, the Egyptian way, the Chinese way. These ways, as impressive structures of social facts, provide elaborate systems for individual experience. By the same token, they also form the basis for individual encounters. They contribute force to the vectors of individual invention and reaction. In this sense they serve as "exciting" factors in human potential. The great creators of history derive in an important sense from the cultural forms, although in mode of derivation they may be arranged along a continuum from concordance to discordance. Confucius may serve as an example at the concordance end of the continuum and Nietzche as an example at the other.

To grapple with culture is the stuff of the human enterprise and the basis for the emergence of potential.

The Dynamic Within the Self

Potential cannot be read in biology until we have a referent in terms of which potential can be measured. Among the Arapesh the men follow a social form that is, from our standards, more female than male (13). If there is a "natural" master of men among them, we will never know. They are nonaggressive and given to weeping. It is hard for us to imagine what kind of a person Napoleon would have been had he been brought up an Arapesh. We do not doubt that his biology would have infused elements that would have influenced his personality, whether Arapesh or

French. But we know that he would not have been the Napoleon of history. What would have been the potential of Napoleon as an Arapesh? It would be read in the record of his Arapesh personality. Society participates in self from the earliest time, and it is in the product that we read the potential. And, of course, the potential we see is a percept obedient to our own cultural ideas.

The order in the human self is derived from the materials of the social system, and this is what Sullivan means in referring to the "tension buildup system." The social system, itself, is structured in terms of behaviors or activities, norms, beliefs, emotions—social facts as we have said. The individual in a society does not, of course, abstract these elements and incorporate them as wholes in his personality. But, in a truly basic sense, he employs them to form those combinations and permutations that build into that unity we call the self. There is fortunately no hypodermic to "biologize" the self with social facts. It is an individual adventure. Through the order thus arising the individual becomes known to himself in the human sense, and through that same order he becomes known to others. This order is prior either to the existence of potential or to the perception of it.

Societies, however, are not content to mingle with the self in terms of its structure. They take a hand also in the self's self-estimate. They establish proprieties for the forms of experience that are admissible. Ruth Benedict has pointed out how the Plains Indians institutionalized the trance and the vision as forms of legitimate experience, while the Pueblo Indians did not (14). Obviously, a trance or a vision among the Pueblos would do little to elevate the self-conception, but the situation would be quite the reverse among the Plains Indians. The Buddhist mystic endures a solitary vigil that could be shattering to the self if it were not supported by cultural elements which define it as an elevated form of experience. In our own society at the present time intense personal religious experiences are not generally viewed with favor. Yet, only a few decades ago, we had a rather enlarged view of the proprieties in this area. Mary Ellen Chase reports that, in her childhood: "Mr. Fisher recruited his congregation slowly and with the utmost vigilance as shown by several documents descriptive of the 'works of divine grace' experienced by those asking admittance" (15). Obviously, these social definitions not only restrict the self's ideas of what it can do but also encourage the development of the potential for experience in defined areas.

The self of course must have a place to stand; it must be socially differentiated as a self. In this respect our society is inclined to feel that it has wrought well. And indeed we may take pride that our limits of legitimate individual behavior have not declined to the levels of Russian or Chinese communism. Yet the fulcrum for leverage we present to the individual may not be as large as we think. Dorothy Lee, in her book *Freedom and Culture,* points to instances of social respect for individualism that run far beyond the limits of approval in our own society (16). Reflection will indicate that, in our own society, it is useful to make a distinction between ideology and practice. We have an elaborate ideology of individual development and fulfillment, but we also place narrow limits on the approved forms of individualistic behavior. Individualism is a concept; conformity is a practice. Our concrete forms are, to an important degree, concentrated on competitive achievement for highly evaluated economic goals. This limits the practical application of the ideology when we think in terms of self conception, for individualism in socially disapproved directions becomes maladjustment. Individualism defined as maladjustment is no encouragement to individual exploration. It colors the self-judgment and booby traps the road to individual adventure. In this aspect it is likely that our own society is not making the contribution to human potential that it might.

There is a further aspect of the society's share in the self; and here again, unfortunately, our own society's contribution to human potential may not be as great as we could wish. We are referring not to the approval of experience nor to the legitimate expression of individualism but to ideas about what the self can do at all. When Max Weber (17) referred to the disenchantment in the modern world he certainly had in mind the increasing secularization and "practicalization" in our social conceptions of what the self is. This calls to mind that societies do, by implication, define not only the structure and experience of the self but its very limits as a self. Experience is not just disapproved as improper but excluded as impossible. The Chinese have always had an open-ended conception of the self. There is in the Chinese cultural orientation an infinite capacity to be surprised by self-behavior. The Boxer Rebellion shows dramatically that many Chinese had been so influenced by the magical aspects of folk Taoism that they defined themselves as able to fly through the air and to call down the forces of the Jade Emperor from Heaven.

If the Chinese prefer a self that may shock by its impudent claims, we favor a self that performs mechanically, conditions easily and consumes enthusiastically. The common parlance emphasizes neuroses, frustrations, Oedipus complexes, achievement motivation. The self is something to be placed on a track marked "progress" and repaired if it stops or goes off the track. A biological-machine model of the self limits the horizon of our social philosophy and our vision of the possible. Our views of the self are, of course, wider than this, but they show a strong focus in this area. And the individual, comfortably and insistently defined within these limits, has little social encouragement to develop his potential beyond these boundaries of the possible (18). Columbus could not undertake a darker journey!

Programs and Play

As individuals we seldom give much consideration to such matters as communication and intelligibility. We assume that people are reasonable enough to understand us; and, if they do not, it is either because of some impediment in their understanding or some defect in their experience. Unfortunately, these assumptions are hardly tenable. The potentials for communication and intelligibility are given in the nature of man, but the content of communication and the understandings which make it intelligible are given in the nature of a social system. The society contributes the basic means whereby the individual can achieve prediction—prediction in terms of the behavior and understandings of others and prediction in terms of the visibility and stability of opportunity.

Social facts, as we have explained, are legitimated behaviors. So they have the probability of repetition or continuity. They can be *depended* upon. A type of social fact is a role, such as the role of teacher, businessman or clergyman; and this role has continuity and predictability. A teacher feels obligated to recognize certain patterns of behavior as legitimate, and his students are entitled to rely on these performances in making their own decisions. The situation is, of course, reciprocal.

Analysis of roles and role structure has shown that they tend to exist in clusters forming institutions such as a church, a family or a college. Roles have two faces; on the one hand they form a general structure which shows us how a given society "gets things done"; on the other hand they serve as referents for individual behavior. And these two faces of roles have important relations to human potentials.

Roles, in their macroscopic aspect, define the types of action available in any society. And this is a complicated function indeed. A role does not merely tell us what a person is likely to do in a certain position; it also tells us what a person is likely to think and what emotional displays he is likely to make. In a sense an individual in a certain role is *at our service*. The obligations of the teacher's role place him at the service of his students. They are entitled to *use* him in their goal-striving behavior. Their potentials are given an enlarged field of action. Role structure is therefore an intricate and important network that relates others to our purposes. In a complex society like our own there are many such networks from which the individual can choose, and these networks form connections through time so that the individual can form a program of action from youth to adulthood. Thus roles which, from a cold analytical standpoint, are mechanisms of social continuity are, from the individual point of view, the roads to achievement, to adventure. They are the means to the development of potential, to enlarged experience, which would be impossible without them.

If we look at a role in its more intimate relation to individual behavior, we see that the role has a play aspect. When we take a part on the stage, we have the experience of doing something not entirely native to us; we are trying on an experience "for the fun of it." It is the same if we make up a game then take the parts we have assigned to ourselves. Our specific motivation may go only so far as deciding to take the part. Beyond that we cast ourselves upon experience to see how it will affect us. We hold ourselves in abeyance and show a disposition not to determine our action but to see what our action will do to us. In a game of poker, of course, it is nice to have a way out if you do not like what the situation is doing to you.

It is not different in society. A role is an adventure in what can happen to you. It is also of course an adventure in what you can make happen to others. Social roles are prefabricated adventures in the sense we have described and thus may stimulate novelty and potential.

When Erving Goffman (19) tells us that we are continually putting on performances in our social roles, estimating the reaction of our audiences and often holding back our real selves in the interest of our goals or the image we wish to present to others, we may be shocked. We may deny that we are capable of such stratagems; or we may feel that this kind of behavior betrays a weak ego, a loss of identity, a discouraging anomie. Nothing could be farther from the truth. Since the work of Freud we know we are all capable of stratagems, and play-acting is a resource of the self, not a disparagement of it. It is the way the self comes in contact with new experience and, by playing at new experience, absorbs within itself any novelty that it relishes.

Therapy

The individual, wrestling with the restrictions and opportunities of the social system and with a novel and complex order of self-demands, finds that the road to fulfillment is paved with frustration. We expect that individuals "worth their salt" will solve their own problems and march ever upward with "excelsior" on their lips. Many problems are not so easily solved, however.

Potential, snared by confusions and contradictions in the social or self-prospect, is often not easily released. Societies, by making some contributions to the solutions of these problems, can pinpoint the area for the most effective employment of individual initiative.

We are all familiar with the modern therapies of psychoanalysis and psychiatry. They are an example of the kinds of structured help a society can offer to individuals. The "cathartic" method developed by Freud represents a modern and refined method of therapy. Existential psychotherapy has been developed by Rollo May and others (20). These modern therapies represent explicit, specialized treatments of individual problems.

Societies, however, have long been offering therapy to their members, although it has not been supported by such glittering conceptualization. Family doctors and religious advisors, to say nothing of "Dutch uncles," have traditionally exercised such functions.

Not all therapy is so explicitly formulated. Benjamin Paul reports a fascinating case in Guatemala where the social structure accomplishes therapy in an indirect fashion. The neurotic manifestation in that society was read, by a shaman, as an instance of possession by malignant, supernatural forces. The patient was not responsible for this possession, however. The cause was conceived to be in the sinful behavior of some unspecified person in the close kinship group. All members of this group had to be whipped in a ceremony of exorcism. Paul explains how the change in the situation brought about the patient's cure. "The significant thing is that the onset of Maria's illness created a marked change in the pattern of interpersonal activity within her kinship circle and that Maria was aware that not she alone but a group of people were locked in battle with the threatening forces" (21). Another example of indirect therapy is reported by Ruth Benedict among the Plains Indians. A person inclined to suicide could take a "suicide pledge." In battle he was staked at an advance position where no retreat was possible. He would thus probably be killed honorably in battle. However, by extreme valor he might survive; and in that case he won "all the kinds of recognition that the Plains held dear" (22). This new life of acclaim tended to discourage the interest in suicide.

In our own society we can find instances of what we might term "transitional therapy." Individuals may encounter difficulties in adjusting to new goals and experiences, and some kinds of social arrangements may facilitate the change. Howard S. Becker and Blanche Geer have pointed out that the social structure of the medical school not only imparts medical knowledge to the student but also gradually initiates him into an attitude of professional idealism that serves him better in professional practice than the romantic idealism that he probably brought to the medical school (23). In quite a different field Burton R. Clark has pointed out that the complex counseling he observed in a junior college served over a period of time to aid the adjustment of the student who was faced with the necessity of lowering his educational aspirations—a process attended with considerable strain on the self-image (24).

We can see that societies are suffused with therapies. It is part of their job to mix aspiration with consolation; while they may emphasize performance, they must have an eye to the integration of the self. The system which has a role in stimulating potential has a reciprocal and crucial role in releasing it from those impediments that are bound to develop in individual experience.

Innovation

A society may not only contribute to individual potential by some aspects of its structure, as we have pointed out in earlier sections, but it may also contribute to individual potential by encouraging changes in that structure. Innovative potential in the individual can profit from the order of legitimacy and the nature of the resources that a society can lend to the enterprise.

One important social resource for innovation is in the institutionalized right to innovation and the institutionalized approval of that type of motivation likely to lead to innovation. Although societies do not glibly acquiesce in their own downfall, some legitimation of radical change often does exist. In Chinese classical society it was possible for the emperor to lose the Mandate of Heaven because of poor or corrupt administration, and in that case a successful usurper who ruled well could claim that he had obtained the Mandate. In American society the Supreme Court of the United States protected the right to freedom of speech in a famous decision holding that dissent could be curtailed only when it was attended by circumstances indicating a "clear and present danger" to the stability of the society itself. At the present time it is being hotly contested whether civil disobedience is a right inherent in a democracy; and if so, what limitations are to be imposed upon it. Although the limits on individual rights to achieve social change, both in terms of goals and methods, are open to contention, the contention itself assumes the existence of rights in principle. Such rights constitute a basic resource for the individual in seeking change and indicate that the society has not only the will to continue but the obligation to merit continuity.

The right to criticize in this society is not an empty formality, for it is attended by an approval of innovating activity. Motivation for innovation and criticism is a highly rewarded potential of the individual. Striving is the stuff of life. So the right to criticize is exercised, and such action is gratifying whether or not it leads to successful innovation. We do not blame a man for trying. We see it as one of the glories of the American way. Thus, individual action *on* the social system, rather than within it, is encouraged by cultural values. The right to innovation and criticism is a direct outlet for potential and an indirect service to others who may profit from innovations that are successful. Of course, the society in granting a right to innovate does not guarantee that it will not fight back. Innovators have paid high prices for success and have sometimes failed grievously. But that is another story.

What we have said is that a society may grant the right to innovate and it may praise the desire to innovate. The individual needs more than this, however. He has rights, but he needs resources. He may find these in cultural and organizational areas.

The cultural values of a society constitute its basic blueprint for approved behavior and its widest definitions of the meaning of the individual and group enterprise. Robin Williams and others have pointed out that these basic orientations are hardly consistent (25). There are not only basic inconsistencies in cultural values, there is also uncertainty about their rank order. When does turning the other cheek take precedence over rugged individualism and aggressive competitiveness? In addition, there is a distinction to be made between values as ideals and values as integral guides to action in concrete cases. The ideal of the equality of man, which is universally accepted in this society at the level of ideal, has hardly been honored in action either with relation to the rights of women or the rights of Negroes. Cultural values have a third complicating characteristic: They differ in their degrees of saliency, and this saliency may vary absolutely over time and relatively in terms of the varying saliency of other values.

These inconsistencies, differences in level and variations in saliency make a confusing picture if we are looking for simplicity in human values. But they are the arsenals of the reformer; they are his enterprise. By manipulating the position of his favorite values he can strive to raise them in rank order, to implement them in action and to increase their saliency. Success in any one of these fields may bring about a measure of success in the others; so the reformer has many strings to his bow. In addition, he can form coalitions, develop symbols of communication and solidarity with others, form an ideology of action and expand into a social movement. Human potential in these fields, without social weapons, would be a lone battle indeed. Many a reformer would, like Roland, wind his horn in vain on some lonely social terrain.

The social encouragement for innovative behavior may also be related in an important manner to role experience. Joseph Ben-David has given two examples of the way in which movement from one social role to another has facilitated the potential for innovating behavior (26). The first example relates to Louis Pasteur and developments in bacteriology. Pasteur was a professional academic scientist at a time when there was no great interest in bacteriology. "For reasons connected with his career," says Ben-David, "he (Pasteur) abruptly left his early work of great theoretical interest and abandoned his self-image of pure scientist for that of a helper of the human race through science" (27). In this new role Pasteur was able to employ the scientific techniques and attitudes learned in the earlier role for the solution of practical problems presented in the later role. The result of the application of the scientific resources of one role to the goal system of another was a signal advance in bacteriology.

The other example is presented by the case of Freud. Freud was trained in German academic medicine. But, "He . . . had to abandon his scientific career because of a combination of lack of opportunity, inadequate means, and insufficient success, owing probably to a limited talent for exact research" (28). This shift of roles was not voluntary, and Freud looked on private practice as demeaning in comparison with his academic role. "He solved the problem," says Ben-David, "by turning the searchlight of research on the neuroses specific to private practice and by making scientific techniques of various elements of the traditional healing role which repelled him" (29). In this case an unsuspected potential was developed through a shift of roles where resources from one role were carried over and focused on the problems of another role. The motivation for this enterprise was not furnished in the first instance by a direct interest in the new field but by a desire to play the medical scientist out of context and thus to avoid the contagion of being a practicing doctor. Societies work in devious ways their wonders to perform!

CONCLUSION

We have tried, in this paper, to indicate some social factors fostering individual potential; we have also tried to present a frame of reference which we hope enables them to stand forth clearly. Is it not true that American society has failed to give sufficient emphasis to that order of experience which we have related, after Durkheim, to social facts? And has not this failure obscured the rich variety of factors that societies may contribute to the individual enterprise?

A society is a special type of empirical datum and requires a special technique of analysis. Yet a society is also individuals in action. This is a paradox that does justice to human complexity.

Biology and society are both aspects of a human being and they coexist in stimulating unease. Immanual Kant has put it well: "The means which Nature employs to bring about the development of all the capacities implanted in men, is their mutual antagonism in society, but only so far as this antagonism becomes at length the cause of an order among them that is regulated by Law." Pascal put it more simply: "Custom is our nature."

REFERENCES

1. For instance, Freud's work easily divides into at least three periods, each of which shows a different empirical and theoretical orientation. See STOODLEY, B. H.: *The Concepts of Sigmund Freud.* New York, Free Press, 1959.
2. Some of the most systematic contributions have been made by Heinz Hartmann. See: Mutual influences in the development of the ego and the id. *The Psychoanalytic Study of the Child, VII*:1952, p. 15.
3. ERIKSON, E. H.: Reflections of womanhood. *Daedalus,* Summer, 1964, p. 605.
4. The Freudian analysis of capacities is examined in Stoodley, *op. cit.,* 253.
5. DURKHEIM, E.: *The Rules of Sociological Method,* 8th ed. (ed., Catlin, C. E. G.), trans. by Salovay, Sarah A., and Mueller, J. H. Chicago, Univ. of Chicago Press, 1938, p. 3.
6. *Ibid.,* lvi.
7. *Ibid.,* lv.
8. *Ibid.,* lv.
9. See SULLIVAN, H. S.: Interpersonal processes and the social order. In Beck, S. J., and Molish, H. B. (eds.): *Reflexes to Intelligence.* New York, The Free Press, 1959.
10. See MEAD, G. H.: *Mind, Self and Society* (ed. Morris, C. W.). Chicago, Univ. of Chicago Press, 1934.
11. See, for example, KUHN, M. H.: Socio-cultural determinants as seen through the Amish. *Aspects of Culture and Personality* (ed., Hsu, R. L. K.). New York, Abelard-Schuman, 1954, p. 45. HOSTETLER, J. A.: *Amish Society.* Baltimore, John Hopkins Press, 1963.
12. Psychologists have been moving toward theories of motivation more consistent with observable facts of social life than the earlier instinct theories. Freud dealt tentatively with a drive for mastery in *Beyond the Pleasure Principle.* See also ALLPORT, G. W.: The open system in personality theory. *J. Abnorm. Soc. Psychol. 61*:301. WHITE, R. W.: Motivation reconsidered: The concept of competence. *Psychol. Rev. 66*:297.
13. See MEAD, M.: Sex and temperament in three primitive societies. In

From the South Seas. Studies of Adolescence and Sex in Primitive Societies. New York, Morrow, 1939.

14. Benedict, R.: *Patterns of Culture.* New York, A Mentor Book, The New American Library by arrangement with Houghton Mifflin Company, 1934.
15. Chase, M. E.: *A Goodly Heritage.* New York, New Avon Library by arrangement with Holt, 1945, p. 115.
16. Lee, D.: *Freedom and Culture.* Englewood Cliffs, A Spectrum Book, Prentice-Hall, 1959, pp. 5-14.
17. See Weber, M.: Science as a vocation. In *From Max Weber* (ed.) and trans. by Gerth, H. H., and Mills, C. W. New York, Oxford, 1946, p. 129.
18. This point is systematically examined by Fingarette, H.: *The Self in Transformation.* New York, Basic Books, 1963.
19. See Goffman, E.: *The Presentation of Self in Everyday Life.* Garden City, Doubleday Anchor Books, Doubleday and Company, Inc., 1959.
20. A good sampling of this position is found in May, R.: *Existence: A New Dimension in Psychiatry and Psychology,* New York, Basic Books, 1958.
21. Paul, B. D.: Mental disorder and self-regulating processes in culture: A Guatemalan illustration. In: Stoodley, B. H. (ed.): *Society and Self.* New York, Free Press, 1962, p. 147.
22. Benedict, R., *op. cit.*, p. 111.
23. Becker, H. S., and Geer, B.: The fate of idealism in medical school. *Amer. Sociol. Rev.* 50 (Feb.), 1958. Reprinted in *Society and Self, op. cit.*, p. 125.
24. Clark, B. R.: The "cooling-out" function in higher education. *Amer. J. Soc.*, May, 1960, p. 569. Reprinted in *Society and Self, op. cit.*, p. 135.
25. Williams, R. M., Jr.: *American Society.* New York, Knopf, 1952, pp. 389-442.
26. Ben-David, J.: Roles and innovations in medicine, *Amer. J. Sociol.*, May, 1960, p. 557. Reprinted in *Society and Self, op. cit.*, p. 323.
27. *Society and Self, op. cit.*, p. 331.
28. *Ibid.*, p. 335 where Ben-David relies on the authority of Jones, E.: *The Life and Work of Sigmund Freud.* London, 1955.
29. *Ibid.*, p. 335.

Chapter 13

RELIGION AND HUMAN POTENTIALITIES

DONALD A. WELLS

THE measurement of human potential is complicated by a variety of factors. The term "potential" is ambiguous. In addition, elements of cultural chauvinism and social conditioning make it difficult to admit that alien beliefs and practices may actually develop human potentialities better than our own familiar ones. Imagine what a shock it would be to discover that voodoo contributed more to human development that conventional Christianity. In addition to these matters there is the fact that potential is always measured in terms of the social milieu. It would be absurd, after all, to have criteria of the developed person which would award merit achievement to the social pariahs. These elements all play some part in our attempts to assess the degree to which religion of some specifiable kind contributes to or detracts from the fulfillment of healthy human possibilities. Our first task, therefore, is to give some meaning to the term "human potentialities."

Gardner Murphy (1) suggested four senses in which we might identify or measure human potential. They were quantitative, qualitative, the discovery of new elements and configurational. As applied to religion this would entail, first, that religious belief or experience was instrumental in bringing about changes in alertness, skill, information or sensitivity. It would imply that religion has been a factor in value betterment and perhaps in the discovery of some new facts about man and his universe, it would presume, finally, that religion is one of the effective means by which old data can be arranged in new ways so as to make them more meaningful.

Now where does religion fit into this scheme? Does religion make men more sensitive, skilled, alert or informed? If so, by what criteria? Is there an evolution in human awareness such that persons with no religion are seen to be more crass and unaware of the finer sentiments than the persons who have a religion? Do we find such a state of affairs part of the history of the human species, or is this more specifically part of the life history of the individual person? If it is the former, we would expect to find later religions to be qualitative improvements over earlier religions. If it is the latter, we would expect to find that there are significant psychic contrasts between the religious and the irreligious persons in terms of their assessments of and adjustments to life. It seems antecedently unlikely that religion will uncover any facts not previously known to the sciences of the day, but it might be the case that in the development of the individual psyche, the introduction of religion may reveal attitudes not previously known to the person so involved. There is little doubt that religions have contributed configurational hypothesis to prescribe meaning to both the grand sweep of the history of the species and to the more limited scope of the experiences of the single person. The important issue in all of this, of course, is whether religion has contributed positively, negatively or not at all in the development of human potential.

For purposes of this type of analysis the definition of what religion is taken to be is not crucial. Commonly, arguments over the definition of religion are actually debates over the "essence" of religion; i.e., they purport to determine what religion "really is." This will never be decided by definition, no matter how precisely we define or how thoroughly we study the word. It is far simpler and, for descriptive purposes, far more informative to allow whoever uses the term "religion" to define it as he sees fit. While we will discover that persons do not use the term in common ways, we will still be able to determine what follows from various types of practice or commitment defined as "religious."

If psychology were a unified science, and if religion were a univocal art, the task of relating these two fields would be relatively easy. As it is, the plethora of answers is matched only by the variety of religious and psychological explanations. There are two general theories about the relation of religion and psychology. One is that religion may be useful to persons with psychic difficulties, but of no use to "normal" persons. The neurotic persons who are religious may, of course, either cure or generate these same neuroses by their religion. Religion may thus be a panacea for the illness rather than the cause of the illness; although, on the other hand, religion may be the ground and sign of the neurosis. The second view of the relation of psychology and religion is that religion meets "normal" essential human needs and may, derivatively, meet neurotic needs. In general, one would suppose that, other things being equal, mature persons would have a mature religion, while immature persons would have an immature religion. One would expect that sick persons would have a sick religion, and healthy persons would have a healthy religion. The causal problem, however, very simply reduces to the question: Does a sick religion make sick people, or do sick people create sick religion? Does one attract the other but each develop independently of the other? Or is all religion basically a sign of an obsessional neurosis (2)?

WHAT PROMPTS PERSONS TO BE RELIGIOUS?

The answers to this question will reflect what religion is believed to be, that psychology is presumed to mean and what mental health and mental sickness are diagnosed to be. Writers like Bartlett (3), Cantril (4) and Flower (5) considered that the desire to understand is what has prompted religion. This has been called the cognitive need theory. Fromm (6) saw the religious need as expressed in the demand for a frame of orientation and an object of devotion.

Freud (7) saw religion as a response to frustration of the basic instincts due to civilization and privations due to catastrophies in nature. In another context Freud remarked: "Religious ideas have sprung from the same need as all the other achievements of culture: from the necessity of defending itself against the crushing supremacy of nature. And there was a second motive: the eager desire to correct the so painfully felt imperfections of culture" (8). The thesis that religion was prompted by frustrations from without was shared by Karl Marx, who saw religion as an opiate for proletarian penury. Argyle (9) stated, however, that economic frustration did not seem to cause increased religious activity. For example, the depressions did not bring religious revivals and, in addition, the middle classes, who are economically adequate, are more religious than the poor. In the case of the small sects, however, there is some correlation in the sense that they appeal to the oppressed, although they do not propose and practical solution beyond promises for a future life. In the same study (10) it was suggested that the increased religious activity of widows over married women may be in response to frustrations. There is evidence that there is a rise of religious interest from the age of thirty on. In one study 100 per cent of those over ninety were certain of an afterlife (11). Does it follow, therefore, that frustrations increase with age?

Many of the older psychologies of religion emphasized this attempt at adjustment with an unfriendly universe. Ames (12) for example, saw religion as basically the sublimated expression of the biological instincts of food and sex. Stratton (13) identified conflict as the basic event in religion. Leuba (14) described religion as a kind of anthropopathic behavior originating in the desire to live well. Coe (15) asserted that religion occurs whenever men identify themselves intensely with anything.

In all of these delineations of religion as man's attempt to come to meaningful grips with his universe we have not indicated whether such an enterprise is a sign of health or sickness. In 1913 Albert Schweitzer published an exposition and criticism of a number of psychiatric studies of Jesus, all of which were designed to show that Jesus, as well as Paul, Buddha, Mohammed, Luther, Swedenborg and Kierkegaard present a picture of sickness which may be diagnosed by the psychiatrist as epileptic psychosis, paranoia, dementia paralytica and possibly hysteria (16). Freud presented the belief in a God as a fantasy of the father-figure, and, thus, an instance of autistic thinking (17). Flugel (18) said that the superego is projected onto the God thesis, while the instinctive desires are projected onto the Devil figure, especially among Roman Catholics. For Protestants it is the desire to reduce guilt which prompts religion.

Much of the early psychological study of religious experience centered around conversion, a phenomenon noted by G. Stanley Hall in his 1881 Harvard Lectures to lie almost wholly within the years of adolescence (19). If we equate conversion with the acquisition of a religion, the hypotheses explaining conversion should apply equally well for the explanation of religion. Hall, for example, saw conversion as a "natural, normal, universal and necessary process at a stage when life pivots over from an auto-centric to a heterocentric basis" (20). Hickman (21) considered conversion to serve as a unifying agency, an energizing force leading to optimism, a new self-evaluation and a deterrence to fleshly temptations. In his assessment of conversion Starbuck (22) concluded that "response to teaching and altruistic motives are the least prominent of all, while fear of death and hell, conviction for sin, imitation and social pressure are the most frequent. Fears are a large factor. Hope of heaven is nearly absent." Starbuck did, however, consider the net result of conversion under normal circumstances beneficial. It liberated fresh energy and brought the converted into sympathetic contact with the world (23). While this intense interest in the phenomena of conversion marked earlier psychologies of religion, neither psychologists nor liberal clergy today find much health in this type of experience. One religiously concerned psychologist admitted that there was a good deal of shamefacedness about the subject but urged that interest be reestablished. He anticipated that use might be made of it for the "creative transformation of human lives" (24), provided that psychology would study the phenomena constructively.

The interest of theological seminaries in clinical psychology and psychiatry suggests that some liaison between the two areas is both hoped for and believed to be possible. The religious ranks do not, however, present a united front. Sheen (25), for example, has felt that psychoanalysts were out to replace the clergy. Liebman (26) on the other hand, believed that each aided the other and that their aims were not mutually destructive. Goodwin Watson (27) surveyed thirty-two texts in psychology currently in use to determine the attitudes of these books toward the possibility of religion making a contribution to mental health.

Ten of the texts approved religion as making a possible contribution to mental health, and of the ten, four were strongly sympathetic. Another ten books condemned religion, usually by using illustrations of pathological behavior associated with religion. Nine texts ignored religion, while three books discussed the pros and cons of religion and mental health. A similar study was made by Allport (28) of the references to the subject of religion in introductory texts. He discovered that most texts ignored religion by giving it the silent treatment. A few texts were openly hostile toward religion. Most of them, however, avoided the whole area by systematically ignoring the terms that have traditionally been associated with religion, such as will, conscience, values and the self. Let us look first at the case which claims that religion does not further the development of man and that it may even destroy what potential men do possess.

The history of religion exhibits a variety of reasons, in addition to the uniquely psychological ones, as to why any person would wish to retain religious ideas, practices or institutions. To a large degree religion survives through lack of diligence. We inherit religion from our cultural milieu and we are generally conditioned to participate in it. Rarely do persons reflect and then choose a religion in the way in which they would choose a particular brand of car. It is in the same sense that, though religion may be used to keep the peasants in line or distract them from their obvious economic discrimination, few if any persons ever sat down to invent a religion with this end in view. While theologians construct arguments for a God or immortality, the believers always antedate the arguments. Psychologically, however, we can assess various reasons for religion; and while this does not affect the truth of religious claims, it does affect the clinical evaluation which we may assign to religious activity.

RELIGION CONTRIBUTES TO THE DESTRUCTION OF POTENTIAL

"On the whole, reliance on man is inversely proportional to reliance on God" (29). Thus Leuba summarized the general milieu in which religious persons operate. If the goal of healthy personality is the development of self-reliance and self-confidence, then, to the degree that theism prospers, human potentialities wither. Leuba believed that the personal relationship nurtured by the conception of a divine Father and in the Roman Catholic Church of a divine Mother is open to all the criticisms which would be pertinent against excessive dependence of the child upon his natural parents. Faith in the "Good Shepherd" is infantile and debilitating. Freud agreed with this general evaluation. If men would face the world without the illusion of a father God, they might more likely come to face and to solve their own problems. At the point of the God notion religion threatens the important values of reason, moral responsibility and the reduction of suffering. Leuba also believed that the expectation of rewards or punishments associated with the belief in heaven or hell constituted a very inferior motive for responsible behavior. He asserted that genuine love of virtue and noble character are not produced by either promises or threats to take effect after death (30). Christianity and Judaism contributed to a further deficiency by virtue of their claims to both uniqueness and eternal truths, for such pretensions promote intolerance. It is in part because of the cognitive claims of some religions, like Christianity, Judaism and Islam, that the chief evils of religion are found to be maximized where the believers are civilized, and, hence, the most convinced of their rational claims. Leuba concluded that "no religion teaching that love is the cure-all and that God, through Jesus, Mary, and the saints, is the unfailing source of help in time of need, can be seriously concerned with the progress of knowledge" (31).

Fromm has been equally critical of theism and of authoritarianism, which he believed to be its natural consequence. He was so suspicious of the God commitment that he asked: "Can we trust religion to be the representative of religious needs; or must we not separate these needs from organized, traditional religion in order to prevent the collapse of our moral structure" (32)? His answer made it clear that he expected humanistic religion to be potentially beneficial, while theistic and authoritarian religion was not to be trusted. All such authoritarian and theistic religions "keep man in bondage instead of leaving him free" (33). In the area of guilt Fromm and others have been particularly critical of theistic religions. "It is usually not difficult to discover," Fromm noted, "that this all-pervasive guilt reaction stems from an authoritarian orientation" (34). Even Mowrer (35), who generally favored the use of both the concept of sin and of guilt in psychiatric treatment, was aware that the stress on the helplessness of man was common to Freud and Calvin, the former whom he opposed while approving the latter. Fosdick criticized orthodox religion for heightening, fruitlessly, the conscience pangs of putative sinners. "Many people worry themselves into complete disintegration over moral trifles," he observed, "and others have consciences so obtuse that they can get away with anything" (36). "Yes, the conscience . . . is ready to condemn us as our most malicious enemy would be. Our conscience is a 'prattler,' bent less upon our regeneration than upon our destruction" (37). Even religiously interested persons are critical of the therapy value of excessive guilt. "We are now beginning to ask whether our wrongdoing is sin or caused by emotional illness. . . . Health of mind depends upon whether we can let these forces come out without feeling excessively guilty or frightened by what erupts from within" (38).

In general these criticisms claim in the Freudian tradition that much, if not all, authoritarian religion is debilitating of human potential. In spite of his general suspicion of both Judaism and Christianity Freud indicated, however, that he was not really sure whether the religious thought-prohibition was as bad as he had assumed, but he did wish to try an experiment in irreligion. If the results were not an improvement over religion, he indicated that he would be willing to return to the old order, conceding that man is, after all, a creature of weak intelligence who is overwhelmed by instinctual wishes which only religion can assuage (39). In spite of his conviction that mental illness was basically a sign of religious alienation, Jung stated that he regarded the religious problems of his patients as possible causes of their neuroses (40).

Experimental psychology has fostered numerous statistical and relational studies of religion and mental illness. Kaufman (41) developed Freud's thesis that the ideas of psychotics are simply individual or private religions. Argyle noted (42) that catatonic schizophrenics in particular are extremely preoccupied with ultimate problems, including religious ones. Obviously, such contiguity is not the same as causality. Slater (43), in a study of neurosis and religious affiliation of noncommissioned servicemen who were admitted to neuropsychiatric wards rather than to general wards, found a slightly higher neurosis rate for religious people. For example, 92 per cent of Jews admitted were placed in the neuropsychiatric wards, 85 per cent of Salvation Army persons and 74 per cent of Methodists. In another study, Roberts and Myers (44) noted that although 9.5 per cent of the population were Jews, 24 per cent of the neurotic patients in New Haven were Jews. Likewise, Dayton (45) analyzed the 89,190 first admissions in Massachusetts between 1917 and 1933 and found that 9.54 per cent were Jews, although they comprised only 3.91 per cent of the population. It should be noted in this context that middle class people comprise most of the neurotic patients, and this factor may be more significant than the religious affiliation of the Jews. In a study by Funk (46) it was noted that there was a correlation of .29 between scores on the Taylor Anxiety scale and the orthodoxy of religious belief. Dreger (47) observed that the orthodox score higher on ego-defensiveness and dependency.

In all such studies, however, the unresolved question is: To what degree are neuroses religiously caused? Are neurotic persons incidently religious, or are they religious because they are neurotic? Are religious persons incidently neurotic, or are they neurotic because they are religious?

DOES RELIGON MAKE FOR HEALTHY PERSONALITY?

William James (48) elaborated on what he called the healthy-minded person whose religion was itself an expression of this healthy-mindedness. He looked on the bright side of life, optimism prevailed, and the future always contained the potential for betterment. The healthy-minded was not preoccupied with sin, guilt or despair, and the presumption of James was that such persons fulfilled themselves better than their sick-minded counterparts. There was, however, a variety of religious experience, and only some of it fitted the category of healthy-minded.

That some religious commitments may make people feel better is undeniable, but this is not really what the issue is all about. J. B. Pratt (49) asked believers what they thought would be the difference if they became convinced that there was no God, and most of them thought that this would be a crushing matter. This sort of information does not signify that their potential would actually be stunted but only that such data would inconvenience them, to put it mildly. What is needed, rather, are data from clinicians or experimental psychologists that would show that man operates more efficiently when he has religious support, that he is freer from debilitating neuroses and that he operates at peak efficiency. There are several ways in which this kind of information has been sought: questionnaire; biography; analysis of religious documents; history; or experience and by statistical correlations of various types of experience. Both the experimental psychologist and the clinician interpret their data in the light of some theory which assigns meaning to what might otherwise be neutral facts. While the psychology which prevailed before experimental psychology arose concentrated primarily on the ultimate nature of mind or the meaning of religious experience in the framework of putative religious truth, experimental psychology is concerned with the laws of human behavior, religious or otherwise.

Hickman (50) studied religious practices such as confession and observed that it aided persons to rid themselves of feelings of guilt, unhealthy repression and to give them a chance to achieve normal balance. Religious confession has its secular counterpart in psychoanalysis and psychiatry, where it may be presumed it has been tested and found useful. Leuba (51) held that religion did serve utilitarian human needs in that it gave psychic satisfactions which aided in the socialization of man. In spite of a basically sympathetic outlook toward religion, Mowrer (52) did not expect confession to bring about unconditional and necessarily enduring benefits apart from the proper clinical assistance. On the premise that emotionally ill persons are typically suffering from real guilt, a view he thought Freud rejected,

Mowrer conceived of the concept of sin and guilt as therapeutically helpful in helping patients to pass from self-rejection to self-acceptance (53). Biddle believed that "the basic tenets of Christianity are sound principles of mental hygiene" (54). Boisen affirmed that "American Protestantism is the foremost representative of the form of Christianity which has gone farthest in meeting the changing conditions of the new age" (55). In the same vein Boisen concluded that "There will always be some form of religion in any enduring social organization" (56). Indeed, as Jung (57) claimed, neuroses grow more frequent as the religious life declines.

Weatherhead tried to show that, by definition, the Christian religion could not possibly be neurosis-producing. In this assumption he concluded: "Where the psychotherapist has no religious experience of his own he will, in my opinion, be found to succeed only indifferently, compared, say, with the therapist with a spiritual insight and faith which help in synthesis as well as investigation. A religious interpretation of life on broad lines seems to me essential to a *complete* integration of personality, and thus to *complete* health" (58). This may very well be, but it still misses a basic point. Christianity may have been established by well-wishers, while, in fact, so-called Christian experience produces or feeds neuroses. The claim that "authentic Christianity" would not produce mental sickness must yet face the brute facts that putative religious experiences by self-styled Christians are frequently signs of neuroses. To plead that neurotic religious practice is not really Christian is no more persuasive here than for a psychiatrist to plead that unsuccessful Freudian analysis was not really Freudian.

Does religion actually prevent mental disorder? Argyle (59) concluded, at least, that there was really no evidence which proved that religion did produce mental disorder. He also observed, more obliquely, that "religious influences may be therapeutic for some patients" (60). Moberg (61) found a correlation between religious activity and adjustment of patients over sixty-five living in institutions. Victor White (62) insisted that soul and psyche are not the same, and that, hence, one can be ill and the other healthy. Thus a sick psyche does not entail a sick soul, nor does a sick soul entail a sick psyche. Notwithstanding this dichotomy, he did affirm that the appropriate religion indisputably functioned as an integrating factor in the whole personality. At the same time, he could admit that "mental and emotional disorder is by no means incompatible with personal holiness as theology understands it" (63).

CONCLUSIONS

Argyle concluded his survey of psychological studies of religion with the note that there was little evidence that religion either caused or cured mental disorders. Is this the result which the facts entail? Is religion, thus, a neutral factor in personal adjustment and does it therefore follow that religion, like analysis, "casts a spell but does not cure" (64)? The variety of psychological reports leads ineluctably to the conclusion that William James' first insight is probably correct. There are "healthy-minded" religions and there are "sick-minded" religions. Some of these religions are causal and some of them are consequential. While Jung may conclude that his patients got well only after they got religion, other psychologists have observed that "empirical results show that religious people are on the average less humanitarian, more bigoted, more anxious . . ." (65). Persons associated with religion seem to be a typical cross-section of the human variations. They include competent and incompetent, aggressive and diffident, sensitive and callous, intelligent and stupid, dependent and independent.

The history of religions reveals that the cognitive beliefs of religious persons imply a variety of intellectual and normative options. Some religious beliefs have been geologically, biologically and psychologically false. Examples of these would be the commitment to the naive Genesis account of creation of the earth and of the animal species, and of the New Testament assessment of mental illness as caused by demons. The moral concern of many biblical figures over murder, theft and false witness must be balanced by the chauvinism with which many of these same moral spokesmen applied their indictments as intended only for their friends.

The most fertile source of evidence from religious history that religion has aided in the development of human potentialities is in the area of what Murphy called the configurational. It has historically been a major function of religions that they supply an overview of the human situation. Where this cosmic map entailed hope and promise, we would expect that the believers would find solace, encouragement, confidence and optimism because of the religious configuration. Where the metaphysical picture entailed hell or eternal damnation, the displeasure of the powers that be with sinful man or a mean assessment of human talent, we would expect that believers here would exhibit either an ennervating despair or take recourse to some flight from the reality thus pictured. It is, perhaps, not entirely facetious to observe that the major claims for the essentiality of religion come from the professional religionists, much as we would expect that claims for the necessity of profit come from investors, that the virtues of thrift are best made by bankers, of insurance by insurance salesmen and the blessings of the single life by celibates.

It is obvious that at least a major part of our difficulty in arriving at a conclusion as to the healthy and sickly properties of religion is caused by the lack of any general notion as to what religion is. Unquestionably, millions of persons get along quite well without accepting any of the unique tenets of the Baptist religion. Millions also are mentally healthy without being Christians in any standard sense. It is possible to be fairly precise about what it means to be a Baptist, though less so for what it means to be a Christian. Who can specify the criteria, however, so that we will know whether we have before us a person who is religious. This means simply that we can experiment to see whether backsliding Baptists exhibit anxiety and whether, if they return to the fold, they experience release from tension. The ambiguity of what it means to be religious, however, seems to leave us in an impossibly unresolvable situation. Even if, for example, all Presbyterians were free from neuroses, we would still wonder if healthy persons are attracted to this Church, if this Church has something which makes healthy persons out of its members, or if perchance their health and their religiosity are independent variables.

If religion were like stamp-collecting, we could perhaps show that philately has been psychically helpful to some collectors and harmful to others without offending the serious collector. Religion, however, must be beneficial to all, for the least chink in the armor of the usefulness of faith usually proves upsetting to those who believe that religion is a necessity for man to express his full potential. What data there are would seem to support a multivocal thesis. Some persons who do develop their potential are also religious. Likewise, some religious persons do live expanded lives. On the other hand, some persons with dwarfed potentialities are also religious, and some religious persons fail to live richly. Our problem is still to confirm what is antecedent and which factors are causal and which consequential. In any case, religion has been a many-colored coat which has warmed persons of varied needs in disparate ways. It has also been a strait jacket of inhibition which has, on occasion, sheltered incompetence and curtailed talents. The picture, thus, is not clear. In Watson's (66) survey of the ten texts which made favorable comments concerning religion, they noted that religion gave a reassuring sense of belonging and security, it enlarged concerns beyond the self and it helped to interpret trans-human forces. While Allport (67) doubted that every person needed religion to be mature, the overall picture for him was favorable to at least some kind of religion. "It is true," he said, "that religion tends to define reality as congenial to the powers and aspirations of the individual, but so too does any working principle that sustains human endeavor. Those who find the religious principle of life illusory would do well not to scrutinize their own working principles too closely" (68).

REFERENCES

1. Murphy, Gardner: *Human Nature and Human Potentialities.* New York, Basic Books, 1958.
2. Freud, Sigmund: *The Future of an Illusion.* New York, Doubleday, 1957.
3. Bartlett, F. C.: *Remembering.* Cambridge, Harvard Univ. Press, 1932.
4. Cantril, Hadley: *The Psychology of Social Movements.* London, Chapman and Hall, 1941.

5. FLOWER, J. C.: *An Approach to the Psychology of Religion*. London, Kegan Paul, 1927.
6. FROMM, ERICH: *Psychoanalysis and Religion*. New Haven, Yale Univ. Press, 1950.
7. FREUD, SIGMUND: *Civilization and Its Discontents*. Chicago, The Univ. of Chicago Bookstore (n.d.).
8. FREUD, SIGMUND: *The Future of an Illusion*.
9. ARGYLE, MICHAEL: *Religious Behavior*. Glencoe, The Free Press, 1959.
10. *Ibid*., p. 150.
11. CAVAN, R. S.: *Personal Adjustment in Old Age*. Chicago, Science Research Associates, 1949.
12. AMES, EDWARD S.: *The Psychology of Religious Experience*. Boston, Houghton Mifflin, 1910.
13. STRATTON, G. M.: *Psychology of the Religious Life*. London, Allen, 1911.
14. LEUBA, JAMES H.: *A Psychological Study of Religion*. New York, Macmillan, 1912.
15. COE, GEORGE ALBERT: *The Psychology of Religion*. Chicago, Univ. of Chicago Press, 1916.
16. SCHWEITZER, ALBERT: *The Psychiatric Study of Jesus*. Boston, The Beacon Press, 1948.
17. FREUD, SIGMUND: *The Future of an Illusion*.
18. FLUGEL, J. C.: *Man, Morals and Society*. London, Duckworth, 1945.
19. HALL, G. STANLEY: *Adolescence*. *I*, p. 292, New York, Appleton-Century-Crofts, 1904.
20. *Ibid*., *II*, p. 301.
21. HICKMAN, FRANK S.: *Introduction to the Psychology of Religion*. New York, Abingdon Press, 1926.
22. STARBUCK, EDWIN D.: *The Psychology of Religion*. New York, Scribner's, 1903.
23. *Ibid*., p. 128-130.
24. CLARK, WALTER HOUSTON: *The Psychology of Religion*. New York, Macmillan, 1958.
25. SHEEN, FULTON: *Peace of Soul*. New York, Whittlesey House, 1949.
26. LIEBMAN, JOSHUA L.: *Peace of Mind*. New York, Simon and Schuster, 1946.
27. WATSON, GOODWIN: Psychiatry. In *College Reading and Religion*. New Haven, Yale Univ. Press, 1948.
28. ALLPORT, GORDON: Psychology. In *College Reading and Religion*. New Haven, Yale Univ. Press, 1948.
29. LEUBA, JAMES H.: *God or Man?* New York, Holt, 1933.
30. *Ibid*., p. 272.
31. *Ibid*., p. 281.
32. FROMM, ERICH, *op. cit*., p. 34.

33. *Ibid.*, p. 85.
34. *Ibid.*, p. 90.
35. Mowrer, O. Hobart: *The Crisis in Psychiatry and Religion.* New York, Van Nostrand, 1961.
36. Fosdick, Harry E.: *On Being a Real Person.* New York, Harper, 1943.
37. Michalson, Carl: *Faith for Personal Crises.* London, Epworth, 1959.
38. Anderson, G. C.: *Man's Right to Be Human.* New York, Morrow, 1959.
39. Freud, Sigmund: *The Future of an Illusion.*
40. Jung, Carl: *Modern Man in Search of a Soul.* New York, Harcourt, Brace, 1933.
41. Kaufman, M. R.: Religious delusions in schizophrenia. *Int. J. Psychoanal., 20*:373-376, 1939.
42. Argyle, Michael, *op. cit.*, p. 108.
43. Slater, E.: Neurosis and religious affiliation. *J. Ment. Sci., 93*:392-398, 1947.
44. Roberts, B. H., and Myers, J. K.: Religion, national origin, immigration and mental illness. *Amer. J. Psychiat., 110*:759-764, 1954.
45. Dayton, N. A.: *New Facts on Mental Disorders.* Springfield, Thomas, 1940.
46. Funk, R. A.: Religious attitudes and manifest anxiety in a college population. *Amer. Psychol., 11*:375, 1956.
47. Dreger, R. M.: Some personality correlates of religious attitudes as determined by projective techniques. *Psychol. Monogr., 66*:3, 1952.
48. James, William: *The Varieties of Religious Experience.* New York, Collier, 1961.
49. Pratt, J. B.: *The Psychology of Religious Belief.* New York, Macmillan, 1907.
50. Hickman, Frank S., *op. cit.*, pp. 296-298.
51. Leuba, James H.: *God or Man?* p. 21.
52. Mowrer, O. Hobart, *op. cit.*, p. 97.
53. *Ibid.*, p. 54.
54. Biddle, W. Earl: *Integration of Religion and Psychiatry.* New York, Macmillan, 1955.
55. Boisen, Anton T.: *Religion in Crisis and Custom.* New York, Harper, 1945.
56. *Ibid.*, p. 246.
57. Jung, Carl, *op. cit.*, p. 230.
58. Weatherhead, Leslie: *Psychology, Religion, and Healing.* New York, Abingdon Press, 1951.
59. Argyle, Michael, *op. cit.*, p. 117.
60. *Ibid.*, p. 119.
61. Moberg, D. O.: The Christian religion and personal adjustment in old age. *Amer. Sociolog. Rev., 18*:87-90, 1953.
62. White, Victor: *Soul and Psyche.* New York, Harper. 1960

63. *Ibid.*, p. 189.
64. Mowrer, O. Hobart, *op. cit.*, p. 121.
65. Rokeach, Milton: Paradoxes of religious belief. *Trans-Action, 2*:11, 1965.
66. Watson, Goodwin, *op. loc.*
67. Allport, Gordon: *The Individual and His Religion.* London, Constable, 1951.
68. *Ibid.*, pp. 25-26.

Chapter 14

HUMAN POTENTIALITIES AND THE HEALTHY SOCIETY

JOSEPH BENSMAN and BERNARD ROSENBERG

LET us freely admit that our title is redundant: the healthy society, by definition, is one that enlarges human potentialities as the sick society blocks them.

Even if we posit widely shared Western values it is not possible to venture far beyond this tautology. Furthermore, the common device by which a concept is explained in terms of its opposite in this case creates more difficulties than it dispels. We cannot simply say, as too many of our Nineteenth Century forebears did, that health is the absence of pathology, for by pathology they meant isolable symptoms located in specific political, religious or economic spheres. Such analysis encourages segmentalism, concentration on aspects of society and not on organic interdependence, which is a condition so marked that to "tamper" with anything is to affect everything. Impeding a holistic or structural view of man-in-society, this limited focus also relieves the observer of any need to assess the full implications of his position. From his point of view it is impossible to contemplate the broad outline of a good and healthy society.

To supply such an outline is, of course, a colossal task which requires much more than a statement of opposition to existing evils. The bitter lesson that man has had to learn and relearn for ages was never clearer than in our time: that the removal of evils may be followed by greater evils. Therefore, to rehearse social symptomatologies as we perceive them, while necessary and desirable, is an insufficient exercise. For our purposes it does not suffice merely to *define* the unhealthy society.

Nevertheless, it should be said that, beyond a basic split to be dealt with presently, there is remarkable agreement about those social evils whose extirpation would presumably lead the way to some kind of *summum bonum.*

Although no such phrases were used or known, "the enlargement of human potentialities" was critically important to classical Greek (or Athenian) philosophy. The ideal polis, as it comes down to us in literature, is one dominated by education, in which individual capacities for civil government, physical prowess, philosophical speculation, science and the arts may be brought to an exquisite bloom. This tradition emphasizes balance in the cultivation of all these potentialities, an Appolonian ideal that does not always hold sway. At times it is supplanted by a familiar stress on specialized and intensive development of particular faculties or talents—with heightened sensibility and excitement as the spur.

By contrast there is the Spartan tradition which sets as its goal neither the balanced nor the specialized *individual,* but the strengthened polis.

Ancient civilization, with comparable cases East and West, set the stage for a titanic conflict, yet to be resolved, over the role of the collectivity, "society," or the state. In many guises and forms this conflict is a permanent feature of Western thought. The liberals who were our immediate intellectual progenitors exalted individualism—as had *their* progenitors in the Renaissance. They were naturally fearful of government, which seemed to them to be either an instrument of oppression or, at best, a mechanical arrangement which, if properly contained, could allow for fulfillment in other areas of life.

Collectivist ideologies, left and right, from Sparta on down to the present, result in subordination of the individual to the group, of one's personal proximate ends to distant societal ends. In pursuance of those ends the individual has had to be restrained, directed, controlled and subdued.

With the spread of modern technology and other manifestations of applied science this ideological conflict has taken on global proportions. There is thus no point any more in discussing the healthy society except as it encompasses all mankind. The many subdivisions into which our species is organized provide so many arenas for much the same battle. Doctrines are pitted against each other. Sometimes the same doctrine is so latitudinarian that its own elements may be pitted against each other.

This is certainly so for Marxism, which, as Marxist-Leninism, has become a major world religion. There are strands and strands in Marx himself, so many indeed that we may speak in his own terminology of Marx's internal contradictions. The game of "Marx *versus* Marx" is an amusing pastime which, if played in the founder's day, could easily have provoked him to exclaim on more than the one occasion we know of: "*Je ne suis pas Marxiste.*"

The young Marx (the only one Erich Fromm would like us to remember) was something of a liberal. He also believed, early and late, that history was teleological. In his youth he expressed the belief that man was moving toward a society in which each of its members would be a creative and autonomous being. By and by he saw in the class system and in government—its constant handmaiden—an insuperable barrier to human development. He viewed the propertied, who owned land, capital and chattel or wage slaves, as a force which prevented the propertyless and exploited classes from becoming fully human, while the exploiters and their minions were transmuted into "monsters." Indeed, for him, class war boiled down to war between dehumanized "brutes" and dehumanized "monsters."

As young men, Marx and Engels allowed themselves the luxury of a Utopian blueprint. It is set forth in *The German Ideology*, where we learn that once the expropriators have been expropriated, that is, when private property is abolished, the state (like the division of labor, the family, the church and all other institutional encumbrances) will disappear. Prehistory will finally end; and, as history begins and the whole range of creativity inherent in man comes to flower, a truly healthy society will emerge at last.

Marx's understanding of the past, although obviously deficient in some ways, was much better than his vision of the immediate future. In fact, so-called Marxist totalitarianism, employing means not totally alien to the more mature Marx, has in this century produced an absolute idolatry of collective values—still, to be sure in the name of other values forever postponed. No system is more inimical to individual development than that which has been spawned under the auspices of men who call themselves Marxists. All the same, Marx's theory of personality has had its positive consequences, albeit ironically in non-Communist countries.

The proponents of that theory, in harmony with liberalism, strove even more radically than their predecessors to democratize the development of human potentialities which had previously been monopolized by privileged, leisured and ruling classes. Such development was to become universally accessible, and Marx assumed that all classes were capable of achieving it. He and Engels believed that whether self-actualization did or did not take place was largely, if not wholly, a social question. Indeed, for them what we now call "personality" stemmed from the work situation where men were obliged to cooperate; and, when not allowed to grow, they were inevitably stunted. The humanization of man could occur only as society itself was reconstituted so that all systems of exploitation were ended once for all.

Whenever a people is liberated from mercilessly exploitative practices and begins to produce thousands of cultivated and creative individuals, we see that Marx and Engels, as sociologists of work (if not as agitators and economists), were substantially correct. Besides those hitherto impoverished and brutalized societies that suddenly "take off" into productivity and creativity, there are even now in the most economically advanced countries whole strata in which talent, ability, motivation, interest and possible genius are systematically obliterated. Their partial "liberation" is wonderful to behold.

The creative person is still a mystery to us; his total makeup is special and personal and probably unique. Yet, even if he is inordinately productive, under adverse social conditions only a minuscule fraction of his potential can be realized. We know, then, how seriously suffocating society can be, what deformations it makes in character-structure. We do not know, however, how a society would function if everyone were allowed to reach and enjoy the full measure of his biological and cultural capacity. We may never know. Almost certainly no one now alive will see such a society. We suspect it would have to be a quasi-anarchist order such as that once envisaged and foolishly predicted for the day after tomorrow by Marx, that it would require the deepest transformation of man and all his works and that it would, fortunately or unfortunately, fall far short of Paradise.

Nor can anyone know at this moment, with real specificity, what there is about all historical societies that has made it impossible for them to tap much that lies within man. Everywhere the potential is present; and this is, so to speak, our constant. Our variables are the social sources of development and of retardation.

They are most obviously present in the family, that irreducible unit of social organization within whose confines we are raised or maimed, cherished or crushed. Unconditional love, warmth, affection, intimate care and attention are literally priceless; their absence inflicts overwhelming and irremediable damage. Anna Freud and René Spitz have demonstrated in horrendous detail what the loss of mother-love does to children in their "pre-Oedipal" stages. Some languish and die; others are deranged for life. The more fortunate are exceedingly, i.e., cripplingly, neurotic. Problems a relatively healthy child easily surmounts are insoluble for those who have been traumatized in impaired or disorganized families. The healthy family enables children to mobilize their energies, to face life and deal with it. By identification with mature adult models they learn how to use the almost unlimited psychic energy at their disposal.

The strong, confident and loving adult makes meaningful identification possible not only because of traits he brings to his offspring but also because of the restraints that he imposes on them. These restraints force the child to surrender his purely biological, amorphous and asocial impulses, which, with luck, will ultimately be redirected into constructive cultural activities.

Precisely because socialization operates in large part through restraints, it is always an imperfect process, the more so in times like ours which are characterized by rapid social change. Opportunities for innovation, reinterpretation, selection and re-creation of culture tend to appear and multiply. The child undergoing socialization resents and rebels against the very process that is making him human. If the repressive force brought against him is not overwhelming he can reject some of the cultural items presented to him or modify them and experiment with new forms. The selective acceptance, rejection and reinterpretation of culture may operate on a wholesale or retail basis but can never be completely eliminated. We would argue that it is the major source of all creativity. Where, if not here, lies the genesis of a unique image of the world? When early independence coincides with strong ego development and socially defined media for self-expression are at hand, circumstances favorable to substantial self-fulfillment may be said to exist.*

These circumstances, mostly but not exclusively generated by the family, may be reinforced by the larger society which can affirm one's aspiration to mastery of materials and techniques, can supply them and offer as exemplars those who personify past accomplishments while praising and encouraging work well done. Contrariwise, society may and usually must present the developing person with restrictions, distractions, alternative rewards and penalties, incomprehension, resistance, alarm and hostility.

It follows that the potentially creative human being must "use" society to extract from it all the support it has to offer while mustering his resources to repel available "solutions" manufactured for him as well as attractive or oppressive alternatives to his own natural unfolding. All this implies that one needs to develop in childhood the psychological strength to define his own tasks, to create his own vision and not to let himself be deflected from it.

The family, as we have already indicated, can best supply this strength by providing love *and* a sense of limits, but mostly by allowing the conflicts inextricably involved in socialization a certain freedom from overrepression. And yet the family has only a preliminary and fragmentary role to play, at least in contemporary society.* It acts as a primary agency for the entire complex of social relations and institutional patterns that cross our

* In so brief an essay, we must leave most of this in elliptical form. See, however, a recent attempt to document the theory for one group of creative men and women: *The Vanguard Artist* by Bernard Rosenberg and Norris E. Fliegel (Quadrangle Press, 1965).

* See chapter on the family in *Mass, Class and Bureaucracy* by Bensman and Rosenberg (Prentice-Hall, 1963).

path. Hence, it is the total structure of society which determines the possibility of successful socialization (in our sense).

If the family is seriously defective, if adults are absent by reason of death, desertion or divorce, and neglect or abandonment is the result, human potentialities are snuffed out just as they begin to flicker. If the parents are available but suffer from extreme weakness, brutality or frigidity, human potentialities are diminished beyond repair. By the same token, if a given society coerces parents into a position from which they can only transmit deprivation—by allowing poverty, misery, race prejudice and the raw struggle for survival to prevail—the loss is immeasurable.

A solution to the intolerable problems of poverty, inhumanity and exploitation—at present within our reach if not our grasp—is a minimal precondition for the release of that vast human potential that has never been touched. In our own country, for the first time, a national administration is now in power which has committed itself not just to the patchwork amelioration of poverty but to its elimination.

So far, despite many programs and plans, mere tokens have appeared, apparently to spread limited funds over the largest possible number of bodies in the shortest period consistent with inadequate annual budgets. There has already been considerable striving to assure positive public relations. Washington has strenuously sought leaders of the poor and found them in an assortment of self-serving politicians, bureaucrats, social workers and academicians who, as their appetites are whetted, will soon invoke Parkinson's Law and demand the steady expansion of antipoverty programs. Short of total war (and we are not so short of that fatality right now), the Administration will find it difficult to set these programs aside. Given war, we can learn just how extensive man's inhuman potentialities really are. Otherwise, pork barrel and all, we are in a fair way of releasing many hitherto unsung, undetected and unknown capabilities in many millions of people.

To overcome poverty and concomitant forms of deprivation, while a difficult and delicate task, is also a rationally attainable one. Other worthy objectives, as yet dimly perceived, may be less realizable. What to do, for instance, after everyone's stomach has been filled? For two thirds of the world's population grappling with problems of subsistence such a question seems not only premature but obscene. *Yet it is the comparatively well-fed superpowers with their deliverable thermonuclear weapons that currently menace our existence as a species.* Moreover, the Chinese masses, as well as those of the rest of Asia, Africa and Latin America, could be adequately fed by a reorganization of the international economy. By the end of this century, provided that we have not all become radioactive dust, there will only be pockets of economic underdevelopment. And then what?

Then men everywhere will have to look to the *quality* of their lives, as those of us who live off the fat of the land have long had the opportunity to do. When this happens, we will grow interested in those ideals, objectives and visions radiating out of society, to link them if we can with our personal perception of the world. That postmodern society will so provide for us is not to be taken for granted. Monolithic value systems, allowing for no ambiguity, no elbow room, no alternative, are also possible. They are guarantors of further instability at a time when civilization is most precariously balanced. In a monolithic straitjacket, the individualist (and there is one in each of us) squirms until he is exhausted, finally deriving whatever comfort he can while relinquishing his manhood. The only option that may be available to him is to break the straitjacket by striking out blindly at "society" in the interests of self-preservation. *This nightmare can be avoided only so long as a sufficient number of human beings are permitted to express their individuality by rebelling against the accumulated wisdom or dominant values of their society.* There is no other way by which the avenues of self-development can be maintained.

A paucity of ideals circulating in society makes it so much harder to combat the widespread tendency toward cynicism, careerism and professionalism with their passionate involvement in external rewards and their disdain for immanent meaning. Within this technological perspective human development signifies no more than the acquisition of specific skills and techniques which are designed to produce competence or expertise for any and every purpose. The upshot is devaluation of those media by which self-development can take place. When instrumental ends are unduly exalted, there is very little of social value to which we can tie our private visions.

Here there is a counterforce at work. Again it is the providentially imperfect process of socialization by which a child sees his parents' cynical and fraudulent behavior and, revolted by that sight, is forced to construct values of his own mostly out of those to which an older generation is formally but hypocritically committed. In this manner youth continuously recreates the half-forgotten ideals of their parents—which is not to say that the well-nigh universal spread of adult cynicism is anything but an enormous obstacle to potentially idealistic and altruistic human development. Youthful zeal is too often smothered in a society which handsomely rewards its countless frauds and heavily penalizes those who persist in going their own way. Discouragement, capitulation and conversion to fraud are likely reactions in an environment that may preclude anything like the self-imposed discipline and devotion required for genuine creativity.

Marx and his followers were not entirely insensitive to this range of human problems. They were, however, tragically mistaken in their hope that History was just about to solve them all. The specter that haunts us more than a hundred years after Marx first loosed his revolutionary bolts is surely not that of capitalism which, insofar as it exists at all, would be unrecognizable to any Nineteenth Century man. And the *soi-disant* Communist Revolution—a cover for totalitarian and authoritarian dictatorship—has brought once-backward states up to and beyond the levels of bureaucratism and mass manipulation which several non-Communist societies have managed to reach at a slower and less gruesome pace.

Human society, much freer here and much more restricted there, tends everywhere to become overmechanical. By revolution and by evolution, despite morally decisive differences in terror, bloodshed and misery, men make large-scale organizations with bureaucracies to tend and nourish them, as they urbanize and industralize, adding mass communication to more and more specialization and impersonality.

The triumph of bureaucratic technological society brings with it a host of new values, personnel requirements and skills. It confers a kind of social centrality on adminstrators and technicians; they then bring unbearable pressure on traditional institutions which are required to refashion personality to make it fit the new regime. To the fore come mechanical efficiency, value neutrality, personal efficiency and "interpersonal" competence and disciplined amiability. These are the traits that old-fashioned critics excoriate as evidence of other-direction and overconformity. Within the emerging framework of society such traits represent some development of potentialities, but they are elicited by squelching others and ultimately threatening us with the creation of another monstrosity. The new society has new functions that are rightly considered indispensable. They do not include "idle" contemplation, the accumulation of "useless" knowledge, "pure" science or any of the "impractical" arts and crafts.

There is little room in this order for the articulation of creative potentialities among men who, while at work or at their leisure, must respond to the vast bureaucratic apparatus that grips them. It is dehumanizing if the individual's substantive interests are blocked either because his chosen field is artificially narrowed or for lack of opportunity to stretch toward some destiny other than that of becoming a bureaucrat himself.

There are other subtler hazards. Eric Homburg Ericson has pointed to one which, paradoxically, involves overacceptance or overidentification. In this instance, college-educated parents who function in the bureaucratic milieu wish to support their children's artistic or academic talents for reasons extraneous to the children and dear to the parents. Parental anxiety, coupled with a desire for the addition of middle class social graces, may propel children willy-nilly into the half-hearted pursuit of activity which, whatever spark within them set it off, is no longer theirs. Should the spark really ignite with a manifestation of serious interest in an unremunerative medium of self-development, conflict will ensue at just that point. Psychologically, this danger is much to be preferred over the passive response to parental wishes and the attendant loss of any initial drive that may once have been nurtured.

Such are the hazards of good fortune in this world. To the

extent that they are peculiarly contemporary, most of them are derived from the disenchantment and bureaucratization of society. These are phenomena that have to do with the human spirit, its perils and possibilities. The vast majority of human beings live even now in a state of semistarvation. We have said that their redemption from this brute existence is a matter of the first importance. How is such redemption to be achieved? By economic development, which is to say by the extension and expansion of huge bureaucratic structures. There is probably no other way to administer and coordinate the institutions that must come into being if poverty is to be banished.

The problem is: How can we chart a course between animal underdevelopment and mechanical overdevelopment? Knowing this problem *may help us to dream up improvements, to concoct experiments, to try innovations.* It would be a monumental irony if man's newly liberated potentialities had to be suppressed, perverted, lost or turned against the self. The human predicament—suffering and death and the conciousness that they exist—is our perpetual lot. The rest is excrescence, which Sisyphus—or Man—may help to erase with his giant boulder as he rolls it uphill once more.

REFERENCES

1. Fromm, Erich: *Marx's Concept of Man.* New York, Ungar, 1961.
2. Rosenberg, B., Gerver, I., and Howton, F. W.: *Mass Society in Crisis.* New York, Macmillan, 1964.
3. Rosenberg, B., and Bensman, J.: *Mass, Class and Bureaucracy.* Englewood Cliffs, Prentice-Hall, 1963.
4. Rosenberg, B., and Fliegel, N.: *The Vanguard Artist.* Chicago, Quadrangle, 1965.

PART III

THE ROLE OF EDUCATION

Chapter 15

THE DEVELOPMENT OF THE CHILD'S POTENTIAL

RUDOLF DREIKURS

IS it feasible to make any statement about a child's—or any person's potential? By definition, potential—or perhaps better, potentiality—refers to abilities, qualities and properties which cannot be observed; one can only speculate that qualities which are not overtly discernible may exist in a person. We say that a child does not live up to his potential. Certain observations make us believe that he could function on a higher level than he does. Or, qualities which a child displays may suggest future developments going far beyond what he can do today. We can only be certain about skills and abilities which the child *has* developed; but there is no assurance about those which he may be capable of acquiring.

This makes any discussion about a child's potential utterly unscientific and speculative. One may actually ask whether such an inquiry is worthwhile or even permissible, since any prediction is based on highly subjective and untestable assumptions. However, educated guesses are recognized as a valid basis for exploration; and there are sufficient and observable phenomena which can serve as a basis for meaningful speculation.* We have seen the sudden emergence of qualities which were dormant and previously unobservable. Under certain circumstances, through efforts to remove obstacles, qualities appeared which one would never have considered possible. Therefore, we can say that we *know* that what is, is no indication of what could be. *The mere absence of qualities does not imply that they could not be developed.*

* In this "subjective" appraisal, present and possible future developments are viewed only from the author's own and necessarily biased point of view.

The development of qualities which are presently not observable can be of two kinds. Dormant qualities may exist but need favorable circumstances to bring them to view. Therefore, overt performance of behavior is not a precise measure of underlying abilities. Situational conditions affect the degree to which the unobservable inner events become observable. On the other hand, the organism is capable of developing types of skills and qualities which require favorable circumstances for their development. Such an optimistic point of view is essential if we want to explore the potential of our children. Only those who share such confidence in man's untapped resources can contribute to their development.

Through correctional efforts in counseling and therapy, many children develop abilities which ordinarily would never have emerged. We will concern ourselves here with a clarification of the obstacles to growth as well as with the steps necessary to remove them. Limitations of development are not only evident in children who are deficient in their performance; even children who seem to be successful reveal, under closer scrutiny, unnecessary restrictions in their functions. They, like the rest of our children, encounter handicaps which must be recognized before they can be removed.

One cannot visualize the consequence if parents and teachers were sufficiently trained to stimulate growth and development instead of stifling it, as they often do. We can recognize wrong and deficient motivations in children who present problems and do *not* function as well as they should. However, few realize the faulty motivation in *excellent* students and apparently well-adjusted children; they are vulnerable despite their high level of performance, often because of it. They do not study in order to learn, nor behave well because they like it. They are good only because they want to be better than others. And their overambition keeps them in constant fear of either not reaching their extended level of aspiration or of slipping. The rush for personal superiority leads to the vulnerability of the best and to the deficiencies of the failing.

What are the requirements for full growth and development,

and which experiences and procedures retard or misdirect them? There is, first, the self-concept of the child, the belief in his strength and ability, both to contribute and to stand up under adversities. A high tolerance level can only be established through a sense of belonging, what Adler called *social interest.* Only if a child feels belonging can he be sure of his worth; then he is willing to contribute and participate *under all circumstances,* concerned with the needs of the situation rather than with his own status, worth and prestige. Restrictions of his feeling of belonging constitute the major obstacle to his full self-realization.

When children become deficient or maladjusted, one looks for individual and social pathology, both in the parents and the community. We usually overlook our *cultural* predicament which adversely affects the development of *all* our children. Misbehavior, social and academic failures, are similar throughout the country; therefore, we cannot assume any special pathology in each case and must recognize a cultural handicap of all parents and all teachers. They want to do a good job and do not know how to do it.

Children were always raised by tradition; but the traditional methods, evolved in an autocratic society, have become ineffective in a democratic setting with its high degree of equality. Tradition and autocracy have greatly limited the freedom of choice of action; they need efficient *controls* of behavior, which are one step above "instinct" as a deterministic direction-setter for behavior. Democracy emphasizes not merely equality, but vastly expanded opportunities for freedom of choice and action. The *belief* in such a freedom and the *skill* either in using it or in training children to use freedom are two different things. Parents and teachers who grew up with traditional and autocratic concepts do not themselves have the skills to use freedom wisely, and they do not know how to teach children such skills either. Freedom of choice involves problems of decision making, which is not learned fully in the system of tradition and autocracy. This is the reason that the self-concept becomes even more important in a democracy than in an autocracy. Inner resources and strengths and the person's perception of them become a major directing principle when external direction is minimal, i.e., when tradition and autocracy no longer exist.*

Since the traditional methods fail them, neither parents nor teachers know how to cope with their ever-increasing problems. The educators are excellent as long as the child applies himself and behaves well; if he decides not to do so, neither teachers nor parents know how to motivate him. For this reason, we can speak of a bankruptcy of our educational institutions, the family and the school. Both present the child with a sequence of discouraging experiences. We either overprotect him, by doing for him what he could do for himself, thereby depriving him of the realization of his own strength and ability, or we correct, scold, admonish, nag, punish and humiliate the child, undermining his self-respect and sense of worth. Defeated in our tasks as educators, we suffer from what one may call an "unrecognized prejudice against children." We underestimate their abilities to an unbelievable degree. We distrust them and fail to evoke *their* trust. We are at war, without being aware of it.

This warfare exists between our whole generation of adults and children; it defeats our best educational and corrective efforts. This must be understood in the light of our culture dilemma. Hostility is rampant wherever a previously submissive group claims its equal rights (women-men, colored-white, labor-management, children-adults). As a consequence, we witness in our children a "continuum of norm-violating behavior" (Kvaraceus [1]). There is the child whom we cannot get up in the morning nor to bed in the evening, who will not dress himself, eats either too little or too much, refuses to put his things away or to study, fights with his brothers and sisters—in other words, the "normal" child; and at the other end of the continuum is the defiant juvenile delinquent. Instead of winning the cooperation of our children, we drive them only deeper in deficiency and defiance, when they need help and support. The more encouragement a child needs, the less he gets. Correctional efforts usually aggravate the situation, because parents and teachers know little about

---

* I am indebted to my daughter, Dr. Eva Ferguson, for some of these formulations.

motivation, about psychodynamics and even less about group procedures which could be used to prevent and to correct deficiencies. Few recognize that reward and punishment are no longer effective; they are necessary means of influencing subordinates in an autocratic society but wasted and actually damaging in a democratic setting (2). The child regards a reward as his "right" and will not do anything unless another is forthcoming. If punished, the child takes his punishment in his stride as part of the fortunes of war; and he assumes the right to retaliate. Acts of mutual retaliation fill our homes and schools. In vain did Maria Montessorri sound the call for "disarmament in education" (3).

Hardly any child grows up with the realization that he *has* a place and is good enough as he is. He is driven to be more and better; *then*, perhaps, can he amount to something. Unfortunately, he never can reach this peak. The mad rush for higher status and increased prestige leads to lasting insecurity and perpetual anxiety because one can never be or have "enough." Whatever one has, one may lose. The competitive strife stimulates a mistaken motivation. Instead of moving on the *horizontal* line (Sicher [4]), growing through interest, curiosity and practice, children are induced to move on the *vertical* line, up and up. Their abilities serve more to gain personal success rather than to be useful. True enough, one can achieve progress on the vertical line, but at what price? Stimulating competitive strife between students, between siblings, neither brings optimal results nor prepares children for living in a competitive society. For every child who succeeds, many more give up in discouragement. The more competitive a person is, the less he can stand competition unless he wins. The less competitive, the better he can function under *all* circumstances; he is willing to do his best regardless of how others may be doing. The worst aspect is the antisocial attitude which such competitive strife fosters; it increases feelings of inferiority and restricts the development of social interest. Competitive children have false incentives and perverted motivations, leading to what appears to be a "low frustration tolerance." Consequently, their parents are more concerned with satisfying their "needs" in order to soothe their unwillingness to function if they are not on top instead of teaching them to cope with stress and with environmental adversities. And they are often supported by experts who also stress need-satisfaction and need-reduction. Self-satisfaction, rather than being useful, becomes a primary goal.

The striving toward being important and significant never stops. If the child becomes discouraged and feels defeated, he merely "switches to the useless side of life" (Adler [5]) and gains his significance through defeating adults and/or through putting them into his service. In current educative methods, creativity and imagination, the greatest sources of growth, are either stifled because they hinder conformity and render the job of the educator more difficult; or they become perverted as mere means for more effective disturbance and mischief.

Many children fail to develop an adequate sense of responsibility because parents and teachers take on full responsibility for them. An increasing number of children come to believe that they have the right to do as they please, regardless of the consequences, and that only the adults have the responsibility to see to it that unpleasant consequences or dangers are avoided. This is the children's perception of democracy; thrill and status appear to them often as the only important values in life. Studying and cooperation with parents and teachers are often regarded as disloyalty to the peer group, especially by boys who may regard such behavior as unmanly. And those who seek knowledge, skill and excellence do so often merely as steps to personal aggrandizement and do not regard it as implying greater responsibility. The system of grading and the newly recommended ability grouping intensifies the development of an educational aristocracy which looks down on those who do not keep up and fall by the wayside, partly just because they feel stigmatized as inferior and thus become only more antieducational. This is the cultural matrix which leads to increased deficiency, in frequency and in intensity, and prevents rather than enhances the development of our children's potential.

Under these circumstances many children become deeply convinced of their limited ability. This may, in extreme cases, make them perform as if they were retarded; and the special attention and care which retarded children receive at home and in the community induces many children with normal intelligence to behave as if they were retarded. In the absence of reliable diagnostic tools—IQ tests are only reliable on the upper score but not on the lower; and performance may be influenced by the child's assumption of being stupid—the distinction between real or pseudoretardation is often difficult. Many children succeed in convincing the adults of the correctness of their own low self-evaluation. This holds true for a wide segment of our normal children who function below their ability because they do not expect to succeed and are reinforced in their expectations by the critical and punitive treatment they receive.

It is of the utmost importance what we, the whole generation of adults, think about children in general. Contrary to our professed benevolence, we have a low opinion of them, are impressed with their frequent lack of responsibility, unwillingness to cooperate and refusal to do their part. This state of affairs can change only after we begin to recognize our present prejudice. It will require a reorientation of our educators, of parents and teachers, before we can mobilize the heretofore untapped resources in our children. We seem to be on the verge of discovering the means by which we can help children to function on a considerably higher level than they presently are able to reach. This development may soon lead to a drastically different concept of children, nay, of man (Matson [6]).

It is not accidental, but probably part of the contemporary cultural development, that we are discovering the tremendous power within the heretofore smallest and most insignificant particle, the atom, at the same time that we are beginning to visualize the power and strength within each human being. The term "atom" turned from the lowest possible denominator to become one of the most powerful symbols; equally, the term "human" or "childish" may soon shed its humble or feeble implications. It required the emergence of a democratic revolution to free the small and insignificant—and the deficient—from the stigma of worthlessness. This opened the door to new vistas which made new discoveries possible.

The democratic evolution permitted the individual the freedom to decide for himself. However, this freedom could not have been recognized without the advances in theoretical physics which ended the period of strict causal determination in our concept of life, of the universe. Today, it is becoming acceptable, scientifically, to recognize man as a decision-making organism and not as a mere victim of forces from within and from without. This change in basic concepts has not yet progressed sufficiently to alter the opinions of our adult population and even of a large segment of our scientific community. But we are on the way.

The new concept of man, as it is now emerging, has far-reaching consequences for our perception and treatment of children. The child is not a passive object, either of his hereditary endowment nor of environmental influences. Very early, long before he can think consciously, he injects himself actively. He observes carefully, draws his conclusions and acts upon them. Adler demonstrated in 1907 (7) the relative freedom of the child from hereditary influences, from organ deficiencies with which he may be born. *It became obvious that it is less important with what the child is born than what he does with it afterwards. Similarly, it is less important in what situation the child finds himself than how he responds to it.*

This is difficult to perceive because we are not accustomed to recognize the perceptibility of infants and their ability to manage their environment. Too deeply ingrained is the assumption of the infant's passive helplessness, his assumed lack of cognitive ability, which leads many to regard an infant as a parasite. We begin to see how they choose their actions in line with their perception, although not on the conscious level. Normal infants born to deaf parents usually cry without making any sound; they do not waste any effort. Later, when they lose their tempers, they stamp with their feet or cause vibrations when they want to attract their parents. We have innumerable examples of how infants can size up a situation correctly, knowing how to get the attention of their parents and responding instantaneously when parents change their tactics.

The child determines the role which he intends to play through life in his transactions with his brothers and sisters; the parents afterwards merely reinforce his decision of being good or bad, productive or deficient. He depends less on what his mother does to him than his mother depends on what he is doing. It is usually the child who prompts mother's behavior toward him, since he knows how to influence her, while she usually displays little ability to change him. Contrary to prevalent opinions, the mother does not cause the child's disturbing or deficient behavior; she merely makes it possible through her compliance with his unconscious schemes.

The development of personality, of a *style of life*, is based on the opinions which the child forms about himself and others and of the goals which he sets himself in order to find a place. He probably begins with random decisions, perceiving and evaluating the reactions, each decision limiting the remaining possibilities of choice. But, even after he has established his frame of reference within which he operates, his life style, the child is free to choose from a great variety of alternatives and makes full use of this freedom, to the disadvantage of adults who usually neither recognize his decisions nor know how to change them if they are objectionable.

The realization that each child can decide and *is deciding* what he is going to do opens new vistas for child psychology and pedagogy. It implies the child's ability to change, to learn, since the emphasis is put on the here and now, on his *present* movements in the social field. This refutes the common assumption that the child is the victim of past experiences. They certainly have contributed to his development and to the present circumstances; but there is a profound difference whether one regards the past as the "cause" of his deficiency or difficulty, or as antecedents which explain how he developed his present ideas and concepts. What he thinks and believes *today* is the basis for his behavior. This opens the way to his changing the sequence of events in his life through new and more adequate concepts and goals. This is the basis for a more optimistic outlook.

It is not easy to change the convictions of a whole generation of adults who affect a generation of children with their pessimism. While teachers and parents sincerely try to help the child, their culturally fostered pessimism defeats their best intentioned correctional efforts. They look for pathology if the child fails academically or socially. *They cannot visualize that wrong behavior and deficiencies are merely errors in the child's evaluation of himself and his situation, that he merely uses wrong methods, without being pathological in any possible meaning of this term.* (This holds true for all children except those who are psychotic; and even they follow a private logic which can be understood.)

The usual belief today is that the "disturbed" child differs in terms of underlying pathology from the "normal" and healthy child. We find in contrast that achievement and deficiency differ not in their underlying processes, but only in overt behavior. The same motivation stimulates them both. Each child seeks significance and status, either through excellence or through deviation. The overambitious child will either be the best or try to be the worst. Weakness and deficiency only thinly veil the strength and accomplishment which a child achieves in this way. He either uses them to keep adults busy, to get service from them or to defeat them and demonstrate his power over them. Or, he wants to hurt as he feels hurt by others or to be left alone so that his real or assumed deficiencies will not become obvious and undermine his status. These are the four goals of disturbing behavior which need to be recognized by everyone who deals with children (8). Those who seek "deeper" causes and reasons for the child's deficiencies will object to such "superficial" explanations of his behavior. To us it seems they do not see the forest for the trees.

Mistaken approaches, based on faulty self-evaluations, imply a lack of self-confidence; otherwise, the child would not have abandoned proper approaches which are much more gratifying. Therefore, encouragement is essential for any corrective procedure (9).

Parents and teachers need instruction in the process of encouragement, since their competitive attitudes lead them to become more interested in the faults of others than their virtues. Lack of respect for others prevents us from distinguishing between the deed and the doer; but without truly respecting the child *as he is,* giving him recognition for his accomplishments, even if they are on the useless side, one cannot provide the badly needed encouragement. It opens the door for growth and development as discouragement closes it. Unfortunately, the more encouragement he needs, the less he gets.

Another consequence of the low opinion which adults have of children is their inability to share responsibility with them. They try to manage their children's lives without giving them an opportunity to participate in planning and in finding solutions to their common problems. In our democratic era children become aware of their state of equality. Therefore, we can no longer run schools *for* them, only *with* them as equal partners. Their sense of responsibility needs to develop through their involvement in the affairs of the home and the school. This does not imply that adults should abdicate and let children make all decisions. The opposite is true. *As long as they are not invited to participate fully in the school program, the children actually do decide what happens; they decide whether they want to study, to behave, to be contributing or disturbing—and no power of adults can force them to change their minds.* Responsibility cannot be "taught" by condescending adults—it has to be given to be learned. New methods of raising children permit a relationship of mutual respect. There is no need to fight or to give in, violating either the respect for the child or the respect for oneself (10). To permit and to help our children to develop their potential requires educational and corrective approaches which in many regards are contrary to the principles which presently are used in dealing with children. What is needed is not essentially new; everything has been suggested before, in one way or another, from Rousseau to Pestalozzi, Herbert Spencer, Montessorri, Piaget and many others. Yet we are standing at the threshold of an educational revolution. We can hardly foresee what will happen if and when children are exposed to new experiences which until now were inconceivable.

It has been suggested that children could, within the first ten years, acquire all the knowledge presently obtained through higher education. Until most recently this was considered unrealistic, wishful thinking. The question has been and still is being raised whether such development would be desirable or harmful. During the last few years new observations have been made with increased frequency which seem to substantiate the assumption that early learning is not detrimental. Innovations are so numerous that mentioning a few would be unfair to others perhaps equally significant. And, since the author had no opportunity to test the claims made about the unbelievable learning ability of very young children, no specific method is mentioned here. Throughout the ages we had examples of unusual intellectual and artistic abilities coinciding with very early training. The question arises whether early activities are the consequence or the cause of special talent. We have indications that activity usually precedes ability. For some time one assumed that toilet training should be postponed until an age when the neurocerebral development would permit control. Then we found out that the physical development was the *result* of the training. Under these circumstances one can hardly foresee the development of children—and of mankind—if the unusual and highly revolutionary experiments would actually evoke abilities in the very young which today seem nothing less than miraculous.

One of the most important and far-reaching "discoveries" concerns the ability of newborn infants to swim. A gag reflex, which disappears after the age of six months, supposedly prevents them from drowning. If this is true, and the many reports of parents who tried it would indicate that it is, it would revolutionize the whole life and development of children. One merely has to visualize its effects on the self-concept of a child which he develops in his early experiences. Presently, the human infant is one of the most helpless creatures in the world (like the birds who also need training and development before they can reach mobility). This would change as the infant would become free in his actions and directions, using his limbs and muscles and developing his brain as he is free to decide where to go. He will no longer be impressed with his state of passive helplessness which led many to the assumption that the infant is a parasite. This assumption was always incorrect, since we know how infants can manage their surroundings, observe clearly what goes on and choose their actions accordingly, although not on the conscious level. Apparently, the infant's physical immobility impressed parents and many experts with his general lack of ability so that they could not perceive the clever and well-directed social activities of infants. Our whole concept of children would be altered if we recognized the obvious mobility and even self-directedness of the infant during the first months of his life. And one can hardly visualize the effect of such early activity on the speed of the child's physical and mental growth.

One can only wonder why the tremendous learning ability of young children has not been "discovered" before. Many have witnessed the speed and facility with which very young children learn foreign languages, without any instruction and apparently without any effort. Such early "knowledge" and "skill" never did any harm to a child or spoiled his childhood pleasures, even if he managed to talk several languages. However, we did not take much notice, nor did we know the ways by which very young children learn foreign languages. Whatever their method of learning is, it certainly is different from the language instruction to which our children are exposed in school. Now we suddenly discover that the child can learn reading, writing and arithmetic with the same ease and speed at a very early age. Several years ago, Moore startled the educational world with his experiments which indicated that children two and one half years old can learn to read and write—through play (11). This upset the current educational trend. Many educators were impressed with the difficulties of six-year-old boys to learn reading and writing. One heard the suggestion that reading instruction may have to be postponed until the age of eight, since many boys do not show "reading readiness" at the age of six because of their slower development. In other cultures, *all* boys learn to read at the age of four; but there one does not know yet about the slow development of boys.

Moore's experiments, while startling, still emphasize a difference between the gifted and the average child. Experiments of others indicate that *all* children may be able to learn to read at the age of two an one half years. We are told that this is the optimal age for learning to read; and the later one begins, the more difficult learning becomes. While we had no opportunity to verify these claims, our experience would tend to support them. The customary practice is simply absurd. We let the child grow up for most of his formative years with the conviction that he cannot read nor write. And after he is well settled in this belief, at the age of six we suddenly demand from him that he learn. If this is artificial and unnatural, how can one then explain that most children do not reach their "reading readiness" before? It seems that children themselves accept the "norms" of adults, that one has to be of a certain age before one will be able to read. Many children do not accept this dictum and want and can learn sooner. This is then attributed to their greater intelligence. However, children often learn to read prematurely, not because they are necessarily brighter than their brothers and sisters. A frequent reason for their early interest and exhibited ability is an older sibling, mostly a brother, who has difficulty in learning. This gives the next child a chance to show how much smarter he is.

We may have to revamp our present notions about the learning abilities of very young children. They probably have a tremendous capacity for absorbing knowledge. We are becoming aware of how early children can learn arithmetic, far before the present age level set for them. But the methods of instruction of the very young are entirely different. What distinguishes them all from present indoctrination is the use of play, of visual and tactile experimentation. *Children learn through play.* In our opinion this is the most important characteristic of the newest developments in teaching children.

Previously, one distinguished between play and duty. Learning was supposed to be a duty. It was even deliberately made more unpleasant, so that children would learn to accept unpleasant tasks. This was possible and probably even necessary in an autocratic era when submission to demands was the law of the land. Today's children only do what they want and what they decide to do. Many are unwilling to do anything that is unpleasant. The sad fact is that in our schools we make learning for those who refuse to learn even more unpleasant and then are surprised that we fail to overcome their learning resistance.

No such struggle can be found in any of the new methods, if the reports are correct. Learning seems to become fun and achievement pleasure. There is no honor nor failure, no grading, no superiority nor inferiority, no exhibition of deficiency—all simply enjoy what they are doing and progress through pleasant practice. It is possible that *all* normal children can learn in this way, not only the gifted, as all children learn to speak and all children learn a foreign language in a foreign country. This seems to indicate that learning deficiencies of normal children are artificial and unnecessary. Conversely, the early learning seems not to deprive the child of his "childhood." He continues to play, only on a more significant level.

We do not know to which level of achievement learning through enjoyable activities can be carried out. We are accustomed to believe that high achievement requires strenuous effort. However, some of our best students learn "easily" and enjoy the studying. The question is whether they are enjoying learning because they are talented or gifted, or whether they became talented because they enjoyed learning. Today the greatest stimulation comes from the striving for importance and superiority. Excelling appears to many as a main goal in life; and, therefore, all energies are devoted to the attainment of superiority regardless of the sacrifice in other essential aspects of living. But perhaps similar accomplishments are possible on the horizontal line, without struggle and inner friction, when children are liberated from fear and threat of failure. Time will tell.

Any achievement, skill and knowledge, requires training. But does this training have to be unpleasant? And what takes place when the child—or for that matter anyone else—"learns"? It is always based on a change of concepts, of perceptions; these changes probably occur instantaneously. At a given point, the child suddenly "catches on." Then he knows what to do. In between these periods of sudden development, a great deal of time is wasted with meaningless practice, supposedly training muscles, movements, isolated details of improvement. Actually, all minor improvements, like the major, are based on the same process of suddenly finding out what to do. Under proper instruction, children can learn skills far ahead of what presently is offered to them. Unusual feats of memory can be achieved in this way. We know of a music teacher in Jamaica who taught all of her very young students to compose music of considerable quality, such as sonatas and fugues. The Japanese Susuki is teaching unselected groups of children, ages three to five, to play the violin, with startling results which are noticed by the musical world. It is quite possible that many other skills and abilities, far beyond those presently experienced, can be acquired in this way, such as time perception, orientation in space, a deeper grasp of people and the perception of new patterns of various kinds. There may even be a chance that children can learn to perceive events beyond the tridimensional world of our five senses and perhaps through extrasensory perception break not only through the space barrier, but perhaps even through the time barrier. Any new ability would increase the child's—and mankind's—mastery of life. These, of course, are mere speculations. Some will heartily endorse them and others as vehemently object to them. But who knows what is possible?

We are standing on the threshold of a new social order, the age of democracy, of equality for all. As at the beginning of our civilization eight thousand years ago, the transition of one fundamental culture to another is characterized by rapid change. When primitive tribal society gave way to regional heterogeneous communities, man's skills developed within a few centuries (agriculture, writing, mathematics, architecture, etc.). The tremendous speed and extent of the changes which we experience today indicates the second fundamental change in human relationships and social organizations. We are not only developing a new culture, but a new type of humanity, through children who can learn what was impossible for our ancestors. If we can remove the obstacles to intellectual growth, to social and moral development—and it seems that we are on the verge of achieving this—then we may, in a relatively short period of a few generations, experience such a high degree of knowledge, skill and performance that man may be as different from us as we are from the most primitive people found anywhere today.

REFERENCES

1. Kvaraceus, W. C.: *Delinquent Behavior.* Washington, D. C., National Education Association, 1959.
2. Dreikurs, R.: The cultural implications of reward and punishment. *Int. J. Soc. Psychiat., 4*:171-178, 1958.

3. MONTESSORI, MARIA: Disarmament in education. *The Montessori Magazine, 4,* 1950.
4. SICHER, L.: Education for freedom. *Amer. J. Individ. Psychol., 11*:97-103, 1955.
5. ADLER, A.: *The Education of Children.* New York, Greenberg, 1930.
6. MATSON, F. W.: *The Broken Image.* New York, Braziller, 1964.
7. ADLER, A.: *Studie uber die Minderwertigkeit von Organen.* Wien Urban and Schwarzenberg, 1907. *Study of Organ Inferiority and Its Psychical Compensation, Nervous and Mental Disease.* New York, 1917.
8. DREIKURS, R.: *Psychology in the Classroom.* New York, Harper and Brothers, 1957.
9. DREIKURS, R., and DINKMEYER, D.: *Encouraging Children to Learn: The Encouragement Process.* Englewood Cliffs, Prentice-Hall, 1963.
10. DREIKURS, R., and SOLTZ, V.: *Children: The Challenge.* New York, Duell, Sloan and Pearce, 1964.
11. MOORE, O. K.: *Autotelic Responsive Environments and Exceptional Children.* Hamden, Connecticut, Autotelic Responsive Environments, 1963.

Chapter 16

IDENTIFYING CREATIVE POTENTIAL IN CHILDREN

E. PAUL TORRANCE

IN the summer of 1964 I asked approximately two hundred experienced teachers in my class in "Creative Ways of Teaching" at the University of California at Berkeley to recall and describe in writing an incident in their teaching careers in which they had allowed or encouraged someone to express himself creatively and then observed that the experience made a marked difference in future achievement and behavior. Eighty-two per cent of these teachers were able to recall such instances. In 86 per cent of the incidents described, it was judged that the incident that made a difference was triggered by the teacher's recognition of creative potential. These incidents are truly exciting descriptions of explorations in human potential and indicate the critical importance of identifying creative potential in children.

John in the second grade was a nonreader, a poor listener, rejected and ignored by his peers. His teacher recognized his tremendous capacity to create exciting stories. One day she took the time to let him dictate to her a lengthy story. His choice of words, sentence structure and use of suspense were vivid, imaginative and mature. When his story was read to the class, reaction was wildly enthusiastic. John was starry-eyed and learned to read his own story, created other stories and became a good reader. His behavior improved and he made friends.

Bill was reported to be the culprit of many a weekend shambles at his school. He was an almost permanent fixture in the principal's office because of his undesirable behavior. A teacher recognized his ingenuity in things mechanical and in getting things done. She suggested that he be made chairman of the Lunchroom Committee. Bill organized a team of boys who spent half their noon hour cleaning, moving tables and helping the janitor. He noticed many other things about the school that needed improving and organized groups to take care of them. Vandalism in the school faded out completely. At age twelve Bill was able to say for the first time, "I like school." For the first time he began to read, and his art work was outstanding.

David in kindergarten began earning a reputation as a trouble-maker. In searching for the key to unlocking David's potentialities, his third grade teacher recognized his outstanding creative thinking ability and his preference for learning in creative ways. Instead of making him work with someone else on an imaginary tour of some country for Christmas, she permitted David to work alone. He chose Sweden and wrote several very neat letters to his Swedish grandmother for various items of information. For two weeks he walked to school instead of coming by bus in order to get in extra writing and painting in preparation for his presentation. His Swedish fairy tales were wonderful, with colorful paintings as illustrations. He taught his classmates a game Swedish children play and how to make little "goodie" baskets to hang on Christmas trees. Thereafter David was too busy learning, creating and teaching to misbehave.

Mark was frequently a nonparticipator in class projects and seldom handed in written reports. His fifth grade teacher recognized that he was an extremely creative boy and developed an enormous respect for him. He had not volunteered to prepare a report on one of the Latin American countries because he wanted to work alone, was interested in Ecuador, and two other classmates had volunteered for Ecuador. The teacher discovered that Mark had been reading Darwin's journals and was fascinated by the Galapagos Islands, and she permitted him to prepare a separate report on the Galapagos Islands. Three weeks later, Mark had not begun his report, in the sense that he had nothing on paper. He was too busy reading books, interviewing anthropologists at the University and thinking. The teacher tried hard to get Mark to get something on paper but finally decided that his would have to be an oral report. He delivered a magnificent account of Darwin as a person, his voyage on the *Beagle* and various forms of a single species as they appear on different islands, drawing pictures of the variants on the chalkboard, complete with describing the different environments the various islands offered and asking his fellow pupils to guess what variant they would imagine would result. Mark obtained such satisfaction from this experience that he was willing to write his next report complete with a very proper bibliography.

My experience in developing tests of the creative thinking abilities and in conducting research on the development of these abilities through school experiences indicates that tests may be used to help teachers sharpen their perception on creative potential in children. In our longitudinal studies we have seen dramatic changes take place in the functioning of a child identified as being creatively gifted. During the first year of these longitudinal studies I was told by most fourth, fifth and sixth grade teachers that there were some pupils who could not take a test of creative thinking because they could not read or write. Usually we tested these children individually and orally. In almost every class at least one of these "hopeless cases" turned out to be creatively gifted in some way. When this was discussed with the teacher, he usually showed curiosity concerning the potential of the pupil, later started asking the pupil questions he would ordinarily never have dared ask and giving him assignments to test potentiality. Almost always the teacher was amazed that the pupil knew so much, thought so deeply and could produce such excellent solutions to problems. In some cases, such occurrences became turning points in a child's school career.

IDENTIFICATION AS A BASIS FOR INDIVIDUALIZING INSTRUCTION

Some teachers and laymen argue that it is useless to identify potential because "what is good for the average is good for all." This argument is simply not true. The results of practically every educational experiment which has taken into consideration different levels and kinds of ability provide an argument in favor of the importance of individualized instruction. It is true that in most classrooms the so-called "average" may demand most of the teacher's time and effort. This leaves the problem of motivating and guiding the learning and thinking of those who are different from the average.

Whether we are concerned about identification as a basis for individualizing instruction within a classroom or grouping children for instruction, an effort should be made to consider those kinds of potential that make a difference in the way children should be taught. One of the major reasons that I have been interested in developing measures of the creative thinking abilities is that I believe that they provide one useful basis in differentiating instruction. Since abilities at least to some extent constitute a basis of needs and motivations, knowledge about a child's creative thinking abilities seems to reveal differential preferences for ways of learning.

A variety of convergent bits of evidence from the research of investigators such as McConnell (4), Stolurow (5), Burkhart (1) and Hutchinson (3) supports the conclusion that whenever the way of teaching is changed different children become the star learners and thinkers. Similarly, whenever methods of assessing the outcomes of educational experiences are changed, different children emerge as stars. Stolurow, for example, found that with certain strategies of programming instruction posttraining achievement is more closely related to measures of originality than to measures of mental age derived from intelligence tests. Hutchinson (3), by changing regular classroom instruction to give opportunities for different kinds of mental functioning, obtained similar results.

SOME TEST WAYS OF IDENTIFYING CREATIVE POTENTIAL

The history of the development of tests of creative thinking is a long and interesting one (Torrance [6, 7]). There has been so little sustained interest and support for the variety of rather promising efforts of the past that there is not yet on the market a standardized test of creative thinking for children. After over six years of sustained work, we believe that we are approaching a point where this can be done.

At first we sought to adapt for use with children some of the tasks developed for adults by Guilford and his associates (2). Our first work was with two alternate forms consisting of the following six Guilford-type tasks: unusual uses; impossibilities;

consequences; problem situations; improvements; and common problems. Adaptation was accomplished by substituting objects or situations more familiar to children. Thus, subjects were instructed to think of unusual uses of "tin cans" or "cardboard boxes," instead of "bricks," and to imagine all of the things which might possibly happen "if animals and birds could speak the language of men," instead of what would happen "if all national and local laws were suddenly abolished."

Almost simultaneously, experimentation was begun with several other kinds of tests. Test tasks were constructed on the basis of analyses of the reported experiences of scientific discoverers, inventors, writers and other types of creative persons. An attempt was made to construct tasks which would be models of the creative process, each involving several different kinds of thinking.

We have tended in the direction of fairly complex tasks which have features which make use of what we know about the nature of the creative thinking processes, the qualities of creative products, the creative personality and conditions which facilitate or inhibit creative behavior. Very early we began to include both verbal and figural tasks. We have continued to increase our repertoire of figural tasks. To the Circles Task we have added Squares and Parallel Lines, various versions of the Incomplete Figures Test, the Picture Construction or Shape Test, a Manipulative Design Task and the Science-Toy Test.

Verbal tasks have involved a variety of objects and materials which stimulate the senses of sight, hearing and touch. The Ask-and-Guess Test calls for questions about gaps in knowledge about the events occurring in a picture and hypotheses about possible causes and consequences of the pictured events. Similar uses have been made of excerpts from films. The Product Improvement Test calls for novel ideas for improving such objects as children's toys. We have adapted the concept of the well-known Consequences Test by presenting new improbable situations along with drawings for what is called the "Just Suppose Test." The "Sounds and Images Test" makes use of tape-recorded sound effects, a progressive series of warm-ups and other built-in features based on research findings. We are now developing tests based on tape-recorded dramatized accounts, using both fantasy and reality materials. As an example of the former we are using the story of "Giovanni and the Giant." Each time the Giant maneuvers Giovanni into a tight spot, we stop the tape for pupils to write their solutions. We are using "Polar Pilot," the story of Richard Byrd, in a similar manner.

Some individuals respond more creatively to things which they hear, while others achieve greater heights when responding to visual stimuli. Some individuals are free, spontaneous and bold in their thinking when permitted to transmit their ideas in some nonverbal form but are paralyzed and impoverished if they have to express their ideas in words. For others, the reverse is true.

In general, test-retest reliabilities after two weeks, three months, eight months and twelve months have been reasonably satisfactory. Battery totals have in general been satisfactory in the intermediate grades and with college students (reliability coefficients of around 0.88, even with alternate forms of the stimulus materials). In the primary grades reliability coefficients for battery totals ranged from the upper 0.40's to the 0.70's. I am not so concerned about the lack of reliability of the tests in the primary grades as I am about some of the conditions that cause this low reliability in scores.

In designing test tasks, instructions and scoring systems, we have endeavored to build into them characteristics which make use of what we know about the creative processes as they have been revealed in the history of invention, discovery and other kinds of creative achievement, as well as the results of experiments. Most of our attempts to establish validity for these measures have involved one or the other of the following two approaches:

1. Identifying high and low groups on some test measure and then determining whether or not they can be differentiated in terms of behavior which can be regarded as "creative"; and
2. Identifying criterion groups on some behavior regarded as creative and then determining whether or not they can be differentiated by test scores.

During the past six years we have accumulated a variety of evidence under each of these approaches. Most of this evidence has been summarized in other sources (Torrance [6, 7]). In general, it can be said that individuals identified as high or low on the measures can be differentiated in terms of behavior which can be regarded as creative, and children so identified have been found to have characteristics similar to those reportedly displayed by eminent creative individuals at the time they were children. It can also be said at least for a variety of groups that individuals identified as being creative on some criterion can be differentiated on the basis of these measures from individuals not so identified but similar in other ways. Much more developmental work is required, but it is my opinion that this field of measurement can now aid teachers and others who work with children to identify creative potentialities that might otherwise be unrecognized.

NONTEST INDICATORS OF CREATIVE POTENTIAL

Teachers need not be dependent upon tests for identifying creative potential. Nontest indicators may be obtained both in regular classroom activities and by creating classroom situations especially designed to call for creative behavior.

From a list of signs of creative learning compiled by the two hundred students in my class in "Creative Ways of Learning," I would like to suggest the following checklist of behaviors indicative of creative thinking ability and preference for creative ways of learning: intense absorption in listening, observing and doing; intense animation; use of analogies in speech; bodily involvement in writing, reading, drawing, etc.; tendency to burst out to complete teacher's sentence; tendency to challenge ideas of authorities; habit of checking many sources, taking a close look at things, etc.; eagerness to tell others about discoveries; continuing creative work after the bell; showing relationships among apparently unrelated ideas; continuing ideas begun at school; manifestations of curiosity; spontaneous use of discovery or experimental approach; imaginative play; excitement in voice about discoveries; habit of guessing outcomes; honesty and intense search for the truth; independent action; boldness of ideas; low distractability; manipulation of ideas and objects to obtain new combinations; tendency to lose awareness of time; puzzled looks; penetrating observations and questions; self-initiated learning; tendency to seek alternatives and explore possibilities; tendency to test guesses and verify information; willingness to consider or toy with new ideas; and many others.

Taylor has offered a number of illustrations of how teachers can create situations to identify creatively gifted children. The following are a few of them.

1. At times, let students do most of the planning on their own and make their own decisions and observe which ones are most dependent and which ones have the least need for training and experience in self-guidance.
2. Develop exercises through which children report their inner feelings and impulses and then have them see how well they can intuitively anticipate a correct course of action. (Example: Which is the quickest way to go from school to some remote part of the city, town or county?) Then check accurately to see whose hunches were best.
3. Pose complex issues and see which children take a hopeful attitude rather than a position that things are in an impossible state of affairs and nothing can be done about them.
4. Have idea-generating sessions to see who comes up with the most ideas, whose ideas bring out the strongest negative reactions from their classmates and who tends to lead in expressing strong negative reactions. Observe who has the most courage to hold his ground or even move ahead instead of retreating or giving up in the face of negative reactions.
5. Ask students to do a task which they have done before, but take away most of the facilities previously available to see who will be the most resourceful in improvising or in accomplishing the task without the usual facilities.
6. Structure some classroom task where those who tolerate uncertainty and ambiguity do better than those who are unable to do so—in other words, a situation in which the rewards go to those who keep the problem open and keep working on it with their own resources until they eventually attain a solution.

These are examples of the countless opportunities teachers can create in evoking and identifying behavior that will reveal glimpses of creative potentialities. A teacher could not even identify outstanding jumping ability if he depended only upon his observations of how high children just happen to jump in ordinary activities. In order to identify children with oustanding jumping ability he must create a situation which will motivate and/or require them to jump.

REFERENCES

1. Burkhart, R. C.: *Spontaneous and Deliberate Ways of Learning.* Scranton, International Textbook Company, 1962.
2. Guilford, J. P., Wilson, R. C., Christensen, and Lewis, D. J.: *A Factor-Analytic Study of Creative Thinking. I: Hypotheses and Descriptions of Tests.* Los Angeles, Psychological Laboratories, Univ. of Southern California, 1951.
3. Hutchinson, W. L.: *Creative and Productive Thinking in the Classroom.* Doctoral dissertation, Univ. of Utah, Salt Lake City, 1961.
4. McConnell, T. R.: Discovery vs. authoritative identification in the learning of children. *Univ. of Iowa Studies in Educ.*, 9(5):13-62, 1934.
5. Stolurow, L. M.: Social impact of programmed instruction: Aptitudes and abilities revisited. Paper presented at the annual meetings of the American Psychological Association, St. Louis, Missouri, September 3, 1962.
6. Torrance, E. P.: *Guiding Creative Talent.* Englewood Cliffs, Prentice-Hall, 1962.
7. Torrance, E. P.: *Education and the Creative Potential.* Minneapolis, Univ. of Minnesota Press, 1963.
8. Torrance, E. P.: Education and creativity. In C. W. Taylor (ed.): *Creativity: Progress and Potential.* New York, McGraw-Hill, 1964, pp. 49-128.

Chapter 17

CONTRIBUTIONS OF EDUCATIONAL PSYCHOLOGY

FREDERICK J. MCDONALD

GARDNER MURPHY'S conception of *teaching as a force for freeing intelligence* challenges the educational psychologist, not by giving him experimental data, nor by describing a new methodology for investigating human behavior, nor by enunciating a new principle; rather it challenges him because it projects a new approach to defining what we mean by teaching—at once complete and radically different. Such a challenge will and has received a sympathetic response. It has received and will receive a critical response. Many psychologists will reject it; others will accept it.

This ambivalent reception is inevitable because educational psychologists are divided among themselves on what they mean by psychology, by the origin of behavior, by intelligence, by teaching and by learning. This ambivalence and its related conflict must be accepted to assess realistically what contribution educational psychology has made and may make to the development of Murphy's conception of teaching. To do this we begin by exploring the historical antecedents of educational psychology and some of its pattern of growth and development.

THE ORIGINS OF EDUCATIONAL PSYCHOLOGY

Educational psychology was established as a distinctive aspect of the larger science of psychology by E. L. Thorndike who, at the turn of the century, defined its scope and characteristic method (1). For Thorndike the basic problems were: first, how did people learn; second, what part of their learning was controlled by native endowment; and third, how did people differ from each other and what were the correlates of these differences. The inductive method was the device that was to yield the facts on these problems.

The general scope and methodology of educational psychology has not changed in fifty years. The theories dominating the research, the emphasis given to problems have changed. The methodology is greatly advanced. But the tone given to the field has determined its approach to the problems of teaching.

Thorndike's ideas are in the tradition of science as it was conceived at the beginning of this century (2). This was an age of faith in progress, particularly in the progress that science would produce. Men in those times could believe that scientific knowledge not only made men wise but good. Science was revolutionary, changing man's whole conception of himself and the universe; invention, not always the child of science but mixed with it in producing change, revolutionized the conditions of living. Not even a war to save the world for democracy, one of the greatest holocausts in the history of mankind, could completely dim this faith in progress, in its inevitability, in its goodness.

Thorndike was the robust investigator, the model of this way of thinking. He is personally responsible for more changes in educational practice in this century than any single man. His theories dominated educational thinking for years. In these ways he set the direction of educational psychology and demonstrated to educators what values psychological thinking and inquiry might bring to educational practice.

This devotion to the scientific method has characterized educational psychology, particularly in the study of intelligence and variations among individuals. Even recent studies in creativity, seemingly venturesome and ground-breaking, take the same approach (3). A lengthy period of test development precedes the investigation. The requirements of design are adhered to. Critical reviews invariably evaluate methodology.

This scientific character of educational psychology cannot be underestimated. Some people feel that it is scientism, not science. Others feel that it is pedantic, that the scientific approach has made significant problems trivial. Yet large numbers of educational psychologists adhere to belief in the value of the scientific approach.

It would be easy to polarize an issue that has many sides or to attack a straw man. Much of the history of educational psychology has been that, the scientists against the humanists, the "softs" against the "hards," "the nothing-buts" against the "something-mores." Murphy's position in the argument is clear though he goes far beyond the petty carpers and even the more responsible critics of scientific method applied to the psychology of human learning. His point of view also is part of the history of growth in educational psychology.

THE INFLUENCE OF JOHN DEWEY

It is hardly necessary either to point out or to describe the influence of John Dewey on American education. However, it is not so clearly recognized that Dewey's intellectual influence was heavily psychological. Dewey effectively gave education a different kind of educational psychology than Thorndike's. In time the two views came to be pitted against each other (4).

Dewey's view was more speculative, more philosophical, but he wanted it tested in the laboratory of experience. It was not a humanist's view of the world because Dewey quite clearly rejected traditional modes of thought. He, too, wanted to bring the scientific method to bear on the problems of his times. He saw science as the tool for changing and improving the welfare of mankind.

Some of the intellectual enemies of Dewey and Thorndike were the same—inadequate knowledge parading as truth, *a priori* stipulations, speculators who were not problem solvers. But they differed considerably in their conception of man. Although these differences have been considerably exaggerated (5), they came to be seen as differences between the mechanistic and the purposive; between affectivity and rationality as illustrated by an anecdote Murphy cites (6).

Bode was the first to point out the congruence between Dewey's ideas and those of Gestalt psychology. This theoretical position came to be the preferred one of many educators because they saw it as embodying Dewey's ideas. Educational psychology became a mixture of Dewey's ideas and Gestalt theory, with the latter usually serving as the justification of the former.

Dewey's ideas won out in the long run, not because their validity had been demonstrated beyond cavil, but because they appealed to people. People liked them. The times were right for them. They were part of the *Zeitgeist*.

Yet the two traditions live on; conflict is sporadic. Adherents of both points of view exist in large numbers in education, many of them are teachers of educational psychology. Both kinds of ideas are in Murphy's thinking, but this view is sufficiently different from each. It represents a point of view that has not had a spokesman in educational psychology.

THE PERSONALIST TRADITION

The caption is only a trick to call attention to a point of view that has no spokesman within the establishment. This view is best expressed by Murphy, who combines a feeling for the interplay between rationality and affectivity with a sensitivity to the demands of intellectual and scientific rigor.

The personalist tradition has its roots in dynamic psychology. This approach to human problems was for years the approach of clinicians, most of whom worked with patients. Freud has had no advocates among educators of the the stature of Thorndike or Dewey. Freudian ideas have yielded little if anything in the way of practical educational procedures.

The reasons for this neglect are obscure. Probably Freudianism and its derivatives are too strong a brew for the conservative institution of the school. Dynamic psychology yielded clinical techniques not readily adapted to the classroom. Moreover, teachers have largely had a nonclinical viewpoint and have resisted adding a clinical dimension to their already burdensome task.

The practical consequence of this lack of a tradition, of a school, is that the premises of Murphy's view, as he himself has noted, as well as their derivations remain to be tested as they apply to education. Practically also, the Gestaltist tradition, which supports Murphy's view in part, has been largely assimilated and modified into cognitive theory (7). The best of experiments that need to be done in classrooms, with teachers, to test Murphy's hypotheses have yet to be done; nor are there good models yet of how they might be done.

This observation should be related to the earlier one describing the emphasis on scientific method in educational psychology. Further, the times have changed again; and the tradition begun with Thorndike was revived. A new conception of teaching is emerging and needs to be placed against the backdrop of the history reviewed and alongside of Murphy's view. In the end we will suggest how new directions may be taken out of what has been conflict and shifting tides of opinion, conviction and commitment.

THE COMPUTER AS TEACHER

The computer revolution is a well-known fact. Hardly anyone is surprised when some task is taken over by one. Although its capacities may be overestimated, the computer is producing a social revolution that will eventually impinge on education.

That a computer will teach strikes some as a contradiction in terms. The problem here is what is the relevant model of teaching behavior? When a computer is used the principal components of the teaching system are a stimulus presented to the student, his response and the feedback to him on the appropriateness of his response. In these respects the computer is simulating elements of teaching behavior. For example, a teacher asks a question, the students responds, the teacher indicates in some way whether the response is appropriate or not.

The state of the art, teaching by computer, is such that predictions about the future of this way of teaching are largely speculative. But, in principle, there seems to be no reason why computers, linked in complex audiovisual systems, cannot assume many teaching functions. The art of computer simulation is advancing with sufficient rapidity for this possibility to be taken seriously (8).

The underlying theory of some computer-teaching is based on Skinner's ideas on learning. Skinner applied his conceptions of shaping behavior by operant conditioning to human learning in the form of programmed instruction (9). This idea received an enthusiastic response, even to claims that teachers would be replaced. Skinnerian ideas about programming have received a pragmatic test—programs can be built which teach. How much and what they can teach remains to be seen.

Educational psychologists, as might be expected, have taken programming seriously. The theory behind it appealed to many. Still others saw in it a way of testing fundamental ideas about learning in a controlled way. For the first time the "teacher variable" could be controlled and still provide systematic and identical instruction for each learner.

It will strike some readers as strange that controlling the teacher variable should be desirable. Murphy's view makes the teacher an intimate part of the teaching act. Clearly an issue lies here—to what extent teaching needs to be mediated by humans in close proximity to and frequent interaction with the student. Can teaching be defined in such a way that such interaction is not necessary and may even be undesirable? The development of computer technology will remove the teacher from much of the teaching act; but students will continue to learn. Is this teaching?

COMPETING MODELS OF TEACHING

Murphy and Skinner provide two contrasting and competing models of teaching. History is repeating itself in the clash of views. But the memory of ancient controversies has dimmed enthusiasm for renewing them. There are still committed devotees of each view who would gladly do combat with their opponents. But there are probably more pragmatists who prefer to fuse the views or to find in what ways each is a viable approach to some aspects of teaching and learning.

The difference between the two views is difference about individuality, what is meant by it, whether it is a meaningful concept in a psychology of learning. Again it would be easy to polarize the views, to see freedom and respect for the individual on one side and authoritarian control on the other, or to see chaos in learning opposed to predictability and sureness. These stereotypes only serve to confound the issue.

The issue is whether one starts with variation as the given or whether one sees it as a consequence of learning. Actually, both conceptions are correct; but Murphy stresses the biological, evolutionary character of individuality. So for him, "the teacher must help the learner to believe in his own individuality and his capacity to learn." Skinner sees each person as learning in the same way; they acquire a response repertoire by associating reinforcing events with responses. It is the variation in the reinforcing events that produces individuality. When you, as teacher, want certain changes you help produce them by controlling reinforcing events.

It follows logically from Skinner's general conception that any method of controlling reinforcers (within well-recognized ethical limits) may be used to produce learning. The surer the control, the more desirable the method. Programming procedures guarantee that the student will be reinforced for each response. Using the computer increases the flexibility of the system. A Skinnerian would say that it is responsive to the learner's individuality.

It should be clear by now that Skinner and Murphy are talking about two different kinds of human beings. Murphy wants to pull from the richness of the resources within; Skinner is building a response repertoire and is unwilling to make assumptions about what goes on "inside the skin."

These differences generate different kinds of problems, different research methodologies. What each regards as evidence differs. In theory, each would explain what the other thinks he explains.

Can these dilemmas be resolved? Are we doomed to another twenty years of conflict with eventually another shift in direction? I think not. These two points of view represent a fundamental dilemma in American society which ultimately will have to be resolved. It is likely that the dilemma will be worked out in some way other than by having psychologists resolve their theoretical conflict. Further, the computer revolution will force everyone to face the fact that many teaching tasks can be taken over by computers. The challenge facing us is to find in what ways teachers are uniquely necessary to the education of the young.

RESOLVING THE DIFFERENCES

To this point this article has said little about the specific contribution of educational psychology to the problem described above. At one time educational psychologists became embroiled in resolving differences of this kind so that learning theory could be used profitably by teachers (10). The attempt was interesting but largely unproductive, partly because differences could not be reconciled, partly because people pick their theories on other than completely rational grounds.

The research literature of educational psychology does not resolve the problem. There are no critical experiments demonstrating that one view is better than the other. During Thorndike's day Thorndike-type problems and experiments were performed. During the ascendancy of Gestalt psychology experiments characteristic of that theory were performed. And now we have a resurgence of experiments on operant conditioning and, in education, on programmed instruction.

What the educational psychologist can do is what he has always done: clarify problems, state hypotheses in testable form, devise methods of measuring changes, experiment to produce knowledge. For this he has been trained, as have other kinds of psychologists, many of whom are now working on educational problems. This training and talent might more profitably be put to use testing the hypotheses generated by these differing points of view.

As Murphy has said, his position needs rigorous examination. Other positions also need such examination—not competitively, but by determining if the changes claimed as products do in fact occur. A real need for the fullest application of the scientific method exists; not less research, not less theory, not less observation and clinical experience. Lest this comment be read as, "We need more research," I hasten to add that the kind of research now needed is not necessarily more of the kind that has been available. This research must involve analyses of long-term teacher-student relations, of the effects of teacher characteristics on achieving specific kinds of learnings, of the effects of radically new subject arrangements. The goal should be to find those combinations of teacher characteristics, student characteristics and subject organization which produce desired changes in students.

EXPERIMENTING IN EDUCATION

Murphy's view cannot be tested by simple experiments in ordinary classrooms. The kind of relation between teacher and student he wants simply cannot be built in the standard classroom. Murphy calls for an identification of the student with the teacher as an integral part of the process of learning. This identification "incorporates" the teacher into the personality of the learner, assuming his attitudes and values both consciously and unconsciously. In this way the teacher affects the student's whole life, not just those parts of it involved in subject matter content. Nor are all teachers likely prospects for establishing the kind of relationship Murphy envisions. Further, the whole conception of the curriculum must be changed and teaching methods devised that probably do not exist.

Although a reform movement is now sweeping the schools, it is questionable and debatable whether the reforms are sweeping enough or envision all dimensions of change. As Sizer says, the main criticism of present reforms is that they accept the schools the way they are (11). Murphy's suggestions would entail new curricula, new methods of organizing schools and a different kind of teacher. Thus, change to be effective, to achieve the goals of any of the reformers or theorists or prophets has to be drastic.

To bring these changes in the conservative institution of the school will require a social movement of significant proportions. No such movement is apparent now. However, the means for generating one lie in utilizing the research skills of psychologists, the imagination of theorists and the experience of practicing educators. The funds are now available to support such enterprises. Hopefully, they will be used to try radically new experiments in education. Available money is specifically marked for supporting new enterprises utilizing the cooperative efforts of the researcher and the practitioner.

TRAINING OF TEACHERS

The educational psychologist participates actively in the training of teachers. Educational psychology courses have been part of teacher training programs since Thorndike's days. Because he has shared the training task with others, the psychologist has not had the freedom to shape the kind of program he might like. Most programs for educating teachers divide the labor among psychologists, subject matter specialists and methods experts. Programs are likely to be potpourri of courses and training experiences.

Research of teacher training has been carried on by comparatively few psychologists (12). This research has almost always been designed to test the effects of existing programs. Other experiments in teacher training have worn the label of experiment proudly but unwisely, for their effects were rarely tested.

Again, marked departures from the past are needed. At Stanford University, a research and development center on teacher education has recently been established. This center combines the talents of psychologists, educators, university professors in the humanities and the sciences and the active cooperation of practicing educators. The purpose of the center is to experiment boldly, to mobilize resources to find ways of educating the kinds of teachers that seem needed or desirable.

Interestingly, the first several sessions of the Seminar on Teaching brought out that the two views of teaching described earlier existed in the center. But rather than revive old bickerings the group has committed itself to finding ways of bringing the divergent points of view to bear on problems. Such is the model, in my opinion, of the kind of collaboration that teacher education badly needs.

Certainly, if Murphy's conceptions of teaching are ever to be tested they will have to be tried out with teachers working with pupils. To achieve all of his conception of teaching would require a massive social revolution. But, though that seems presently unlikely, the beginnings of testing these ideas can be made.

CONCLUSION

We have ignored a large number of specific aspects of educational psychology here (such as how psychologists measure intelligence). It is clear that what Murphy is calling for simply has not been done in any extensive way. Nor are the mass of educational psychologists likely to do so. As in the past, those to whom Murphy's ideas appeal will test them.

Basically, what Murphy is calling for is utilizing the full potential for creativeness in the individual. He is willing to visualize new arrangements of curricula, such as specializing in the high school and early years of college, but generalizing in the later years. This provocative suggestion shows Murphy's concern with the creativeness of the individual. Unlike many suggestions for change, this one visualizes a true interdisciplinary creativeness to give the individual depth of insight both into himself and the world in which he lives. Integration needs to be planned for in the educational system, creativeness and imagination stimulated. These are Murphy's goals and hopes.

In such experiments, hopefully large in scale, massive in extent of change, educational psychology can make its greatest contribution to teaching. Further, through continued experimentation with teaching, some advances may be made in finding how humans can be educated to their fullest.

REFERENCES

1. See THORNDIKE, E. L.: *Educat. Psychol.*, Vols. *I, II and III.* New York, Teachers College, Columbia Univ., 1913.
2. Thorndike's ideas are available in selections in JONCICH, G. M. (ed.): *Psychology and the Science of Education: Selected Writings of Edward L. Thorndike.* New York, Teachers College, Columbia Univ., 1962.
3. GETZELS, J., and JACKSON, P.: *Creativity and Intelligence.* New York, Wiley, 1962.
4. See MCDONALD, F. J.: The influence of learning theories on education (1900-1950). In HILGARD, E. (ed.): *Theories of Learning and Instruction,* Sixty-third Yearbook of the National Society for the Study of Education, Part I. Chicago, Univ. of Chicago Press, 1964.
5. See BAGLEY, W. C.: *Determinism in Education.* Baltimore, Warwick and York, 1925. BODE, B. H.: *Conflicting Psychologies of Learning.* New York, Heath, 1929.
6. MURPHY, GARDNER: *Freeing Intelligence through Teaching.* New York, Harper and Brothers, 1961, 28-29.
7. HILGARD, E.: The place of Gestalt psychology and field theories in contemporary learning theory. In HILGARD, E. (ed.): *Theories of Learning and Instruction,* Sixty-third Yearbook of the National Society for the Study of Education, Part I. Chicago, Univ. of Chicago Press, 1964, 54-77.
8. FEIGENBAUM, E. A., and FELDMAN, J. (eds.): *Computers and Thought.* New York, McGraw-Hill, 1963.
9. SKINNER, B. E.: The science of learning and the art of teaching. *Harvard*

Educ. Rev., 24:86-97, 1954. Teaching machines. *Science, 128*:969-977, 1958.

10. HENRY, N. B. (ed.): *The Psychology of Learning,* Forty-first Yearbook of the National Society for the Study of Education, Part II. Chicago, Univ. of Chicago Press, 1942.
11. SIZER, T. B.: Classroom revolution: Reform movement or panacea? *Sat. Rev. Lit.,* 52-54 (June 19), 1965.
12. BELLACK, A. A. (ed.): *Theory and Research in Teaching.* New York, Teacher's College, Columbia Univ., 1963.

Chapter 18

HIGHER EDUCATION AND HUMAN POTENTIALITIES

PAUL HEIST

THE SETTING AND THE OBJECTIVES

DURING the present decade the opportunities for American youth at all educational levels have reached a point undreamed of in most countries of the world. We have long taken pride in a very extensive elementary and secondary school system, both public and private. Since the end of World War II we have seen a tremendous expansion in the facilities and provisions for further education beyond the first twelve years, at least in many states with rapidly increasing populations. In numerous areas the development of community colleges has literally extended the education and training for almost all youth into the thirteenth and fourteenth years. Public colleges and universities now provide four and more years of higher education for unpredicted numbers of young men and women.

When viewing the modern panorama of expanding institutions and programs, much of America must still appear to residents of other countries as a wonderland where the potentialities of the mass of mankind can be realized. This "goodness-for-all" perspective involves an assumption, however, that the various systems and levels of institutions are staffed and programmed to bring all variations in ability, talent and motivation to a greater state of fruition. To judge by the growing demand to enter college this is an unquestioned assumption, and advanced education is probably being seen by most as the essential experience which will lead to the attainment of life's goals.

Human potentialities, particularly those which are capable of being nourished and furthered through formal, educational experiences, can be considered from several perspectives. The generally accepted and often quoted *objectives* of education may appropriately serve to provide one structure for examining the matter of potentialities. Some of the most frequently listed objectives, the attainment of which are proposed as a realization of a whole gamut of potentialities, are the following: attainment of knowledge and skills; growth in wisdom and the ability to reason; understanding of the cultural heritage; acquaintance with the world of ideas; increase in esthetic sensitivity and appreciation of the arts; development of talent and creative expression; preparation for the role of a politically responsible citizen; and psychological growth to greater maturity, autonomy and personal integration.

Educational objectives such as the list above, and especially when they refer to hypothetical developments for a *variety* of people, should perhaps be seen as ideals and guidelines rather than as attainments or results to be realized by all.

Education of all to the optimum level of their ability and interest is something of a cliche. But, the potentialities of human beings that can presumably be furthered through post-high school educational experiences are sundry and diverse. Traits and characteristics which may be developed in the college setting, supposedly representing a shift from potentiality to actuality, have their origin in the unique possibilities of each student. But, simultaneously, much more than is promised in the stated objectives must be accomplished for the mass of youth in a democratic society.

THE LIMITED IMPACT OF A COLLEGE EDUCATION

Most college faculty members are not so naive as to suggest that the majority of students attain the changes in behavior implied in the usual set of objectives. However, there is a persisting "folklore" about the presumed accomplishments of higher education which appears to be contradictory to the suggested or existing facts. Apparently some leaders and administrators continue to believe that important, common goals are achieved for those students who finish four or more years. Numerous institutions, large and small, of great and of little fame, receive financial support and assistance by propagating a myth about the benefits and values attained by the students who graduate from their programs.

Many colleges and universities, as well as the whole educational establishment, can probably provide a body of evidence that would imply general success and acknowledgeable attainments—to the satisfaction of taxpayers in the mass, legislatures and other supporting constituencies. In fact, such "proof" is frequently attempted by many specific institutions and some state programs. But it should be noted that the evidence submitted is invariably of a "headcounting" nature; for example, data are often presented about the *number* of graduates who continued in graduate or professional schools, entered established service professions or became prominent businessmen, research scientists and/or governmental leaders. Generally lacking is any information about the quality of an education received or the resulting caliber of the graduates, individually or as a group; also lacking is information about the activities of graduates in their roles as citizens or about their lives as *educated* men. One major study that may be cited as providing some exceptions to these criticisms is embodied in the report by Haveman and Salter (3).

The effect and influence of college, especially as related to *change* in specific characteristics and the furtherance of certain potentialities, has received somewhat more rigorous investigation and evaluation than may be implied in the above comments. The work along these lines has been reviewed and summarized in a number of publications. At least two of these represent comprehensive surveys of the research conducted over several decades (Jacob [8], Webster, *et al.* [18]). A more recent review encompasses the studies completed since 1960 (Boyer and Michaels [1]).

Among the studies reported in these surveys are a number in which the measured "potentiality" of persons at one point, for example, entrance to college, is compared with attainments at some future time. For the most part, the measurements in such studies of what might be defined as potentialities are rather limited. Except for the inclusion of tests of academic ability and measures of a few selected attitudes and values, the complex of human behavior is never assessed. However, better studies have included human traits and characteristics which are relevant to academic motivation, learning activities and modifications in thinking or behavior and supposedly related to formal college experiences.

The most repeated finding indicates that students do change on a general dimension of conservatism *versus* liberalism. This appears to be the case whether the particular focus is on political attitudes, religious beliefs and practices or social concerns (Webster *et al.* [18]). Since early studies by Newcomb (12) on the effects of four years at Bennington, later research has confirmed that a majority of students become significantly less conservative. However, for the mass of students in the respective educational settings, changes in attitudes and values appear to be far from extensive.* Thus, consistent with the finding about some change in attitudes and values during the college years is the concomitant finding regarding the relatively limited change in the majority of cases.

An increasing concern about the true effects of college has led to some studies in the past decade in which the first respectable provisions have been made to deal with effect of maturation. An initial investigation by Plant (13) represented a serious attempt to compare the extent of the influence of college experiences with other influences outside of the formal educational setting. As a control or reference group Plant used samples of students who had withdrawn from college voluntarily. He found that for matched samples, the students who remained in college for two years became less ethnocentric while those who withdrew did not change.

Plant found a basis for a little different interpretation, however,

---

* The findings on change in attitudes, values and general orientations are confounded in most studies with the fact that all students in a sample are treated as *a group* through the use and comparison of average scores. Very seldom have the analyses of data involved categorizations among students on initial measurements, for example, "liberals" *versus* "conservatives" or "very bright" *versus* "less bright," to enable measurement of the amount of change for different "types" of students. The different experiences, due to different curricula or peer relations, have also been overlooked too often, that is, as they relate to amount of change on designated variables.

in the findings of a later study in which persons in a noncollege comparison group also showed a change in their attitudes in the same direction as those who attended college, though not to the same extent (Plant [14]). These results led him to suggest that the changes found in college students are mostly an acceleration of the normal developments for young persons in the general population. A more recent investigation by Telford and Plant (16) provided evidence to substantiate this previous interpretation. In a comprehensive study of junior college students, including several comparison groups, the lack of significant differences among the groups in the amount of measured change led them to question the hypothesized or expected impact of college, at least as far as effectively influencing attitudes and values.

In an extensive investigation of high school graduates, followed as college-going and noncollege-going samples, Trent and Medsker (17) did find significant differences between the two samples in the amount of change measured after four years, with the youth who completed college showing considerably greater change. Those who only completed two years of college also changed, but the amount differed significantly from those who received their B.A. degree. Since the results of these recent and more adequate studies by Telford and Plant and Trent and Medsker lead to dissimilar findings and unlike conclusions, we are left with continuing uncertainty about the impact of college on nonintellectual characteristics. Some reasons for this may be found in the different types of colleges involved in the respective studies. But great changes are not reported, in any case; and Plant contends that careful analyses or use of better control groups will show most differences to be nonsignificant.

Obviously, the studies briefly reviewed do not begin to provide answers to questions such as the following: To what extent do the typical college experiences bring the average student to greater personal involvement in the world of art and music, to higher levels of aesthetic awareness and appreciation, to a more satisfactory avocational life and to new bases for continuous living as an educated or intellectual person? To this question one can safely hypothesize a simple answer, and it is very much in the negative. The expectations implied may be achieved for a minority; but the size of this changed minority, graduating from most public and private institutions, would probably prove to be a shocking surprise to the interested educators and citizens.

To what extent does a typical college education lead to interested and participative citizenship, to active leadership and involvement in our democratic society, to an intelligent concern for local, state and national issues and to ethical concerns about the welfare of all citizens and the equality of opportunity? To this multi-faceted query the answer is less simple than to the one above, if one is to judge by the findings of recent studies at the Center for the Study of Higher Education at Berkeley; but the response is also very much in the negative. A minority of students appear to change positively, in some colleges more than others, and their interests and inclinations in this political area are brought to a level of greater involvement. However, greater political and human concern for most students, to the extent of taking constructive stands and leadership, cannot be inferred from the small measured changes in attitudes and opinions between the first and last years of college. Perhaps the more telling evidence, also in the way of a negative answer, can be obtained from some of the conditions in our society where a "sophisticated maintenance" of social incongruities or failures to resolve social problems is part and parcel of the lives of our *educated,* adult public.

To those who may not concur in the above questions or answers, who may argue that the importance of education centers essentially in acquiring knowledge and skills and in gaining preparation for a vocation, there are a few fairly obvious rebuttals. But, granting for the moment the merit and importance of acquiring knowledge and vocational training, the fallacies and inadequacies of formal education in this respect also are easily pointed out. For most undergraduates, much of what they study is only indirectly related, if at all, to their future occupations. Thus, one might ask what much of the course work is supposedly related to and whether the myth of a liberal arts education for large numbers of college youth should continue to be perpetuated, especially since the evidence shows limited effectiveness along these lines.

SOURCES OF INADEQUACY AND FAILURE

Underlying the proposed approach to viewing human potentialities in higher education is the assumption that the implied expectations, that is, the attainment of specific objectives, are possible to varying degrees for all college-going youth. An effective educational program, supposedly taking the differences among students into consideration, would help all students to develop in the *direction* of the ultimate goals, thus at least approaching the potential of all individuals. Obviously, the objectives are or must be seen as relative since the potentials of students are exceedingly diverse. Their attainment will be represented in relative changes in attitudes or increments of knowledge and understanding rather than in common performance criteria or specified levels of achievement.

The Enigma of Individual Differences

The reference to both the relativity of goals and the fact of individual differences brings into focus one of the persisting and perplexing problem areas of all education. The tremendous human variety in all intellectual and nonintellectual characteristics has been called to the attention of countless administrators and faculty for the past half century (Learned and Wood [9]). The importance of recognizing the diversity among students has been given increasing emphasis in the past decade (Stern and Cope [15], Heist and Webster [5], Heist [4], McConnell [10], McConnell and Heist [11], Darley [2]).

However, in actual practice, even currently, recognition has been given only to the significant variations among students. A few colleges, such as Antioch, Goddard and Bennington, to name a few, make special provisions to accommodate their students by diversification and flexibility within their overall programs. A growing number of colleges appear to respect the diversity among students chiefly by admitting only those above certain levels of ability. Other colleges utilize honors work and independent study as partial accommodations for the variety of students they admit. Except for these examples, in which the attention to the problem is actually fairly specialized and directed to limited numbers, most college faculties continue to teach as if all students were of one mold or at least very similar. In reality, the latter is never the case, and failure to understand human dissimilarities is too often directly related to successes and/or failures in particular institutions.

It is being suggested here, perhaps a little too mildly, that the goals and objectives of education are a much lesser determinant of what happens to students than are the important differences among students. Several investigations have provided strong evidence that the students who attain the most in college enter with a readiness to gain and achieve more than other students (Holland [7], Heist *et al.* [6]). It is more strongly suggested that the very limited attention, if any, given to the distinguishing student characteristics serves as one significant reason for the very limited development of much human potential. The transmission of knowledge and the development of reasoning capability are definitely handicapped where and when teachers will not attempt to look at the variations in students' perceptions and motivation. Appreciation of the arts and/or increasing interests in citizenship are similarly curtailed when the differences among students are ignored, when specific objectives are not implemented in the operative program and when appropriate opportunities are not included among students' experiences.

Resistance to Change

Successful or effective learning leading to behavioral change has been described as a process involving some rejection of previous learning and a certain amount of intraindividual conflict. It could be argued that when some rejection or questioning of earlier learning and some conflict are not involved, at least at the college level, reeducation and true change have probably not taken place. This suggests that the learning or relearning process is not an easy one, thus introducing another reason for the results of studies which show that college students do not change much in the way of basic commitments, attitudes and learning habits. This matter of the difficulty of effecting significant changes draws support from the fields of social work and psychotherapy, chiefly indicating that most persons after certain ages seem to persist in basic behavior and thinking previously established.

The early "building blocks" of sound personality development have literally resulted in overlearning and anchoring "fixations," at least for a majority. The early and later provisions for experiencing trust, security and important identifications (family, religion, peers and significant models) effect an essential stability and concomitant inflexibility that will withstand many potent influences, good and bad. Consequently, a normal childhood may result in a "negative" carryover. For far too many youths an enduring basic pattern has been established by seventeen years of age. This inhibiting, human condition and its effect are not lessened by the situational factors.

Few institutions are blessed with enough challenging and constructive teaching to sufficiently free the individual from his past, to induce conflict gradually and to prepare him, according to *his* fears, needs and aspirations, for meaningful psychological rebuilding and reexamination of guiding attitudes and values.

It is not impossible to educate individuals to change, even those with the strongest anchorage in their past. This is not being suggested or maintained. But the difficulty of changing, after certain age levels, is an imposing, determining factor, especially under the pervading ways and means of modern higher education. Because of the nuclei for problems and difficulties inherent in the individual students, the faculty and the inadequate learning procedures, the potentialities of many are sidetracked time and again.

INSTITUTIONAL DETERMINANTS

The two major sources of difficulty just described, acting to prevent the optimal education and development of most students, can chiefly be seen as such in existing, institutional contexts. It has been intimated that the prevalent problem centered in individual differences was largely one of lack of awareness, limited perception and disinterest on the part of the faculty. The problem of resistance to change, as it effects education and learning, was also introduced as contingent upon ineffective learning experiences and a paucity of dynamic instruction. Closer focusing on the faculty is in line with the growing trend to investigate a number of institutional characteristics as academic influences of considerable importance.

More and more the conditions or situations that stem from the operation and environmental aspects of colleges and universities are being examined and criticized. The conditions and situations include such as the following: the matter of excessive enrollments; large classes; rigid adherence to formality and regimentation; traditionalism of procedures; lack of experimentation and innovation; uncommitted and disinterested faculty; poor or faulty instruction; lack of integration among areas and different learning experiences; strict supervision and regulation of student activities; conforming or restrictive nonintellectual peer cultures; and predominant majorities of poorly motivated students. The last two are examples of secondary social-environmental "forces" in that they have an origin in the traits of students but directly and indirectly exert influences on many members of a student body.

Only two aspects of the contextual climates, both centered in the faculty, will be briefly examined to illustrate environmental sources of negative effects on students. A combination of faulty institutional conditions are probably basic to a very frequent, current criticism regarding student-faculty relations and a great depersonalization in college and university settings. Psychological growth and development is, to a very great degree, a social or interactional process. And, effective learning for many demands a relational involvement. This involvement, when present in the learning process, obviously takes numerous forms, depending in part on individual personality and characteristics. The criticism about lack of personalization has been expressed repeatedly by students from both large *and* small campuses. Apparently, there are different sets of conditions underlying the atmospheres of colleges and universities which cause many campus climates and classroom situations to be generally perceived as cold, impersonal and not conducive to intrinsic involvement in the learning process.

Campus social climates and classroom atmospheres represent a growing concern, since the means of obtaining reward and necessary reinforcement, so essential in the learning of many students, may be very limited or lacking, if not entirely impossible.

In institutions of very large enrollments, especially of a nonresidential nature, and in others with a heavy emphasis on academic competition, desirable contacts and relationships between students and adults are either nonexistent or severely jeopardized and limited. In a growing number of schools the possible constructive changes in individuals become chiefly a matter of fortuity, and serious thoughts and efforts from faculty about the furtherance or the development of human potentialities are few and far between.

According to the findings from two studies at the Berkeley Center, the sustaining intimacy of human relationships is gained mostly through and with peers, but unfortunately these associations have usually developed by chance and happenstance. Thus, roommates and a few friends become the major source of reward and approbation, provide most of the counsel and advice and are the only ones to lend a ready ear in time of trouble. For the mass of students the possibly valuable influence of significant adults is rapidly becoming restricted to the questionable classroom situation of large lectures and very infrequent seminars.

As a second aspect of the institutional context, relevant to the question of personalization and influential experiences, faculties in their generally perceived instructional role are seemingly becoming an agent of decreasing importance and can be viewed as a problem variable. Since other sources of impact are persistently more effective in determining what happens to students, one might ask about the problems inherent in the faculty as a professional group that derive from the circumstances of their current position?

This question actually opens up an area for separate attention, too voluminous to give more than cursory treatment here. Some pertinent problems related directly to the subject at hand can, however, be listed. For example, most college teachers have never studied nor shown an interest in learning about teaching methods, the principles of learning nor the dynamics of classroom or seminar procedures. They perform over the years as stumbling, naive amateurs, presumably confident that whatever they do or say will serve or can be credited as teaching. A majority in most faculties, whatever their degree of interest in pedagogy and its improvement, can never be described as anything but mediocre lecturers or discussion leaders and second-rate teachers.

An increasing consideration in the lives of professors in numerous institutions is the growing complexity of their involvement in matters beyond scholarship and instruction. Recently this has become a real concern of students and not a few administrators on scattered campuses. What has become known as "the withdrawal from the classroom" had its origin in the expected research and scholarship for most men. Investigations and publications led countless faculty into new vistas in the years following World War II. This was abetted by the long-established "publish or perish" milieu now in some way affecting almost all college teachers.

The total picture for thousands of college teachers today, confounded by matters of recognition, status and advancement, includes emphasis on research, deadlines on papers, speeches and reports, service on intramural and extramural committees and extended time given to consulting work and traveling. Some of the remaining time may be given to preparation of course work and to occasional meetings with individuals and student groups. The great institutional accommodations for the "loss" of numerous professors is, of course, the use of teaching assistants and new instructional techniques. And, in this way, "school is kept," with little planning or effort given to recognized failures in the teaching of students and with only isolated attempts at innovation or renovation.

CONCLUSION

The chief thesis in this chapter is that the system of higher education, with all its diversity in structure, facilities and types of organizations, is not up to the task "assigned" to it and does not provide the setting or program for the realization of a variety of human potentialities. The objectives of higher education, which are accepted as general goals by most educators, might be utilized as genuine models of important potentialities and characteristics to be achieved through college experiences. Before student potentialities can become actualities, however, certain negative and distracting factors which affect the academic process and student-faculty relationship will have to be changed.

REFERENCES

1. Boyer, E. L., and Michael, W. B.: The outcome of college. In Pullias, E. (ed.): *Higher Education. Rev. Educ, Res., 35*:4, 1965 (forthcoming).
2. Darley, J. G.: *Promise and Performance: A Study of Ability and Achievement in Higher Education.* Berkeley, California, Center for the Study of Higher Education, Univ. of California, 1962.
3. Haveman, E., and Salter, P. S.: *They Went to College.* New York, Harcourt, Brace, 1952.
4. Heist, P.: Diversity in college student characteristics. *J. Educ. Soc., 33*:279-291, 1960.
5. Heist, P., and Webster, H.: Differential characteristics of student bodies—implications for selection and study of undergraduates. In *Selection and Educational Differentiation.* Berkeley, California, Center for the Study of Higher Education, 1960, pp. 91-106.
6. Heist, P., McConnell, T. R., Matsler, F., and Williams, P.: Personality and scholarship. *Science, 133*:362-367, 1961.
7. Holland, J. L.: Undergraduate origins of American scientists. *Science, 126*:433-437, 1957.
8. Jacob, P. E.: *Changing Values in College.* New York, Harper and Brothers, 1957.
9. Learned, W. S., and Wood, B. D.: *The Student and His Knowledge:* A report to the Carnegie Foundation on the results of the high school and college exams, of 1928, 1930 and 1932, Bulletin 29. New York, The Carnegie Foundation for the Advancement of Teaching, 1938.
10. McConnell, T. R.: Problems of distributing students among institutions with varying characteristics. *North Cent. Ass. Quart., 35*:226-238, 1961.
11. McConnell, T. R., and Heist, P.: The diverse college student population. In Sanford, N. (ed.): *The American College.* New York, Wiley, 1961.
12. Newcomb, T. M.: *Personality and Social Change.* New York, Dryden, 1943.
13. Plant, W. T.: Changes in ethnocentrism associated with a two-year college experience. *J. Genet. Psychol., 92*:189-197, 1958.
14. Plant, W. T.: *Personality Changes Associated With a College Education.* San Jose, California, San Jose State College (Final report, U. S. Office of Education, Cooperative Research Branch Project 348), 1962.
15. Stern, G. G., and Cope, A. H.: Differences in educability between stereopaths, non-stereopaths, and rationals. Paper presented at the American Psychological Association Convention, Chicago, September, 1956.

16. Telford, C. W., and Plant, W. T.: *The Psychological Impact of the Public Two-Year College on Certain Non-Intellectual Functions.* San Jose, California, San Jose State College (U. S. Office of Education, Cooperative Research Branch Project 8646), 1963.
17. Trent, J. W., and Medsker, L. L.: *The Emergence of America's Young Adults* (Characteristics and Backgrounds of High School Graduates and Their Subsequent Personal and Educational Development). Berkeley, California, Center for the Study of Higher Education, University of California (U. S. Office of Education, Cooperative Research Branch Project 1328), Publication forthcoming, 1965.
18. Webster, H., Freedman, M., and Heist, P.: Personality changes in college students. In Sanford, N. (ed.): *The American College.* New York, Wiley, 1961.

PART IV

CONTRIBUTIONS OF THE DISCIPLINES

Chapter 19

THE THERAPIST AND HUMAN POTENTIALITIES

C. H. HARDIN BRANCH

IN general, psychotherapy has been directed at the patient with the general formulation that the patient was an intact person before he was incapacitated by some sort of noxious element or stress situation. This presumably occurred at some time or other in the individual's life, and the therapist takes the position that once the effects of this stress have been eliminated, the individual can return to his previous good level of adjustment. It is obvious in many instances that the person has never really attained a very good level of adjustment, but certainly the intent of the therapist is to eliminate blocks to healthy activities. What happens when the blocks are eliminated is largely left up to the initiative of the patient.

Unfortunately, there is very little concern with the healthy factors in an individual's life. Presumably, it should be possible to correct a situation by pressure on one or the other end of the seesaw which has been tipped in the direction of ill health. In other words, if stresses have pushed the individual down toward incapacity, it might be possible to push on the "up" end of the seesaw or to lift the "down" end, either effort eventually resulting in a restoration of balance. In this connection it might be well to note that there has long been a tendency on the part of psychiatrists and others to equate pathology with incapacity. The two things may certainly exist at the same time, but it is not always true that an individual may be incapacitated by the pathology. It may be entirely possible that a person may be incapacitated by social maladjustments which are only indirectly related to the psychopathology and considerably more accessible to therapy.

For instance, a young lady with a history of a great deal of sexual experience with her father and all the resultant difficulties and attitudes toward growing up, toward sexually mature behavior, etc., complained of loneliness and social incapacity. It seemed to the therapist that while there was no question that there existed in her considerable deep-seated difficulties, largely stemming from her willingness—if not actual eagerness—to engage in sexual practices with her father and her inability to deal with these ideas, her real social incapacity arose from social awkwardness and a considerable naivete in social matters. It was suggested, therefore, that along with an attempt to deal with the deeper seated problems, she get contact lenses, obtain some training in cooking and entertaining, take dancing lessons, etc. Since she had excellent intelligence, charm and knowledge of music, it was not too difficult for her to establish a social life which vastly increased her appraisal of herself as an individual and was probably largely if not entirely responsible for her eventually achieving a good marital adjustment and a success as a wife and a homemaker.

It is perfectly obvious that a good many people find these strengths for themselves. Cole (1) has found that a large number of individuals who are not diagnosed as mentally ill actually do have psychopathology which should be incapacitating; but these individuals have found ways of dealing with life's situations which depend upon religious support, the support of individuals in the neighborhood, recreational outlets and various character strengths which exist in themselves and which are sufficient to prevent their being overwhelmed by the psychopathology. There have been too few surveys of this sort, but an interesting one was reported by Bond (2) who said: "Many neurotic traits in families and many faults in persons can be compensated by abilities of other family members or in individuals and . . . the normal is the person whose abilities allow neurotic traits and other faults to be managed." I had an opportunity to participate in this study which in summary involved psychiatric and psychologic evaluations of members of the student bodies of three Eastern schools, and I remember well that a fair number of these people had either physical disabilities or some emotional difficulties which would have been considered incapacitating and probably would have been if they had not been so courageously handled by these individuals.

It is certain that there are many strengths which the individual could realize in himself if he were only given the opportunity. I am speaking now about those individuals who do show up for psychotherapy. It is unnecessary to belabor further the point that we could learn a great deal by the study of those individuals who have maintained themselves without recourse to psychotherapy, by the use of these strengths which they have found either accidentally or with the help of others.

It is unnecessary to list these various strengths in a personality. Religious faith can be a strong supporting factor, as can imagination and flexibility in an individual, the capacity to accept success without undue humility, the capacity to gain from constructive relationships with other people (and sometimes the luck to find such friends), technical training which fits into the social needs and consequently leads to economic satisfactions, etc.

My concern, however, is not with these factors which people find for themselves. I have already indicated that my concern is primarily with the ways in which the psychotherapist should concern himself with the strengths in the personality rather than with the pathology. A good discussion of the behaviors of individuals who find help outside the standard psychotherapeutic channels may be found in "Americans View Their Mental Health," Series No. 4 of the Joint Commission Report (3), and a smaller report carried in the article by Cole, already referred to.

On the treatment side it is certainly obvious that there is much less preoccupation with the strengths in individuals than should be the case. There has even been a tendency to depreciate the normalcy of individuals and to have a sort of impression that every individual has some neurotic activity at work, whether or not it is obvious to the observer. What is not so obvious is that the vast majority of people are functioning in spite of or even because of this neurotic activity, and presumably the therapist might be able to help others function better if he identified and exploited the strengths in their personalities rather than attempting to ferret out the neurotic difficulties. Fleming (4) says: "Freud . . . was rubbing out any sharp line that might be thought to divide neurotics from 'normal' people. In fact, it was he, more than anyone else, who put the quotation marks around *normal* and made people sheepish about saying it." The present day psychotherapist must, in my opinion, deal not so much with the normal *versus* abnormal continuum but with the functioning *versus* incapacitated continuum and attempt to determine from his study of the patient what is the optimum point of therapeutic approach, what might be called the *locus minoris resistentiae* for the therapeutic attack. The question of the psychotherapist is, of course, how best to identify these strengths and how best to make use of them. It is impossible to go into all the ways in which the psychotherapist might help the individual locate and develop the strengths which will enable him to handle his personality difficulties in a more efficient way. It might be well at this point to insert a plea for further investigative work in these areas. The various criticisms directed at psychotherapy, usually surrounding the obvious fact that this is a time-consuming and expensive process with sometimes uncertain or at least unproven results, have made many of us wish for research in attempts to ascertain which, if any, factors in the psychotherapeutic process are most useful, what results can be expected, how those results can be predicted, etc. Of one thing we may be sure: The doctrinaire psychotherapeutic approach, however reassuring it may be to the psychotherapist, has not—at least for any "school" of which I have any knowledge—sufficient *demonstrated* superiority to justify our choosing one approach to the exclusion of others. The crying need is for flexibility, but we should somehow or other be able to measure the usefulness of experimental or new approaches to psychotherapeutic problems. Without this we are guilty of a "shotgun" type of therapy in which no evaluation is possible. We are not yet so rich in psychotherapists that we can afford this lavishness.

Perhaps it would be useful to focus on one area—that is the appraisal which the individual has of himself in relationship to his environment, including the people in it. Environmental manipulation in psychotherapy has always had a rather low status value;

but since most of the patient's difficulties will stem from some disturbance in his relationships, in the final analysis there must be some alteration of the individual-environment interreaction, whether this change comes from working with the individual himself or with the environment around him. As Howell (5) puts it: "All forms of psychotherapy, regardless of the approach of the psychotherapist, depend upon the quantitative improvement of self-esteem in the subject being treated. Self-image can be improved in many ways. Good fortune, accomplishment, acceptance by others, and 'religious revelation' are some of the environmental forces which may effect a change in the individual's feelings toward himself." We have previously touched on some ways in which an alteration in an individual's attitude toward himself can be achieved (6). Even so, admittedly some individuals are much more comfortable in feeling that the psychotherapist should somehow or other magically produce these changes without their having to take the responsibility for it. Patients have often become accustomed to looking at themselves as inadequate, ill-favored or unlucky people, and it sometimes requires a great deal of perserverance on the part of the therapist to identify the real strengths which exist and then patiently to help the individual himself to see that there are these assets which can be turned to account. As Jaspers (7) says: "The individual is always more than he knows or can know himself to be or than anyone else knows him to be."

Bettelheim (8), in discussing his attempt to reach an understanding of the phenomena he observed in a series of concentration camps, came to the conclusion that the strengths were far more important than the neurotic difficulties in determing whether or not an individual would succeed under these very stressful conditions. He says: ". . . What counts or what constitutes the good life under normal conditions is living a subtle balance between individual aspirations, society's rightful demands and man's nature . . ." and he comments specifically on ". . . the Jehovah Witnesses who not only showed unusual height of human dignity and moral behavior but seemed protected against the same camp experience that soon destroyed persons considered very well integrated by my psychoanalytic friends and myself." He adds: "To prefer compensation for pathology to the normal . . . is a dangerous moral position, both in psychotherapy and in society. It emphasizes the tragic and spectacular and slights the salt of the earth—what makes the common happiness and the good life, namely, living a sane and relatively happy life with one's family and friends."

It is, of course, not easy for the therapist to be sure of his ground in recommending a course of action for his patients. It is obvious that he can suggest changes toward the development of social skills and he possibly may be able to suggest increased technical training or vocational guidance which may make the individual more likely to improve his economic condition and his satisfaction with the world about him. The mere fact that he believes sufficiently in his patients to insist that changes can be made is in itself a supporting and reassuring thing.

Unfortunately, however, most psychotherapists are inclined to be comfortable only within their own socioeconomic experiences, and these may be quite narrow as compared to the range of problems presented by their patients. Considerable imagination and inventiveness may be necessary if the psychotherapist is to suggest changes in approaches in areas which lie outside his own experiences. Redlich (9) feels that psychiatrists have a good deal of difficulty with individuals from "the lower classes." He says: " . . . They dislike these patients, were particularly annoyed and dismayed by their crudeness and aggression, their sex mores, their inability to express themselves, their need to be reassured and supported and their unwillingness and inability to help themselves by understanding themselves." It may be that it is precisely because these people do openly demand reassurance and support that those of us who are inclined to insist that psychotherapy consist only of their developing an understanding of themselves—which involves a preoccupation with their psychopathology rather than in their understanding that side of themselves which is positive, supportive and helpful—may well be uncomfortable with these people whose attention at least initially, is focused away from the areas with which we are accustomed to deal.

There are two types of patients in whom this approach, namely that of concentrating on the strengths in the personality, seems particularly applicable. These are the old people of both sexes and the mature woman in the fourth to sixth decades of her life.

With reference to the elderly people, there is usually considerable preoccupation with what the individuals cannot do. It is certainly true in our culture that the elderly are not valued as depositories of wisdom since we have better records than their memories; and since, in any event, life changes so rapidly that what they remember of the "good old days" is more than likely to be boring rather than enlightening. We are inclined, in fact, to depreciate their repeated stories of significant family events by referring to Grandpa's "anecdotage." Actually, many geriatric living arrangements have been successful simply because they focused on the fact that these elderly people do have interests which can be developed and new skills which can be exploited. Even in such matters as placement in a hospital, for example, the ability of the older person to live much in the past can make hospital adjustment much easier if we allow the old person to surround himself with the mementos, photographs, etc., which play into his wealth of thoughts about individuals and happenings in his past. Refusal to consider the dreary aspects of one's existence and the insistence that a knowledge of the World Series or an interest in any television show or the ability to walk two and a half blocks are far more significant than the individual's physical frailties—this therapeutic approach may well make the difference between a crippled older person and an older person who is making the most of what he or she has.

In the case of women in the fourth to sixth decades it is essential that the physician who has an opportunity to see these people before they reach the psychiatrist make every effort to prepare them for the period when they will no longer be able to think of themselves as mothers or potential mothers, as heads of growing households or as useful, energetic housekeepers. As the children move away and as the woman can no longer bear children and also as the increase in mechanization or the increased use of apartments and similar living arrangements make her contribution to the care of the house less important, she may wind up in a situation in which she is making inordinate demands on her environment for the sense of self-esteem which she had when she was more active in these other areas. Since her environment is quite often made up of individuals who are undergoing some of these same stresses, it is unlikely that she can find in her bridge group or her social organizations the sort of individual support which she needs. Theoretically, of course, it is precisely at this time that the real strengths in her personality should be most available to her, when she is no longer tied to her own physiology, and it is precisely here that the physician who has seen this event coming or the psychiatrist who is called upon to advise her regarding the various neurotic difficulties is in a position to utilize the real strengths in her personality by insisting that she make arrangements for additional technical training, that she get a job, that she move into completely new areas of activity, etc. It would, of course, be optimal if some preliminary training for this period were undertaken years before. A very worthwhile experiment in this area is being carried on by Lazar (10) and others who are employing women in this age group to act as volunteer workers in various kinds of mental hygiene clinic activities. An important element in this project is the screening of the people for the positions and an equally important point is the fact that they are being paid for the work they do. Exploration of the labor market possibilities for these mature, sophisticated and physically active women would undoubtedly open up many avenues and areas where their skills could be used. The psychotherapist who attempts to treat difficulties of this sort by focusing on the realistic elements of the individual's despair or the nervous symptoms is concentrating on entirely the wrong aspect of the total situation.

In summary, it is an obvious though often neglected fact that all individuals contain strengths or potential strengths which help them achieve a flexible and efficient adjustment to living, and in those individuals who, for one reason or another, reach the psychotherapist's office, these strengths are still available for use in the psychotherapeutic process. The occupational hazard in psychotherapy is to concentrate on the psychopathology. Every effort must be made to determine whether or not the individual's incapacity is due to the psychopathology alone or whether there are other elements more accessible to therapeutic approach which can be used to restore the individual's balance and his capacity to deal with his environment. In many instances, a few of which are briefly discussed, it should be possible for the psychotherapist to concentrate on the strengths in the individual's personality, exploiting the potentials existing in the individual's personality structure and thus support his reestablishing the balance which he needs to function again as an efficient human being.

REFERENCES

1. Cole, N. J., Branch, C. H. H., and Shaw, O. M.: Mental illness—a survey assessment of community rates, attitudes and adjustments. *AMA Arch. Neur. Psych., 4*:393-398, 1957.
2. Bond, E. D.: The student council study. *Amer. J. Psychiat., 107*:271, 1951.
3. Gurin, G., Feld, S., and Veroff, J.: *Americans View Their Mental Health.* Series No. 4, Joint Commission Report. New York, Basic Books, 1960.
4. Fleming, D.: The meaning of mental illness. *The Atlantic Monthly,* 72-76 (July), 1964.
5. Howell, I. L.: Delinquency and sociopathy. *Rocky Mountain Med. J., 61*:29-34 (Oct.), 1964.
6. Branch, C. H. H.: *Therapy Sine Psychotherapy.* In Masserman, J. H. (ed.): *Current Psychiatric Therapies,* Vol. *II.* New York and London, 1962, pp. 1-9.
7. Jaspers, C.: *General Psychopathology.* Chicago, Univ. of Chicago Press, 1964. Translated by J. Horning and M. W. Hamilton, p. 767.
8. Bettelheim, B.: *The Informed Heart.* Glencoe, Free Press, 1963.
9. Redlich, F.: Psychoanalysis and the problem of values. *Psychoanalysis and Human Values.* In Masserman, J. H. (ed.): *Science and Psychoanalysis,* Vol. *III.* New York and London, Grune and Stratton, 1960, p. 87.
10. Lazar, I.: Personal communication.

Chapter 20

TESTING FOR POTENTIALITIES

ALFRED B. HEILBRUN, JR.

TRAVELERS between two communities in southeast Iowa have recently encountered a series of highway signs sponsored by a furniture store in one of the cities. These signs boldly exclaim, "Keep bullfighting out of Cedar Rapids." Surprise and perplexity rather quickly merge into amused contemplation of the incongruity and illogic of the frenetic bullfighting scene materializing in this conservative farmbelt. In a real sense, the title of this chapter is equally incongruous and illogical. Considering psychological tests as they are typically conceptualized and potentialities as Webster defines them, one cannot test for a potentiality. Why this is so will be discussed in the first section. The next section, in a more constructive vein, will propose what would be required to measure human potential. Finally, the problem of testing for educational potential will be considered in way of translating the issues of potentiality testing from the abstract into more socially significant terms.

BASIC PROPERTIES OF A TEST

A psychological test can be considered as an economical procedure by which human behavior can be rendered predictable. Since it is commonly accepted that the best basis for predicting future human behavior is past human behavior, economy has applied to the question *how much* behavior is to be examined before we assume to predict. The impetus for the psychological testing movement can be traced historically to the social-military conditions of World War I which required the crude screening of large numbers of military recruits to identify those who were least likely to make the adjustment to service. The Woodworth Neurotic Inventory, crude by present testing standards, nevertheless served a purpose in demonstrating that a set number of questions inquiring into past and present behaviors offered at least limited utility in predicting behavioral events.

The requirements that a test be an economic sample of behavior only begins to tell the story. Obviously the test must be a sample of some behavior in particular. The test behavior (content) is selected because it bears relationships to the variable to be measured either in the judgment of some expert or as an empirically demonstrated fact. In either case the relationship may be in the nature of a sample or a sign.

A *sampling* test elicits responses from the person which are qualitatively the same as the responses to be predicted. For example, the Wechsler Adult Intelligence Scale (13) includes subtests designed to measure various aspects of intellectual functioning. If the person performs capably in these circumscribed intellectual tasks, it is expected (and predicted) that he will perform capably in more extensive naturalistic situations requiring the same or related intellectual functions.

Test content as a *sign* of the variable being assessed would be indicated when the content is qualitatively distinct from the behavior to be predicted but related to it for some known or unknown reason. Intentional instances of sign-type tests are relatively infrequent, although the incidence of tests that "work" for which the sampling premise is erroneously accepted may be higher than we think. Obviously, if we can predict behavior from test content and we have not sampled that behavior, the test is of the sign variety. The Rorschach Inkblot Test (12) is one well-known illustration of a sign-type test. Chromatic color responses are interpreted as indicants of emotional responsiveness, yet no one would argue that perceiving a green worm *is* an emotional response.

Now what has all of this to do with testing for potentialities? To paraphrase Webster's dictionary, a potentiality can be defined as "that which exists in possibility, not in actuality." However, test construction has traditionally proceeded, whether a sample or sign approach is used, with the requirement of test validity in mind. Simply stated, validity requires that performance on a test relate in a specified manner to a behavioral criterion, the predictive target. An intelligence or achievement test should predict the formal educability of the child, a personality test of dominance should predict the leadership behavior of the person, and a vocational interest test should predict the future job satisfaction of the individual. Each validity criterion represents an observable (and thus measurable) dimension of behavior, for if psychometrics has learned anything from behavioristic psychology, it is that test-based inferences must be rooted at the prediction end in observables. The failure to adhere to this tenet most certainly has made it possible for tests to remain available for usage long beyond the time that rigorous validation procedures would have clearly sounded the warning signal.

Accepting as we must the necessity for validation of our testing instruments, it becomes clear that we test for the opposite of a potentiality, namely, "that which exists in actuality, not in possibility." That is true because the meaning of "actuality" to behavioristic science is given only in terms of what we can observe and in principle can reduce to measurement. As stated above, this is a procedural requirement for test validation.

Certain testing procedures may beguile us into believing that we are going beyond the predictive limitations of "actual" behavior in the direction of behavioral potential. This is especially the case with projective techniques which purport to (and probably do) delve into less accessible fantasy and preconscious tiers of cognitive function. Extreme caution is necessary, however, before we assume that potential is linked in any important way to less accessible mental activities. Although psychoanalysis has provided a strong influence in behest of this assumption, the scientific jury is still out. Perhaps the safest stance to assume in this regard would be that projective devices like the Rorschach or the Thematic Apperception Test (11) merit continued scrutiny as possible avenues toward predicting potential.

THE MEASUREMENT OF POTENTIAL

The basic problem for testing behavioral potentiality, as discussed in the section above, is that the construction and ultimate evaluation of psychological tests are tied to their ability to predict actual performance criteria. To point out the inappropriateness of using available tests in their standardly applied manner to estimate potential is not tantamount to saying that tests cannot be employed for this particular prediction problem. It simply means that we must use new procedures to make a different type of prediction. Let us first examine in more specific detail what the nature of the differences are between the prediction of actual behavior and the prediction of potential behavior.

When a prediction is made as we standardly employ tests, the predictor assumes that the conditions which exist at the time of testing will be the same as those which will hold when the predicted behavior will occur. The term "conditions" here subsumes both the naturalistic life conditions of the person and the specific conditions under which he took the test. That this premise of constancy rarely, if ever, is satisfied remains as a major limitation upon the effectiveness of tests. To illustrate this point, suppose a person receives a high score on a test of mechanical aptitude and his success in a technical school is forecast. Between the time of testing and entry into the school, however, this person is involved in an automobile accident in which he incurs some brain damage. The prediction of success in the technical school is very likely to be attenuated by the altered physical status between the time of testing and that of the predicted performance. Variable states of motivation represent a more subtle and more common source of inconstancy. The person's level of motivation on the test may be discrepant from his motivational status at the time of predicted performance.

Given the task of testing for potentialities, even more extensive problems are encountered. Not only must the tester face the inconstancy of conditions between the test and predictive situations, but the formidable problem of distinguishing between some future actual and potential level of behaving must be resolved and translated into his testing procedures. Stripped of elegance, the distinction between actual and potential behavioral outcomes resolves itself into identifying the factors which tend to inhibit the full realization of some hypothetical state we term a capacity. The hypothetical quality of this upper limit to a potentiality is stressed. We never know for certain what the potentiality limit is but must settle for specifying this limit under a given set of boundary conditions. For example, if educational potential of a student were being considered, we would have to restrict our statement to the conditions under which educational performance is evaluated in American colleges. One cannot have a higher potential than being a straight-A student if graded classroom performance is the criterion of success in college. Again, if job potential were being considered, no matter how well a man performed at work we could never be certain that he had reached an upper limit of proficiency.

Despite the fact that the concept of a potentiality has a disturbing open-endedness to it, probably no one would deny that a discrepancy often exists between the performance we observe in others and what could be elicited given more optimal boundary conditions. The first problem, therefore, which requires our attention if we wish to test for potentiality within a given behavioral domain is to identify the most important of these optimizing factors. Specifically, what environmental or organismic changes must occur before behavior will be altered from a lower to higher level of competence? (For purposes of convenience in the present discussion, it is presumed that a potentiality refers to a level of behavior which would be generally more valued than that level we have chosen to call actual. It is recognized that potentiality for negatively valued outcomes such as mental disorder or delinquency represents an equally important problem for testing. The principles involved in either case are assumed to be the same.)

The procedure for developing a test of potentiality suggested by the preceding discussion can be illustrated as follows. Suppose we are interested in testing for potential in some specific vocation. We first identify a relevant skills dimension which when sampled allows us to predict actual vocational performance. We then devise our test of dimension A, say, manual dexterity. Then, concerned with vocational potential, we establish in some way that job performance can be systematically enhanced if workers are placed in competition with one another (X), are encouraged to develop a loyalty to the management (Y) and are made aware that promotion to supervisory positions will be determined solely on effectiveness as workers (Z). X, Y and Z become boundary conditions mediating potential of the worker. By translating the competitiveness, loyalty to authority and need achievement variables into additional tests, the X, Y and Z scores can be used to modify our prediction from the initial test A. Identifying the factors which optimize performance and reducing them to measurement allows for a multi-factor prediction of potentiality *under the specified conditions of the particular work situation.*

Two implications emerge from this example of potentiality testing. The first is that once the factors responsible for the discrepancy between some observed level of functioning and a more competent level are identified and rendered susceptible to measurement, one is no longer testing for potentiality. Rather, a new predictive "formula" is available which will more effectively specify actual performance under more complex but clearly delineated conditions. Thus the term "potentiality" is meaningful only so long as performance-limiting factors remain unidentified, unmeasured and unavailable for prediction. The second implication is that reference to a potentiality without specifying the conditions under which it is to emerge is a rather useless exercise; potentiality is always conditional.

HIGHER EDUCATIONAL POTENTIAL— A CASE IN POINT

Few areas of human endeavor have attracted greater attention with regard to actual and potential behavior than the educability of our youth in colleges and universities. Although college dropout and academic underachievement cannot reasonably be attributed solely to failures in potentiating upper limits of competence among our students, it is safe to assume that many educational casualties would be averted if conditions could be implemented which would partially accomplish this goal.

Now where do tests fit into the problem of enhancing the performance of students in higher education? The primary basis for recommending the employment of potentiality testing is a temporal one. The earlier students can be identified as potential problems, the earlier that steps can be taken to alleviate the problem. Tests can be administered at any time, including prior to matriculation; if problems are to be identified only after they develop, it is often too late to rectify them. It is one thing to identify a potential college dropout before he takes his first class but quite another to discover him when he fails to return for his sophomore year.

The plan in this section is not to present a survey of the extensive literature on the relationships between tests and educational process variables. Rather, an attempt will be made to present some speculative proposals of how the proposed prototype for potentiality testing could be applied in a college setting and to supplement this speculation with illustrative evidence from research with college students.

The first order of business must be to specify clearly the nature of academic potential as it applies to the higher educational experience. It would seem that any consideration of such potentiality must subsume two very obvious facts about college. The student is there to learn and he cannot learn (what is taught) unless he is there. Thus, prediction of college potential must incorporate both the educability and continuation factors. These factors are clearly not independent of each other (e.g., students with poor grades are often required to drop from college early in their academic careers), yet there is good reason to believe that the reasons for college dropout and poor classroom performance are often distinct. Data from a study of college dropouts (4) illustrate this point graphically. Table I presents the percentage of girls from two consecutive freshman classes at the University of Iowa who failed to return for their second academic year, these percentages being listed by decile levels on the freshman intellectual ability test. Since the academic performance of the student is best predicted from such intelligence tests, it is not surprising to find that continuation at the institution into the second year is fairly predictable at the extremes of intelligence.

TABLE I

PERCENTAGE OF COLLEGE DROPOUT BY INTELLECTUAL ABILITY LEVEL

	Ability Level Decile									
	1	2	3	4	5	6	7	8	9	10
Percentage drop	75	56	41	35	41	30	32	30	27	21

However, it can be noted that ability differences within the lower half of the intelligence range (1st through the 50th percentile) bears a far greater relationship to college dropout than do ability differences in the upper half (51st through 99th percentile). To illustrate, 34 per cent more students in the bottom decile of the lower intelligence range drop out of school than do students in the top decile of that range. In contrast, only 9 per cent more students in the bottom decile of the higher intelligence range drop out of school than is the case for students in the highest decile. These data suggest that the psychological antecedents to college dropout are distinguishable from the intellective contribution to classroom performance for the relatively more capable student.

Proceeding then on the assumption that college potential can be usefully conceptualized as involving both an educability and continuation factor, a program for potentiality testing modeled after our prototype can be proposed. Priority in such an enterprise must be placed upon educational research which will identify the behavioral variables relating to our potentiality factors. Intellectual ability would clearly maintain its status as an effective predictor; but the status of such variables as personality attributes, personal values, interests or childrearing history remains in need of clarification. Even in the case of intellectual assessment, the problem of what type of test to use (e.g., achievement *versus* more abstract intellectual functioning) and the conditions under which the test is to be administered warrant further investigation. In the latter regard, it should be determined whether or not it would enhance prediction if the conditions of intelligence testing were made as comparable as possible to the conditions which prevail when classroom performance is evaluated via examinations. One perhaps impracticable suggestion would be to establish a precollege entrance examination which would involve the dissemination of standard materials covering a variety of subject matters at some fixed period prior to the examination. Each candidate would have the same opportunity to study the same material in preparation for the examination. The performance of potential college students upon the examination would reflect not only their level of intelligence but also their motivation, ability to study and organizational skills. Since the intrusion of the family and friends in the preparation would represent an undesirable variable, the program of preparatory study would have to be placed under the supervision of high school personnel who would be responsible for maintaining uniform but sufficient preparation time allotments during the senior year. Such a proposal would seem to guarantee a better relative evaluation of the capacity for learning than present procedures allow.

Once research has fixed the factors contributing to college achievement, the next major problem is to select or develop appropriate tests which will serve as measures of these factors. Other refinements would follow, of course, including weighting and determination of the prediction formula to be used for each school.

Since research was stressed as a preliminary to establishing an effective college potential testing program, it is of some interest to examine where we stand with regard to scientifically established "laws" of higher educational performance. It is probably safe to say that among the nonintellective behaviors studied, the relationships between personality and educational outcomes have received the greatest attention. The results, taken piecemeal, have failed to attribute any major role to personality; but, taken in combination, they offer some promising hypotheses. In way of illustration, let us examine the results of several studies bearing upon the relationships between personality traits and both college academic underachievement and dropout (Table II). One high school study of intellectually gifted children is included (personal communication from Professor Anthony Davids of Brown University). These studies were selected because the personality tests employed provided measures on the same fifteen variables. Most of the studies also controlled for the contribution of intelligence to the criteria of college adjustment. Inspection of the summarized data offers several instances of consistency and inconsistency among the studies. For one, the pattern of findings suggests that inconsistencies exist not only between the personality correlates of academic achievement and dropout but also between the two sexes and among levels of ability. *Achievement motivation, endurance, order* and *change* are the only personality traits which impressively cut across both outcome variables for both sexes; and even these variables do not appear to be important for low ability students. *Intraception* (except for one reversal) is a fairly consistent correlate of academic achievement for both sexes but not of dropout, whereas *affiliation* is shown to be an important personality dimension for predicting only male academic achievement. Unrelated to classroom performance, *deference* assumes importance from both sexes when dropout is considered.

One might well ask whether this summary of empirical findings

TABLE II

RELATIONSHIPS BETWEEN PERSONALITY AND COLLEGE ACADEMIC ACHIEVEMENT AND DROPOUT

	Males								*Females*						
	Academic Achievement Studies							*Dropout Studies*	*Academic Achievement Studies*					*Dropout Studies*	
Personality Variable	*(1)*	*(8)*	*(10)*	*(2)*	*(5)*	*(6)*	*(HS)*	*(7)*	*(3)*	*(10)*	*(2)*	*(6)*	*(HS)*	*(4)*	*(7)*
Achievement	+	+		$+^{b}$	+	+	$+^{c}$	$+^{c}$		+			$+^{c}$	+	
Deference								$+^{a, c}$						↑	$+^{c}$
Order	+	+			↑		$+^{c}$	$+^{c}$					$+^{c}$	+	
Exhibition								$-^{c}$				−			$-^{a, c}$
Autonomy				$-^{a}$				$-^{a, c}$				−			−
Affiliation	−	−		$-^{b}$											
Intraception	+			$-^{b}$			$+^{c}$				$+^{c}$	+	$+^{c}$		
Succorance			+		not tested			$+^{b}$						not tested	$+^{c}$
Dominance							$+^{c}$			+					$-^{c}$
Abasement										−	$-^{a}$	+			$+^{c}$
Nurturance	−			$-^{b}$		−					$-^{a}$	+			
Change	−			$-^{b}$				$-^{b, c}$					$-^{c}$	−	$-^{c}$
Endurance		+		$+^{b}$		+	$+^{c}$	$+^{c}$	+			+	$+^{c}$	+	
Heterosexuality		−			↓		$-^{c}$							−	
Aggression				$-^{c}$				$-^{c}$				−		↓	

Note: Plus (+) indicates a significant positive relationship between the personality variable and college adjustment (i.e., classroom achievement and continuation); minus (−) signifies a significant negative relationship between the personality variable and college adjustment (i.e., underachievement and dropout). The HS columns include the unpublished data from the high school sample.

[a] Low ability.

[b] Middle ability.

[c] High ability.

should represent a source of hope or dismay for those who entertain the possibility that testing can hope to contribute to the assessment of educational potential. The decision must ultimately rest upon further research which will indicate whether the continuities and discontinuities among the personality-educational outcome relationships mirror the actual complexities of the behaviors in question. The alternative conclusions that these contingencies are not substantial enough to allow for replication or that tests are in principle not up to the job of measuring behavioral variables like personality traits would obviously command far less optimism. Before a verdict is rendered, however, educational research must be upgraded so as to be more definitive in character. Somehow, experimental manipulation of carefully considered variables must be taken to the actual educational setting, be it the classroom, dormitory or the dean's office. The work cited by McKeachie (9) represents some fruitful beginnings in this direction.

POTENTIALITY: AN EPILOGUE

Although the concept of human potential can be meaningfully segmented in a large number of ways, as the format of this book demonstrates, it would not be surprising if many contributors fail to resist the temptation to express somewhat more general observations. These closing comments will be of this nature.

Every effort has been made to treat the concept of potentiality as objectively as possible in this chapter. That is, a potential has been regarded as behavioral outcome which differs in some specifiable way from the outcome which would be expected if certain relevant conditions were not met. Sometimes in the discussion a different but consistent interpretation of potentiality has been employed: the probability of some specified behavior outcome as given by scores on measures of the relevant conditions. In either case, potential is reduced to observable and measurable phenomena. Approached in this way, potentiality loses some of its conceptual elegance. Yet, lacking objective specification the term becomes more a subject for faith than science, since it embraces not only unknowns but unknowables. If one concedes to this definitional procedure, it is more accurate to say that a given person has potentiali*ties* for any behavioral outcome rather than a potentiality. Potentiality changes as the relevant conditions change. A boy's academic potential, using graduation as the outcome criterion, will vary depending upon the caliber, size, and locale of the school, the classroom structure, his athletic prowess, the nature of his peer and interpersonal relationships, including the quality of the relatedness established between him and specific teachers, etc. His potential at school A differs from that at school B.

A second general observation is concerned with why potential should be measured at all. It is certainly not enough simply to predict potentiality from a test. If we wish to capitalize more effectively upon our human resources in this country, it follows that measurement would serve as a prelude to attempts to alter potential among those who are identified as being in need of it. *The point to be made here is that modification in potential may be mediated not only by changing the individual but by changing the environment.* Too often, for example, academic potential even within a single institutional setting is considered unilaterally to reside within the student when, in fact, a more flexible curriculum or social structure might enhance overall performance of students. The solution to the problem of potential, in the realm of education at least, becomes partially a matter of resolving barriers imposed by tradition and practical demands of increasing enrollment. The question of whether the instigation toward realizing individual potentiality is to stem principally from changes in the individual or changes in the setting seems equally apropos to the domains of vocational or social behavior.

REFERENCES

1. Gebhart, G. G., and Hoyt, D. P.: Personality needs for under- and overachieving freshmen. *J. Appl. Psychol.*, *42*:125, 1958.
2. Goodstein, L. D., and Heilbrun, A. B.: Prediction of college achievement from the Edwards Personal Preference Schedule at three levels of intellectual ability. *J. Appl. Psychol.*, *46*:317, 1962.
3. Guttman, H. E.: A study of the Edwards Personal Preference Schedule in relation to over- and underachievement. Unpublished doctor's dissertation, Univ. of Washington, 1959.
4. Heilbrun, A. B.: Prediction of first year college dropout, using ACL need scales. *J. Counsel. Psychol.*, 9:58, 1962.

5. HEILBRUN, A. B.: Social desirability and the relative validities of achievement scales. *J. Consult. Psychol.*, *26*:383, 1962.
6. HEILBRUN, A. B.: Configural interpretation of the Edwards Personal Preference Schedule and the prediction of academic performance. *Personnel Guid. J.*, *42*:264, 1963.
7. HEILBRUN, A. B.: Personality factors in college dropout. *J. Appl. Psychol.*, *49*:1, 1965.
8. KRUG, R. E.: Over- and underachievement and the Edwards Personal Preference Schedule. *J. Appl. Psychol.*, *43*:133, 1959.
9. MCKEACHIE, W. J.: In JONES, M. R. (ed.): *Nebraska Symposium on Motivation*. Lincoln, Univ. of Nebraska Press, 1961.
10. MOGAR, R. E.: Competition, achievement, and personality. *J. Counsel. Psychol.*, 9:168, 1962.
11. MURRAY, H. A.: *Thematic Apperception Test*. Cambridge, Harvard Univ. Press, 1943.
12. RORSCHACH, H.: *Psychodiagnostics: A Diagnostic Test Based on Perception*. Berne, Huber, 1942.
13. WECHSLER, D.: *Wechsler Adult Intelligence Scale*. New York, Psychological Corporation, 1955.

Chapter 21

GROUP METHODS AND HUMAN POTENTIALITIES

MILTON M. BERGER

ALL group methods of relating—family, educational, spiritual, recreational, counseling, therapeutic and others may allow for the development of some of the potentials in each individual. However, because a psychotherapy group provides the greatest opportunity for a person to experience nonexploitive relationships, it is the most meaningful setting for human potentials to develop to the maximum. Therefore, I shall focus primarily upon the potentials developed within that slice of life we call a psychotherapy group. The group is a laboratory of life for being and becoming in which each patient can be helped to move toward a clearer definition of himself, his potentials and his road toward self-fulfillment while contributing in the same vein to others.

No man is an island. Alone, no man could survive as a psycho-socio-biological animal. For survival—let alone for the development of human potential—relationships are required. Interaction in groups allows for dependence as well as independence, giving as well as receiving, touching and being touched and a dialogic encounter which includes subjective-objective-participation in a spirit of caring, mutuality and affective honesty.

Each individual personality has an inner potential for constructivity and for destructivity. Societal practices aided by law enforcement agencies attempt to prevent or check the activation and expression of destructive elements of human behavior. However, in the group therapy setting the individual has a unique opportunity to experience, reveal, act out, examine and work through his destructive potentialities; this is a direct contrast to his experiences in other group situations such as family, school, work, church or recreation. At any one moment healthy constructive forces may be in ascendancy, and at another moment these forces may be eclipsed by the forces of destructive neurosis or psychosis. Horney states: "The analyst helps the patient to become aware of all the forces operating in him, the obstructive and the constructive ones; he helps him to combat the former and to mobilize the latter. . . . The undermining of the obstructive forces goes on simultaneously with the eliciting of the constructive ones" (1).

A psychotherapy group actively cooperates in the development, elaboration and exposure of all human functioning, whether healthy or unhealthy. In the group, free-floating pervasive intrapsychic and interpersonal anxiety has a chance to become magnified to the point almost of becoming palpable, then clarified as to its causes and eventually worked through, hopefully. Following the exposure of latent constructive or destructive potentials, the group is highly motivated to help each group member to use his energies to develop his constructive potentialities, for here it is possible for a corrective attitudinal and emotional reeducation to occur. Group support, stimulation, encouragement and sharing in responsibility can help a fellow member to take a constructive giant step forward in being and becoming more authentic and real-self-fulfilling. Somehow in a group there is a feeling that responsibility for the action of one member is shared by the others. Gardner Murphy says: "Growth is more than the release of a potential. It is actually the interaction with a personal-social reality" (2).

It has been my experience that the group milieu provides a background for the following significant maturing processes and peak experiences to a greater degree than anywhere else: truth, beauty, goodness; caring, feeling, belonging; raw pain, bleeding and despair, helplessness, weakness; fantasies, irrational thoughts, confusion; factual ignorance, wrong conclusions, inability to understand or comprehend—or simply communing with oneself and others in silence, without having to make empty, superficial conversation. In an atmosphere of interacting human beings gathered together in a spirit of mutuality while learning about oneself and others, it is possible freely and spontaneously to commit oneself, express one's innermost feelings and develop the courage to risk as one finds that others do this successfully and are enriched while becoming more truthful and able communicators.

As the optimally functioning group gradually "reaches" the patient, it calls forth an obligation from each person to make the utmost effort to energize his or her latent potentials and to give up neurotic patterns. The group, perhaps more than the individual therapist, can act as a catalyst in motivating a stronger commitment on the part of each patient to change. The group focuses upon the need for each individual to change and "demands" that he change as the price for remaining. During a group session one member confronted another group member with, "We were talking about you last night at our alternate meeting and decided that you have changed the least in the year we have been together. We know very little about you. Are you aware of this? You frequently speak about your wife or your son and your business, but we rarely hear about what is going on inside of you." This was a group expression of one of the most important reasons for a group's existence, namely, that it is our duty to go beyond what we are and have been as we risk becoming what we can be.

Underachievers who amble through life in low gear because they have not previously experienced an accepting, supporting, encouraging human environment are forced in the group experience to examine their neurotic, idealized or hateful self-image and to acknowledge a more truthful self-image as they begin to function more authentically.

Some people first learn that fantasy is available to them when they listen to someone else's fantasy in a social or therapeutic setting. There are a whole host of people, patients and nonpatients, who are "emotional illiterates," i.e., they are afraid to risk feeling and constructive fantasy-making because of a deep-rooted alienation from self or the lack of stimulation of their potential for fantasy-making. Just as we meet in group people who have given up wanting or wishing something for themselves, we also meet those who are unable to fantasy for themselves but can do so for others. For example, a man can express his fantasy of succeeding in a new business venture so that he may purchase a larger home for his family, provide private schools for his children or buy mutual fund growth stocks to secure his children's future. We must not forget, however, that while some people need to learn to dare to fantasy, paradoxically some of society's sickest members live in imagination to such a degree that they are ill-equipped for functioning in reality.

I believe that we should pursue with special vigor research on finding ways of freeing man to utilize more of his imaginative potential, e.g., to free him to "imagize" and to express ideas, wishes and wants which will not be all too quickly edited out of consciousness by fear that these productions will be declared irrational. We need greater freedom to express what is and what might be—that which is beyond classification as rational or irrational; that which exists before we have the tools and knowledge to truthfully declare it as being rational or irrational! I have found that amongst "professional helpers," such as psychiatrists, psychologists and social workers, there is a deep-seated inhibition against or an actual inability to acknowledge to themselves and others their very personal fantasy of going off to some island alone for an indefinite period to commune with themselves, or of becoming a scuba diver in the warm, coral-reefed Caribbean or Pacific waters, or of racing a sports car, or taking a course in Chinese cooking or bread-baking or simply learning to play the guitar or some other musical instrument for fun.

In psychotherapy groups a patient can identify with those who have freed themselves enough from the shackles of their constrictive "brain washing" neurotic system of functioning to feel, to want, to wish and to fantasy.

In therapy groups it has been found that very disturbed patients and/or those with relatively little ego strength may have strong inhibitions against verbal communications of their inner experience. Flexner states: "In an art therapy group where all the patients mutually participate in the creation of a single work of art, a patient may find it easier to expose himself through the valuable nonverbal tool of painting" (3). Creative activity can at times replace words as the medium of communication, and patients can be encouraged to discharge pent-up feelings symbolically through artistic expression. An art program can be designed to help patients discover their inherent talents and unresolved problems through the emergence of their creative flow.

A therapeutic group experience can nurture certain elements of human functioning which allow for the expression of simple talent as well as genius on rare occasions. In therapy a high valuation is placed on spontaneity, a capacity for an entirely fresh and different ways of looking at things—a willingness to give up looking at things with old eyes, a love of the unexpected, nonconventionality, patience, intuitive inspiration, power to concentrate—both inside and outside, personal courage, love of truth, self-surrender to the point of being almost in a trance and an attitude of passive surrender towards the flowing in of valuable ideas—in the therapist as well as in the patient.

In testing intelligence or knowledge, most of the tests probe mainly the informational and memorized "capital" of the individuals, and much less their creative potentials, their specific abilities and their capacity for logical, mature and original thought (4). In a recent survey of highly talented graduate students fifteen years after graduation, it was shown that the majority of the people were primarily interested in achieving freedom, autonomy and self-expression (5). In contrast to the goals of these bright students, the average so-called healthy person today is probably functioning at only 10 to 15 per cent of his actual potential; and the multitude of those afflicted with more or less of a character neurosis are operating with even less of their total potential. This does not preclude the well-known fact that many neurotics can function at a high level of creativity in certain specific areas; e.g., artists, writers, theatrical people, business people and even social scientists.

Buttressed by the legend that without illness the creative spark will die, many psychologically ailing artists, writers, musicians, teachers and scientists refuse therapy. It has been the experience of therapists that creativity without illness is both possible and desirable; in fact, the toll which neurosis exacts of a person's creative potential cannot be overemphasized. When man learns how to free his creative processes from the drag and bias of covert neurotic influences, he will have achieved the highest degree of spiritual freedom and personal creativity. It is Kubie's contention that potential creativity is as universal as the neurotic process (6).

For people to be involved holistically with other humans, it is necessary that they learn nonlexical aspects of communication. In a group the potential to become aware, plus the opportunity to practice utilizing and interpreting body language to self, as well as the varying facets of nonlexical communication to others, is markedly enhanced (7). In the group there is an opportunity to learn that nonlexical communication, alone and in conjunction with lexical language, is of major importance, not only as a medium of expression, communication and imparting information, but also to establish, maintain or regulate relationships (8).

In individual psychotherapy the silent patient rarely develops much of his potential, but in the group therapies even a silent group member is able to realize much of himself as he identifies with and participates in the emergence of many new feelings and experiences. He may gain insights which permit him to abandon his myopia while he expands his vision of his assets and liabilities and his life as a whole. In listening to and seeing others we may begin to hear and see ourselves. Sartre states: "In order to get any truth about myself, I must have contact with another person." A thirty-eight-year-old female patient states it another way: "Even when silent I get reactions and I think about them. I then stay inside myself and don't listen to the others for a while—and get confused at times—and then clearer too—but I feel alive when I leave the sessions." In the group people realize, *through a geometric rather than through an arithmetic progression, a profound increase in awareness that how we are being is more significant than what we are saying or even doing.*

It has become almost axiomatic that you cannot have an emotionally sick child from an emotionally healthy family. The treatment of the family seemed to be a logical and necessary development for those therapists who wished to identify more accurately healthy, distorted and sick family attitudes, values and behavior patterns by experiencing them in the here and now of a family group meeting. Firsthand observation and experiencing of a family's interaction offers the therapist a more complete diagnostic continuum so that he may more realistically evaluate the family gestalt, thus minimizing secondhand reporting about family happenstances from individual members of a family. By our focusing on a "What and how in the here and now?" approach to the family, by our experiencing the whole family or parents and child, by our becoming less afraid to bring our own inner experiencings into the dynamic therapeutic process, we can more rapidly come closer to knowing the family multi-dimensionally and helping the family to fulfill its potential together in more constructive ways.

For example (9), an adolescent girl, an attractive sixteen-year-old high school senior, was referred to me because of repeated friction between her and her parents. Her father, a successful forty-seven-year-old accountant, and her mother, a forty-year-old former schoolteacher, were intelligent, well-meaning people caught in the conflict between being consciously interested, loving parents and unconsciously directive, tyrannical, domineering and overprotective parents. At one and the same moment their daughter Susan was expected to act like a grown-up young lady, but also in fact treated as if she were a baby or perhaps a too trusting innocent Little Red Riding Hood type of girl who could hardly be trusted to stay out after eleven at night without being swallowed up by some of the wolves in our society.

After six weeks in which a positive relationship was built up between the patient and myself, we decided we were ready to risk having her parents join us for a session. Midway during the session the patient looked at her mother and addressed her as "Mommy." I interrupted the verbal communication between daughter and mother at this point to focus my attention and that of mother, daughter and father on the communication that had just occurred. I am referring, of course, to Susan at this moment calling on her mother to be, in fact, "Mommy." Yet for six weeks Susan had been openly telling me how her mother keeps treating her as if she were a little girl. This moment of encounter—this moment of existence—this moment in which I was privileged to be in with the family group—was the moment in which the family as a group most closely approximated a moment similar to the behavior of the family at home. We then learned from Mommy that she was aware that Susan refers to her at different times as "Mommy," "Mom" and "Mother." When Susan calls her "Mommy," Mrs. B. knows she is being called on to be mothering and understanding and helpful to her "little girl." When Susan calls her "Mom," Mrs. B. knows the relationship between them is friendly and relatively realistic and with real mutuality and affection. When Susan calls her "Mother," Mrs. B. feels her own adrenalin working overtime, tightens up and prepares for overt or covert hostility.

All this came as a surprise to Susan, who now began to sense her own role at certain times in bringing forth the very same parental domination and overprotection which she claimed to hate. Susan also had a fresh sense of respect and appreciation for her mother, learning that her mother was really with her on levels and in ways she was not even conscious of. The mother was relieved to learn that the therapist was interested in the clarification of distortions for the benefit of the whole family and not engaged in collusion with Susan to point the finger of responsibility and blame at the parents. They left with a greatly enhanced feeling of being a family together.

Group methods, such as group process and T group seminars, are becoming increasing valuable for training psychotherapists and other community, educational and business leaders in sensitivity to the human processes involved in being in relationship with others, e.g., in individual and group psychodynamics. Referring to professionals, Rosenbaum states: "The practice of individual psychotherapy often makes the procedure barren and clinical because it denies the *person* who is in the patient and reinforces the therapist in his feelings of omniscience. The entry into a group experience enables the patient to feel how much *person* he is and how much potential resides within him to help other 'patients-persons.' This procedure then, following the concept of the philosopher, John Locke, finds a group of 'patients-persons' joining together in a compact to be of aid to one another. Beyond the more limited clinical applications, the patient becomes aware of his potential as a person, his capacity for growth and his ability to tap his own strengths and be of help to other distressed 'patients-persons.' By placing professionals, trained as individual psychotherapists, in a group experience they may become sensitized to the impact of themselves on others and of others on themselves. It teaches them that the people they formerly conceived of as solely patients are really *persons* whom they may have forgotten or overlooked in the course of training which reinforces feelings of omnipotence" (10).

CONCLUSION

The traumas of life in the twentieth century have resulted in emotional repression and deadening in many people and in an increasing compulsive intellectualization as man attempts to live by brain alone. Participation in a group experience offering a cluster of provocative and creative stimuli confronts the intellectual with his self-seduction and encourages him to risk shedding his armor and his neurotic controls, to risk developing his emotional potential and to risk real feeling as he moves toward finding and developing himself as a whole person. According to Mullan: "One of the great potentials of a psychotherapeutic group experience is that people have an opportunity for actual self revelation, with affective honesty, of something they have never revealed to others or perhaps even to themselves" (11). Whether or not this leads to insight, it may lead to change. It may lead to that sharpened perception of man which allows one to actualize his potential by accepting that living is adventuring in experiencing. To the degree we own self and are authentic, we do not have to hide behind the costly mantle of status and neurosis which keeps us empty and alienated. Through group experiences patients as well as therapists learn to know and respect the impact of those life forces which, without rigid shapes, shape those who are exposed to them. Involvement with others in educational, counseling, activity, therapeutic or other constructively motivated groups allows for greater fulfillment of our potential for subjective-objective participation in the great adventure of living—if, as the drafters of the Declaration of Independence said, we are willing to commit "our lives, our fortune and our sacred honor" (12).

REFERENCES

1. Horney, K.: *Neurosis and Human Growth.* New York, Norton, 1952, p. 341.
2. Murphy, G.: Psychology: New ways to self-discovery. In White, L.: *Frontiers of Knowledge in the Study of Man.* New York, Harper, 1956, p. 29.

3. Flexner, L.: Personal communication, November, 1964.
4. Sorokin, P.: *Fads and Foibles in Modern Sociology and Related Sciences.* Chicago, Henry Regnery, 1956, p. 64.
5. *New York Times,* Oct. 19, 1964, p. 25.
6. Kubie, L.: *Neurotic Distortion of the Creative Process.* New York, Noonday Press, pp. 2-6.
7. Berger, M.: Nonverbal communication in group psychotherapy. *Int. J. Group Psychother., VIII*:161-178, 1958.
8. Sheflin, A.: Communication and regulation in psychotherapy. *Psychiatry, 26*:126-136, 1963.
9. Berger, M.: *Group Counseling: Its Values for Families.* Paper presented at the Annual Meeting of the Family Service Association of Westchester, White Plains, New York, May 16, 1960 (unpublished).
10. Rosenbaum, M.: Personal communication, Oct., 1964.
11. Mullan, H.: Personal communication, Nov., 1964.
12. United States Declaration of Independence, July 4, 1776.

Chapter 22

HUMAN COMMUNICATION AND HUMAN POTENTIALITIES

RAY L. BIRDWHISTELL

THE anthropologist, searching for a point of departure for a discussion of the relationship between new knowledge about human communicative processes and man's potential, could hardly find a better starting point than that provided by the enigmatic myth in the eleventh chapter of Genesis. The reader will recall that Noah had been instructed to build his ark to preserve the heterogeneity of the animal kingdom. However, with the flood mankind was reduced to but a single family. The members of this highly reproductive family sought to preserve their identity by building a city with a great central tower which would reach up to Heaven, lest they be "scattered abroad upon the face of the whole earth." The Deity came to visit them and, after viewing the products of their labor, said:

> . . . Behold, the people *is* one, and they
> have all one language; and this they begin
> to do: and now nothing will be restrained
> from them, which they have imagined to do.—Gen. 11:6.

He then went down and confounded their language so that they could not understand one another and scattered the sub-families "upon the face of all the earth." The ninth verse tells us that:

> Therefore is the name of it called Babel;
> because the Lord did there confound the
> language of all the earth: and from thence did the
> Lord scatter them abroad upon the face of all
> the earth.—Gen. 11:9.

The elusiveness of the ideas contained within these verses is not unusual either in biblical or other folklore. While it does not really matter whether it is the metaphoric language or mistakes in translation which leave these passages so provocative, some biblical scholars have suggested that *bab-el* translates as "the gateway of God" and that the tower was a connection between the city and the Deity. However, it is surmised that the ancient Semites confused or punned upon this word with the verb *balbel*, "*to confound*." Whatever the linguistic truth may be, and even though "babel" in certain usages still implies great aspirations, the "Tower of Babel" has come to stand for confusion of communication and has even been used as a colloquialism for a madhouse or insane asylum.

The chapter is particularly interesting because there is nothing in it which implies that the post-Noahites were scattered as a punishment. Rather, and succeeding chapters lend support to this interpretation, this seemed to be a way of ensuring or rationalizing heterogeneity in mankind. The sixth verse contains lines which tempt the modern student of human communication to marvel at the perspicacity of the Lord or, at least, of the Hebrew storytellers: ". . . and they have all one language . . . and now nothing will be restrained from them, which they have imagined to do." The enigma, it seems to me, lies here. Does this imply that if men spoke in a single tongue and had words with totally shared and absolute meaning that man's achievements could be boundless? Or, does it, in the clause, "which they have imagined to do," somehow recognize the debilitating effect of provincialism, the limiting and stifling influence of a monolithic signal system and of a single body of experience and belief? The scientist concerned with human communication, who turns from the description and analysis of communicational behavior to apply his knowledge to a calibration of man's future, finds the problem familiar.

The babelian enigma can be raised to the level of a dilemma by the recognition that if human beings *cannot* communicate and cannot share effort and information, change and development must be left to the exigencies of biology and the larger environment—that individual contributions would remain private and untransmittable; and cumulative change and social inheritance, matters of happenstancial imitation. On the other hand, even relative homogeneity of perceptual organization, particularly if shareable only through a closed and absolute code, could concretize adaptation. Any species, so limited and so rigidified, would be condemned to a life span determined by the stabilities of the surrounding systems of nature.

Review of social organization tells us that the logical choice between chaotic and atomistic individualism and crystalloid homogeneity of structure is no more than a *logical* choice. Humanity and, in varying degrees, all social species, if they are to survive in a changing environment, must have a membership with varying capacities, subject to exploitation by the group as the need arises. We may state this in the form of a two-level proposition: (a) Every viable group must have within its membership individuals with *special orders of sensitivity and desensitivity, which increase the likelihood of differential experience;* and (b) the group must have *methods for ordering, testing, discarding, transmitting and preserving* these products of differential experience. This must be the crux of any discussion which would pertain to human potentiality and human communication—if communication is seen as the immediate structured system requisite to interorganism connection—and if self-extinction is seen as the polar extreme of human potentiality.

There are some immediate dangers in such a formulation as this. Sensitivity and insensitivity, if conceived as a series of points on a calibrated scale, can divert our attention from their functional relevance. Unfortunately, it is all too easy to stress the more easily measured gradations of sensory acuity than it is to calibrate the systems in which special orders of perceptual organization have consequence. "Potentiality" at one level of examination for me is conditioned by considerations of "possibility" and "necessity" at others; in the real world, potentiality is always a multi-context, a multi-system matter. For example, it is erroneous to conclude that the communicative potential is 99 per cent unrealized because no spoken language utilizes more than, say, 1 per cent of the audible vocalic range. This is to jump from system to system without regard for organizational principles at either level. Comparably, it would be trivial to propose that since the musculature of the face has the possibility of some 25,000 permutations, no society utilizes more than .005 per cent of its potential in structured visual communicative activity. Obviously, this same objection could be extended to statements about the relationship between the variety of taste buds and gustatorial communication, the number of pressure and heat and cold buds and tactile communication, the range of chemically sensitive receptors and olfactory communication and so on. The aeronautical capacity of a plane is not measured, even though it is limited, by the tensile strength of the various metals used in its construction.

The unused portion of any *aspect* of an abstracted system cannot, without theoretical safeguards, be regarded as potential expansion territory for that system. On the other hand, while it may be an interesting pastime to ruminate on the inefficiency of nature, as limited observation reveals behavior whose function we have not yet been able to discover, only innocence would permit us to count this "wastage" as behavior potentially "useful" to itself or to a neighboring system. Unless we are aware of the teleologs we are applying, this order of computation can lead us to a theoretical cul-de-sac about "potential" identical to that from which we have so recently escaped in the concept of "vestigial." Moreover, it is not easy, even for the most determined cultural relativist, to evade the Calvinistic temptation to measure the universe in level-jumping calculations about "waste" and "inefficiency." It is one thing to recognize that chickens are more efficient converters of vegetable energy into edible animal energy for humans than are cattle. It is quite another to anticipate man's potential in simple terms of a reduction of ranching and an increase in chicken farming.

To summarize, even though it is quite evident that man or, at least, many men could be trained or released to be more visually sensitive, to be more auditorially acute, to be more gustatorially or olfactorially receptive, we cannot use the unused sensitization range as a measure, *in itself,* of man's potential to communicate with, to interact with or to contribute to or learn from other men. In fact, we could very well hold that such sensitization, *untranslated and unaccommodated* to, might increase the likelihood that the individual, so "realized," would perish or, at least, be subjected to an institutionalization which would negate any potential contribution. The tendency to regard potential as measured only in terms of possible *increase* in function is to ignore the fact that certain roles in society are probably more adequately performed by individuals who are desensitized to certain cues. The concentration demanded of the specialist in many fields and the special action demanded of the leader may require special orders of desensitization. The acquisition of "more" information provides, depending upon the context, either a positive or a negative potential for purposive or adaptive action.

The proposition about capacity and utilization, as stated above, turns upon the ability of a social group (*with or without awareness* of the process) to convert perceptual innovation into social usage and to preserve these *explicit* or *implicit* adaptations for application, *appropriately or inappropriately,* in later situations. The communicative system of the group must provide for these operations. The communicative system of any group is a storage-retrieval as well as a transmissional system. If it is conceded that communication does have a storage-retrieval aspect, the student must take great care in the construction of his model of this aspect of the communicative system. Common culture (prevalent folk belief) provides him with an atomistic model in which the head of each member of the society has a storage vault which contains frozen packages of words and sentences which can be located, thawed and transmitted. Such a model operates upon the assumption that each head is a receptacle containing discrete wholes of information which are emitted, transmitted, shuffled and dealt in individual or group operations of decision or continuity. It seems to me that such a model is completely inadequate to the task of providing a theoretical base for comprehending social continuity because it deals with such a small portion of registerable, transmittable and shareable experience.

Part of our difficulty here lies in the vulgar conception which defines communication as a passive mechanism, active only in that it somehow transports word-shaped ideas from head to head and contributory only in malfunction. If our models of the communicative process are based upon telecommunicative devices, which are, after all, only part of the technology of interaction, we are blinded to the productive and regulative functions of the communicative process. It is going to shape our consideration of man and his potentiality if we see man as locked in his own head and connected only by carriers of messages in the form of sound and light waves or their surrogates. In a sense, such a conception as this locks "thought" inside of individual heads to be emitted intermittently for group consideration. "Negotiation" or group decision or nondecision, if we so limit ourselves, can only be explained by some variation of contract theory at one level, by a complex model of trial and error at another or, more dangerously, by social valence theory, in which the "power" of individuals or groups of individuals determines which of a set of head-produced decisions prevail. These are not erroneous theories; they are simply insufficient.

An alternative model would conceive of the possibility that while, as individuals some of what we store constitutes entities of information, much of what the individual member of a group registers and stores are incomplete aspects of multi-sensory patterns, *partials,* which gain completion only by the contributions of others within the group (1). From this point of view, the ikons or bits of the code which are transmitted *along whatever combination of sensory channels* serve to cue both or either the partials and the wholes requisite to continuous and shifting activity. Such a model as this permits man a richer heritage, a more adequate larder for preserving continuity and for meeting crisis than does one which can retrieve and transmit only whole pieces of information. It is also more consistent with the observed, out-of-awareness, interdependence of man. The communicative system as a system becomes a productive, a regulative and a contributory process. Interaction is more than a sum of the component actions.

The communicative system operates as a transmissional device in that it serves to transmit and organize both the completable partials and the wholes which are held in common within the group or selected segments of the group. This is another way of saying that a group makes decisions or performs the activity of not making decisions according to operations and upon experiences which are both in and out of awareness. "Decision making," in this case is defined operationally as a perceptible shift in patterned response in a structured situation, "non-decision-making" being the absence of a shift in patterned response as the structured situation perceptibly shifts.

A swell of studies of animal societies have vitiated the anthropocentric definition of man as *the* communicator. However, since, at the time of this writing, no animal communicative code has yet been cracked, cross-speciational comparisons designed to gain perspective upon *human* communication leave us with admiration for man's invention of language but with inadequate cross-speciational data to determine its import. Yet, we can gain assistance from these data. Their primary contribution may be in the fact that they compell us to take account of possible continuities in evolution (2). The more data we accumulate either about animals or humans, the more unlikely it appears that man is a mono-channel communicator. That is, there seems no support for the almost universally assumed position that as man developed language, he loaded all of his communicative eggs in the verbal basket—that as man became man, he became an exclusively audio-aural communicator, at least, insofar as significant information is concerned.

Research over the past two decades has demonstrated that human beings in particular societies respond regularly to patterned cues along several if not all sensory pathways, pathways which are not merely intrapersonal but are demonstrably interpersonal. Investigation of body motion behavior has revealed that such behavior is just as ordered (although not in identical manner) for communication as is vocalic behavior. And, more important, it has been possible to demonstrate that this is not merely an alternative to vocalic communication, but that it is interdependently interwoven with the vocalic behavior. Our knowledge about gustatory, olfactory, tactile and other sensory channels remains rudimentary. However, there is at present no evidence which would permit us to ignore such behavior as necessary elements in the communicational system. The fact that we are but marginally aware of the function or even the orderliness of such behavior in our day-to-day intercourse is trivial as to its importance. Everything we do not know how to say must be conveyed by other aspects of the communicational system. And, what we do know how to say is given flexibility and malleability by the larger system. However, as we shall see below, for the first time man now has the technology which, by its exclusive emphasis upon the input from one channel, could reduce the contribution of these other channels. If this happens there is no alternative but to anticipate an impoverishment in the state of man.

The anthropologist, when he is asked to predict or evaluate, turns for perspective to cross-cultural and historical data. Unfortunately, cross-cultural material about *communication* (notwithstanding the elegant linguistic data) is almost as sparse as cross-speciational data. In fact, I have the feeling that some of the results being reported by the primatologists, the ornithologists and the icthyologists are going to send anthropologists back to the field to try to get data which are even equivalent to that which the social biologists are presenting. Yet, there is one overriding set of evidence that is completely relevant here. Anthropological linguists have made it manifest that there is no correlation between the *complexity of the socioeconomic adjustment* of any people and the *structure* of the languages they speak. While the psycholinguists have demonstrated that language A may more easily lend itself to certain communicational tasks than does language B and that language C may more easily distort the understanding of certain of its speakers about certain matters than does language D, there is no evidence that the speakers of any language may not with their language say anything they are *able to verbalize* and *need to say* (3, 4).

Anthropological and ethnological data are pertinent in the sense that they demonstrate that all men whom we can investigate *communicate* and seem able, at least at a translation level, to be able to learn the system of other men. They do not give us much evidence for evaluating "good"–"bad" communication. Perhaps we can speak with more security about the potential of modern, urban, literate man, particularly if we limit ourselves to reference to certain aspects of his special condition. It is true that man over the ages has adapted to the most diverse conditions. A survey of man's condition, society by society across the world, is an impressive record of man's toughness, resiliency, malleability and inventiveness. This is one measure of the adaptability, the capacity and the productivity of man's equipment for information collection, problem solution and for the recognition, accumulation, preservation and transmission of these solutions. On the other hand, intensive studies of man in his multifarious situations are equally revealing as to man's capacity for blindness to opportunity, his stubborn devotion to nonsense, the depth of his resistance to nonconforming innovation and his rigidity in the face of evidence in unfamiliar or nonapproved form.

In whatever manner we may interpret or evaluate the life-ways of the world's societies, there exists the fundamental point that those societies which are extant today survived. As we look at ethnological data, written with disciplined historical perspective, we are aware that even within the past century societies have perished. Moreover, such accounts make it unavoidable that there are a number of societies extant today that are probably lethals. This is deceptively self-evident. If we are not exceedingly cautious we may be lured into a dichotomy in which we measure potentiality on the one hand by the fact of the survival of some groups and employ a different yardstick for those in whom traceable progress and potential for progress can be seen. It is easy to ignore the potential for nonsurvival in those groups which we have selected to measure in terms of progress and potential for progress.

We can say that in his modern state literate man is dependent upon literacy for survival. A survey of history reveals the fantastic organizational ability which man has achieved through the development of reading and writing and through the development of technologies for the exploitation of these skills. It would not be extravagant to say that the accelerated velocity of recent history is a direct function of these developments. Through literacy even the most isolated men have become participant if not contributory to the course of history. Yet, to measure progress in terms of numbers of literate men or in terms of the accessibility of books or to measure man's potentialities in terms of the increase in either of these is to fail to see some of the cost of hypertrophic literacy.

Many scholars have recognized that literacy, man's greatest achievement for information storage retrieval and for telecommunication is not an unmixed blessing. The written word and its accompanying conventions for definition and transmission have served to reify limited, inept and inaccurate abstractions of and plans for experience even as they made possible great advances in the abstraction, analysis and accumulation of experience over time. Philosophers and semanticists have long been troubled by the fact that words and their derivation can gain greater status than the experiences for which they stand. Thus, concretized words often enervate the very solutions they have enabled to come into being. Literacy can have a self-limiting productivity. We know much more about how to read and write than we do about what portion of experience these skills permit us to transmit. And, we know very little about what they do not permit us to transmit. *If we are to free literacy* to perform its task more adequately and more productively and to gain control of its screening shape, we need to understand both the structure of reading and writing and the relationship between this form of derivation and the more fundamental systems of social interconnectedness for which they are in some measure representative. Linguists are already aware that we do not write all we can say. We are aware that we can write only that which we can verbalize, but we do not yet know what we add to that part of what we say when we write it. We can safely say that we know that literacy has been a boon to data collection, storage and transmission, but we do not know enough about it to relinquish all of communication to its conventions.

As the division of labor in modern society became increasingly insecularized and complex, the role of the defined word became increasingly important in intra- and intergroup *official* decision-making. And with the advent and spread of literacy, the written word gained increasing status as *the* receptable and vehicle for legitimate and negotiable experience. Burgeoning religious, political, economic and educational institutions, with their increasing power to determine the course of history, rely increasingly upon experience which can be codified into words and which can be abstracted into and stored within and manipulated by the conventions of literacy. Even the most barbarous reactionary cannot fail but acknowledge that science, law, art, theology and philosophy have enriched life in the course of their attempts to verbalize experience and to turn these verbalizations to the tasks of civilization. However, as humanists have long complained, all too often the price of this codification has been high. Codification exercises, like word play, can become an object in itself. Removed from experience, it can bar new experience and preclude the reappraisal of the old.

Recent research which indicates that man is a multi-channel communicator and which provides evidence that verbal communication is only a special form of the larger communicative process gives substance to the humanist's demurrer. Man, as a multisensory animal, is connected with his fellows by a number of channels. In the daily task of becoming a human, of sharing his humanity and of making or rejecting one's own or the experience of others, *much of man's continuous activity is beyond his recall or purposive transmission*. This is forcibly demonstrated in the educational process; we have learned to teach but a small portion of all that must be learned to be accepted into humanity.

The assumption that only that portion of experience is real which can be put into words is *nondestructive only so long as there exists ample opportunity for the utilization of experience which we have still not put into words*. Society does not maintain itself merely by support and taboo of expressed ideas or demonstrated action. Every society is self-sustaining as it shapes the input of the data which is regarded as reliable by the member or the membership. As long as non-verbalizable experience is considered inadmissable as evidence, society's decision-making or non-decision-making will rely upon implicit and limited information. Obviously, even the most devoted lexophil lives in, responds to, contributes to and learns from a multi-channel system. And, let me make this absolutely clear, this is no pastoralist plea for the illiterate. Literacy and its derived conventions have made it possible for man to be purposive in decision and have enabled him to check the effects of his decisions in a way which has revolutionized man's condition. However, there are negative potentialities inherent in the overdevotion to a monochannel interpretation of communication, to its derivations in literacy and, finally, to the derivations of these derivations in other telecommunicative activities.

While scholars have been at least ambivalent about some of the side effects of literacy, few have been anything but enthusiastic about the increased velocity of the transmission of information within the society. Radio and television transmission, apart from a fairly general despair over the content of most programming, has been seen as a boon to the society as a means of reducing the relative distances between communicants. Even the newspaper, as science writers have gained skill in popularizing scientific discoveries without bowdlerizing them, has been gaining grudging respect as a dispenser of reliable and high status knowledge. Within the formal educational structure, many teachers and administrators, confronted with a flood of students and the strong demands of a technologically accelerating society, have welcomed new equipment which speeds reading, writing, memorization and word problem solution. Again, no serious student of modern civilization can avoid the recognition that this makes both mass education and specialist training possible in a manner inconceivable before this century. However, I believe that very serious consideration should be given the fact that *speed and acceleration in problem solution, information transmission and education can contain a negative potential if they serve to reduce the likelihood of learning that which we do not know how to teach because it is not yet verbalizable.* As the status of an increasing proportion of the public depends upon word manipulation, the words they manipulate can become less subject to question—particularly if that which is verbalizable structures the test of the reality of that which is yet unverbalized to the exclusion of other reality-testing systems.

It would be improper to overstate this position. Men are not likely to become unisensory in perception or to communicate only by a single channel simply because of an instruction program or its paraphernalia. Men in all societies and ages have probably bootlegged learning. And, no brainwashing technique works for long without reenforcement and probably does not work at all on those who have access to nondictated environments. On the other hand, a qualitative shift in our investigating, problem solving, learning and transmissional environment has been provided by the development of the most recent addition to the word acceleration system, the computer. Completely dependent upon a lexically-shaped input system, the computer presents increasingly isolated and powerful decision-makers with data and conclusions far removed from the operations of experience.

And, more importantly, decisions are made and implemented at a rate which precludes our utilization of that proportion of the out-of-awareness equipment which have made social survival possible. Inevitably, the decision-making function of the society passes into the hands of those who feed the computer. If we forget that the computer-feeder's information is always partial, are overimpressed by the fantastic capacity and velocity of his machinery, we are likely to elevate his status to the point that we overevaluate the information which he presents us through his machine. Stuart Chase's forebodings about a tyranny of words could become a reality—particularly if we limit the nonlexical perceivers and contributors to the role of providing us with diversion or with pleasurable but impractical aesthetic experience.

The assumption upon which all of this discussion rests is that man has survived because he could collect and share information and could make individual and group decisions of which he was not aware because he could utilize the strengths in the unconscious and because he could respond to information before he could verbalize it. And this argument further rests upon the assumption that a viable social grouping contains within its membership individuals with special capacities for special response which contribute to the adaptibility of the group as a whole. The potential of any group is shaped by the presence of special talent and by the structure of the milieu which screens out, shapes, utilizes or rejects the products of these talents. Any society which reduces the opportunity for pluralistic contribution reduces or at least limits the adaptability potential of the group. Although this chapter may read as a Jeremiad, it is not so intended. Man has the potential to communicate on purpose. We need to have more information about man as a communicator, and we need to be able to translate more of man's experience into a form where it becomes useful in purposive decision-making. We need to search out those whose perceptions, insights, decisions and contributions have been hitherto nonverbalizable, and we need to find ways to weigh their contributions. Otherwise, the machine-equipped verbalizer will be given and forced to use more power than history indicates he should bear alone.

The socially powerful machine can become a social homogenizer or it can become a device which allows us to test our experience (the limitations of which we recognize) in a way which permits us pluralistic and heterogeneous contributions to social planning and to life. ". . . they have all one language; (concretized and reified by literacy and its derivations) . . . and now nothing will be restrained from them, *which they have imagined to do.*" I do not feel that it is necessary to scatter man or destroy his tower in order to survive or to achieve a more productive life—but we must understand the price of monopoly, the cost of unity.

REFERENCES

1. For a more extensive discussion of "partials" see Communication without words. In L'Aventure Humaine. Paris, France, Societe d'Etudes Litteraires et Artistiques (in press, 1966).
2. Mead, Margaret: *Continuities in Cultural Evolution.* New Haven and London, Yale Univ. Press, 1964.
3. See Whorf, Benjamin Lee: *Collected Papers on Metalinguistics.* Washington, D. C., Department of State, Foreign Service Institute, 1952.
4. For extensive discussions of the "Whorfian" hypothesis see Hoijer, Harry: *The Sapir-Whorf Hypothesis.* In Hoijer, Harry (ed.): *Language and Culture.* The Univ. of Chicago Press, Chicago, 1954, pp. 235-247.

Chapter 23

THE CONTRIBUTIONS OF PSYCHOANALYSIS TO HUMAN POTENTIAL

O. SPURGEON ENGLISH

THE greatest degree of human potential, in my opinion as a doctor engaged for more than thirty years in psychoanalytic theory and practice, lies in that energy deriving from the fruitful union of two instinctive forces: *love* (Eros); and *aggression* (the death instinct).

This succinct formulation has been phrased in numerous ways both by professional psychoanalysts and by those outside the ranks who often care little for psychoanalytic theory and practice. Actually, the idea was clearly formulated long before Freud. Freud, however, sharply clarified the results of combining these two basic forces and presented to the world the most cogent examples of their interaction in every day life.

Let us examine the elements of *love* and *aggression.*

Love, reduced to its simplest form, requires two essentials: to enjoy; and to provide the best conditions for the growth and welfare of that which is loved. True, enjoyment may be passive. But to "provide the best conditions" requires positive activity in varying degrees.

This derives from *aggression,* which in turn derives basically from energy essentially destructive in nature until subjected to the creative forces of affection, good will and other manifestations of love.

A real life incident amusingly illustrates the fundamental relationship between constructive and destructive forces.

> A church group of a certain denomination in a certain community decided to raze their old, dilapidated church in order to build a new one on the same site. In his campaign to raise funds, the pastor made bold to ask the leader of a church of another denomination (which by reputation was not always kindly

disposed toward his own) for a contribution toward the erection of the new church. The rival pastor, somewhat surprisingly, responded with a check, and this note: "Traditionally it is not the policy of my denomination to aid in the creation of rival religious denominations, with whom we naturally do not agree. However, it seems possible for me to enclose a check for one hundred dollars to be used in the destruction of the old church."

By this gesture and this act, the rival, who actually had respect for his colleague, could display a spirit of cooperation rising above the often destructive spirit of rivalry. Nevertheless, by specifying that his donation be used to *destroy* the old church (an action that had to be taken at considerable expense before the new one could be built) he was able to participate constructively in the total creative effort of his rival.

This, for our purpose here, is a perfect parable—for destruction must play a part in human affairs. The old, the superfluous, the outmoded, the inefficient ways and values must be pushed aside (or destroyed) in order for the new and the better and the more effective and creative to find their place and prosper. Individuals and groups, therefore, must entertain feelings of dissatisfaction, annoyance, discontent, even hate toward the useless, or whatever impedes progress, in order to find the energy necessary to bring about a change for the better—that is, to realize their maximum human potential.

How does psychoanalysis theory and technique aid in this process?

COMMENTS ON THE OPERATION OF PSYCHOANALYSIS

Psychoanalysis is a treatment, a process, an interaction between two people. Its aim, viewed largely, is the redistribution of psychic energy. However, psychic energy is not a free floating commodity like oxygen in a cylinder, which can be wheeled from place to place and applied in pure form. Nor is it stored energy, like radium, uranium, plutonium, which are mined, confined and kept on a shelf until there is a need to put their expansile and beneficial properties to work in a well-focused, mathematically calculated operation.

According to theories of psychotherapy, the psychic energy of the human being arises from the two instinctual sources, love and aggression, mentioned above. The human being functioning according to the love, or pleasure principle, perforce invests himself in another human being: first the parent (mother), followed soon after by the father and later the siblings, if any. Next come teachers and contemporaries. The investment of this energy, identified in psychoanalytic writing as *libido,* is necessarily tenacious and affective; it should be a lasting investment of both depth and power. The word *depth* connotes both intensity of relationship and the feeling associated with the relationship. It connotes also a mutual dependence to enable the growing human being to continue to pay the necessary amount of sustained attention (sometimes known as loyalty) to the older and more experienced person. Only thus is the young one assured of benefiting from the protective devices built into the role of protector and teacher. The mother, first protector from physical dangers, who nourished the child's body, not only imparts a variety of information about life from day to day, but also provides a number of successful techniques for dealing with people. Thus early the young human being has the fortunate experience of having invested his interest, or loyalty, well; he receives daily a good return on his investment. Such a human investment in another person is far more complex than a banking operation, yet there are certain analogies: a sound, long-sustained investment, in terms of the human libidinal relationship as well as in terms of finance, produces positive, long-sustained results.

THE PHENOMENON OF MATURATION

The phenomenon of maturation—that is, becoming an adult, independent individual—is, as yet, no more than a word to most of the people in our society. Mr. Average Man holds the opinion that people "just grow." Growth, to him, is mainly a matter of the body. In order to grow he must eat his vegetables, try to keep looking attractive and, after a certain age, see his doctor once a year. His chief concern, other than the purely physical, generally is for the cultivation of "good habits" and possibly for seeking out the "right company."

The phenomenon of maturation might be compared to the establishment of a branch bank, removed from the large parent organization. Almost the same operations must be carried out by the branch. But, to be successful, the branch personnel must be trained by the parent organization; they must know the same methods of operation and have acquired the ability to function with equal or even better efficiency. Those in the *Filiale*—as they are called in the German language—must be aware of values learned at the source, which enable them to make decisions in doing business from day to day.

So it is with parent and child, in human terms. When the young person, who has "invested" in the parent, has derived from him dividends of knowledge, judgment, a sense of values and skill in operation, he can go forth into the world and become an independent center, engaged in work of his own, yet closely related to the parent operation.

What, you may wonder, has all this to do with the human potential? A great deal, for it is well known that a firm, solid, personality foundation as described above gives rise to the greatest human potential, which may include strength, integrity, courage, flexibility, reliability, interest in one's fellowman, leadership, humor, sensitivity, spirituality, etc. Ideally, all of these positive qualities should have their beginnings in early life. To develop them to their fullest, the maturing human being needs to practice, to build layer upon layer of experience and to be exposed to the example of others.

THE PSYCHOLOGICAL GROWTH PROCESS

It has been demonstrated over and over again, during the treatment experience known as psychoanalysis, that when the maturation process, which should follow a definite pattern, has been ignored, slighted, rejected or tainted strongly with shame, guilt or fear, the goal of independence, personality strength, flexibility, etc. cannot be attained. In such a case, depending on its seriousness, just so much human potential is wasted within an individual and thus lost to the world. Let us therefore further reflect upon the psychological growth process.

Freud concentrated much attention upon the psychological

training for maturation. He noted the need in the young human being for nourishment and close contact with the parent "organization" during the first year, the highly dependent "oral" period when nourishment and the various phenomena connected with lips, mouth, esophagus, stomach, skin and related activities are the prime objects of attention. As the child becomes reasonably assured that his operational system works fairly well, with an accompanying sense of security, he is invited by the parent into the second or "anal" period, during which he adds the responsibilities of cooperation in toilet training, with its corollaries of neatness, cleanliness, punctuality and conformity to the expectations of those in whom he has invested himself or his psychic interest. Often he would prefer to ignore these expectations, which are sometimes in the form of appeals or demands, because living up to them requires thought energy, a more mature effort for which he may not be altogether ready. Usually, however, he realizes that conformity will guarantee further security and, thus aware that the energy is well spent, capitulates more or less gracefully to parental appeals or demands. The result then is a pleasant, friendly, enjoyable cooperation continuing safely through this second phase of maturation.

When the individual has arrived at the point of feeling that bed and board may be safely counted on and that he can conform sufficiently to count on pleasant mutual relations with his parents, a new problem emerges: the problem of sexuality.

THE MANIFOLD PROBLEMS OF SEXUALITY

The human psyche (which has a tendency to oversimplify whenever possible), having successfully gone through the first two stages of the maturation process, would understandably conclude: "Now I know how to get along in the world." But the world has a surprise in store—a higher excitement and greater pleasure than any yet experienced: the twin phenomena of *sexuality* and *love*. True, both have eventually to be paid for in terms of responsibility involving the care of others and possibly of their procreation. But to function successfully in a healthy way, no individual can ever ignore the most fundamental prerequisite to rapport with and enjoyment of the opposite sex: taking care of others. Whether or not he wishes to go further and bring into the world others of his own flesh and blood is a matter of choice and sometimes of fate. But a life confined merely to receiving nourishment and conforming to demands (the essentials of the oral and anal periods of maturation) seldom provides the individual with anything better than a low-keyed, humdrum existence and is likely to leave him vulnerable to life's complex negative scourges of discouragement, apathy and retreat. The development of human potential requires going beyond the first two stages in order to give to and reciprocally draw from other human beings.

Sexual differences, sexual manifestations develop a heightened sense of the meaning of life and its pleasures over and above the pleasures of eating, sleeping and conforming to the demands of the body and those in the environment. In short, no one will go far on the basis of merely living to eat, or eating to live. Neither will he go far on the basis of pleasure derived from merely conforming to the wishes, expectations or appeals of others.

There must be a still higher regard for greater and sustained achievement. This is latently within the sexual function, lived out in its most congenial relationship with one of the opposite sex. The sexual act provides the brief moments of joy on the highest level known to mankind. An individual with versatility of imagination and discipline of emotions will be able to apply this capacity for pleasure on a high level, in varying degrees, to other aspects of life. Lacking this imagination and discipline, he may compulsively desire (and in actuality) merely repeat the sex act over and over with either the same person or a variety of persons and never get beyond what may seem to him a dull routine. Perhaps some may scoff at the words "dull routine," but deep within them they acknowledge it. Such people may never be able to "sexualize" (or "sublimate"—perhaps a better-known term) their sexual pleasure into other life activities and therefore, it is obvious, need instruction, guidance and encouragement to do so. Such help may apply both to growth activities prior to age twenty-one and to conduct of later life.

Thus, one of the many contributions of psychoanalysis to the expansion of human potential lies in emphasizing the fact that a high level of emotional gratification during the oral period tends to create a personality, however young, that is warm, buoyant, hopeful, expectant of what is to come next. If the nursing period has been satisfying and interesting, the child will find in the more demanding anal period, with its toilet and other training, a challenge to his young spirit; and he will cope with this with the greatest degree of "problem solving" versatility in relation to what is asked of him. As often as possible, such a young personality will turn the challenge into an experience in which he is the winner, the successful one, the victor, the blessed cooperator. He even may learn a few useful tricks about handling people (mother and her aides) in the bargain.

These two phases successfully lived through should put a young person into the best possible position for avoiding or at least minimizing the heavy load of shame, guilt, disapproval and actual threat of punishment and even psychological death by ostracism or partial death by castration (real or one of its symbolic representations) which can in the unconscious mind amount to the same thing. Should he reach the period when sexual feelings are beginning to spread from the gastrointestinal tract—one might say all the power for pleasure inherent in the entoderm and its derivatives of ectoderm—to blend themselves in the genital area, without an outlet for the expression of self in this third and final area of sensuality, he will become an unfinished organism, many times worse off than a fine-looking car with a defective motor or a beautiful building with a faulty foundation. Deprived of the warm glow of sensuality seeking its highest expression, he is like a healthy young plant which withers and dies before reaching natural nourishment and adverse weather conditions. Any one of these natural forces, in moderation, can bring the plant to full maturity. In excess, or in partial or total absence, they bring disaster.

In the young human organism, an excess of moral zeal, stark discipline without empathy, overinsistence upon rules of conduct that screen out the joy of living for too long will starve the soul and effect a withering or retreat from life which might end in insanity or produce hatred that might end in delinquency or despotism, their degree depending upon how high on the ladder of power the person has ascended.

THE GROWTH OF HUMAN POWERS *VERSUS* THE GROWTH OF DISEASE

As we pointed out earlier, love has very humble beginnings—that is, in the infant's gratification of his hunger, repeatedly and on demand to the point of satiation. Many people feel that this leads to dependency. On the contrary, the more gratified or secure is the child, the greater, when exposed to the variety of life's joys, beauties, challenges, opportunities, will be his capacity for that sense of well being generally called happiness. Since a creative life, as pointed out above, must grow out of love combined with enough aggression to produce necessary action, so adroitly does the "happy" individual, at whatever level, devise his own way to combine work and pleasure. For this he will need to cultivate *order* and *concentration*. Only thus will he achieve a sense of success and accomplishment.

At any stage of development self-expression or creativity can be blocked, hampered, forbidden, discouraged, negatively criticized. Thus, the sensitive, developing ego may be humiliated, wounded (traumatized) by mockery, threats, frustrations, so as to stop, (or fixate) it completely. And there it will remain, unless released by treatment.

For example, a ten-year-old girl often wanted to read her mother verses she had made up. "Who wants to listen to poetry written by a child that age?" the mother would say, in refusing. A boy of nineteen lost the urge to try to do anything whatsoever because whenever as a child he wanted to start something, his father would ask suspiciously, "Do you think you can do it?"

Similar intimations of doubt, suspicion or other negative attitudes are cumulative in nature and have tremendous power to counteract human potential.

THE TECHNIQUE OF PSYCHOANALYSIS

Since its inception as a science sixty-five years ago, psychoanalysis has been oriented towards knowledge of what destroys, cripples or limits human potential rather than towards its release or expansion. Positive results occur more or less as a by-product of the two by four years (400-800 hours) spent in surveying the growth history and the phenomena which have suppressed, blocked or smothered joy in living and the potential for self-expression in the patient. The philosophy of psychoanalysis is permissive; it is slanted toward freedom of the individual; it encourages development, self-expression. Its techniques are versatile, varying with the need and psychic state of the patient.

In most cases the analyst relies upon the strength and persistence of the conscience (superego), and his task is usually to soften the tendency of the superego to be severely repressive—that is, to prevent the individual from growing. Through analysis of the patient and his growth matrix and all that went into it which prevented the fullest expression of self, the situation is changed. That which has retarded or warped the development of the person is recognized, and he can then realize his human potential. In this process the capability of the analyst to help the patient clarify the meaning of his dreams (which are a distorted but decipherable presentation of his history, personality, conflicts and potential) can be an important aid to the process of achieving insight and consequent maturation.

The technique of psychoanalysis allows adequate time for the individual to arrive at knowledge of the nature of his feelings and ideas by providing an atmosphere of relaxation (on the couch) in the presence of someone (the analyst) who is a living, breathing representative of mankind. This person has trained himself, for five or more years, to respond as uncritically and unprejudicially as possible to what the patient has to think and say about himself. In encouraging this untrammeled self-expression, new combinations of ideas and feelings are created.

When the psychoanalyst is aware that attitudes, ideas, wishes and desires are being stifled by the patient's own repressive forces, he helps him to speak them away and allow his true feelings and ideas to emerge. This process is known as the *analysis of resistance.* Behind this iron curtain of resistance much of the unused human potential is confined. When the curtain is breached, through the "trial experience" of being fully oneself in the analyst's office, the patient can decide how much of his newly released or discovered self he wishes to apply or put into action on the outside. Sometimes he may, in his eagerness, rashly attempt too much and find that he must pull back and rethink the problem. Or, going more slowly, he may look around and listen and tentatively explore before he sets his full potential into effective action.

In the phenomenon known as *transference,* the patient under treatment re-enacts the basic patterns of his thinking and much of his behavior. What he recognizes as useless and futile, he tends to discontinue; what is more useful and less productive of tension, he expands. To what he has never thought of before, he gives expression. Here, then, is the second phenomenon of great importance to the freeing of the spirit and the awakening of consciousness to a potential of which the patient previously was unaware.

Over the years there has been growing discussion of just what degree a psychoanalyst is involved in leading the awakened to consciousness to new thinking and behavior patterns. It stands to reason that this varies from analyst to analyst. One must also bear in mind that patient and analyst constitute a *team,* a pair of individuals each equipped with numerous potentialities which, brought into close contact day after day, are in fact capable of possibilities unlimited.

There are, in general, three definite stages or levels of "patient feeling" recognizable between the beginning and end of analysis. The first concerns the patient's pain, suffering or misery, whether due to a phobia, a psychophysiological headache or depression. The first objective is to alleviate or cure the pain. In the process of doing this, he moves toward the second stage of wellness, or relief. But meanwhile he has glimpsed the possibility of living at a still higher level of well-being, has sensed ideas and feelings within himself which could be developed to bring more meaning to his life.

As can well be imagined, some patients are more content than others to stop at an early stage. It is also true that analysts vary in their interest and skill in helping patients work for, attain and develop the third stage.

Of course, all patients do not come to analysis for the relief of pain. Many actually begin at the second level of reasonable wellness, but motivated by dissatisfaction with themselves or by a sense of boredom or unfulfillment to explore the possibilities in psychoanalysis for making their lives more creative and meaningful. This is well within the scope of psychoanalysis, since, as we have pointed out, discontent with the inner status quo is a primary force. A world so wide and varied in scope offers infinite chances for the investment of self, with an almost certain guarantee of a splendid return on the investment. In fact, one might say a *written* guarantee, since so many writers, whose creative powers have been released and enhanced by psychoanalysis, have testified to this in the fact of their works.

A PATIENT'S SUMMING UP

It seems appropriate to close with a statement by someone who has gone through the experience of psychoanalysis. When she came to me for help she was twenty, suffering from a phobic condition which had forced her out of college work in the middle of senior year. Twenty-five years later, in answer to my question about what psychoanalysis had done for her she wrote:

> Analysis taught me one strong hard fact: i.e., *face up to what is!* You held up the "mirror of my reality" to me during my ten months with you. I've kept it there, staring me in the face and scrubbed clean for the past twenty-five years. I never intend to let go of it. You cut the umbilical cord of my beginnings. You untied the apron strings of which I felt were obligations to the people-of-my-life when I was twenty. You held me before that mirror until I knew completely and with total acceptance that "I was female and that this was a good thing to be." You excused me from my preconceived conception that I "must be outstanding or I was a failure" and substituted the idea that "normal average" was enough to keep anyone busy for a lifetime. *You freed me to be myself!*—even though this meant being different than what my parents expected. At first this seemed to me a great disloyalty. It was hard for me to adjust to. And yet, twenty-five years later, it has meant great comfort to them. Their one child has been strong and sure enough to really meet their aged needs.

> You *cared* about me . . . like I'd never been cared about before. You were audience to my every *positive* effort. You were my cheering section and my champion. *You* were my incentive. You opened the gates of a territory called "Miss X" and helped me walk into it and claim it for my own.
>
> I have complete unself-consciousness about having been a patient. Everyone who really knows me knows that I've been analyzed by you. It is a fact I have never concealed. Nor is it a false banner that I wave. It is just one of the most basic facts of my life. In spite of "family schooling" (private school and a well-known girls' college), the major, foundational tenets of my education-for-life were learned in analysis. I will tell this to anyone who needs to know.

Whenever any analyst suffers a moment of impatience or doubt—as which of us does not in a profession so unpredictable and demanding?—it is good to reassure himself with some similar generous response to his effort and resume work with renewed faith in his own human potential which psychoanalysis originally activated for him.

Chapter 24

HUMAN POTENTIALITIES FROM THE VIEWPOINT OF EXISTENTIAL PSYCHOLOGY

ADRIAN VAN KAAM

AS a human being I am always involved in the world, in a field of thought, feeling, imagination, expectation, movement and action. I am in this world as an oyster is in its shell, a fish in its pond or a fetus in the womb. For I can exist only in and through the world.

The world does not present the same image to all people. For example, the world in which I live differs from that of the Indians, Bantus or Eskimos. Things have other meanings for them. Thus it seems that we ourselves to some degree make our own world. For reality does not appear the same to men of different periods and cultures. Animals, on the other hand, seem to carry on the same ways of life from generation to generation, from century to century. We do not see much change in their patterns of building shelter or their ways of rearing their young. But we are changing all the time: We dress in new fashions, cultivate the earth with improved machines, build new types of homes, establish new sciences, create new forms of artistic expression and even attempt to fly to the moon. As a human person I do not seem to be so dependent on one life situation as animals seem to be. I make, as it were, my own situation; I take my existence into my own hands and, so doing, I shape my own world. I cannot realize my own potentialities without realizing the potentialities of the world in which I live. Self-actualization always means actualization of both myself and my world. For one cannot happen without the other. Humanity shapes itself by shaping the world.

We changed ourselves into city dwellers by building cities, for example, and into miners by sinking mines; we became readers by printing books, travelers by producing trains, cars and planes, astronauts by creating space craft and satellites. The world is the domain of our possibilities, our field of self-realization. Our human potentialities are ours in and through the world. Without the world we would be nothing potentially. We experiment with the world in an almost infinite variety of ways because this is our only road to becoming. Each time that I am in touch with the world in a new manner I realize a new mode of my humanity. When I probe the world I actualize my potentiality for empirical investigation; when I care for people I grow in love; when I admire the beauty of a sunset I foster my esthetic sense. When I dig a hole, chop down a tree, fly a kite or shovel snow I gain in practical insight, strength and agility. In short, I become human by my manifold engagement in the world.

Thus we realize that our potentialities for growth are not closed up in us but rather bound up with our involvement in reality. In the past people believed human life to be far less changeable than we now know it to be. They thought, moreover, that the development of their potentialities had little to do with changing the course of events around them. As a result they indulged in much speculation but in little scientific investigation, social action, planning and production. They assumed that their immediate way of life would prolong itself through generations without alteration. Instead of improving on adverse situations they considered them natural and unavoidable. Today, on the other hand, we perceive the possibility of amending undesirable conditions of life. As a result we are witnessing an age of change never before known in the history of evolution.

We may conclude, then, that human potentialities are always potentialities involved in a life situation, that they are realized in that situation and not in man's interiority.

Speaking as a psychologist, I do not use the word "potentiality" as meaning lifeless or inert. A human potentiality is a driving force, a dynamic tendency striving toward actualization. A person may be oblivious to this urge, but such unawareness is actually due to repression which inevitably leads to disturbance.

As an existential psychologist I do not accept that viewpoint of the classical psychology of consciousness according to which dynamic tendencies were thought to be neatly tucked away as "things" in the "locker of consciousness," just as perceptions and emotions were supposed to be stored up in this "mental container." For me, a human potentiality is a dynamic tending which is a real mode of human life, of presence to the world. This "tending" permeates my personality, my perception of the world and my behavior, whether or not I actualize this potentiality. Every human potentiality I have is so real that it is impossible for me to totally obscure its traces in my personality. As I sometimes tell my patients, no person can be whole so long as he is unaware of these dynamic tendencies to self-fulfillment and does not come to terms with them realistically in the light of his life situation.

The emergence of a human potentiality thus implies a powerful motive to actualize this potency. The potentiality for walking, for example, which emerges at a certain age is experienced by the child as a tendency toward movement in playpen or living room. His world becomes momentarily structured as a field of realization for this new ability. To a child who is eager to walk, the world becomes different in the light of this potency which presses for actualization: the open arms of his parents become a harbor to which he can safely dare to travel, chairs become instruments to lean upon in his first awkward attempts, belts with which he is bound are now resented as obstacles.

Later on in life we may experience similar reconstructions of our world when we are driven by other strong potentialities. Consider the worlds of the adolescent who experiences his first love, of the executive who strives to reach the top, of the scholar or artist who feels that he can achieve something great in his field. At such peaks of experience other meanings of the world seem to recede into the background. The person involved has an eye only for that which will lead him to his desired goals.

In the past psychology gave much attention to the reduction of various motivations to earlier motivations. For example, the incentive of a hard-working surgeon was sometimes reduced to a sublimation of earlier sadistic inclinations. In certain cases such a reduction may have been totally or partially true. I think, however, that psychologists sometimes overlook the fact that a special ability for surgery in and by itself might play a motivating role in the complex constellation of motivating forces which sustain a person in this particular profession. When a potentiality is actualized, the motivation loses its urgency, the world loses its one-sided structure and becomes reorganized in terms of other potencies. The scholar who has finished this book may go on vacation and experience the world anew; he may feel the urge to dance, sail, swim, race a car or enjoy a lively party. All kinds of other potentialities which had temporarily receded into the background remind him again of their presence. We may call attention here to a hierarchy of human potentialities, a hierarchy which differs somewhat in each individual, a hierarchy according to which certain potentialities are prior in actualization to others. This hierarchy is dependent, first of all, on the developmental structure of man's nature. Certain potentialities, such as the potentiality for bodily movement, hold high rank for all human beings. We learn about this type of hierarchy from developmental psychology. Moreover, culture and environment influence the establishment of the hierarchy of potentialities. Cultural anthropology is very enlightening in this respect. The potentiality for muscular prowess, for example, has a priority among primitive tribes which it could not have in the city of Paris. Accordingly, the meaning of the world is different, in this particular sense, for primitive tribes and for the Parisian. I found an interesting illustration of this principle when I studied a mixed group of North and South American high school seniors in California. The South American girls complained about the absence of potential masculinity in the young men they dated, while North American girls found little potential manliness in the small, polite, agitated young men from below the border. When the matter was discussed in a group therapy session, it became clear that the two national groups had different concepts of what should come first in the hierarchy of potentialities for manly existence. For the South American girls, it was potential "fire" that made a masculine man; for the North Americans, it was a complex of characteristics derived partially from the Hollywood model of movie hero.

Still another influence on this hierarchy of potentialities is inborn affinity. Recently I had the good fortune to interview the parents of one of the great pianists of our time. They described to me how, even as a baby, he almost frightened them with the unusual rhythmic sense which he manifested in his little body when he heard music on the radio or a simple tune whistled in the street. The affinity to sound, rhythm and melody was so intense in him that it soon became an overpowering need, taking priority in the hierarchy of potentialities of this gifted boy.

Finally, there is the impact of personal decision on this hierarchy. For a man may freely decide to give priority in his life to the actualization of one potentiality over others.

Thus we see that a human potentiality—as a mode of existence—is a conscious or unconscious dynamic tendency toward a specific form of self-actualization in the world. As a motivating force it colors personality, perception of the world and behavior; it tends to structure the life-world (Lebenswelt) of the person in its own terms. Which particular potentiality has priority in a person is dependent to a large extent on his prereflective hierarchy of potencies. This hierarchy, in turn, is influenced by man's developmental structure, culture, inborn affinity and personal decision.

Having described its main structures, we may now analyze human potentiality as a concrete process. What are the dynamics at work in a person who under the influence of a potency, tends toward self-actualization? Let us examine further the behavior of the child who experiences the emerging potency for walking. First of all, the child is dissatisfied with sitting still or mere creeping; he is displeased with this confinement. Sitting up and creeping once meant a great mastery for him, a delightful actualization of a pressing potency. But now he no longer feels contentment with what he has achieved. He says "No," as it were, to his state. Affectively, he negates his satisfaction with what he already is; he eagerly anticipates a new fulfillment. If he were satisfied with what he is, he would not feel inclined to seek further accomplishments. This emotional discontentment, this affective declaration of "not enough" is an essential aspect of the dynamics of any human potentiality. We may call this the negative or negating aspect of human potentiality. The positive or affirmative aspect of potentiality, then, is the tendency toward the realization of that which is not yet achieved.

Because man is always human potentiality, his fullness is at the same time emptiness; his contentment is pervaded by discontent; his ease, peace and enjoyment are affected by constraint, anxiety and dissatisfaction. No matter what values I experience in the realization of my potentialities, my experience is never such that my "yes" is definitive and no longer infiltrated by my "no." This negation is present on every level of my existence. Whether I actualize my potentialities in the political, scientific or artistic realm, my "no" will always be present. A technical, social or economic project of my society may attract me as a real possibility for self-actualization of my world. However, I can never give a consent to this project which would not also imply negativity. For, the fact that it cannot fulfill me completely is hidden within it as a worm within a delicious fruit. Therefore, I am never finished in the realization of my potentialities, whether I realize myself as an athlete, philosopher, painter, musician, lover, father or in any other mode of existence. Something similar may be said of my world which I actualize in actualizing my own potentialities. I shall always be dissatisfied with that which is established, determined, finished, completed in the world. My "yes" to my world can never be final. I am urged on constantly. As human potentiality, I am in the world not as a rock, massive, closed, without movement outward and forward, but as a task, open, always in progress, always in encounter with what is not yet me.

The negating aspect of human potentialities would be harmful to me if it led me to the denial or total depreciation of my former achievements, which remain true attainments no matter how limited they may be. If I deny all my qualities and accomplishments and if I am not yet able to realize my further potentialities, I may become depressed, bitter and rebellious. In the extreme, this negation of what I am could even lead to suicide. For, in the light of what I desire to become, I may not only negate but even hate what I am at present. This hate is self-destructive. In a mature person, to be sure, the aspect of negativity is increasingly experienced as one of relativity. That is, the person realizes that his past accomplishments are neither fulfillment nor emptiness but real attainments which are *relatively* valuable in the light of the potentialities which he should yet realize. This attitude leaves room for a certain peace and for further achievement, while preventing self-disparagement and self-destruction.

When we say that man is always potentiality, we mean that man is always "ahead" of himself. For, as we have seen, human potentiality means that man is always tending toward that which he is not yet. Things, on the contrary, are closed in upon themselves; they do not look ahead of themselves; they do not go beyond what they already are. A bookcase does not desire to do something tomorrow or to prepare for something next week; but man lives always in the "not yet." Insofar as I experience myself as not-yet-fulfilled, I tend toward the actualization of my human potentialities. This very tending is a being-ahead-of-myself as I am now. I *exist*, literally, "stand-out" beyond what I already am, toward the realization of that which I am not yet. Because I am never totally satisfied and am always urged on by emerging human potentialities, I am always in the process of becoming. I am "becoming" because I am not merely a determined factual personality; I am also always potentiality for becoming more than I am at a given moment. As soon as I have realized one potentiality, I reach out for the actualization of another. I am always "on the go." I cannot say this of the world of things, of my table, chair or ashtray. As a human person I may actualize a certain passive potentiality of a thing. I may give a certain shape to a piece of wood so that it is changed to a chair or a table. But once it has received this shape, it remains what it is, closed in upon itself. I do not observe in it the restless spontaneous search for new forms of self-actualization which is so obvious in myself and my fellowmen. The table is what it is, finished, factual, determined and measurable in all its dimensions.

But I cannot say about myself that I am as the table is. I experience myself as unfinished, not totally determined, not measurable in all my dimensions. I am circumscribed and measurable in so far as I am determined; I am not circumscribed, I am immeasurable insofar as I am not yet determined, insofar as I am human potentiality, becoming. As long as I live, my shape is not final. This experience of the urge of my human potentiality for new actualization causes me to experience myself not as something that "is" in a final sense, as a stone is a stone: I experience myself as "having to be," as "a being towards," as "becoming," as "project." Each time that my having-to-be or my project is fulfilled, it is only a relative fulfillment, leaving room for tending toward the next realization of myself. Indeed, if I could actualize all my potentialities, I would no longer be man. For it belongs to my very essence as a human being to be human potentiality and not merely factual determination, to be dynamic tendency toward self-actualization and world-actualization.

In short, the fact that I am man implies that I am human potentiality. However, I am not potentiality alone. I am also actualized potentiality. That which exists in my world as a result of this actualization becomes in turn a factual determinant of me and my world. When I have developed my muscles by actualizing them in exercise, for example, my gain in muscle tone and structure is a factual determination of mine that can be measured scientifically. Moreover, this measurable determination of my personality implies many kinds of further human potentialities. Because of the new power of my muscles, I may become an athlete, a porter or a stevedore. The personality which I am as measurable determination is also, as human potentiality, always nondetermination, an "I am able to." I must even say that the factual determinants of my personality are not *real* determinants of myself without this implication of new kinds of potencies. I did not *really* develop muscular strength if my actual muscular development does not imply many capacities for muscular achievement. I did not *really* actualize my potentiality for intellectual thought if I am not able to realize my newly gained capacity in the solution of various problems. Intelligence and aptitude tests are based on this principle. They measure the innate and acquired factual determinations of a person in order to predict whether or not these factual determinants are a basis for many kinds of new potentialities to be realized in specific studies, accomplishments or professions. They do not predict that the person *will* realize these potentialities but only that he *can* realize them.

The above assertion concerning possibility of realization applies to any one of the factual determinants of my personality at any moment of my existence. For example, I am never merely hungry as a factual determinant. Even my hunger implies possibilities. I can use my hunger as a means of protest as Ghandi did; I can seize upon it as a motivation to reorganize my life economically; I can experience it as a stimulus to fierce rebellion against those who never go hungry; I can accept it in passive indifference or as religious mortification. A hunger which does not include any other human potentiality is not a *real* human hunger.

We may conclude that "human potentiality" or "being-able-to" is a necessary characteristic of man. In short, I cannot find a human being who is not at the same time human potentiality for something more than he is at the present moment. Human potentiality is far more than a logical possibility; it is a concrete, actual potency rooted in man's concrete personality and in his actual determinations; it is an active tending. It is the very stuff of my humanity which I can never leave behind me, which will accompany me as long as I live. Therefore, human potentiality is an *existential. Existentials* are the typical necessary characteristics of man as man.

Consequently, a most sordid crime against man is to rob him of his possibilities of self-actualization, which also imply, as we have seen, his possibilities of actualization of his world. Whether a human being is member of a racial minority, a prisoner, an employee, a marriage partner, a child, a student or a patient, he is always a human potentiality tending toward self-actualization by freely actualizing some possibility of his world. My first duty toward my fellowman, then, is to treat him as a human being. This means that I create room for his self-actualization, that I enable him to act freely in the world in which we live together. Industrialization, mass education, mass entertainment, central administration would all be crimes against humanity if they did not allow for the actualization of human potentialities. The individual within modern mammoth organizations must have some opportunity to be himself. I should not smother my fellowman as human potentiality by either overwhelming care or overpowering restraint. Whenever possible, I should allow him to perform awkwardly by himself what I could perhaps do more swiftly and more expertly for him. I should not freeze him into becoming a "thing" by permitting him no creativity.

The deepest revolt of the adolescent, the "layman," the colonial, the minority race, the proletariat, is a revolt against the impossibility to actualize themselves and their world, even though in an unwieldly way. The primary desire of the social "underdog" is not for better food, clothing and shelter, even though he may think so; it is a desire to be simply man, human potentiality. Often, rebellious groups are worse off materially after they have revolted. But they choose to actualize their potentialities in poverty in preference to being kept splendidly in a vegetable state. They do not wish to be debased to the status of well-polished instruments for the self-actualization of a few organization men who desire to change the world on their own.

A brilliant administrator may in fact actualize himself through the creation of almost ideal economic conditions for large numbers of people without leaving them any room for self-realization through full and free participation in the very creation and maintenance of such conditions. Such an administrator commits a crime against mankind, for he destroys what man basically is: human potentiality. He may attempt to hide from himself the magnitude of his crime by maintaining that he is most altruistic because he works day and night for the welfare of others. But precisely in doing so much for others he proves his self-centeredness. While enjoying the actualization of his own potentialities by constantly realizing a world of welfare for others, he paralyzes his protégés as human potentiality in so far as he does not allow them free voice and action in his enterprise. Paternalism and patronage can be attacks on the very being of man.

When people cannot fulfill their potentialities in reality, they will often attempt to do so in fantasy. They will spend much time in the movie theater or watching TV, identifying themselves with heroes who realize themselves freely and impressively. Or they may escape into an artificial dream world created by drugs, or drink themselves into a stupor or "explode" in destructive, senseless acts. Herein, perhaps, lies the explanation of so much "unexplainable" violence among certain groups in our contemporary society.

From an existential psychological point of view, then, human potentiality is a necessary characteristic of man as man. Its free development or its criminal abuse is crucial both for the individual and for society.

REFERENCES

1. Calon, P. J. A., and Prick, J. J. G.: *Psychologische grondbegrippen.* Arnhem, Holland, Van Loghum Slaterus, 1962.
2. Dondeyne, A.: *Contemporary European Thought and Christian Faith.* Pittsburgh, Duquesne Univ. Press, 1958.
3. Gurwitsch, A.: *Field of Consciousness.* Pittsburgh, Duquesne Univ. Press, 1964.
4. Kwant, R. C.: *Encounter.* Pittsburgh, Duquesne Univ. Press, 1960.
5. Kwant, R. C.: *The Phenomenological Philosophy of Merleau-Ponty.* Pittsburgh, Duquesne Univ. Press, 1963.
6. Luijpen, W. A.: *Existential Phenomenology.* Pittsburgh, Duquesne Univ. Pres, 1960.
7. Luijpen, W. A.: *Phenomenology and Atheism.* Pittsburgh, Duquesne Univ. Press, 1964.
8. Maslow, A. H.: *Motivation and Personality.* New York, Harper and Row, 1954.
9. May, R., and van Kaam, A.: Existential theory and therapy. *Curr. Psychiat. Ther., Vol. III.* New York, Grune and Stratton, Inc., 1963.
10. Strasser, S.: *Phenomenology and the Human Sciences.* Pittsburgh, Duquesne Univ. Press, 1963.
11. Strasser, S.: *The Soul in Metaphysical and Empirical Psychology.* Pittsburgh, Duquesne Univ. Press, 1957.
12. van Kaam, A. L.: Assumptions in psychology. *J. Individ. Psychol., 14*:22-28, 1958.
13. van Kaam, A. L.: Clinical implications of Heidegger's concepts of will, decision, and responsibility. *Rev. Exist. Psychol. Psychiat., 1*:205-16 (Fall), 1961.
14. van Kaam, A. L.: Commentary on "Freedom and Responsibility Examined." In Lloyd-Jones, Ester, and Westervelt, Ester M. (eds.): *Behavioral Science and Guidance, Proposals and Perspectives.* New York, Teachers College, Columbia Univ. Press, 1963.
15. van Kaam, A. L.: Counseling and existential psychology. *Harvard Educational Rev.* (Fall), 1962.
16. van Kaam, A. L.: Existential psychology as a theory of personality. *Rev. Exist. Psychol. Psychiat., 3* (Winter), 1963.

17. VAN KAAM, A. L.: The fantasy of romantic love. *Modern Myths and Popular Fancies.* Pittsburgh, Duquesne Univ. Press, 1961.
18. VAN KAAM, A. L.: Freud and anthropological psychology. *The Justice.* Brandeis Univ. (May), 1959.
19. VAN KAAM, A. L.: Humanistic psychology and culture. *J. Hum. Psychol., 1*:94-100 (Spring), 1961.
20. VAN KAAM, A. L.: The impact of existential phenomenology on the psychological literature of Western Europe. *Rev. Exist. Psychol. Psychiat., 1*:63-92, 1961.
21. VAN KAAM, A. L.: *A Light to the Gentiles.* Detroit, Bruce, 1962.
22. VAN KAAM, A. L.: The nurse in the patient's world. *Amer. J. Nursing, 59*:1708-10, 1959.
23. VAN KAAM, A. L.: Phenomenal analysis: Exemplified by a study of the experience of "really feeling understood." *J. Individ. Psychol., 15*: 66-72, 1959.
24. VAN KAAM, A. L.: A psychology of the Catholic intellectual. In, HAZO, SAMUEL (ed.): *The Christian Intellectual.* Pittsburgh, Duquesne Univ. Press, 1963.
25. VAN KAAM, A. L.: A psychology of falling-away-from-the-faith. *Insight, 2*:2, 3-17 (Fall), 1963.
26. VAN KAAM, A. L.: Religion and existential will. *Insight, 1*:1 (Summer), 1962.
27. VAN KAAM, A. L.: Review of *The Divided Self* by R. D. Laing. *Rev. Exist. Psychol. Psychiat., 2*:85-88 (Winter), 1962.
28. VAN KAAM, A. L.: *Religion and Personality.* Englewood Cliffs, Prentice-Hall, 1964.
29. VAN KAAM, A. L.: Sex and existence. *Rev. Exist. Psychol. Psychiat., 3* (Spring), 1963.
30. VAN KAAM, A. L.: *The Third Force in European Psychology.* Greenville, Delaware, Psychosynthesis Research Foundation, 1960.
31. VAN KAAM, A. L.: *The Vocational Director and Counseling.* Derby, New York, St. Paul Publications, 1962.

PART V

CURRENT INVESTIGATIONS IN HUMAN POTENTIALITIES

Chapter 25

TOWARD A PSCHOLOGY OF TRANSCENDENT BEHAVIOR

SIDNEY M. JOURARD

A PSYCHOLOGY of transcendent behavior in man is long overdue. We have a very detailed psychology of man as he is usually perceived; this psychology, well grounded in systematic research, permits us to understand how a man or animal has become as he is now. It can even serve as the basis for prediction of his future condition, action and experience.

But our current psychologies concern themselves with only half of man's potentialities for being, the half he shares with animals, objects in nature and man-made things. Our psychologies view man as *determined* by his structure, his past or the forces of the present. The thesis is that if these factors are specified, variance in man's action and experience can largely be explained. This approach neglects, even undermines the other, peculiarly human and more important half of man's being—his capacity for freedom, his possibility of transcending determiners of all kinds and actualizing projects of his own choosing.

Every goal, every project a man sets *for himself* and sets about achieving—whether it is making something, getting somewhere or becoming somebody—is a gesture of defiance in the face of forces that make fulfillment of this project improbable. The world has an inertia and a momentum of its own; so has the body, as a natural object. This matrix of simultaneously acting forces or "determiners" will pull, push or mold man's experience and action in the way a current carries a twig, or wind and rain sculpture a rocky outcrop—but only if man *chooses to be an object* in the world. This way of being is experienced as "familiar," "habit," "the path of least resistance," "resignation," etc. It is a choice of being what is available to us at every moment of our existence; but just as man can choose to be shaped, pushed, pulled or carried by the thrust of past and present forces, so can he transcend this way and propose goals and projects that would never come into being if he had not chosen to risk actualizing them. Man's intentionality, will or decision to do or be something is a force in its own right, a force that exists under the sun as surely as do wind, biological pressures and social norms. If this will or freedom of choice is renounced, repressed or resigned, then behavior will indeed be the resultant of specifiable, natural forces.

Each decision, choice or project transcends the specifiable determiners that would make man predictable. If a psychologist knew all the forces and determiners that were operative and bearing upon the person and he could measure the strength and direction of these forces, he *still could not* predict the action, experience or condition with precision unless the individual revealed whether he intended to "rise above" or acquiesce to the operative determiners. If the person's goal were known, the psychologist could weigh forces and make some prediction about the probability of fulfillment. Man's predictability is either proof of the extent to which he has become alienated from his intentional will or testimony of the degree to which he has confided his projects to the psychologist.

A psychology of transcendent behavior is based on a psychology of the will, such as Rank attempted to develop, or a psychology of the *experience* of freedom. It also includes description of *possibilities* of being or an estimate of the ever-receding limits of human potentiality. The present psychology of man as a determined being portrays man in his modal state, his most usual way of appearing to others and to himself. A psychology of transcendent behavior assumes there are possible levels of experiencing and behaving that *go beyond* the modal level. It postulates that, under most conditions of existence, man functions at a level which is the outcome of his acquiescence to "forces" and "determiners," especially his socialization. From time to time, however, he gets glimmerings from his own experience and that of other people, of *higher* ways of being that are possible for him. He sometimes experiences the world in greater richness, feels upsurges of strength or accomplishes goals so atypical of him that even he is shocked. He learns of the amazing accomplishments of others, feats that give proof of apparently superhuman experience, beyond the reach of mere mortals like himself—works of art, music, invention, athletic prowess and the like that defy all forces militating against them. These are the focus of a psychology of optimal functioning or transcendence. They are ways of being that call for description, explanation and for specification of the conditions under which they will emerge.

One reason we have no psychology of transcendence or optimal functioning may lie in the relationship between the individual and the social system. There is ample reason to suspect that man, as we encounter him, is fundamentally estranged, alienated from his own experience and possibilities. He has renounced his experience of freedom and his freedom to experience. In order to conform to the social systems in which he exists and to a sclerosed concept of himself, man feels obliged to conceal much of his experience from others. If he conceals too effectively, he becomes alienated from his experience. Phenomenologists are discovering that typical human experience is fragmented, serialized, objectified, separated from action—in short, reduced from its earlier promise of richness and wholeness. Indeed, we denigrate as infantile, mentally ill or primitive those persons who report experience in which fantasy, memory, feeling, perception, conceptualizing and action are all integrated into a rich syncretic unity. We reward the man whose experience of himself and the world is fragmented or intellectualized and schematized, like a blueprint or map. He is studied by psychologists, while "transcendents," those who have "peak experiences" or a deviant experience of the world are not studied or conceal their offbeat experience. *Thus, the possibility arises that our psychology is a faithful report of human beings who have complied with social pressures and have reduced their experience of themselves and their world in order to "play it safe" and conform.* If this is true, there is all the more reason for developing a psychology of transcendence or optimal functioning. If man functions typically in the "reduced" state, but has the potentiality for transcending it, then we are called upon to explore the conditions under which such potentiality can be fulfilled. Toward this end there are included here some attested examples of human functioning beyond modal limits and some of the conditions for their emergence. It is hoped that this may provide a beginning of an era where such a special field will not be needed but is instead included in "general psychology." Actually, the study of transcendent functioning is a misnomer. Man doesn't transcend his real being; he transcends only someone's *concept* of his being—his own concept or that of an investigator or a witness to his conduct. Man cannot go beyond his ultimate limits. He only reveals powers beyond someone's *concept* of his limits. If modal man's actualizing of possibilities is a feeble hint of what he might be, do or become, and if man might become what he (or someone) is capable of *imagining* he might become, then wild imagination about human possibilities must be encouraged, both in individuals and in those who function as consulting specialists. Surely it is a sad commentary on the profession of psychology that writers of science fiction, certain leaders, poets, mystics, inspired teachers of the young all have been more productive of concepts of human possibility than psychologists. They also may know more about the ways of bringing them into being than psychologists do. Too often psychologists have "sold" knowledge of determining factors in human behavior and experience to "highest bidders" (in business, industry, government or other institutions) who want, not to enlarge man's freedom *to* and freedom *of* experience, but rather to confine his being to an expedient, safe and profitable range.

TRANSCENDENT BEHAVIOR

To describe the examples of man's revealing unsuspected capacities, the term "transcendent" was chosen because it embodies the idea of "going beyond" or "surpassing." Accordingly, "transcendent thinking," "transcendent survival" or "transcendent learning," as used in this chapter, refers to human experiences or actions which to an observer or to the person himself seem improbable or even impossible. *The use here of the term "transcendent" is related to but not identical with its use in philosophical writing.*

Transcendent behavior, in contrast with habitual behavior, carries with it an element of surprise or unpredictability. In transcendent behavior, the person is literally "rising above" forces thought to be determinants, e.g., social pressure, habit, physical limitations, such as blindness or lameness, all of which predispose some highly probable range of responses. In transcendent behavior the individual adds his own latent powers to the array of impersonal forces affecting him, and thus the behavior he manifests may impress the observer as unexpected. Transcendent behavior implies a release of latent potentialities, of capabilities to perceive, invent, create, achieve, endure or perform. In most people these capacities lie buried under the "crust" and inertia of habit, rigid role definitions and confining self-concepts. First, in transcendent behavior, the individual is transcending himself or, more literally, his concept of himself. Some conditions or situations *release* or evoke latent resources in him, resources which ordinarily are suppressed and hence unconscious. He responds to situations in novel, unusual, valuable ways, and these ways depart from those which have been most typical of him up to the moment of transcendence. It is also possible that the transcendent performance of the person will exceed the performance of many other persons who have been confronted by similar challenges.

Some Examples of Transcendent Behavior

Transcendent Thinking: Creativity and Originality

There is inertia associated with all levels of functioning, both behavioral and experiential. Forces predispose toward continuation of sameness in thinking, feeling and overt behavioral responses to situations. Freud referred in this connection to a "repetition compulsion" that seems inherent to man. He implied that this "compulsion" is instinctive. Modern behavior theorists are able to show that persistence of behavior is in large measure explainable in terms of reinforcement histories and schedules of reinforcement. That is, behavior (including perception as well as overt motor responses) tends to persist so long as it is reinforced or rewarded. Sociologists point to constraint on the individual imposed by "agencies of social control." Personality theorists see the self-concept and the need to maintain a sense of identity as factors in persistent behavior and modes of experiencing the self and the world.

Inventiveness is a departure from the usual. Novel solutions to problems, new ideas in art, literature and science all seem improbable at first. They arise in the mind of their creator spontaneously, effortlessly and sometimes playfully. New ideas seem to crop up when the artist or inventor is *not* trying. Zen Buddhists refer to this experience as "no-mind" (4). They mean by this not empty-headedness or stupidity but rather a cessation of active striving or searching for novelty. The inspired acts of creation seem to occur *after* a person has struggled hard to discover a new truth, a new idea or the solution to some vexing and pressing problem. Once the new invention has come into being, it carries with it the quality of transcendence. The inventor has transcended his own and sometimes all mankind's present limitations.

Here we have a hint of a condition for release of transcendent behavior and experience, namely, the ability to "let oneself be," to "let go," to "stop trying," to let our thoughts play or flow spontaneously, without seeking to guide our thinking process. It goes without saying that novel, original ideas must be criticized and tested for their utility. Not all that is original is immediately useful for human purposes.

Transcendent Perception

Generally, we see the world in its conventional rubrics. We see someone and identify the person as a woman because she has the hair, curves, voice and gait of women in general. We look at her long enough to assign her to some categories—e.g., pretty or ugly, willing or unwilling, marriageable or not, and then look at her no more. We usually observe the world under the impetus and direction of our needs, values, feelings and purposes of the moment. Such need-steered perception certainly serves a vital role in our survival and adaptation, but it also tends to blind us to all features of the world that are not immediately relevant to our present hungers, desires and values. "Desireless," or "undriven" cognition—when we simply open our eyes, ears, noses, taste buds, kinesthetic and organic receptors and let stimuli play upon them and impress them—seems to be the condition for the enriched mode of perception. This mode of perception (Maslow calls it "B-Cognition," or "cognition of 'Being,'" and Schachtel refers to it as "allocentric" perception) (5) adds new dimensions to experience or, rather, it permits new dimensions to happen. Colors are seen more vividly; and things, animals, people or scenes are perceived in their "suchness," in their concrete uniqueness, almost transfigured.

Moments of such perception are experienced by people as unforgettable. In fact, when people recall the past with vivid imagery, the content of their recollection is almost always the moments when they let the world impress itself upon their senses without selection. They let the world disclose itself to them. When two people fall in love and are truly open and unguarded in their communication with one another, they come to see one another as unique, irreplaceable, quite *unlike* any other human being in the world—certainly not as mere representatives of the classes, men and women. And though it is true that "lovers" who are merely starved for companionship, are in fact somewhat "blind"—they see in the other only the means of sating present appetites and hungers—it is also true that happy, fulfilled lovers see one another *and the world* more richly and more veridically. In this sense one can say that people who are in love, people who are open and spontaneous in relation to their loved ones, are *at that time* also more open to their own experiencing and more perceptive of the real world. Their senses all seem keener, and the world discloses itself more vividly to their eyes, ears, skin and olfactory lobes, to their experience. Their imaginations, too, are released, and their capacity for metaphorical, poetic description is aroused, hence the plethora of poetry on love. Incidentally, it may be that the capacity to think metaphorically is an index of one's access to transcendent powers. Such cognition, then, because it is rare and valued, may be called transcendent perception.

We may well ask: Why is it so rare? Why is rubricized perception, perception of things and people as mere members of categories, so common and usual? The answer probably lies in the fact that average people are most often in the midst of many simultaneous conditions of privation, of need, and so their egos, their perceptual apparatus, remain servants of unfulfilled desires. Here, then, we have a hint for yet another condition for transcendent functioning in general; namely, it may presume the fulfillment or devivifying of most of the person's pressing needs. Once these needs have been met the person has, as it were, been released from the urgencies of the quest of gratification—he doesn't want to consume the world or exploit it. He can be content to let it be and let it impress him with its "suchness."

So far we have proposed that "letting oneself be" and basic-need gratification are conditions for the release of transcendent experience and behavior in a person. Now let us explore further.

Transcendent Remembering

Most people have some difficulty recalling things when they are asked to do so or when they have some need for information from the past. Like perception, remembering is an act of the total organism, and it is controlled to some extent by the pressure of immediate needs and interests. Hence, one's recall of the past is highly selective and highly subject to the shaping and distorting influence of present needs, sets and wishes (6). Sometimes, too, persons have a need *not* to remember selected aspects of past experience; so they will have large lacunae in their recall of the personal past. These gaps may be filled with fabrications and lies, and at other times the gaps are experienced as such. It was to explain these failures or inabilities at recollection of the past that Freud proposed his theory of repression. Memories will be actively repressed when their recollection would yield anxiety, shame or assaults to one's present self-esteem.

Yet, the experience of psychoanalytic therapists and of hypnotists, has shown that under certain conditions, massive and vividly "imaged" recollection of past events—even of early childhood—is sometimes possible. Certain drugs, viz., sodium pentothal, likewise release vivid and unresisted recall of the past. So do certain sensory triggers, such as an odor, a sound or, as occurred with Proust, the feeling of an uneven cobblestone under his feet. These *unresisted* acts of remembering occur under special conditions, which we will explore, since they may throw further light on our quest for the conditions of transcendent behavior in general.

When a patient undergoing psychotherapy finally arrives at a stage where he trusts his therapist utterly and feels fully accepted by him, he drops his defenses, relaxes and *lets himself be* while he is in the presence of his therapist. "Letting himself be," in this context, means that he lets his thoughts, his memories, his feeling and his fantasies unfold *spontaneously*. He does not try to direct or steer the content of his cognitive field. Rather, he lets the process happen. Under these conditions remembrances will arise that surprise even the patient. He will relate events from his past with remarkable detail and then say with some surprise: "I haven't thought of these things in years." He may be able to recall entire passages of poetry that were learned in grammar school and long since "forgotten"; he may recall scenes in which he and his parents or friends shared some experiences and be able to narrate entire conversations.

Hypnotists have been able to "regress" their subjects to younger age levels. They are able to suggest to their hypnotic subjects that they are now nine years old, or six. If the subject has truly been cooperating in the hypnotic experiment, he will begin to behave in a manner that resembles that of a child; and he will frequently bring forth, on request, vivid narratives from his own life of events that truly happened in that age interval (7).

There must be something in common between the condition of "letting oneself be," that arises in conventional psychotherapy and responding to a hypnotist's invitation to experience oneself as younger. The similarity appears to lie in the *dropping of defenses;* the relaxation of defenses is in turn a by-product or concomitant of *trust* that has been elicited or earned by the professional person, such that his invitations will be complied with. In addition to the relaxation of defenses and the trust, there appears to be a factor of focusing, of undivided, undistracted, fascinated attention to the flow of one's experience. In everyday, modal living one can seldom concentrate fully upon any one thing for long. Indeed, to do so invites a stupor akin to or identical with hypnoidal state (8). Furthermore, the average person has many interests, needs and wishes simultaneously operative;

and no sooner is one need fulfilled than another tension arises. These pressures seem to preclude or prevent the uprush of the past into the present; probably this serves adaptive functions in that it permits people to live in the present. But the ability fully to recall episodes from the past can also serve adaptive functions in the present, and it can enrich experience. Consequently, an enlarged capacity to recall has value. Novelists and playwrights depend on it for the practice of their art. Transcendent remembering thus is seen to share certain factors in common with transcendent perception, namely, a relaxed, "need-free," undriven, secure present state. Further, in addition to "letting be" and need-gratification, we have added *focusing* and *trust* (of another and of the self) to our list of probable factors in trancendence.

Transcendent Learning

The process of learning some skilled performance or a list of nonsense syllables or some meaningful verbal material is usually described in psychology textbooks with learning curves. If it is errors that are being plotted against trials, a gradual dropping-off is portrayed. If it is number of correct responses that are being plotted, these are shown to increase up to some maximum level; and at this point, the curve becomes horizontal. The person who is seeking to learn something generally experiences considerable effort as he struggles with the demands of the task. If someone addressed a skill to be learned, a poem to be memorized or a technique to be mastered and "absorbed" it almost instantly, it surely would be marvelled at. It could truly be called transcendent learning. Insight in learning appears to be a special case of transcendent learning.

Such transcendent learning falls within the experience of most people, but only rarely. The reason, again, is not to be found in the "difficulty" of the task, but rather in the *resistance* to full focusing and attending to the problem at hand. Testimony of persons who have mastered complicated learning assignments with transcendent ease shows that they reach these moments when they have gotten "warmed up." The "warm-up" process (9) is not unlike a process of "purging"; in this instance, purging one's experience of all thoughts, fantasies, interests and feelings save *fascination* (10) with the problem. The subjective experience of fascination is probably what learning theorists have attempted to explain with the concept of "motivation to learn." But motivation to learn has generally been provided for by rewards and punishments that follow the outcome of the learning process. When a person has become fascinated by a poem to be memorized, a concert to be played, a technique to be learned (and assuming he has already mastered prerequisite basic skills), he addresses the problem with undivided mind. His very being, from hair to toenails is focused upon the problem; and its solution or mastery comes effortlessly.

Again, the factor that seems inherent to transcendent learning is that of "letting be"—in this case, letting oneself become fascinated or absorbed. When one is so absorbed, all else is excluded from awareness, *one "opens up" to the information being disclosed by the problem or task,* and one "lets" one's problem-solving apparatus work by itself.

Another factor that seems inherent to transcendent learning is that the task or problem must have *meaning* and value to the person who is addressing it. It must have meaning in and for itself, as well as meaning in the sense of a means to other ends. Probably the instrumental value of the learning provides the incentive for selecting the task in the first place. Whether or not the learning that takes place is transcendent depends upon the availability of the fascination response. Thus, we add value and meaning to our list of factors in transcendence.

Transcendent Achievement

Why was Sir Edmund Hilary able to climb to the peak of Mount Everest when other climbers failed, though they were apparently as well trained and comparably supported by helpers and technical gadgetry? Why were the Wright Brothers able to get a motor-driven plane off the ground when others failed? Why does an ordinary football player sometimes make an inspired run which wins a game?

If we assume that such inspired and transcendent actions occur in some people who have been adequately prepared or trained and not in other people with comparable preparation and training, we are left in a quandary. Presumably, since the remarkable achievement was accomplished, the *capacity* to accomplish it lay dormant in the several contenders for the goal. Why did the successful act emerge from this person rather than that? Let us set aside the factor of luck, although it is important.

The most plausible hypothesis is that the remarkable achievement occurred in the contender who was most fully *committed* to its attainment. Commitment is a curious and little-understood phenomenon, one to which the term "motivation" hardly does justice.

When one is "committed" to some course of action, some goal or some mission, one can roughly gauge the degree of commitment in terms of the *price the contender is willing to risk to attain the goal.* The ultimate commitment, of course, is to stake one's life or safety. Before one is willing to expend one's time, energy or money in pursuit of some mission, one must believe utterly that it is worth it; hence values and meaning are involved. When one's reputation or one's life or anything else is being risked in pursuit of some mission, then the person must believe the goal is worth it in order to be able *to release his inner resources* (viz., inventiveness, resourcefulness, endurance, strength, self-control, etc.) fully for the task. If he only half believes in the worth of the mission, he will hold back (12). Such commitment, indeed, seems to be one condition for such release. Perhaps here we have another hint of a condition for transcendent achievement—the capacity to see accomplishments as having so much intrinsic importance that they are worth staking everything of value in the attempt to achieve them. This is not to underestimate the importance of making preparations, taking safety measures, having equipment and downright luck. Rather, the element of commitment seems to induce or inspire the contender to go where others fear to tread, there to find not danger but rather the means to the end. Further, commitment seems to release hitherto latent and unsuspected capacities in the individual. It is an "integrator" of the person, from toenails to fantasy, such that no muscle works against muscle, and mental processes are synchronized with physical processes.

The one factor which most great achievers saliently share is this capacity to commit themselves, bordering on fanaticism (13). The absence of self-doubt and the absence of doubt about the worth of the mission seem to be essential to such commitment, while the commitment itself seems to be necessary to the release of inner resources that bring success. Probably the modal personality is less able to commit himself fully to a given mission and is obliged by the facts of his life to "spread himself thin"—to make a living, protect his reputation, etc. In fact, he may be committed to some role or status, and this commitment precludes new ones! This is not entirely a bad thing, and it seems necessary to effective living within society. Such division of purposes, however, seems to preclude "magnificent achievements"(14).

Transcendent Survival

Another category of transcendent behavior is sheer physical survival under conditions where death is the best possible estimate of the outcome predisposed by the given conditions.

The successful voyage in 1916 of Sir Ernest Shackleton and his five companions in an open boat across fifteen hundred miles of Antarctic Sea, with scant rations, skimpy clothing and subzero temperatures illustrates transcendent survival, notwithstanding the technical know-how in seamanship of the six men.

Perhaps better illustrations of transcendent survival are provided by the tragic, infinitesimal percentage of Nazi concentration camp inmates who managed to live under conditions cruelly designed by the administrators of the camps to hasten death. The horrifying and yet inspiring accounts of Bettelheim (15), Frankl (16) and others offer evidence both of wholehearted, dedicated bestiality on the part of captors and transcendent survival powers on the part of the prisoners who escaped death.

How did the survivors do it? The consensus appears to maintain that survival was contingent, among other things, upon a powerful commitment to life, upon the conviction that survival had purpose and meaning in spite of the incredible hardships of daily existence. The concentration camp survivors were persons who were capable of finding new meanings and reasons and purposes for life when the usual purposes and meanings had gone by the wayside. Frankl, who survived the death camps and went on to become a spokesman for the "existential psychiatry," summarized his view of the values which can sustain life, even in death camps, as follows (17):

> Man has the freedom and responsibility to pursue *creative* values, that is, to work, to make things, to use his energy and resources to produce wealth, or goods. He has the freedom and responsibility to pursue *experiential* values—the good things that life provides, such as beauty, food, pleasure, etc. When creative and experiential values can no longer be fulfilled, as occurs, for example, under conditions of the death camps, or as occurs when one knows that he will soon die, then man has the freedom and responsibility to fulfill *attitudinal values.* This last term has reference to the attitude with which one faces the certainty of death, or extreme hardship. Ideally, one will face these extremities responsibly, seeking to give them meaning, and seeking to address them at a *human* level rather than at a level of less responsible functioning.

Another type of transcendent survival is illustrated by persons who recover from illnesses or injuries which are diagnosed as fatal or incurable. There are many instances of persons who, as it were, defied the best medical opinion and survived cancers thought to be incurable and inoperable. To the best of my understanding, based on available literature, interviews with physicians and nurses and some contact with patients who displayed this talent for survival, the decisive factor was again a strong desire and reason for living. Probably, given such a strong commitment to life, *healing capacities that ordinarily lie dormant are drawn upon or released.* Doubtless, the maintenance of hope and of determination to live can promote survival, whereas hopelessness and loss of a sense of meaning or purpose for existence can suppress these latent healing reflexes (18). The capacity of a physician, minister, relative or of the patient himself to elicit in him a determination to live and to maintain hope for a meaningful existence has been relatively ignored by scientific students of factors in health (19). In spite of the lack of scientific understanding of the underlying process, any efforts to mobilize hope and a "fighting spirit" in sick people have good promise of tilting the balance of forces in the direction of recovery. We can call this capacity the capacity to inspire or to "inspirit," and it seems to be a capacity found in so-called "charismatic leaders."

Transcendent Personality Reorganization

This category of transcendent functioning is drawn broadly, to cover such diverse occurrences as: the rehabilitation of confirmed criminals to responsible social living; the achievement of Helen Keller at establishing linguistic communication with other people in spite of deafness and blindness; the many instances of people who have risen above environmental forces that predisposed to the development of delinquency, criminality, ignorance, superstition, to attain high standards of achievement, etc.

In all such instances, a common thread may be discerned, namely, a refusal to submit to the apparently overpowering forces of the environment and to apparent limitations (as defined by somebody) of one's own organism. Some of the "transcendents" were able to release their powers by recourse to prayer or other religious practices. Others were inspired or challenged to rise above limitations by another human being who saw potential in them. Still others made the transcendence by sheer faith in their own potentials, when no other human being seemed to share this faith. Perhaps it is at this point that a personal relationship with one's God serves its purpose—the individual feels that, though no human loves him, God does and, moreover, God expects him to keep trying.

The best therapists of personality may have this capacity to discern potentials for transcendence in a patient when neither the patient nor others can see such capacities. Further, the effective therapist is able *to communicate this belief in the patient's potentials to the patient.* Finally, the therapist is able to provoke or inspire the patient not to resign in conformity and acquiescence to the limiting forces of his environment, his past or his perhaps defective body, but rather to see these apparent limits as *challenges.*

This analysis suggests that the concept which a person has of himself (his self-concept), as well as the concept of him held by other people in his life can be factors in transcendence or in the inability to transcend present modes of functioning. If a person *believes* himself to be weak, helpless or doomed to some fate or other, he will tend to behave or suffer in the way expected. If, on the other hand, he has a concept of himself as a being with much untapped potential to cope with problems and contradictions in his life, then when these arise, he will persist in efforts to cope with them long after someone who sees himself as ineffective and impotent has given up.

When some significant other person, such as a teacher, coach, therapist or minister, believes he sees potentials for functioning in an individual which the latter cannot presently see in himself, he can sometimes convince or inspire the pupil or patient to efforts which bring success. Under those conditions, the pupil or patient undergoes of necessity a change in self-concept, so as to encompass his perception of new capacities, hitherto not imagined. In fact, there is something in common between an effective hypnotist (20) and an effective teacher, leader or therapist. A hypnotist is able to capture the attention and confidence of his subject; and, through verbal suggestions, he can modify the subject's perceptions of self and the world and his beliefs about self and the world. Ordinarily, a person cannot lie outstretched between two chairs spaced two feet apart, and then support another person who stands on his body over the space. Under hypnosis, the subject believes he is as rigid as a board, behaves that way and, indeed, supports the unaccustomed weight. The hypnotist knows that the subject's body has the capacity to support the unusual weight, and he elicits and focuses his subject's strength for the task at hand. A good teacher, therapist or minister knows (or profoundly believes) that all men have unplumbed capacities for learning, achievement, health or goodness, and through the relationship with their students or patients these specialists modify the latter's beliefs about their own potentials and the consequent performances. If a person will not permit his present concept of self to be shaken, then of course it remains a constraining influence on his behavior; and transcendence will seldom occur in his life.

Review of Factors in Transcendent Behavior

Let us bring together into one section the factors that seemed to be involved in the emergence of the different examples of transcendent behavior and discuss them in a little more detail. Perhaps in the process of so doing we shall increase our understanding of this valuable mode of functioning and become better able to elicit it in others and in ourselves.

Letting Be

One of the factors which we mentioned in discussing transcendent thinking or creative endeavor was the attitude of letting be (21). This term is difficult to define in abstract terms, for it refers to a mode of experiencing that must be experienced to be known. As close as I can come to defining it is to describe some common occasions when average people are most likely to be in a state of "letting themselves be." For example, when one has soaked oneself for half an hour or so in a hot bath, one becomes extremely limp, relaxed and passive. One's mind or thoughts, so long as one does not fall asleep, are most likely to drift or play about, without conscious direction. If that is the case, then one is letting himself be. In the state of letting be, the individual does not seek to steer, guide or direct each thought as it arises, but instead permits it to arise and be followed by whatever thought, image or memory comes next. *If* the person who is thus letting himself be has "plugged in" a problem that is to be solved and has previously exhausted all conscious, logical, methodical efforts at its solution, the probability is increased that the problem will "solve itself" when the man is letting himself be. This will be true, of course, only if the question or problem falls within the realm of solvability by humans.

Letting be, however, cannot be attained so long as a person is in a state of vigilance, anxiety or conscious *trying* for the attainment of some goal or other. These latter states seem to channel or steer the thinking processes and do not permit the free flow of all kinds of thoughts. Instead, under privation, anxiety or striving conditions only those thoughts arise which are directly relevant to unfulfilled needs or the successful completion of the task in process. Thus, letting be seems most likely to arise only when most pressing problems in existence are *temporarily in abeyance*. Probably, a person who is able, at will, to effectively suppress his ongoing concerns so as to permit "letting be" to arise in himself has more chances of experiencing it, since few people are ever, for long, in a need- and problem-free state.

Openness

A man makes himself "open" to other men when he reveals to them what he is thinking or feeling—when he discloses his experiencing to the other person. In order to do this fully and freely the disclosing person must, of course, trust that he is in no danger when he is thus unguarded, defenseless and open. Yet, as we indicated above, in our discussion of transcendent cognition, when man is that trusting and open, he is also simultaneously in the state when his sense receptors are maximally open to be impressed with what is there to be seen, heard, tasted, smelled or felt. When a person is guarded and defensive before other men or nature his sense organs serve a searching function, and they are highly selective, seeking sources of danger and safety. This means that the man will be relatively blind to all things that are irrelevant to his present concerns. Thus, a sense of safety, a sense of trust in the good will of other people in the situation seem all to be essential to openness which, in turn, permits transcendent cognition to take place. Persons who have been competent in coping with their needs and problems and who are interpersonally competent—able to establish safe relationships with others—will be most able to experience moments of openness.

Focusing and Fascination

When one has become fascinated by something—a problem, a person, a book, a scene—then the object of fascination fills a person's experience, and nothing else exists for him. This is the case, for example, in "true dialogue" between persons as Buber has described it (22). The participants in dialogue are "fully there"—their thoughts are not preoccupied with unfinished business or fantasy that is irrelevant to the ongoing conversation. Under conditions of fascination, when the fascinated person is fully focused upon the problem with which he is dealing, he is at that time wholly *unself-conscious.* He is wholly single-minded (as opposed to two-minded). When a man is thus "single-minded," his total organism seems to become integrated or organized into its most efficient mode for full functioning, and so it is little wonder that the fascinated person is the one to whom occurs the inspired actions, guesses, solutions and creative thoughts. But the capacity to become fascinated and hence fully focused upon some one thing, person or problem is not easily regulated. It seems instead to require freedom from customary role-definitions, convention and habit. It calls for the courage and freedom to get out of one's ego, one's self-concept, even out of time and space as usually fragmented.

Persons are most likely to display some form of transcendent behavior in situations where they have the freedom to become fascinated with what truly does fascinate them. Unfortunately, not all things in which people spontaneously become fascinated are of equal social value; indeed, some targets of fascination may endanger a man's reputation or job. Therefore, many people may be ashamed or afraid to pursue their fascinations and decrease thereby their opportunities for transcendent functioning.

Commitment and Values

Transcendent behavior has been shown to occur most usually in persons who are committed to some goal to which they assign high value. Commitment implies price. The more fully a person is commited to some project, problem or outcome, the more of his time, energy and personal resources he freely devotes to the quest on which he is launched. The conditions under which people are able to become strongly committed to their work or to truth, justice, beauty or goodness are not as yet fully understood. Since values are created by man it is most likely that an individual will become committed to some goal, achievement or task when there have been leaders or predecessors who provide an inspiring example to imitate. Another factor which seems to promote commitment is the promise of large rewards, whether immediate or remote, concrete or symbolic. The persons who become committed to some unpopular cause, who have to fight public opinion, poverty and even danger to life without support are more difficult to explain.

Self-confidence and a Concept of Self as Transcendent

People in whom transcendent behavior is a relatively frequent occurrence likely are persons who trust themselves and have developed some measure of confidence in their powers to cope with situations as they arise. That is, they attribute power to themselves (23). Self-confidence seems to derive both from a history of graduated successes in coping with increasingly difficult and complex problems and from the experience of being seen by other people as competent and trustworthy. Lack of self-doubt is often characteristic of explorers, daredevils and others whose achievements transcend their own previous exploits as well as the achievements of many of their fellowmen. Any experiences which permit average people to diminish their distrust of their own capacities and their own worth and which permit them to attribute power to themselves probably would contribute to the frequency with which they transcended their own usual levels of functioning.

The self-concept which, as we have seen, is a limiting factor in behavior can also be a freeing factor for transcendent achievement. If it is true, as existential thinkers insist, that man cannot define himself in any fixed way but is always in process of creating and then recreating himself, then it follows that the most accurate self-concept is one which permits a man to see himself as a being with relatively unplumbed capacities for all modes of function. One of the conclusions announced by Dr. Elie Cohen, a Dutch physician who survived almost four years' imprisonment at the Auschwitz death-camp, was that "man has powers of survival and adaptation which he had never imagined" (24). The very fact that he and a few others survived conditions calculated to produce death was the evidence for his assertion. It seems likely that *any person who formulates a fixed concept of himself, including a concept of his powers to cope, is doing himself an injustice.* Since man tends to behave in accordance with his concept of himself, then he will not rise to meet a challenge that calls for behavior in conflict with his present self-concept. If a man sees himself as weak, he will not take challenges posed by life but will instead avoid them. If a man sees himself as always in the process of being challenged and "tested" by life and his capacities as always in process of unfolding, he probably has a self-concept more closely in tune with reality.

Symbols and the Release of Transcendence

Transcendent behavior has been portrayed as the release of modes of behavior that ordinarily are suppressed by habit. Challenges can release transcendent behavior in a person but so also can *symbols* and metaphors such as the flag, the Star of David, the name of a cause in which one believes (25) or the image of a loved person to whose well-being one has pledged himself. Frankl (26) has reported that the image of his wife, which he "saw," or thought about many times during the course of his imprisonment in death camp, helped inspire him to the actions which kept him alive. Doubtless, many of the feats of exploration and conquest carried out in the name of the king, country or the Glorious Cause all illustrate the release of transcendent functioning in the persons who pursued those exploits. The fascinating question for research is: "*How* do symbols release energies, resourcefulness and the other requisites to transcendent functioning?" According to conventional psychological terminology, such symbols function as motive-arousers; but the psychophysiological mechanisms by means of which this comes about are poorly understood. Indeed, excessive analysis and intellectualizing about symbols seems to rob them of their inspiring (or, at times, dispiriting and depressing) powers. They can only be meditated upon, revealing thereby new possibilities of meaning. Symbols are a variety of metaphor, and metaphor, not rational words, may be the idiom of man's self in process of transcending itself. Symbols and metaphors are experienced as irresistible images of possibility, and we need to learn more about them.

Challenge and Transcendent Behavior

The concept of "challenge" has been mentioned throughout the foregoing discussion of transcendent behavior, and it will be useful for us to examine this phenomenon in more detail. To be challenged—by a person, by God, by a possibility that has been imagined, a problem or a crisis—means that an individual *cannot* ignore the situation at hand and devote his attention elsewhere (27). Challenges, almost by definition, are attention-grabbing. A challenge is similar to a call for help. It entices or demands a full focusing of attention and resources to the matter at hand. Effective leaders, teachers and personality therapists are all exceedingly forthright in challenging others (and themselves) to transcend present levels of functioning.

The individual who responds to problems and crises as challenges to be addressed rather than as threats to be avoided is likely to display transcendence with higher than average frequency. Deeply religious people report that they experience God as a Being who perpetually challenges them; and, under the instigation of this challenge, they continually bring forth from themselves achievements and feats of endurance which might be impossible for persons less challenged. It may be proposed as a hypothesis that challenge, however brought about, is a highly important condition for some types of transcendent behavior.

Transcendent Behavior and Healthy Personality

The foregoing sketch of transcendent behavior and conditions for its emergence is intended to provide a glimpse of potentials for functioning that lie beyond the average or usual levels and some hints as to means of releasing them. Since all of the classes of such behavior have occurred in some few people, the promise is implicit that they can occur in more people more of the time. One of the aims of the field of personality hygiene, beyond that of preventing mental illnes, should be to understand and master the conditions for transcendent behavior, so that ultimately the average personality will be not a mere noncandidate for a psychiatric hospital, but instead a being who can release his capacities for transcendent functioning as needed. Therapists of personality then would be not experts at restoring those with neurosis or psychosis to "normal" levels of function, rather they would be more like those few inspired and inspiring teachers who are able to elicit transcendent performance from their students to the surprise and delight of all.

Perhaps the element of mystery, surprise or unpredictability that seems associated with most of the examples of transcendence implies that man, to function most fully, must transcend the "programming" and shaping of his behavior and become less predictable and controllable. This is not to glorify caprice in human affairs. Rather, it is a suggestion that, when man reaches impasses in his existence and becomes ill, perhaps the solution lies not in seeking to train him so he will become "better adjusted" and more predictable. Instead, the solution may lie in so supporting and challenging him that he acquires a greater ease in entering himself and releasing the unpremeditated, spontaneous action which we have called transcendence.

Some Experiments in Transcendence

There is already a great deal of work that is daily being done by a class of people that I will call "transcendence experts." With or without their knowledge they are capitalizing on the efforts of predecessors who have groped for centuries to transcend "the ego," their own or the egos of the thinkers of their time, viz, the Yogis, the Zen Buddhists, the Hindu mystics, the Chassidim, the alchemists, the Sufis and others. I will not mention the experimenters with psychedelic drugs, because their work will have been described elsewhere in this volume. And, certainly, it must be regarded as a forgivable oversight for the editor of this volume to neglect inviting spokesmen for the various approaches to the mystic experience, e.g., D. T. Suzuki, Idries Shah, Martin Buber, etc.

The transcendence experts whose work I have observed (but not evaluated in any systematic way) are "teachers" of various kinds. First, let me mention the work of Roy Hart, a voice teacher in London. This man has a clientele composed mostly of people in the performing arts—singers and actors. By a series of progressive exercises, he is able to get persons to vocalize through a continuum from a heavily vibrating basso to a piping soprano, but with true tone. I listened to a quartet at his studio in which two women sang the bass and baritone and two manly men sang soprano, with beautiful effect. I saw persons utter unearthly (transcendent) grunts, shrieks, cries—using their voices for expression that goes well beyond that which is customary in polite, middle-class society. The persons who took part in these exercises and performances told me they derived considerable personal, psychotherapeutic benefit from extending the use of their voices.

Now let me report on some observations made in a morning visit at a mental hospital near Paris, where the physiotherapy program enjoys an importance in the rehabilitation of psychotics that is equal to the psychotherapeutic program. Patients are introduced to a program of exercises and games and movements which literally get them back into their bodies. They are given massages; they take part in games which permit them to regress to early levels of childhood; they make bodily movements which go beyond the movements which typified their prehospital existences. They are touched by others, and they touch others' bodies in a natural way, as part of the games and as part of everyday discourse. These patients literally are brought back into their skins and become less afraid to feel and use their bodies as, in psychotherapy, they become less afraid to acknowledge and admit their feelings, fantasies and memories. It seems fair for me to state that, through the physiotherapeutic program, the patients transcend their concepts of their own bodies and come to reexperience their bodies and to integrate them into human relationships in ways that permit ongoing growth of self to occur.

A deliberate exercise in transcendence occurs in the Peace Corps "outwardbound" training camp in Puerto Rico. There trainees are exposed to a variety of challenges that most of them have never encountered before, viz, rock-climbing, "drown-proof" procedures that permit them to stay relaxed in water for hours on end, childhood games that call on them to let go their "adult" demeanor and play patty-cake with gusto, five-day treks through the jungle with only a four-ounce piece of salt codfish and a teabag for provisions. The trainees discover to their amazement that they can meet these challenges that go beyond their previous, comfort-ridden American life-styles and beyond their concepts of their own capabilities. In many ways the successful Peace Corps volunteer is an embodiment of the potentialities of young (and not so young) Americans to transcend both their own upbringing and the concepts of the "typical American" which are endemic in host countries abroad.

If we add to this list brief mention of the coaches of people who produce magnificent performances in sports, in the musical, dancing and other performing arts, we have an impressive source of possible information about the conditions of transcendence. There is no reason to suspect that the champions, the superb performers on stage, platform or screen are a special breed of human beings. Rather, they are persons who committed themselves to an avenue of self-expression and presented themselves to teachers or coaches. The latter presumably shared the contender's images or possibility and set about releasing and actualizing these. I suspect that our heroes of playing field, of the cultural arena, of the study or the laboratory are persons whose fulfillment is a proof or pledge of hidden potentiality *in the broad mass of the population.* Too few people have any idea of their latent possibilities. Perhaps their concepts of their powers are false, and perhaps they are false because our educational procedures indoctrinate people with a view of themselves as beings with sclerosed possibility. If it is possible for a multi-billion dollar education program to train people to see themselves as limited beings, it should also be possible for that program to encourage people to see themselves as embodiments of the capacity to transcend their present concepts of themselves and their powers.

An Epilogue

Throughout this chapter we have implied that transcendent behavior transcends not human possibility, but rather someone's *theory* or *concept* of possibility. (We have also suggested that the theories of the investigator may be self-fulfilling because of the peculiar balance of power that obtains in a typical setting where research into human behavior is carried on—a high-status investigator with a theory to test [prove] invites and often gets behavioral collusion from the low-status people who are the subjects in his study [28]. This notion, if valid, implies that investigators with daring theories about human possibility may well be able to invite or elicit astounding performances from subjects as well as they elicit behavior that proves their hypotheses.)

Indeed, a "compleat psychologist" of the future will resemble the "incompleat psychologist" of the present in one respect. He will continue to seek to specify the determiners of man's condition, his behavior and experience, as befits a scientist committed to the assumption of a deterministic universe. But he will also be a *man,* committed to freedom and respect for man's capacities for transcendence and fuller functioning. Consequently, as each new determiner is discovered and studied, he will seek ways by which the "thrust" of this determiner's impact on man can be subverted, neutralized, surmounted or enlisted in the support of individual man's freely chosen projects, his intentional will. As things now stand it is only the psychotherapists who seek to learn about man's "thrownness" in its myriad dimensions in order to help him transcend it. Research psychologists must take some responsibility for the uses to which their demonstrations of "lawfulness" are put. They must show men how to beat these laws by transcending them, lest other men capitalize on the predictability that psychology reveals. They must, indeed, seek to learn more about helping man to experience his will and to eschew resignation to the thrust of determining forces. They must explore the path to those possibilities for optimal functioning that lie buried beneath habit and socialized being, so that more can realize the experience of liberation, satori, awakening or the attainment of selfhood. (Finally, if they are to get man to reveal the secrets of his being for scientific purposes, they must stop treating people as "subjects" and enter more fully into a mutually self-revealing dialogue with them.)

SUMMARY

This chapter is devoted to discussion of transcendent behavior, that is, behavior that transcends the usual or expected behavior shown by a person. Examples of transcendent behavior were taken from the realms of thinking, perception, remembering, learning, achievement, survival and personality reorganization.

The following factors were proposed as conditions for the emergence of transcendent behavior in an individual: Letting be; openness; focusing and fascination; commitment and values; self-confidence and a concept of self as transcendent; symbols; and challenge.

REFERENCES

1. See ROSENTHAL, R.: On the social psychology of the psychological experiment: The experimenter's hypothesis as unintended determinant of experimental results. *Amer. Scient.*, *51*:268-283, 1963, for a review of studies which confirm the notion of the experimenter's influence on his subjects' responses. The possibility that subjects may dissemble is noted by Bakan in BAKAN, D.: A reconsideration of the problem of introspection. *Psychol. Bull.*, *51*:105-118, 1954.
2. See JOURARD, S. M.: *The Transparent Self*. Princeton, Van Nostrand, 1964, for a discussion of self-disclosure.
3. A number of authors have explored transcendent behavior, and the present discussion has been influenced by: Jung's concept of "the transcendent function." See JUNG, C. G.: *Two Essays on Analytical Psychology*. New York, Meridian Books, especially pp. 126-127, 232, 1956; SHAW, F. J.: The problem of acting and the problem of becoming. *J. Human. Psychol.*, *1*:64-69, 1961; Also, SHAW, F. J.: *Reconciliation, a Theory of Transcendent Behavior*. Unpublished manuscript; Also his *Creative Resources: Their Care and Nurture, Etc. 16*:303-311, 1959; FRANKL, V. E.: Dynamics, existence, and values. *J. Exist. Psychiat.*, *2*:5-16, 1961; MASLOW, A. H.: Health as transcendence of environment. *J. Human. Psychol.*, *1*:1-7, 1961; HORA, T.: Transcendence and healing. *J. Exist. Psychiat.*, *1*:501-511, 1961; LAING, R. D.: Transcendental Experience in Relation to Religion and Psychosis. Paper presented to International Congress of Social Psychiatrists, London, August, 1964. See also PRIVETTE, GAYLE: A Factor Analytic Study of Transcendent Behavior. Unpublished Ph.D. dissertation, Univ. of Florida, 1964.
4. See WATTS, A. W.: *The Way of Zen*. New York, Mentor, 1959, p. 35 for a discussion of "no-mind," or effortless thinking and action. Compare also the accounts of creativity in ANDERSON, H. H. (ed.): *Creativity and Its Cultivation*. New York, Harper, 1959.
5. MASLOW, A. H.: Cognition of being in the peak experiences. *J. Genet. Psychol.*, *94*:43-66, 1959; SCHACHTEL, E. G.: *Metamorphosis*. New York, Basic Books, 1961. This is also the quality of experience reported by mystics, and by those who have ingested LSD, mescaline, hashish, etc. See also the papers by Maslow and Landsman in COMBS, A. W. (ed.): *Personality Theory and Counseling Practice*. Gainesville, Florida, College of Education, 1961.
6. *Cf.* BARTLETT, F. C.: *Remembering*. Cambridge, Cambridge Univ. Press, 1932.
7. The issue here is not whether hypnosis is some special state or tech-

nique; rather, it is concerned with a person's willingness and ability to comply with a request or invitation.

8. The importance of diversified stimulation to insure alertness and wakefulness was noted by Blatz, who described it as evidence for an "appetite" of change. See Blatz, W. E.: *Understanding the Young Child.* New York, Morrow, 1944, pp. 100-113. An overview of research dealing with the effects of varying degrees of stimulus input, see Fiske, D. W., and Maddi, S. R. (eds.): *Functions of Varied Experience.* Homewood, Illinois, Dorsey Press, 1961.
9. See articles by Moreno, J. R., for remarks on the role of "warming up" for role-playing in therapeutic psychodrama.
10. Shaw has written in a fascinating way about fascination in Shaw, F. J.: A Program for Finding Out What People Are Good For. Unpublished manuscript, 1960.
11. See Becker, H. S.: Notes on the concept of commitment. *Amer. J. Soc., 66*:32-40, 1960.
12. This notion of "holding back" when one is pursuing a goal, the value of which does not seem fully worthwhile, can be derived from Festinger's theory of "cognitive dissonance." When one's actions and beliefs are consonant or congruent with one another, behavior will be "wholehearted." When actions and beliefs are "dissonant," the action is less likely to be so whole-hearted or inspired. See Festinger, L.: *A Theory of Cognitive Dissonance.* Evanston, Illinois, Row, 1959, for a more formal statement of Festinger's theory.
13. See Hoffer, E.: *The True Believer.* New York, for an excellent account of fanaticism.
14. *Cf.* Shaw, F. J.: Laughter, paradigm of growth. *J. Individ. Psychol., 16*:151-157, 1960.
15. Bettelheim, B.: *The Informed Heart.* Glencoe, Free Press, 1961, esp. pp. 107-235.
16. Frankl, V. E.: *From Death Camp to Existentialism.* Boston, Beacon Press, 1959.
17. *Cf.* Frankl, V. E.: *op. cit.*, also the reference in footnote 1.
18. See Schmale: The relation of separation and depression to disease. *Psychosom. Med., 20*:259-277, 1958. Also Jourard, S. M.: *The Transparent Self.* Princeton, Van Nostrand, 1964.
19. See Jourard, S. M.: The role of spirit and inspiritation in human wellness. In *The Transparent Self.* Princeton, Van Nostrand, 1964.
20. See Barber, T. X.: The necessary and sufficient conditions for hypnotic behavior. *Amer. J. Clin. Hypnosis, 3*:31-42, 1960, for a superb formulation of the more salient features of hypnosis.
21. See Hora, T.: The process of existential psychotherapy. *Psychiat. Quart., 34*:495-504, 1960, for a discussion of letting be in psychotherapy. Letting be as a more general way of life is well described

in the various works of Watts (e.g., reference footnote 2, and also WATTS, A. W.: *Nature, Man and Woman.* New York, Mentor, 1960).

22. *Cf.* BUBER, M.: *Between Man and Man.* Boston, Beacon Press, 1955, pp. 1-39.
23. See HEIDER, F.: *The Psychology of Interpersonal Relations.* New York, Wiley, 1958, pp. 237-242, for a discussion of attribution of power.
24. COHEN, E.: *Human Behavior in the Concentration Camp.*
25. Compare WEISSKOPF-JOELSON, E.: *Psychotherapy and Ideological Problems.* Unpublished manuscript, 1961. Also her paper, written in collaboration with PERRUCCI, R.: *The Half-way House, an Antidote Against Separation.* Neither of these papers was published at the time of writing, but copies can be obtained by writing to Dr. Joelson. In these two papers, Dr. Joelson explores the important role played by symbols and ideology integrating man and in releasing latent powers within him.
26. FRANKL, V. E.: *From Death Camp to Existentialism.* Boston, Beacon Press, 1959.
27. *Cf.* BUBER, M.: *op. cit.*
28. It would be well if researchers interviewed their subjects' room-mates, spouses or friends to get a more complete picture of the subjects' response to the condition of the experiment or to the experimenters' questions and tests. The subjects will often disclose more that is of scientific value to these confidants than they do to the investigator. It seems to me that a research psychologist must, if his data are to be complete, take greater pains to establish a relationship akin to dialogue with his subjects, so that they will more freely reveal the breadth and depth of their experience in the research setting.

Chapter 26

REPORT FROM ACHIEVEMENT MOTIVATION

JOSEPH VEROFF

JOHN GARDNER, in his provocative book *Excellence* (18), makes an appeal that this country should encourage individual effort. He suggests that the pursuit of excellent individual performance is the basis for the innovation and gratification that enables a democratic society to flourish.

Research findings strongly support the proposition that people who have high achievement motivation pursue and attain excellence, thereby meriting not only a sense of self-fulfillment, but also the approval of a society dedicated to its own enrichment. Research in the achievement setting has shown that people with high measured motives for achievement will seek out (Atkinson [1]) and be gratified by challenge to their capacities (Atkinson and O'Connor [4]), will solve problems effectively (McClelland [26]), further their own education (Veroff, Atkinson, Feld, and Gurin [49]), and their children's education (Morgan [33]), make realistic vocational goals (Mahone [25]), will attain eminence in entrepreneurial occupations (McClelland [26]), innovate in their work (McClelland [27]), be occupationally mobile (Crockett [12]), and yet have reasonable aspirations in their jobs (Veroff and Feld [51]). These people with high measured achievement motives are pursuing excellence. Can they not be the examples for others to follow? Are they not the people social practitioners should study to discover the bases for a highly valued motivation?

These questions become particularly pointed when we face certain social dilemmas in decisions about human beings in this country and in other countries. I am thinking particularly about the historic move toward integration of public schools in this country which raises practical and strategic problems about how to develop the achievement motive in Negro children when this motive has not been an apparent part of the experience of the majority of Negroes. I am thinking about the encouragement of achievement motivation in females in our society where the housewife role has become less demanding. I am thinking of the social engineering possibilities in underdeveloped countries in the world for raising the achievement motivation of people which in turn could act as a spur to economic development. I mention these social possibilities as "dilemmas" because I see achievement behaviors in people as just one of many human potentials. For the majority of people in this country achievement has an especially strong value, and therefore Gardner's plea to America to demand excellence is not untoward. To unleash the potential for achievement, narrowly defined as excellent performance, in American Negroes, or in females, or in India or in a newly emerging African country would be betting on one form of human potential over another. Who is to say that we should not be encouraging affiliative concerns in people or love of beauty?

In this report about work on achievement motivation, I will place my bets on the achievement potential of human beings as a goal we wish to enhance in most people. If the social practitioner asks what we know about achievement motivation that might help unleash this potential in human behavior, then I can begin to give him some answers. But in no way does this report suggest that building achievement motivation is the only route, or even the most important, for realizing the greatest potential in human beings.

Let us examine the social engineer's question: How do you raise the level of achievement in a human being? If, by achievement, the practitioner means certain types of persistent behaviors, certain qualities of action we call excellent, then the motivational theorists can answer by saying that practically any type of motivation can elicit achievement behaviors. Men strive for excellence for many reasons. Atkinson and Reitman have shown in a very important experiment (2) that men with high affiliation motivation will perform more persistently for affiliation reasons, that is, when the experimenter asks the subject to perform as best he can for the sake of the experimenter. Other studies corroborate (Atkinson and O'Connor [4]) this finding. What we have in these instances are achievement behaviors being elicited from affiliation incentives. If we wanted to heighten achievement behaviors, therefore, we would tell the social practitioner to measure the dominant motivation of an individual, structure a situation so that the incentive in the situation is relevant to the dominant motivation and then make achievement behaviors instrumental to this incentive. Such manipulation is common enough in life, but to enact such control with scientific backing we would need from the psychologist's laboratory: first, the study of the functions involved in linking instrumental behaviors to incentives; and secondly, the study of the diagnostic procedures that would get at measurement of dominant motivational concerns in individuals. These would be excellent research possibilities for future study of achievement behaviors; little has been done on these questions systematically to date.

Although, as is noted above, it is theoretically meaningful to envision any behavior as being instrumental to any incentive if a situation is so structured, life experiences are not often manipulated in that way. Men and women are not often confronted with situations that are specifically directed towards one incentive or another. Men and women are usually confronted with life situations where the cues for achievement, affiliation, power, sexuality, aggression, are *all* potential. Hence, the way in which incentives become structured for achievement may ultimately depend upon the *dispositional* characteristics of individuals who are in such situations. Men whose dominant motivation is achievement are more likely to structure an ambiguous situation for achievement than men with low achievement motivation or men whose dominant motivation is affiliation. Once a person structures a situation for achievement rather than for other incentives, then he is very likely to pursue excellence. If this assumption is accurate, people with high achievement dispositions are the ones who will structure ambiguous situations for achievement incentives and hence are more likely to perform achievement behaviors in general. If so, the focus of our concern for the social engineer's interests in developing the human potential for achievement shifts from studying achievement behaviors to studying achievement motivation. And this will be the focus of this paper.

We will ask a number of questions about achievement motivation. I will draw particular attention to the determinants of individual differences in achievement motives or in the disposition for finding achievement incentives attractive. It is this motive that has been found to underlie individual variation in achievement behaviors in so many different settings. We may thus be in a position to guide a social engineer who is interested in promoting excellence in our own society or in other societies.

To clarify the significance of the term "achievement motivation," let us step aside and look at the general theoretical structure used by researchers in achievement motivation to conceptualize achievement. Atkinson has been the most insightful of all workers on achievement motivation about the theoretical relationship of determinants of motivational "tendencies" to achievement behaviors (Atkinson [1]). When applied to particular situations, such tendencies are theoretical constructs that presume to underlie the choices a person makes and how energetically or persistently a person acts in those situations defined by the tendencies. The achievement tendencies are presumed to be a function of the interest in achieving in general (the achievement motive), the person's probability of achieving in that situation (achievement expectancy) and the person's attraction to achievement in that particular setting (achievement incentive). Atkinson has postulated that attraction to achievement is an inverse function of the probability of success in the situation; the more difficult a task is to perform, the more attracted the person is to accomplish it for achievement. Recently Brown (8) has corroborated this common sense assumption in an experimental laboratory study. Atkinson has also taken cognizance of the motive to avoid failure and the incentive to avoid failure. The latter is presumed to be a direct function of the probability of success—the higher the probability of success, the more disastrous and repulsive the failure. In a theory of achievement motivation which examines both tendencies to approach success and avoid failure, Atkinson has presented a risk-taking model (2), deducing that a person with high positive achievement motivation would be most attracted to situations of moderate risk. It is with moderate risks that people in general find the greatest challenge, for in such tasks a person is neither guaranteed success nor denied its possibility. Those with high positive motives should be attracted to such a challenge, while those with high avoidant motives should avoid such a challenge.

Atkinson's risk-taking theory has carried considerable support in research studies. (For a summary, *cf.* Atkinson [1], pp. 240-263.) Many predictions about shifts in aspiration or persistence after success or failure are possible. Feather (14) has used such predictions to explain individual differences in persistence at impossible tasks; Moulton (36) has used this theory to explain individual differences in shifts of levels of aspiration after success and failure. Atkinson's risk-taking model thus seems to be one of the most provocative theories of achievement motivation that has emerged from the psychological laboratory during the past decade.

The greater attraction to moderate probabilities of success among people high in positive achievement motivation can guarantee that these people are likely to accomplish success and pursue excellence. Choosing performance levels with moderate probabilities of success gives the person practice with activities that improve his performance and hence should lead ultimately to success. With success, the potency of responding to challenge increases, and thus a self-maintaining circle begins where interest in challenge produces success which produces greater interest in challenge and so forth. This sort of thinking can probably account both for the mobility *aspirations* and actual occupational *successes* in people with high positive achievement motivation.

With this theory one would suggest that the problems for the scientist in helping the social engineer are: (a) to pinpoint what is thought to be successful performance in a situation—*clarifying achievement incentives;* (b) to locate people's expectancies about performance—*clarifying subjective probabilities of success;* (c) to get adequate assessment of the motives for success and avoidance of failure—*clarifying the meaning of motives;* and (d) to take account of people's capacities to enact achievement behaviors in particular settings—*clarifying the importance of capacities in relationship to motives.* Thus, we can have all the ingredients for making predictions about achievement behaviors in situations under achievement motivation. There are many theoretical problems that are of interest in working out the ingredients for this analysis on incentives, on expectancies, on motives and on capacities. The focus of this paper will be on those ingredients that are traditionally within the domain of the topic of motivation—motives and incentives. In thinking about these two motivational variables, we will indirectly come in contact with the other ingredients, expectancies and capacities. But in this paper they will be ignored.

CLARIFYING THE NATURE OF THE ACHIEVEMENT INCENTIVE

What is the nature of the achievement incentive? *Competition with standards of excellence* was a criterion introduced early in the research on achievement motivation (McClelland *et al.* [29]). But, as such, it is an ambiguous criterion. Further questions may be asked of it. Is achievement competing against others or against self-standards? How important is society's evaluation of the excellence of the individual's performance? How much is an individual's *own* performance important, or can he use help on the way to accomplishment? We have begun to accumulate some answers to these questions and the most important researches related to these questions are listed below. Five summary points about achievement incentive can be made.

1. *Performance by the individual seems to be important in eliciting any achievement incentive.* Raynor and Smith (38) have found that achievement-related motives predict risk-taking according to Atkinson's model for games of skill but not for games of chance where the person's own performance is not a factor in success. The achievement incentive is not attained through luck or by an act of fate. Individual performance of competence is required.
2. *Performance by an individual does not necessarily mean rejection of aid on the route towards accomplishment.* Koenig (22) found that subjects with high achievement motives faced with very difficult achievement problems will seek out aid from another, if such aid is available, more often than those with low

measured achievement motives. Without assistance, the achievement would not be possible.

3. *Concrete feedback about good performance seems to be more relevant to the achievement incentive than feedback of general approval for accomplishment in the achievement setting.* French (16) found that subjects with high achievement motivation are more likely to respond to specific information about how well they may have been performing than to general approval. The clearest relationships about achievement motivation to performance seem to be in those performance settings where feedback about the quality of performance is subjectively apparent to the performer and does not require an additional evaluation from the experimenter.

4. *Subjective probability of success is more important in determining incentives than objective probability of success.* Smith (43) reports that the perceived difficulty of a task, although controlled by the experimenter, will vary depending upon the IQ of the subject. His evidence for this is that, compared to subjects with low achievement motivation, high achievement motivated subjects with high IQ's are *more* persistent the more difficult the task, while those subjects with low IQ's are *less* persistent the more difficult the tasks. These results are in keeping with Atkinson's risk-taking model only if one assumes that the subjective expectancy of success is different for the same task for the different IQ levels.

5. The effect of competition with self as opposed to competition with others is an open question for research, but Veroff (48) has some indication that these two types of competition are separable phenomena. *From some research it seems that the behavior most clearly tied to the achievement incentive, as Atkinson discusses it, reflects competition with the self.* Wendt (54) has results that indicate that performance of those high in achievement motive is best when subjects are not bombarded with cues about competition with others. Some of Veroff's measures of achievement motivation with children based on competition with the *self* predict achievement performance in school better than do the measures of achievement motivation based on competition with *others*.

From this list of findings about the nature of the achievement incentive one can conclude that to heighten the achievement incentive in a given situation, social engineers should: present achievement tasks in which the individual is required to assert his own effort if the task is not too difficult or is required to cooperate with another person if the task is too difficult to accomplish on one's own; make sure that the task has immediate feedback for evaluation of good performance inherent in the task itself; structure the task so that a person's subjective probability of success can be apparent; and finally, structure the task so that competition with self is more important that competition with others.

CLARIFYING THE NATURE OF THE ACHIEVEMENT MOTIVE

We will consider two major problems in the clarification of the nature of the achievement motive; first, how to assess it; and secondly, and most important for this paper, how does it originate.

Assessment of Achievement Motives

Most research on achievement motivation has suggested that it is important to take account in assessment of two aspects of the achievement motive—the hope of success, or approach motive, and the fear of failure, or the avoidant motive for achievement.

Hopes of Success

Generally speaking, it has been granted that the achievement motive as measured through thematic apperception (writing or telling stories to picture or verbal cues) is a positive type of motive. Although there are negative characteristics scored in a fantasy production in this device, the theory about thematic apperception suggests that the overall motivation for achievement should be positive in order to allow the person to tell stories with any achievement content at all. There has been one dissenting viewpoint presented about the nature of the achievement motive measured in fantasy. Lazarus and his colleagues have suggested that the measurement of achievement motivation and fantasy is defensive and compensatory for lack of achievement (23). The evidence that Lazarus has offered for this assertion is not convincing, but it remains as an assertion to be dealt with.

Recent advances in the assessment of achievement motive through fantasy focus around taking advantage of the particular nature of the stimuli that are used in eliciting fantasy. Greater validity to the assessment has been attained when the particular nature of the stimuli that are used in eliciting fantasy has been accounted for. Veroff, Feld and Crockett (53) have shown that blue collar workers' responses to pictures of white collar workers and white collar workers' responses to pictures of blue collar workers are more valid predictors than the responses of either group to pictures of their own working situations. Lesser, Krawitz and Packard (24) have noted that they get greater validity to the assessment of achievement motivation in females if they account for the sex of the characters in the stimuli used to elicit fantasy. Female achievement motivation has been particularly difficult to evaluate because of conflicting dispositions against achievement in females. French and Lesser (17) have further demonstrated that it is necessary to measure the female's attitudes toward femininity before accurate predictions to achievement behaviors from achievement motives can be obtained. Systematic research on this problem is underway at the University of Michigan (Fontana [15], Horner [20]). It remains one of the most challenging assessment problems in the problem of achievement motivation.

Fear of Failure

Moulton (34) long ago scored the thematic apperceptive device for fear of failure, but research on this assessment since then has not been profitably continued. Birney, Teevan and Burdick (6) have followed through on this question from an empirical standpoint and have emerged with what they call a *hostile press* scoring system for fear of failure. It is a method for scoring fantasy for fear of failure by noting the blocks or the elements of hostility imputed to the environment within stories. This research has led to a series of important studies on the effect of fear of failure on a level of aspiration and performance. The method seems promising for future investigations of fear of failure, scored directly within the fantasy measure.

Most people wanting to measure fear of failure have relied on the Mandler Sarason Test Anxiety Scale (1961). It calls for the subject's rating of his symptoms of anxiety associated with taking tests. Research on this measure has indicated that this dispositional characteristic is related to debilitative performance in most complex achievement settings. It is related to heightened performance if cautiousness is a characteristic required for good performance (Ruebush [41]). Most often in the research on achievement motivation the two measures, the apperceptive measure of hope of success and the Mandler Sarason Test Anxiety measure of fear of failure, have been used in conjunction to give a resultant motivation score. That is, those subjects who are high in hope of success and low in fear of failure and those subjects who are low in hope of success and high in fear of failure are assumed to be pure groups—pure approach—and pure avoidant-movitated groups for whom predictions about the relationship of achievement motives to behaviors seem most clear. Those subjects who are high on both measures or low on both measures are subjects for whom the resultant motivation pattern is not clear and, hence, predictions are problematic. Using the "pure types" enumerated above, researchers have had continued success in applying Atkinson's risk-taking model of achievement motivation and in testing predictions about the effect of individual differences in motives on achievement motivation and, consequently, on achievement behaviors.

Promising other measures of resultant achievement motive scores have been tried by other researchers. There are: a risk preference questionnaire (O'Connor [37]); achievement values assessment (Burnstein, Moulton and Liberty [9]); differential evaluation of gratification from occupations of different prestige (Strodtbeck *et al.* [45]; Morgan [33]); and an assessment of the repetition choices made by children in the face of both success and failure (Veroff [48]). The body of evidence supporting the validity of any one of these new devices is not large, but each of them has merits to be explored in future research, either because they are easier to administer or code or because they are particularly appropriate for certain populations (e.g., Veroff's measures for young children). It should be noted that the bulk of the research results employing measures of the achievement motive reported in this paper is based on thematic apperceptive devices, often in conjunction with the Mandler Sarason Test Anxiety scale.

Origins of the Achievement Motive

We now turn to what is perhaps the most important question that the social engineer can ask of those interested in achievement motivation, namely how is a strong achievement motive generated? What underlies and supports strong hope of success and/or a strong fear of failure?

The very first study of major consequence in outlining the factors determining a strong achievement motive was the cross-cultural study of American Indian folktales by McClelland and Friedman (30) in which there was a high positive correlation found between the degree of socialization for independence and the level of achievement motive measured in folk stories about the common cultural hero of Coyote. Since that time a number of other researchers have accumulated a much broader perspective on this question. I have found it useful to catalog these new findings under periods of development in individual growth where the effects have been noted. Particular periods of development present particular life problems which in turn affect the development of achievement and interest in particular ways. The socialization of achievement motives has different functions at different ages. Therefore, we will discuss four separate periods of development of the achievement motive: preschool; middle childhood; adolescence; and adulthood.

Development of Achievement Motive in Preschool Period

Callard (10) has extensively examined the achievement motive in preschool age children and found that there is not much evidence at this age for strong achievement motivation as we know it in adults. Preschool children when confronted with choices that represent easy, moderate or difficult performance most often choose the easiest. Or, if they are asked to resume tasks that they failed or did not fail, they elect to resume the most easy or the most difficult task, more so than older age children. It is as if for the four- or five-year-old, steps of difficulty are not a part of their cognitive capacity.

In preschool development one can see the differentiation between "being able to" and "not being able to" master a certain activity, but *steps* of difficulty do not seem to be differentiated. Nevertheless, there were individual differences in the kind of choice behaviors that preschool children made that could be identified as primitive high achievement motive. Some did choose moderate risks. Callard found that in certain subcultures of nursery school children there was a relationship between parental attitudes towards achievement and these precursory evidences of achievement motives in the child. However, the relationships were not straightforward as the McClelland and Friedman's findings would suggest. The relationship was positive (late independence training associated with higher achievement motivation) in one class—middle class boys, negative in another group—middle class girls, and curvilinear in a third group—lower class girls. The results suggest (and we will see similar trends in other studies) that one must take account of the particular sample of subjects dealt with in research before broad generalizations about the origins of achievement motivation can be made. Nevertheless, Callard's results demonstrate that, even in the early preschool period, maternal attitudes towards independence can have some impact on children's achievement strivings.

Let us turn to some results reported in Kagan and Moss' book *Birth to Maturity* (21), for in that research report it seems apparent that it is not maternal emphasis on independence or mastery at preschool age that is critical in the development of achievement motivation for later life. The variable of maternal socialization at preschool development, Kagan and Moss found, correlated with the achievement syndromes in adults was not the attitude towards achievement, but how affectionate the mother was towards the child. A very curious result emerged. Both a mother's *nurturing attitude toward her boy* during the preschool period and *a hostile attitude toward her girl* during this period were associated with a high level of achievement syndromes for boys and girls when they became adults.* What these results suggest is that the affective orientation that children develop toward their own sex role at a very young age may very well be one of the bases for high levels of motivation for achievement in later life. The boy who becomes affectively accepting of his male role, particularly from a nurturant experience with his mother early in life, may fall in line with the expectation for achievement in the male role when he is adult. A girl who develops an antagonism towards the female role particularly from hostile relationship with her mother early in life may develop an antagonism towards femininity and an attraction to achievement when she is adult. This interpretation of Kagan and Moss' findings about the early experiences that may be a factor in the later potential for achievement motivation in men and women is highly speculative, but it can be investigated in future work.

Development of Achievement Motive in Middle Childhood

Winterbottom's often-quoted study (55) of the relationship of ten-year-old boys' achievement motives to their mothers' attitudes and behaviors regarding socialization has been the spearhead of a number of other studies in the past decade. Winterbottom's study reported that boys whose mothers promoted independence at an early age were high in measured achievement motives. Furthermore, these boys have mothers who reported that they rewarded them for accomplishment actively and affectively. Recently, Rosen and D'Andrade (39) have confirmed this finding by observing overt maternal behavior rather than by relying on self-reports by mothers. This study of interaction with their sons observed mothers in actual achievement settings. In Rosen and D'Andrade's study, boys with high achievement motives had mothers who, with considerable affect, actively encouraged higher performance and discouraged bad performance. A recent study shows that an emphasis on punishment for failure at this age can account for strong development of fear of failure (McGhee

* Although Kagan and Moss' assessment of the achievement syndrome is directed towards examining achievement behaviors, the quality of the ratings they use imply a motivational judgment.

and Teevan [32]). Sarason *et al.* (42), in discussing the origin of test anxiety, also emphasize the exaggerated parental criticism of performance that seems to be characteristic of children with high test anxiety.

In Winterbottom's study the measures of independence training attitudes was confounded by a number of different factors. In particular, Winterbottom's assessment of attitudes failed to distinguish between promoting a child's accomplishments as achievements as opposed to promoting a child's independence from the mother's assistance. Sometimes these two attitudes are parallel, but often they are independent (*cf.* Torgoff [46]). Research since Winterbottom's study suggests that it is the component of achievement training and not independence training within Winterbottom's measure of maternal attitudes that is important in determining the relationship of maternal attitudes to the son's achievement motives. Child, Storm and Veroff (11) followed up McClelland and Friedman's studies of cultural differences of achievement motives in folk tales as related to socialization processes with a much larger and more varied sample. They examined cultures from all over the world, taking samples of ten stories from each culture. Scoring them for achievement motive, relating these scores to the Yale cross-cultural file on socialization, they found that there is a strong relationship between the stress on achievement training and the measure of achievement motive, but no relationship between a stress on independence or obedience in a culture and the resultant achievement motive.

McClelland also has done some cross-cultural sampling for the relationship between maternal attitudes and achievement motivation (26). He has accumulated samples of such effects in Japan, Brazil and in Germany. In these studies it was discovered that the direct relationship of early independence training associated with high achievement motive was not apparent in all cultures. Indeed, in one of the cultures, Brazil, the relationship was reversed; the later the independence training, the higher the achievement motive, as Callard had found with the middle class boys. In other cultures the relationship was curvilinear. These results along with Callard's results reported earlier suggest that Winterbottom's finding—the earlier the independence training, the higher the achievement motivation, is not a good empirical generalization. What McClelland suggested in *The Achieving Society* and what Veroff has found further evidence of in second graders in this country (48) is that there may be some absolute critical age period when achievement training is most beneficial in promoting achievement motivation. If achievement training occurs before this critical age, it can induce *avoidant* achievement interest, or fear of failure. But if it occurs after this critical age period, achievement training is not very effective in inducing high achievement motives of either sort. If a country or subculture generally trains early, then a researcher would get a positive relationship between achievement training and achievement motive. If the society or subculture generally trains late, then there should be a negative relationship, and if the sample is quite variable regarding achievement training, the researcher would find a curvilinear relationship.

There is good reason to believe that there would be a critical age in learning achievement motivation during middle childhood. It is a time for considerable emphasis on skill training in children. It is usually during middle childhood that the formal education of the child is initiated, where there is considerable reinforcement of mastery *per se* by the culture at large. Kagan and Moss find that the maternal attitudes and behaviors that have been measured from ages six to nine are those most predictive of the achievement syndrome in adults, again suggesting that middle childhood is a critical time for the development of achievement motivation.

Part of the process of skill learning is for the child to distinguish what his capacities are in relationship to his peers. Such social comparisons should be strongly influential in the development of achievement motivation in the schools. But thus far there has been only one important study of the relevance of such social comparison to achievement motivation. Atkinson and O'Connor (3) have examined the relative effectiveness of heterogeneous and homogeneous ability groupings on the satisfaction of high and low achievement motivated subjects and found that subjects high in positive achievement motivation were particularly satisfied and did particularly well under conditions of homogeneous ability groupings. Such ability groupings were disadvantageous to those with high avoidant concerns. This study suggests that if a child was not anxious about performance, continued contact with peers who are of the same level of competence as the child could help engender strong satisfaction and hence higher motivations for achievement. Such a speculation may be particularly relevant in middle childhood, but could very well continue into adolescence.

A strong generalization which seems to cut across a number of different studies is that a child who has had experience with both success and failure in relationship to his own performance will develop strong interests in challenge. Parental encouragement of achievement during middle childhood perhaps pushes children to the point of experiencing both success and failure, to confront tasks that are not too easy nor difficult for them. It might be argued that manipulations of the classroom experiences of children by teachers should accommodate to children's capacities for experiencing both success and failure. Such a postulation is open to empirical study, and it is hoped that it could be a basis for a number of important developmental studies in the future.

Development of Achievement Motive in Adolescence

During adolescence an orientation towards skill development can be maintained, but other types of interest often become predominant, particularly those related to interpersonal evaluation by the same or the opposite sex. Eriksen (13) and others have pointed to adolescence as the beginning time for identity formation, when children begin to differentiate themselves from their families. If this sort of differentiation is especially problematic for a child it can grossly interfere with his continued orientation toward skill and augment his involvement with interpersonal concerns. Under certain circumstances adolescents strongly concerned about their own sexual differentiation can very well introduce mastery of skills into the arena of their interpersonal difficulties. Such adolescents can use their skills or lack of them as weapons against parents or as vehicles to obtain social approval.

Two studies of adolescence suggest that parents who do not allow their children to operate independently, who do not allow their children to differentiate themselves from the parents, promote lower interests in achievement. Strodtbeck reports a very interesting study in which adolescent boys are brought together with their parents for the resolution of differences of opinions (44). He found that sons with high achievement motives were more likely to be granted power in decision making in the family, especially in comparison to his father. Such a family style should encourage a sense of autonomy and differentiation from the family, which in turn promotes a continued orientation towards skill during adolescence. Another result in keeping with Strodtbeck's findings is an often missed result from some early work on the achievement motive. That result is that high school boys who have high achievement motives were likely to see their fathers as being helpful and friendly, an attitude which would prevail only if the child was able to develop some sense of differentiation from his family (McClelland *et al.* [29]).

A very intriguing book, *Cradles of Eminence* (Goertzels [19]), points out that in the background of eminent male adults there often were mothers who were very involved with them during adolescence. It may be argued that this involvement by an *opposite sex parent* can produce a type of sexual differentiation that is required for the skill orientation begun in middle childhood to continue during adolescence.

Another process which seems to be important in the development of the achievement motive during adolescence is the promotion of identification with models of success. There have been not very many direct studies of fathers and sons to corroborate this assertion, but a number of observations do shed some light on the possible role of identification in the development of achievement motivation. In particular it is interesting to note that Negroes in this culture who are prone to have low achievement motives typically grew up in homes where the father is absent from the family scene. Usually there is no model of a successful father present for Negro sons to emulate. However, a recent study by Moulton (35) of successful Negro junior high school children, those who are particularly achieving in school, suggests that these boys have strikingly competent mothers to use as models of success; their fathers were present, although they were not particularly competent.

In a national study of adults it has been noted that sons who come from families where there was a divorce before the child was sixteen were particularly low in measured achievement motive (Veroff *et al.* [49]). Again it would suggest that emerging from a home where a model for success is absent, low achievement motivation prevails.

Can a father represent too much success for a boy, too distant a goal for the son to emulate? Would the son turn away from achievement if extremely high standards come from the father's example? It would seem that the level of a father's success is not important *per se*, but often what accompanies success in the father is a domineering and authoritative paternal attitude. Authoritarianism undoubtedly interferes with identification and identity formation, as discussed earlier. There are two studies suggesting that a very successful father can interfere with the development of the achievement motive and may stand in the way of continuing the development of the achievement motive. In one study of Princeton undergraduates (Rubin [40]) a curvilinear relationship was found between measured achievement motive and the income level of the students' fathers. The sons whose fathers earned a moderate income (for Princeton undergraduates this meant $10,000 to $20,000 in 1956) had particularly high achievement motives. In another study Bradburn (7) found that among sons of prominent Turkish families those who were sent away from home to school during adolescence had developed higher achievement motives than those who were not sent away from home, presumably because the domineering father was no longer too strong a picture of success for the child to deal with. There were many complications in Bradburn's study, but the results are in keeping with the general assertion posited above.

Development of Achievement Motivation in Adulthood

Until recently, socialization of adult achievement motivation seemed farfetched. It has perhaps been too easily assumed that dispositions to achieve were cemented in early childhood experiences, and later adult experiences were trivial in inducing dispositional changes. Recently, McClelland (27) reported some preliminary findings about the success of a training program directed to increase the achievement motives of businessmen in India. What is the nature of this program? It goes from steps of creating confidence of the program's effectiveness, to emphasizing the relevance of achievement motivation to the person and his life, to clarifying the nature of the motive and its relevance to the person's life experience, to increasing the attraction of having the achievement motive both in the trainer's immediate reference group and the culture from which he emerges. The general rationale for this training program in socializing achievement motivation is based on the assumption that, the more an adult can bring his cognitive and affective associations to the conceptual and affective meaning of achievement, the more achievement motivation he will have in his activity. Three groups of businessmen in Bombay took part in this program. These groups were compared to a control group of men who had applied for the program but did not participate. There was greater increase in "unusual" entrepreneurial activity of the men participating in the program than there was in the control group. These results again are highly provocative but require further study.

There was other evidence for the socialization of the achievement motive in adulthood. Crockett (12) has reported findings in which men who have reached an occupational level above the level of their fathers in either the blue collar or the white collar setting have higher measured achievement motives than those who have not exceeded the status of their fathers' occupations. This finding has been interpreted to be evidence of social mobility in those that have high measured achievement motives, but it also can be interpreted as an increase in achievement motive by those who advance into high, more statusful jobs. The occupation itself can be a socializing agent for achievement. McClelland has discussed a number of findings suggesting that entrepreneurial occupations may have a socializing function for achievement that other occupations do not have. Contrary to this interpretation, however, is a recent report of findings by McClelland (28) that those with high achievement motivation in college will *fifteen years later* be in jobs where entrepreneurial business orientations predominate. A reasonable generalization would be that men with high achievement motivation are attracted to achievement jobs which are prestigeful and require excellence and also are socialized by these jobs once they obtain them.

Veroff and his colleagues (50) have reported one result suggesting that middle age for certain men may be a particularly stimulating time for the achievement motive. For certain groups at this time there may be a strong evocation for the demands for achievement from family pressures or from economic pressures on the job. Middle-aged Catholic men especially seem to be those that have strong evocations of achievement motives during this time. Veroff *et al.* argue that early socialization practices by Catholics have made Catholics sensitive to the kind of external socialization for achievement during middle age.

At older ages men have been found to decrease in measured achievement motive, and women have been found to increase. The demands for retirement, thoughts of approaching death, children off on their own, all can induce new kinds of more dominant motivation which take precedence over the achievement motive for men at old age. For women, however, the lessened burdens of a family may enhance the dominance of achievement motive during old age, while social concerns diminish.

CONCLUSION

Although we can arrive at no formula for how to guarantee strong achievement motivation orientation in people in general, we have come a long way in the last decade in delineating factors that seem particularly important in how achievement motivation is generated for certain groups of people. The findings which were noteworthy in the different developmental periods just outlined are suggestive of a potential program to encourage high achievement interests in most adult males. Such a program would insure that there be: a mother who has a nurturant attitude toward her son in his early infancy; a moderately strong but consistent pressure for achievement or mastery at neither too early nor too late in middle childhood within the context of a group of peers who were as competent as the child; a successful, helpful, but not domineering father during adolescence; an occupation where the feedback about achievement and its general demand promote further achievement; and a maintenance of interpersonal affection with people throughout life so that affection does not become a particularly strong concern in later age.

For females it would appear that the necessary program would include a somewhat rejecting attitude by her mother early in her experience; an appropriate timing of stress on mastery early in experience along with the acceptance of the appropriateness of females to achieve; not too strong and domineering a female figure; and not too strong an emphasis on interpersonal gratification during early adulthood.

The dynamics for the growth of achievement motivations are basically the same for the two sexes. Where there is differentiation in socialization factors, I am accounting for the fact that there is a conflict for achieving for females—a conflict which is minimal for males in our society. The major underlying experience that seems to release the achievement potential in men and women calls for the type of family guidance, of programs for action in schools as well as in structures of occupations and sanction systems in a society where the growing individual can have contact with experiences of both success and failure in performance. Without experiencing any potential for success, without experiencing any potential for failure, no potential for challenge will develop.

From a theory of achievement motivation that stresses both situational and dispositional factors influencing the achievement potential of individuals in life settings, we have examined both the nature of the incentive achievement in *situations* and the nature of the motive for achievement in *people*. There are some very specific research findings that give considerable substance to their characterization; but, of course, much still remains to be discovered. To the social engineer making use of those findings I would reiterate my earlier caution to weigh the achievement capacities in humans along with their other important potentialities.

REFERENCES

1. Atkinson, J. W.: *An Introduction to Motivation.* Princeton, Van Nostrand, 1964.
2. Atkinson, J. W.: Motivational determinants of risk-taking behavior. *Psychol. Rev., 64*:359-372, 1957.
3. Atkinson, J. W., and O'Connor, Patricia: Neglected Factors in the Study of Achievement Oriented Performance: Social Approval as an Incentive and Performance Decrement. Unpublished manuscript, Univ. of Michigan, 1962.
4. Atkinson, J. W., and O'Connor, Patricia: The Effect of Ability Grouping in the Schools Related to Individual Differences in Achievement-Related Motivation (Final Report, Office of Education and Cooperative Research Project, 1283), 1962.
5. Atkinson, J. W.: *Motives in Fantasy, Action and Society.* Princeton, Van Nostrand, 1958.
6. Birney, R. C., Burdick, H., and Teevan, R. C.: Fear of Failure and the Achievement Situation. Technical Report No. 1, Office of Naval Research, 1964.
7. Bradburn, N. M.: N Achievement and Father Dominance in Turkey. *J. Abnorm. Soc. Psychol., 67*:464-468, 1963.
8. Brown, M.: Studies in the Incentive for Achievement. Unpublished paper, Univ. of Michigan, 1963.
9. Burnstein, E., Moulton, R., and Liberty, P.: Prestige vs. excellence as determinants of role attractiveness. *Amer. Soc. Rev., 28*:215-219, 1963.
10. Callard, E.: Achievement Motive in the Four Year Old and Its Relationship to Achievement Expectancies of the Mother. Unpublished doctoral dissertation. Ann Arbor, Univ. of Michigan, 1964.
11. Child, I. L., Storm, T., and Veroff, J.: Achievement themes in folk tales related to socialization practice. In Atkinson, J. W. (ed.): *Motives in Fantasy, Action and Society.* Princeton, Van Nostrand, 1958, pp. 479-492.
12. Crockett, H. J.: Achievement motive and mobility. *Amer. Sociol. Rev., 27*:191-204, 1962.
13. Eriksen, E. H.: Identity and the life cycle. Selected Paper, *Psychol. Issue,* 1959 (monograph).
14. Feather, N. T.: The relationship of persistence at a task to expectation of success and achievement related motives. *J. Abnorm. Soc. Psychol., 63*:552-561, 1961.
15. Fontana, G.: The Achievement Motive in Women: A Thesis Proposal. Unpublished manuscript, Univ. of Michigan, 1963.
16. French, Elizabeth G.: Effects of the interaction of motivation and

feedback on task performance. In Atkinson, J. W. (ed.): *Motives in Fantasy, Action and Society*. Princeton, Van Nostrand, 400-408, 1958.

17. Fench, Elizabeth and Lesser, G.: Some characteristics of the achievement motive in women. *J. Abnorm. Soc. Psychol., 68*:119-128, 1964.
18. Gardner, J. W.: *Excellence*. New York, Harper, 1961.
19. Goertzel, V.: *Cradles of Eminence*. Boston, Little, Brown, 1962.
20. Horner, Tina: *The Motive to Avoid Success. A Thesis Proposal*. Unpublished, Univ. of Michigan, 1965.
21. Kagan, J., and Moss, H. A.: *Birth to Maturity*. New York, Wiley, 1962.
22. Koenig, Kathryn: *Social Psychological Correlates of Self-Reliance*. Unpublished doctoral dissertation, Univ. of Michigan, 1962.
23. Lazurus, R. S.: A substitutive-defensive conception of apperceptive fantasy. In Kagan, J., and Lesser, G. S. (ed.): *Contemporary Issues in Thematic Apperceptive Methods*. Springfield, Thomas, 1961.
24. Lesser, G., Krawitz, Rhoda, and Packard, Rita: Experimental arousal of achievement motivation in adolescent girls. *J. Abnorm. Soc. Psychol., 1*:59-65, 1963.
25. Mahone, C. H.: Fear of failure and unrealistic vocational aspiration. *J. Abnorm. Soc. Psychol., 60*:253-261, 1960.
26. McClelland, D. C.: *The Achieving Society*. Princeton, Van Nostrand, 1961.
27. McClelland, D. C.: Motive acquisition. *Amer. Psychol., 20*:321-333, 1965.
28. McClelland, D. C.: N achievement and entrepreneurship: A longitudinal study. *J. Personality Social Psychol., 1*:389-391, 1965b.
29. McClelland, D. C., Atkinson, J. W., Clark, R. A., and Lowell, E. L.: *The Achievement Motive*. New York, Appleton-Century, 1953.
30. McClelland, D. C., and Friedman, G. A.: A cross-cultural study of the relationship between child-training practices and achievement motivation appearing in folk tales. In Swanson, G. E., Newcomb, T. M., and Hartley, E. L. (eds.): *Readings in Social Psychology*. New York, Holt, 1952.
31. *Ibid.*
32. McGhee, P. E., and Teevan, R. C.: The Childhood Development of Fear of Failure Motivation. Technical Report No. 15, Contract NOR 3591(01) NR 171-803, 1965.
33. Morgan, J. N.: The achievement motive and economic behavior. *Economic Devel. Cult. Change,* XII:243-267, 1964.
34. Moulton, R. W.: Notes for a projective measure of fear of failure. In Atkinson, J. W. (ed.): *Motives in Fantasy, Action, and Society*. Princeton, Van Nostrand, 1958, pp. 563-571.
35. Moulton, R. W.: *Antecedents and Correlates of Achievement Striv-*

ings among American Negroes. Unpublished manuscript, Univ. of California, 1963.

36. MOULTON, R. W.: Effects of success and failure on level of aspiration as related to achievement motive. *J. Personality Soc. Psychol., 1*:399-407, 1965.
37. O'CONNOR, PATRICIA: *The Development of an Achievement Risk Preference Scale;* A Preliminary Report. Unpublished test, 1960.
38. RAYNOR, J. O., and SMITH, C. P.: *Achievement Related Motives and Risk-Taking.* Unpublished manuscript, Princeton Univ., 1965.
39. ROSEN, B. C., and D'ANDRADE, R.: Psychosocial origins of achievement motivation. *Sociometry, XX*:185-218, 1959.
40. RUBIN, M.: *Achievement Motivation and Social Class.* Unpublished junior paper, Princeton Univ., 1956.
41. RUEBUSH, B. K.: Interfering and facilitating effects of test anxiety. *J. Abnorm. Soc. Psychol., 60*:205-212, 1960.
42. SARASON, S. B., DAVIDSON, K. S., LIGHTHALL, F. F., WAITE, R. R., and RUEBUSH, B. K.: *Anxiety in Elementary School Children: A Report of Research.* New York, Wiley, 1960.
43. SMITH, C. S.: Relationship between achievement-related motives and intelligence, performance level, and persistence. *J. Abnorm. Soc. Psychol., 68*:523-532, 1964.
44. STRODTBECK, F. L.: Family interaction, values and achievement. In MCCLELLAND, D. C., *et al.* (ed.): *Talent and Society,* Princeton, Van Nostrand, 1958.
45. STRODTBECK, F. L., MCDONALD, M. R., and ROSEN, B.: Evaluation of occupations: A reflection of Jewish and Italian mobility difference. *Amer. Soc. Rev., 22*:546-553, 1957.
46. TORGOFF, I.: *Parental Developmental Timetable: Parental Field Effects on Children's Compliance.* Paper read at the meeting of the Society for Research in Child Development, Pennsylvania State Univ., 1961.
47. VEROFF, J.: *Assessment of Motives in Children.* Progress Report, Ann Arbor, University of Michigan, 1963 (unpublished report).
48. VEROFF, J.: *Measuring the Achievement Motive in Young Boys and Girls.* Unpublished manuscript, Univ. of Michigan, 1965.
49. VEROFF, J., ATKINSON, J. W., FELD, SHEILA, and GURIN, G.: The use of thematic apperception to assess motivation in a nationwide interview study. *Psychol. Monogr., 74*:12 (Whole 499), 1960.
50. VEROFF, J., FELD, SHEILA, and GURIN, G.: Achievement motivation and religious background. *Amer. Soc. Rev., 27*:205-217, 1962.
51. VEROFF, J., and FELD, SHEILA: *Motive and Roles.* Unpublished manuscript, Univ. of Michigan, 1965.
52. VEROFF, J.: Theoretical background for studying the origins of human motivational dispositions. *Merrill Palmer Quart., 11*:3-18.
53. VEROFF, J., FELD, SHEILA, and CROCKETT, H.: Explorations into the ef-

fects of picture cues on thematic apperceptive expression of achievement motivation. *J. Pers. Soc. Psychol.* (in press), 1965.

54. WENDT, H. W.: Motivation, effort and performance. In MCCLELLAND, D. C. (ed.): *Studies in Motivation.* New York, Appleton-Century-Crofts, 1955, pp. 448-459.

55. WINTERBOTTOM, MARIAN: The relation of need for achievement in learning experiences in independence and mastery. In ATKINSON, J. W. (ed.): *Motive in Fantasy, Action, and Society.* Princeton, Van Nostrand, 1958, pp. 453-478.

Chapter 27

HUMAN POTENTIALITIES RESEARCH AT THE UNIVERSITY OF UTAH

HERBERT A. OTTO

THE Human Potentialities Research Project had its beginnings at the University of Georgia in 1959. At that time the writer was engaged in the study of family strengths, a study which was subsequently extended to include personality strengths and resources. On the basis of interviews with healthy, well-functioning families and family groups, as well as individuals, it soon became apparent that both families and individuals had histories which indicated the presence of latent resources or strengths. Attention was thus drawn to *family potential* and *human potentialities.*

In the course of the Georgia studies it was found that there is a relative lack of criteria or standards for the selection of "healthy" or "well-functioning" family or individuals. As a consequence, selection of family groups for inclusion in the studies was to some extent made by random sampling with the following criteria operative in selection: (a) the family was known to a minister over a number of years and judged by him to be well functioning; (b) the family had no history of separation or pending divorce and was not in the process of same; (c) the family was self-supporting and not dependent on welfare or private agencies; and (d) none of the families were in treatment with members of the helping professions.

In 1960 the work on personal and family strengths and potentialities was continued under the auspices of the Graduate School of Social Work at the University of Utah. Initially, sessions which focused on the development of potential were held with groups of graduate social work students (1) and family groups conducted under church auspices (2). To date the bulk of studies has been based on healthy or normal populations, i.e., individuals or families which functioned adequately and were not in treatment.

The work at the University of Utah is based in part on the pioneering thinking of Gardner Murphy (3), Abraham Maslow (4), Erich Fromm (5) and Carl Rogers (6) and is grounded on the hypothesis first formulated by William James at the turn of the century that man is utilizing only 10 per cent of his potential. This point of view has gained a considerable number of distinguished proponents drawn notably from the behavioral sciences and some of the related disciplines. Research in human potentialities now stands on the threshold of being recognized as a discrete field of scientific inquiry and investigation. Hopefully, the entry of Russian scientists in the field will accelerate this process.

In keeping with the contemporary Russian ethos to exploit the individual and human resources to the fullest, it can be anticipated that considerable research manpower will be concentrated in the human potentialities area. As one would expect, current research appears to be largely related to the development of mental functioning; and a holistic approach is totally lacking. Nevertheless, research in the USSR might accelerate work conducted in this country and *accelerate establishment of research on human potentialities as a recognized discrete area of investigation.*

The approach at the University of Utah has been *holistic,* focusing on the whole man and the development of his interrelated potentialities. From this point of view to single out, for example, the *creative* potential as an exclusive means of development or through a training program, contributes to man's segmentation and denies the fundamental interrelatedness of the human potential—*thus delimiting, encapsulating and establishing definite boundaries to the actualization of human possibilities.* This is not to deny that creativity research is making a most valuable contribution to our understanding of both the nature and development of the human potential.

In more recent times, the distinction between certain educational and therapeutic methods has become more and more academic. It is well to realize that programs devoted to the actualization of human potential combine both educational and therapeutic elements. They are essentially growth-oriented, growth-centered and growth-fostering. *A mandatory and necessary component of such programs is the development of both community leadership and community spirit.*

Purposes and goals of the University of Utah research project have been as follows.

1. To develop initial and pilot frameworks of human potentialities.
2. To develop a theoretical framework of personality strengths and resources, leading in due time to a definitive framework of family strengths and resources.
3. To explore some of the dimensions of individual and family potential.
4. To build theory about factors and forces inimical to the development of human potential.
5. To devise means, methods and instruments to help individuals and families make better use of their potential.

At his present level of development man assumes certain categories or dimensions of what he believes to be his potential and projects his potential essentially within these dimensions. In the course of his development new dimensions are likely to emerge. Thus, in the future, man's potential as well as the realization of his potential will likely be projected against a much enlarged background if not a fundamentally changed set of categories or constructs.

As stated earlier, the development of initial frameworks for the exploration of human potentialities continues to be one of the objectives of the research project. This involves the formulation of *global* frameworks which are subject to continued change and modification based on subsequent studies and findings. The current model of human potentialities will be presented in abbreviated form. It is hoped that from research a theoretical framework of human potentialities will eventually emerge and continuously evolve, serving as a growing edge to extend the frontiers of human inquiry and development. It speaks to the level of man's development that the formulation of a comprehensive framework of human potentialities, based on research, appears not to have been undertaken to date.

HUMAN POTENTIALITIES—AN INITIAL THEORETICAL CONSTRUCT

Human potential is conceived as essentially unbounded in many areas, of which we will mention only four: physiological; social; psychological; and spiritual.

Man's Physiological Potential

The human being as a biological organism has an unexplored capacity for plasticity, self-transformation, adaptation, change, organismic regeneration and organismic self-destruction. Innumerable case histories from the annals of medical science substantiate this.

A survey of the literature of a comparative newcomer to medical science reveals that extensive experimental laboratory work (using hypnosis and suggestion as a major method) gives additional indication of the human organism's capacity for self-modification, its extensibility and malleability.

Hypnosis is now widely used in medical circles, and the professional literature contains numerous clinical reports and studies concerning the use of hypnosis as an anesthesia in both minor and major surgery, in accelerating regenerative and healing processes, as a means of treatment in genitourinary and dermatological disorders, etc. In this connection it is of interest that one of the well-known medical authorities in the field of hypnotherapy offers the following definition: "Hypnotherapy is directed to the patient's needs and is a methodology to tap the 'forgotten assets' of the *hidden potential of behavior and response* that so often lead to new learnings and understanding" (Italics added) (7). Research in psychosomatic medicine has given us some indication of the human organism's capacity for self-destruction. If emotional dynamics play a dominant part in organismic self-destruction, it would follow that the key to organismic regeneration would also lie in this area.

Man has at his disposal a vast reservoir of physical strength and energy, the range and scope of which has been consistently underestimated. This reservoir capacity or resource is presently accessible only under emergency conditions for most persons. (There are cases on record of men and women lifting objects such as an automobile weighing in excess of 3500 pounds under emergency conditions.) Man's ability as a sensing and perceptive organism has also been considerably underrated. He is *consciously* aware of only a small fraction of the stimuli and data which are constantly presented to him. Evidence exists that through training to achieve directive attention, the apertures of perception and awareness can be very significantly enlarged. The human organism is possessed of an extraordinary sensitivity to a very extensive range of cues, stimuli and data but has programmed itself to utilize for problem solving only a fraction of the inputs which pass the screen erected by the life style and cultural milieu in which it functions.

Findings from sensory deprivation research add a new perspective to the understanding of personality function and structure. These investigations suggest *that personality much more than previously suspected is dependent on the whole range of sensory inputs for its operation and is to a large extent a function of the field in which it operates.*

Research indicates that man's neurological structures function at only a fraction of their capacity. There is evidence that one-half of the brain is not being utilized. There is also evidence that use of neurological structure causes growth and extension to take place. For instance, Golgi Cell research indicates that *function (to an as yet unknown extent) seems to create neurological structure.*

Research in parapsychology suggests that man has organismically linked abilities for Extra Sensory Perception and hints at the possibility that he is able to transcend both time and space. Scientists in the U.S.S.R. reportedly conducting investigations in almost a dozen government-supported parapsychological laboratories describe Extra Sensory Perception (notably telepathy) as "cerebral radio communication" which is seen as "effected by a factor present in the structure of the brain," and not as being restricted to the gifted few. Experiments with animals conducted in the parapsychological institutes of the U.S.S.R. seem to imply a phylogenetic distribution of this capacity. Research in bio-cybernetics is currently being pursued both in the U. S. and in the Soviet Union. On this subject one of the eminent Russian specialists in parapsychology, Leonid L. Vasiliev, comments as follows: "In the near future we may expect to utilize at a distance instrumentally amplified radio waves originating from the muscles, heart and brain, in behalf of practical needs of one kind or another" (8).

Bio-cybernetics is a newly emerging area of investigation concerned with the study of man as composed of a multitude of complex and linked energy systems or energy fields. It has been found, for example, that contracting muscles generate high-frequency bio-currents or fields. Some of the research in bio-cybernetics is concerned with the amplification of these fields so that machines, etc., can be operated at a distance through this extension of man's energy system, thus extending the range of his possibilities.

Finally, there is underway a fundamental change in thinking about what medical geriatric experts formerly referred to as "the inevitable organismic deterioration associated with age." Researchers are increasingly reaching the conclusion that personality and its emotional components (and the attitude toward self and life) are integrally if not causally related to the patterns of organismic deterioration in advanced age. One of the leading British specialists recently made the following observation: "I consider that the geriatric illnesses which used to be regarded as organic, permanent, and requiring in-patient admission are only partially organic and partially emotional in their etiology; since the emotional component is the major factor, the time has come for a new look at our attitudes" (9).

Man's Social Potential

That man is a social being is generally accepted and that social institutions, structures and forces are intimately linked to the self-system of individuals is widely recognized. Scientists, however, seem far less aware of the extent to which personality is mediated by social structures and the extent to which personality *and the human potential* are a function of the social milieu or field in which it is embedded.

Man's interpersonal encounters are essentially *social* encounters. (This is recognized by common parlance, we "socialize.") The character or nature of our social encounters is, of course, largely determined by the society in which we live. If we accept the hypothesis that interpersonal relationships or the interpersonal encounter is the major medium for personality development and growth, *then it must be questioned whether the present level and quality of social relationships is conducive to the realization of human potential.* There is reason to believe that the superficial and stereotyped communication which characterizes contemporary social intercourse depresses and delimits the development of potentialities. From a slightly different perspective we can say that pathogenic social vectors and our societal structures and institutions are largely inimical to and delimit development of the human potential. The concept of a "sick society" and dysfunctional institutions has been explored among others by Horney (10), Fromm (5), Kubie (11), and more recently Rosenberg *et al.* (12). Undoubtedly, man's institutions are functioning at a fraction of their potential.

Again, placing the emphasis on the interpersonal relationships field as the main *modus operandi* for the realization of human potential, a differential definition of social institutions is offered. Social institutions can be seen as a matrix of intricately linked and interdependent processes which have a certain historical continuity *with interpersonal relationships serving as the media of transmission lending both form and image to the institutional structure.* Institutions, thus, are both a *process* and in *transition.* For example, an examination of educational institutions will reveal that the teaching function, as expressed in the *relation* of the teacher to the pupil (especially on the elementary school level), has markedly changed from what it was fifty years ago. The administrative structure and administrative function in educational institutions have also undergone considerable change (with similar changes in other institutions).

This is not to deny that an institution is greater than the sum of its parts and that it has a structure and life of its own. However, recognition, if not preoccupation, with these realities of the institutional structure has led to a comparative neglect of the role played by interpersonal relationships and behavior in the maintenance of institutional frameworks. Perhaps the seemingly overwhelming task of bringing about change and regeneration in institutional structures would appear less overwhelming if we began by studying interpersonal relationship processes (and behavior) within the institutional setting vis-à-vis the aims, goals and underlying purposes of the institution. Such a self-directed study and analysis by participants in an institution could be a potent force for change *originating from within* and not imposed externally or structurally, which often leaves the interpersonal and behavioral matrix untouched.

Institutions have but one purpose or function—to serve as a framework for the actualization of human potential. It is possible to evaluate both the institution and the contribution of the institution by asking the following question: To what extent does the function of the institution foster the realization of human potential? Institutional regeneration is inseparable from this question. Finally, implicit in the task of institutional regeneration is the possibility of fundamental change for institutions as well as the development of new frameworks. Much of what is currently described as "problem behavior" or "irresponsible behavior" of individuals is traceable to dysfunctional institutions. These impart to members of society a limited and delimiting self-concept—a crippled image of man which leaves him discontent but not sufficiently so that he will make the mobilization of his potential, *which is the achieving of wholeness,* his lifelong task. The newly emerging concept of human potentialities reemphasizes the individual's uniqueness and adds new dignity and respect to our understanding of the person, *for each member of society, regardless of his status, is seen as having a prodigious potential which we have not as yet learned to unfold.*

From a slightly different perspective, institutions represent values and symbolize man's goals and aspirations; again, they are essentially man's matrix for the realization of his potential.

It therefore becomes a most pressing task to humanize and modify social institutions so that they will function in consonance with man's deepest aspirations, aims and goals. The analysis and study of social structures as they relate to the human potential is a necessary first step for the regeneration of institutions. In the healthy society the primary function of social institutions is to maximize man's potential, to provide him with a matrix which will nurture his evolutionary growth and to help man more fully to become that of which he is capable. Man's social potential remains largely untapped: We have not as yet developed either the art or science of institutional regeneration.

Man's Psychological Potential

The interrelatedness of social and psychological dimensions and forces cannot be sufficiently stressed, and boundaries can be drawn only for theoretical purposes. Man has erected socio-psychological structures and has created value systems (self-understanding, for example, is not a major cultural value) which discourage the exploration of man's inner universe. Yet self-understanding and self-knowledge is a key to man's potential, his development and his becoming.

Paradoxically, we have created a cultural milieu which offers such a multiplicity of stultifiers and "escape opportunities," that flight from the self and from self-knowledge is both a way of life and an obstacle to the actualization of potential. Usually, it is only when a person is in the process of breakdown that treatment and increased self-knowledge is sought from the psychiatrist, psychologist or social worker. To maximize the psychological health of all people, these disciplines need to shift much of their emphasis from the treatment of personality pathology to helping the so-called healthy and well-functioning citizen to mobilize his potential, which includes helping him to achieve gains in self-understanding and self-knowledge. *Programs which focus on the development of the human potential are of the very essence of prevention.* Mass treatment of psychological breakdown is best achieved by fostering psychological health. Man's flight from and denial of his potential represents a denial of his inner reality—an escape into unhealth. Pathogenic social vectors support and encourage this flight from self, from self-understanding and self-realization.

The interrelatedness of man's psychological and social potential is never clearer than when we examine man's capacity for learning, the quality of his intellectual curiosity and the nature of his mental functioning. All these are to a large extent determined and conditioned by the nature of his experiences in our educational institutions. Current educational practice creates strong, deep-seated and, for the most part, enduring emotionally-based resistances to further mental development. If this were not the case, the overwhelming preponderance of our graduates from educational institutions would continue their mental development within the framework of these institutions as a lifelong task. Today education is for the most part sought to achieve a vocational niche and not as a means of sensitively uncovering and developing the potentials of the individual (including his mental development). On the other hand, as Russian scientists have concluded, every man is potentially capable of mastering the required courses of dozens of colleges, of learning forty or more languages, etc. The potential of the human mind, of mental functioning and of learning as a creative process is only beginning to be understood. Research has shown that contemporary educational practice militates against the development of the child's creative potential. Unquestionably, only a very small fraction of the creative potential of the total population ever finds expression. It is safe to conclude that if a larger fraction of this creative potential were "actualized," this could lead to a renaissance and cultural flowering unequalled in history.

The ongoing unfolding of man's psychological potential is expected to include the following.

1. An extension of the ability to communicate and of the communication system, including greatly heightened awareness of various modes of nonverbal communication.
2. The development and amplification of sensory modalities and their transformation into new means of communication.
3. The availability of vast masses of stored data (most ma-

terial in the brain's memory banks appears to be in a type of dead storage) for problem-solving or life-coping purposes.

4. A very marked increase in the range of affective functioning and experiencing, thus adding new dimensions to man's emotional capacity.
5. A greatly expanded understanding of the relationship of motivation (including unconscious motivation) to the realization of individual potential. This will open new ways for people to live nearer to the full limit of what is possible.
6. Utilization of the motivational nexus, in turn, can result in a deeply satisfying involvement of the individual in the process of actualizing his potential so that the need for sleep will be radically curtailed (to four to five hours or less).
7. An enlarged understanding of the role played by man's values and life-goals in relation to the unfolding of his possibilities could give rise to a new branch of inquiry—metapsychology. This new branch of science would also be concerned with the elucidation of the value postulates which underlie *all* studies of personality and human behavior.
8. A considerably augmented recognition and utilization of the psychological forces associated with nourishment (including all forms of nourishment, emotional as well as physical), leading to an acceleration of personality growth processes throughout life.
9. The development of a vastly increased interoceptive and propioceptive awareness—an interior sensing or scanning of the interrelatedness of organismic systems leading to a better understanding (and development) of organismic capacities and abilities as well as increased cognitive control. This advance should also add to our understanding of the processes involved in organismic regeneration.
10. An expansion of the creative, intuitive and imaginative capacities is in the offing in some measure as a result of the contributions from research with the so-called psychedelic

drugs. This work also holds promise of contributing to our understanding of unconscious processes, including their relationship to extrasensory perception.

11. An increased understanding (and utilization) of body rhythms in relation to bio-rhythms and cosmic rhythms leading to a greater attunement with life forces or processes and the mobilization of increased energy and vitality.

The development of this latter aspect of the human potential, linked with a more sophisticated understanding of the nourishment processes, an enhanced capacity of interior sensing (and its implications for organismic regeneration) could lead to an open-ended extension of the life span. This would place the choice of the life span essentially in the hands of the individual, i.e., man's attitudes and basic feelings about himself, life and the world would determine the nature of his continued relatedness to the total environment. Finally, we can anticipate that the findings from research in human potentialities will lead to the emergence of a new (psychological) image of man—a revised and enlarged perception of himself and his relatedness to all which surrounds him.

Man's Spiritual Potential

Both theologians and psychologists who have conducted studies in this area appear to be in agreement that man's spiritual potential has barely been tapped. Religious belief systems and value structures, over and beyond the ceremonial of church attendance, seem to wield little influence on the quality of interpersonal relationships, the conduct of business or vocation and the exercise of social concern and responsibility in the overwhelming majority of individuals holding denominational membership. Our research strongly indicates *that stated life goals of individuals who are members of Christian denominations only in some instances bear any relationship to their religious belief system and value structure.*

The integration of Judeo-Christian values, ethics and principles into the life functioning of denominational members has not been achieved with any significant measure of success. The hierarchic and authoritarian frameworks and didactic experiences (13) provided by the major denominational organizations seem to *actively militate against helping the member to "live what he believes" and help him to achieve but a minute measure of his spiritual potential.*

From another perspective, man's spiritual concerns and values can be experienced by him as a source of strength, inspiration and aspiration. Man's interpretation of his *relatedness* to the universe, to all things, to life and living (and, in turn, the process of building and forming such a relatedness) can be a source of fulfillment and a means of constant growth and development throughout the life cycle. Man's spiritual potential can serve as a matrix for constant growth, since the following are in the nature of lifelong undertakings:

1. The task of relating religious values and ethics to daily living, daily relationships to fellow man and life goals;
2. The task of establishing a relationship to God which emerges from the relationship of man to man (the relationship of man to man as a spiritual process);
3. The process of achieving a deep communion, an atunement or at-one-ment, a state of mystic union or ecstasy, with Nature, the Universe or God. (This is a neglected aspect of man's creative capacity and can produce deeply vitalizing results.) These and many more aspects of the spiritual potential represent a way which can touch the very core of the human potential.

The study of the various states or levels of mystic union (14) and the means and methods (tailored to the specific idiosyncratic needs of the individual) which can be employed to achieve this state constitutes a promising area of research. This is but one of many means through which man's spiritual potential can become both a source and instrument of his transcendence.

The way man experiences and establishes his relatedness to the universe in which he finds himself, *the frame of reference which he creates or adopts to illuminate his passage through life into death,* these congeries of relatedness represent spiritual resources.

How a man perceives his life and death has a very direct effect on how he views and utilizes his potential. There is a great need for exploration of the part played by man's spiritual potential (i.e., his understanding of the meaning of his passage from life into death) in the total range of his interrelated potentialities.

The Laboratory Groups

To date a total of twenty-two laboratory groups have been conducted. Of this number, three were composed of family groups with an average of six couples per group. Laboratory groups are conducted under the auspices of the University of Utah Division of Continuing Education and meet in the evening for two hours. There are an average of twelve meetings per quarter. The noncredit class is listed in the catalog as "Adult Education 31, Developing Your Personal Potential" with the following descriptive material added.

> This program is designed to help you to discover capacities, strengths, talents and abilities which you have but which you may not be aware of or using fully. Emphasis is on discovering your potentialities and developing them, leading to more vital, creative, satisfying living and productivity.

The class is open to the public and draws a varied population ranging from eighteen-year-old employed and unemployed high school graduates to retired persons and members of the professions. The most frequently encountered enrollee is a housewife in her mid-thirties, with one or more years of college education, who is seeking a way to identify or make better use of her personal resources or potential. Enrollment is restricted to seventeen class members, and an informal screening procedure is used so that the class will contain few or no members who are in treatment with psychiatrists, psychologists or social workers. Class members who are in treatment usually remain in the class only when close to termination of treatment or in exceptional instances, *as the emphasis in the research program is on working with healthy and (comparatively) well-functioning populations.*

At the outset, class members are acquainted with the fact that they are enrolled in a laboratory or experimental group. It is pointed out that it is a purpose of the laboratory group to develop as well as to test and explore various methods and means designed to actualize or tap human potential. Throughout the quarter, group members are encouraged to share their thinking and ideas related to the mobilization of human potential. In the course of the first meeting attention is drawn to a poster which states: "We grew into what we are through relations with people. We grow into what we can be through relations with people." The statement on the poster is discussed; and the class then proceeds to its first task, namely to work out how they can "really get to know each other," so that communication will be maximized, free-flowing and centered on the real concerns and interests of the participants. The group usually develops a number of methods designed to "really get acquainted." The DUE (Depth Unfoldment Experience) Method* is then described, and the group chooses which method to use. In 90 per cent of instances the group has selected the DUE Method as a means of getting to know each other.

The group's next task is to undertake an assessment of individual strengths and potentialities. The Otto Inventory of Personal Resources, an instrument designed to provide the user with an overview of his personality strengths is used in this connection. This instrument also provides participants with a frame of reference and orientation to the concept of personality strengths. The concept of human potentialities is discussed at this time, and group members are encouraged to explore how this concept applies to them individually. The remainder of the meeting is devoted to the use, evaluation and development of various methods designed to actualize potential. These methods have been described in detail elsewhere (16, 17, 18).

All sessions are tape-recorded, and tape recordings are used for purposes of analysis and evaluation. An extensive evaluation questionnaire is also filled out at the conclusion of the group ses-

---

* This method has been described elsewhere (15). We have found that through use of this method we can achieve a depth of interpersonal involvement and relationship in one session which formerly took us five to six group sessions to achieve.

sions. Follow-up studies of group members have been conducted (19).

As a part of the Human Potentialities Research Project, studies focusing on the strengths and resources of families (2, 20, 21) and adults (22, 23) have been conducted. An initial framework of family strengths was developed (24), and the Otto Family Strength Survey, an instrument designed to give a family a clearer idea of its strengths and resources, was field-tested. Studies of adolescents (25, 26) have also been conducted. On the basis of the latter studies there is evidence that the personality resources of adolescents differ both qualitatively and quantitatively from those of adults. As one outcome of this research an initial framework of strengths of adolescents is in preparation (27). Open-ended group interviews with varied groups of adolescents were utilized to construct a framework of adolescent strengths, as well as an instrument designed to give teenagers an overview of their strengths and personality resources. This instrument is now in the process of field-testing.

Studies focusing on the personality resources and assets of the aged have also been undertaken (28, 29), leading to the development of an instrument for use by retired persons residing in nursing homes. This instrument, the Otto Inventory of Personal Resources, Form "G," is designed to help nursing home members to gain an overview of their personality resources toward helping them to regain some of their interests and to encourage participation in programs leading to a more satisfying mode of living.

SOME INITIAL FINDINGS AND CONCLUSIONS

The pilot projects and studies conducted at the University of Utah have essentially been in the nature of exploratory investigations. The focus of all studies has been to learn more about personality strengths and assets, family strengths and resources and the nature and dimensions of the human potential. Emphasis has been on three core questions: (1) *How* can potential be actualized? (2) *How much* potential can be actualized? and (3) *Which* specific potential(s) should be actualized? Over a six year period, work has been almost exclusively with healthy or well-functioning populations who have actively participated both in theory formulation and the development of methods designed to actualize potential. Findings and methods from the research project have application to business and industry (30), the professions (31, 32), and other varied programs (33). On the basis of this work, a number of general findings and conclusions have emerged.

1. *A holistic, depth approach to the human potential would seem to be highly desirable.* There is evidence that the study and mobilization of man's interrelated potentialities are best achieved by working with the whole person and by involving as many facets as possible of the field in which he functions. This would include the purposive restructuring of the home environment, the work environment, the interpersonal environment and the constructive use of health vectors in the individual's life space (31) as means of mobilizing potential. Segmental approaches, such as concentrating exclusively on fostering the development of the creative potential are of value but appear to be less effective in triggering personality growth and development than use of a "shotgun" approach, which centers on the development of an individual's multiple potential in the course of an ongoing, total impact or "total unfoldment program."

2. *There are strong indications that the marked resistance to the development and utilization of strengths and potentialities which we have encountered as persistent phenomena is due to a deep-seated and powerful fear-guilt-anxiety cycle, as well as to inimical cultural forces.* The individual fears to develop his strengths, as this would require both exercising leadership, "sticking his neck out," and, more fundamentally, would demand personality change and change in his basic habit and behavior patterns. Intimately linked with this fear is a deep sense of guilt. Such guilt stems from the individual's *awareness on a deep level* (although often partially conscious) *that he possesses specific resources, strengths and capacities which exist only as latent forces and are not being utilized.* The failure to develop and to utilize these resources leaves the individual with a lack of wholeness or lack of self-fulfillment, thereby generating pervasive guilt, which in turn is repressed. Anxiety, the third element, is seen as both flowing from this vicious cycle as well as contributing to

it. Considerable psychic energy is bound up or invested in this process. Freeing this energy or redirecting it to more productive purposes, it is postulated, will enable the personality to move markedly in the direction of more optimal functioning. As yet, however, we have not found an effective means of obliterating the pervasive fear-guilt-anxiety cycle. In turn, closely related to this fear-guilt-anxiety cycle are three basic core configurations. It is our hypothesis that unless these core configurations are investigated in depth, the major portion of an individual's potential must, of necessity, remain in *status nascendi.* These core configurations relate to the individual's basic attitudes and feelings toward sex membership, death, and his value structure.

3. *The average well-functioning individual has an exceedingly restricted self-perception of his personality strengths and a markedly limited perspective of his potentialities.* Research subjects having a background of one year or more of college training, on being asked to list their personality strengths, often identify between five and six strength items but are able to list between two and three times as many "weaknesses" or problem areas. It is hypothesized that pathogenic institutional forces and vectors are inimical to, and to a considerable measure, impede the development of a healthy self-concept. We have repeatedly found that participants attribute their inability to list strengths as being of "cultural origin." As one group member put it: "When I write down my strengths, this is like bragging about yourself, and this is something that just is not done."

4. *The process of "taking inventory" of personality assets, strengths and resources is in itself experienced as strengthening by participants.* The identification of personality assets and resources, particularly if other persons are involved as a part of the process, usually brings about some positive changes in the self-image and self-concept. If "taking inventory" is used as an isolated experience (and not as a part of a total program), or if reinforcement is not employed, the effects of "taking inventory" diminish rapidly and appear to be minimal.

5. *A progressive access effect is noted in the course of actualizing potential.* It has been repeatedly observed that as participants begin to actualize or use latent capacities or abilities, they

seem to discover and recognize more of their possibilities. The process of actualizing potential appears to have made more of their potential available to them. Also consistently reported was an increase in vitality and available energy leading to more productive functioning, both in relation to vocation and home. There was also evidence that there was an increase in social relations and in the enjoyment of these types of relationships.

6. *The concept of a key potential was distinguished.* As a part of the process of "taking inventory," some participants were able to identify a particular potential, the development of which they felt would trigger growth and lead to positive change in various aspects of the personality. It was found that the actualization of a key potential often seemed to result in far-reaching and unexpected change and recognition or unfoldment of other potentialities.

7. *There was evidence that a depleted or impoverished pleasure economy was in operation in most of the group members.* Most of the participants, particularly those having a middle class background, seemed to be engaged in a round of *pseudo-pleasures*—low level, attenuated experiences lacking in the elements of deep and authentic joy and lacking spontaneity linked with a vital relishing and jubilant delight in an experience. There was evidence of a tendency for pleasures to become institutionalized and void of the effort of creativity. It became clear that the low-level pleasure economy and continued participation in pseudo-pleasures was related to the individual's view of himself and the world and appeared to have some influence on his capacity for mobilizing potential. It is currently our hypothesis that a low-level pleasure economy is in many instances directly related to the total amount of energy available for the realization of potential.

8. *There is some evidence that, in most individuals studied, deeply entrenched and ingrained habit systems, which dominate both behavior and perceptions and affect ideational processes, function to delimit spontaneity, creativity and the development of individual potential.* Results from a series of habit analyses undertaken by class participants indicate that the role of habit systems as they affect and delimit personality functioning has, to

date, been underestimated. For example, using a Habit Analysis Form and undertaking a *partial* analysis of habit patterns for one day, an established salesman in his early thirties identified forty-one often-interlocking habits and habit systems which "carried" him through the day and which determined to a considerable extent the nature of his daily experiences. Analysis of work habits was not included in this habit analysis.

9. *The use of posters and sensory awareness experiences has been particularly of value in the program.* We have found that the use of posters, such as: "Every person has a vast potential—let's find yours and use it," "Be sensitive to what others 'telegraph' to you—use your impressions, intuitions, feelings and hunches—and *Communicate* them," is a highly effective tool in facilitating group purposes and aims. Sensory awareness experiences described in detail elsewhere (34) have been used. Effectiveness of the posters varies directly with the depth and quality of discussion (and consequent interpersonal involvement) conducted in relation to the message conveyed. Sensory awareness experiences involving touch, smell and taste, which were largely organized and provided by group members, have a vitalizing effect and seem to add impetus to the interest in mobilizing potential. There is an indication that they enlarge a person's relatedness to his environment and level of perception as he is able to see more and sense more. This appears to contribute to a deeper sense of self and a widening of human experience.

10. *An initial set of criteria for the assessment of family strengths and a pilot instrument (the Otto Family Strength Survey), designed to give a family an overview of its strengths, was developed* (24). A number of methods have been used experimentally (16) in relation to the development of family strengths. These methods appear to have considerable promise, although a detailed evaluation of their effectiveness has not as yet been undertaken.

11. *There are indications that the achievement of an expanded self-concept is directly linked to the ability to actualize potentialities.* A significant proportion of the work conducted in the laboratory groups has focused on helping participants gain an enlarged perception of self, increased self-confidence and a more

positive self-image. It has been our observation that, in the beginning of the group experience, members have a limited self-concept and envision for themselves a narrow horizon of possibilities. Gains in achieving an expanded and more positive self-image seem to take place at an accelerated pace in participants who are actively working on the improvement of their body image through participation in a physical exercise or conditioning program. In turn, these group members appear to have made more rapid progress in realizing their possibilities.

12. *A number of methods which are of particular value in programs designed to mobilize human potential have been developed and extensively field tested.* Included are the Multiple Strength Perception Method which will be described in detail in a subsequent chapter; Action Programs (31) and Strength Role Assignment (17) are other methods which have consistently yielded outstanding results.

To return briefly to the puzzling question: Why does man continue to want to make better use of his potentialities and yet continue to be unable to do so? The fear-guilt-anxiety cycle, the pathogenic social vectors and other hypotheses mentioned previously are only a part of the picture. Much more remains to be discovered and verified. For example, any change or the prospect of change engenders resistance in most people; moreover, most individuals seem to lack a positive self-concept of their potential. To gain something better, something has to be given up—old ideas, the shells of values, etc. Growth and the actualization of potential also mean renunciation, discipline, commitment and responsibility, as well as change in life style. Finally, for man to be fully involved in the continuous act of self-creation he must have both the *vision* of his potentials and the *courage* to realize his possibilities. Unless he has that vision and hope, his courage may never develop. We are at a point of readiness for discarding an outmoded image of man and assuming a new image—the image of man's potentialities.

CONCLUDING COMMENTS

One of the chief values derived from the initial work in the area of human potentialities has been the opening of several promising avenues for further investigation and inquiry. A pressing need exists for rigorous and imaginatively conceived research programs. Equally important is the gathering of data and findings from many discrete areas and disciplines and from all parts of the world. Much of value has been discovered but has never been applied or evaluated in the context of the human potential. The task of bringing together known relevant research and the evaluation of these findings would require an interdisciplinary team approach. The creation of an Institute for Human Potentialities (30) would in all likelihood result in significant advances if not a major breakthrough within the next ten to fifteen years. Research in human potentialities—how to help the well-functioning person function even better—is both one of the most neglected and the most promising research areas in the twentieth century. The history of man is the unfolding of his potentialities—it is also the key to his future.

REFERENCES

1. Otto, H. A., and Griffiths, K. A.: A new approach to developing the student's strengths. *Soc. Casework*, 45:3, 119-124, 1963.
2. Otto, H. A.: What is a strong family? *Marriage & Family Living, Journal of the National Council on Family Relations*, 24:1, 77-81, 1962.
3. Murphy, G.: *Human Potentialities*. New York, Basic Books, 1961.
4. Maslow, A. H.: *Motivation and Personality*. New York, Harper and Bros., 1954.
5. Fromm, E.: *Man for Himself*. New York, Holt, Rinehart and Winston, 1960.
6. Rogers, C. R.: *On Becoming a Person*. Boston, Houghton Mifflin, 1961.
7. Kroger, W. S.: *Clinical and Experimental Hypnosis*. Philadelphia, J. B. Lippincott Co., 1963, IX.
8. Vasiliev, L. L.: *Mysterious Phenomena of the Human Psyche*. New Hyde Park, University Books, 1965.
9. Macmillan, D.: Mental Health Services for the Aged—British Approach. *Canad. Ment. Health* Sup. 29 (May), 1962.
10. Horney, Karen: *The Collected Works of Karen Horney*. New York, W. W. Norton, 1950.
11. Kubie, Lawrence S.: *Neurotic Distortion of the Creative Process*, Porter Lectures, Series 22, Univ. of Kansas Press, Lawrence, 1958, pp. 122-123.

12. ROSENBERG, B., GERVER, I., and HOWTON, F. W.: *Mass Society in Crisis*. New York, Macmillan, 1964.
13. OTTO, H. A., and WIDMER, F. W.: Christian fellowship: Then and now. *The Christian Century, 79*:15, 457-459, 1962.
14. LASKI, MARGHARITA: *Ecstasy: A Study of Some Secular and Religious Experiences*. Bloomington, Indiana Univ. Press, 1962.
15. OTTO, H. A.: *Depth Unfoldment Experience—A Method for Creating Interpersonal Closeness*. Unpublished manuscript.
16. OTTO, H. A.: The personal and family resource development programs —A preliminary report. *Int. J. Soc. Psychiat. 8*:3, 185-195, 1962.
17. OTTO, H. A.: Personal and family strength research and spontaneity training. *Group Psychother. J., 17*:2-3, 143-149, 1964.
18. OTTO, H. A.: *Developing Human Potential: Applications from Research Findings*. Presented at Annual Meeting of American Psychological Association, Chicago, Sept. 6, 1965 (unpublished paper).
19. DOVER, W. B.: *Personal Strengths Research, A Follow-Up Study*. Unpublished master's thesis, Univ. of Utah, Salt Lake City, Utah, 1965.
20. GABLER, J., and OTTO, H. A.: Conceptualization of "family strengths" in *Family Life* and other professional literature. *J. Marriage Family, Journal of the National Council on Family Relations, 26*:2, 221-223, 1964.
21. KINTER, R., and OTTO, H. A.: The family strength concept and foster home selection. *Child Welfare, Journal of the Child Welfare League of America, 48*:7, 359-364.
22. OTTO, H. A.: Self perception of personality strengths by four discrete groups. *J. Human Relations, 12*:4, 525-531, 1963.
23. OTTO, H. A., and GRIFFITHS, KENNETH A.: A new approach to developing the student's strengths. *Soc. Casework, 45*:3, 119-124, 1963.
24. OTTO, H. A.: The family resource development program: The production of criteria for assessing family strengths. *Family Process, 2*:2, 329-339, 1963.
25. HEALY, S. L.: *Adolescent Strengths*. Unpublished master's thesis, Univ. of Utah, Salt Lake City, Utah, 1965.
26. SOUBA, C. E.: *Revision of Inventory of Personal Resources, Form "A."* Unpublished master's thesis, Univ. of Utah, Salt Lake City, 1965.
27. OTTO, H. A., and HEALEY, S. L.: *Strength Concepts of Adolescents*, To be published. *J. Human Relations.*
28. ATKINSON, G. N.: *Personal Strengths, Concepts of Aging Persons*. Unpublished master's thesis, Univ. of Utah, Salt Lake City, 1965.
29. OTTO, H. A.: Human potentialities research: Application to geriatric programs. *J. Amer. Geriat. Soc., 12*:7, 677-686, 1964.
30. OTTO, H. A.: A proposal for an Institute of Human Potentialities. Accepted for publication. *J. Human Psychol.*

31. Otto, H. A.: The personal and family strength research projects—some implications for the therapist. *Ment. Hyg.*, *48*:3, 447-450, 1964.
32. Otto, H. A., and Griffiths, A. C.: Personality strength concepts in the helping professions. *Psychiat. Quart.*, (Oct.), 1965, p. 3.
33. Otto, H. A.: The human potentialities of nurses and patients. *Nursing Outlook, XIII*:32-35 (Aug.), 1965.
34. Murphy, M., and Otto, H. A. (ed.): Sensory unfoldment through smell, touch, and taste. *Ways of Growth* (in preparation).

Chapter 28

EXPLORATIONS IN HUMAN POTENTIALITIES: A GRADUATE SEMINAR ON HUMAN POTENTIALITIES AT STANFORD UNIVERSITY

WILLIS W. HARMAN

IN this chapter we address ourselves to the question of how a graduate seminar, aimed at assisting the individual student in the discovery and development of his own potentialities, might be structured and conducted. The discussion to follow stems from experience gained in conducting such seminars at Stanford University for the past eight years. Rather than describe this particular experiment in detail, however, since each such endeavor will inevitably be the unique individual creative effort of the particular instructor, I propose to discuss the matter in somewhat more general terms.

SOME BASIC PRINCIPLES

There seem to me to be several basic principles which govern such an effort. One of the most fundamental was enunciated in blunt form by Carl Rogers: "*Anything that can be taught to another is relatively inconsequential.* The only learning which significantly influences behavior is self-discovered, self-appropriated learning. Such self-discovered learning, truth that has been personally appropriated and assimilated in experience, cannot be directly communicated to another" (1). That is to say, the endeavor will be successful to the extent that the leader is a "guide, philosopher and friend," not a teacher in the knowledge-imparting sense—to the extent that it is a seminar in the root meaning of the word, as a place where birth and growth are encouraged and facilitated.

Another principle is that, in adult life, the important limitations on the extent to which we realize our potentialities are self-imposed and lie in the deepest reaches of the personality. (Consider the crippling effect which a basic conviction of inadequacy, or impotence or inferiority can have.) It follows, then, that the realization of the individual's highest potentialities comes about through a realignment of the personality at all levels. It is a process which involves the feelings as well as the intellect. Hence, feelings as well as thoughts—perhaps even more than thoughts—are pertinent agenda for the seminar discussions. This is true in two important ways. In the first place, feelings play an essential role because we have resistance, in the psychoanalytic sense, toward the unveiling of the nature of our highest potentialities. Maslow speaks of this as "the need to know and the fear of knowing." "Not only do we hang on to our psychopathology (by repression and other similar defenses), but also we tend to evade personal growth because this, too, can bring another kind of fear, of awe, of feelings of weakness and inadequacy. And so we find another kind of resistance, a denying of our best side, of our talents, of our finest impulses, of our highest potentialities, of our creativeness. . . . It is precisely the god-like in ourselves that we are ambivalent about, fascinated by and fearful of, motivated to and defensive against" (2). Secondly, the experiencing of positive feelings—wonder, exhilaration, affection towards other group members, delight at a new discovery, etc.—typically accompany the self-discovery process.

A third principle is that the effectiveness of the leader of such a seminar depends less on his academic knowledge of such relevant areas as psychology and the humanities than it does upon personal characteristics such as self-awareness, genuineness, warm acceptance of others, sensitive perception, comfortableness with his own feelings and the emotionality of others and integrity—upon the extent to which he has traversed the path upon which he would now guide others.

The implications of these principles are that the seminar for the development of human potentialities, while it may be within the academic framework and sanctioned by centuries of academic tradition, inherently has a very different setting and atmosphere from the familiar lecture hall or classroom. Thus, for example, it seems advisable to sharply limit the group size to the fifteen or so which allows for effective group participation. A seminar with a large table around which all can sit and see one another is a help. Two-hour uninterrupted discussions seem to have a decided advantage over twice as many one-hour periods. If it is feasible, a full-time two- or three-week retreat to a mountain lodge provides a far more advantageous setting than the best that can be arranged on the campus during the regular academic term. A carefully structured, permissive but directed, informality is perhaps a good way to describe the creative atmosphere. The seminar leader needs to be well in touch with his own feelings and to be comfortable with the expression of strong feelings by others. Examinations, grades and even some types of term papers seem quite inappropriate to the nature of the endeavor.

The question of appropriateness is sometimes raised—as by one of my colleagues who protested making the "classroom into a psychoanalytic couch." But this comes about because of the historical development of specialized professions which, whatever its inevitability and advantages, has resulted in an artificial fragmentation of knowledge. Thus the three functions of education, psychotherapy and religion appear in our culture separate and relatively distinct. This may obscure the more important fact that all of them have essentially to do with the recognition and freeing of inner forces that work toward unity, health, fullness of life and purposeful development toward ever higher levels of conscious awareness. (And altering a value system is, in a sense, "deeper" psychotherapy than uncovering a repressed sexual drive.) Insofar as these three areas have to do with the individual's discovery of the wondrous possibilities inherent in the self and of what in life he most wants, they are better viewed together than separately.

THE SELF-IMAGE VIEW OF PERSONALITY CHANGE

Before commenting more specifically on how a seminar on the human potentiality might be organized, let us attempt some general remarks about the processes of personality change. We assume that to make genuine progress in the directions pointed to by such declared aims as releasing creativeness, enhancing ability to communicate, increasing degree of self-actualization, improving intuitive awareness and clarity of perception, establishing consistent and authentic personal values, freeing from such inhibiting reactions as inadequacy feelings or inappropriate anxieties and so on, we must think in terms of rather drastic reexamination of an alteration in the personality structure.

Rokeach (3) provides us with a useful concept for bringing together knowledge about processes of personality change which is found in diverse disciplines and hence discussed in varied specialized jargons. He speaks of the *belief-disbelief system.* By the term *belief* here is meant not what the person consciously thinks he believes, but what one would have to infer that he believes on the basis of all that he says and does. (For example, "I love all mankind" might be a claimed belief substantiated by certain obvious actions, but questionable in the light of more perceptive observation.) "Belief-disbelief systems serve two powerful and conflicting sets of motives at the same time: the need for a cognitive framework to know and to understand, and the need to ward off threatening aspects of reality. . . . The more closed the belief-disbelief system, the more do we conceive it to represent, in its totality, a tightly woven network of cognitive defenses against anxiety. . . . The closed system is nothing more than the total network of psychoanalytic defense mechanisms organized together to form a cognitive system and designed to shield a vulnerable mind." In Rokeach's terms, growth is movement in the direction of the open belief system—open in the sense that any portion of it is available for reexamination for consistency (which consistency includes a tolerance for paradox) and also open to and unthreatened by new data from outside which may prompt revision of beliefs. And this movement is prerequisite to, if not almost synonymous with, realization of one's highest potentialities.

In these terms, central to the personality are the primary beliefs about the nature of the self and its relation to other selves and to the universe in which it exists. This self-image is like the input signal to a feedback control system; the personality and behavior-pattern structure tend to "follow" the self-image. We become as we imagine ourselves to be. "As a man thinketh in his heart, so is he" (4). Thus we can think of personality change as depending upon change in self-image and of the problem of realization of potentialities as fundamentally involving a change in the person's perception of himself and hence of the possibilities open to him.

THREE PROCESSES OF SELF-IMAGE ALTERATION

There appear to be at least three different processes by which these alterations in self-image and resulting changes in personality have been observed to come about. Understanding of these is valuable for assessing the possibilities and limitations inherent in the seminar situation—also for the individual in coming to appreciate the various approaches which he might give trial.

The first process is oriented toward problem solving. Here we mean to include most of what goes on in conventional, verbal psychotherapy (individual and group) as well as the dynamics of "T groups" or "sensitivity training" groups (5). In essence, the individual is helped to become aware of problem areas in his life—difficulties in relationships, value conflicts, failure to feel "fully alive," and so on—and encouraged to search for the genesis of these, either in a historical sense or an existential sense. Through a meaningful, emotional relationship with another or other persons, and in a supportive environment, he comes to an increased intellectual and emotional understanding of himself. He comes to see that his problems are the direct result of unwholesome beliefs included in his self-image: the belief that he is inherently inadequate or inferior; that his feeling of self-worth depends wholly on what he can acquire by way of knowledge, possessions, position and status, esteem of others, etc.; that his existence is threatened when his beliefs or good reputation or financial affluence are threatened; that he is driven by dangerous urges of sex and hostility which must be kept under control at all times; that the criticism or ridicule of others can "hurt" him; and so on (6). He sees also that these unwholesome beliefs are the consequence of his interpretation of life experiences which were possible of other interpretations (7). And "seeing" this in a feeling sense, he is able gradually to revise his self-picture and, as a result, his behavior in problem areas and in stressful situations. The process is characterized by a sort of uncovering layer by layer, as it were, the levels of the psyche, working through problem areas as they come into awareness.

A second process differs from the first in that it bypasses, temporarily, the specific problem areas and centers on changes taking place in the deeper levels of the personality. That is to say, the self-image is changed more fundamentally and directly. Changing of personality and behavior patterns follows, largely without conscious manipulation, through the much-underestimated power of imagination. (The French psychologist Emil Coue wrote: "When the will and the imagination are in conflict, it is always the imagination which wins.")

One approach, used in several executive development seminars and various kinds of self-improvement groups and expounded in some detail by Maltz (8), involves selection of the desired self-image by rational means and autosuggestive techniques for feeding this image into the deeper levels of the mind. Study of "the best that has been thought and said" in humanities seminars and great books courses, contact with great works of art and with religious symbol and ritual are all ways of allowing the experience of those who have gone before to influence the self-image.

The changing of self-image by integrative symbols which the person presents, so to speak, to himself—through dreams, fantasy, directed imagination, in the psychedelic (drug-facilitated) experience (9), etc.—is a powerful technique which is central to the "constructive technique" of C. G. Jung and to the Psychosynthesis of Assagioli (10). It is set forth with particular clarity by one of Jung's students, P. W. Martin (11): "The principal means by which the creative possibilities of the deep unconscious may be reached is the transforming symbol. Anyone wholeheartedly engaged in the experiment in depth will find, as a normal fact of experience, that the unconscious repeatedly produces shapes, objects, phrases, ideas, which have this peculiar quality: if put to their right use they make possible a re-direction of energy and, by so doing, progressively transform the man who uses them." Progoff (12) specifically recommends avoiding attacking personal problems "head-on." Rather, he says, the best progress is made indirectly, by shifting attention "to the depth level of the psyche. There, by permitting the elemental symbol to unfold, a new quality of awareness is achieved by which the original problem is placed in a new perspective that restructures it so that it can be resolved."

If the governing image of the self—the one that is emotionally felt and imagined—is changed from one of worthlessness, or inadequacy or precariously pent-up urges to a self-image centered on an inner self which can be implicitly trusted, then the entire personality structure undergoes (in time) a reorganization in the direction of increased realization of inherent potentialities.

A third process of personality change is described in mystical and occult literature but cannot be said to have formed a part of recognized psychotherapeutic procedures in recent times until the advent of psychedelic therapy (13). It is characterized by the fact that the person's image of himself is changed as a result of his having experiences which he perceives as transcendental and valid, as directly revealing to him higher aspects of himself of which he had previously been unaware. William James wrote of this process of change in *The Varieties of Religious Experience* (14), and Van Dusen has recently summarized:

> There is a central human experience which alters all other experiences. It has been called satori in Japanese Zen, moksha in Hinduism, religious enlightenment or cosmic consciousness in the West. . . . (It) is not just an experience among others, but rather the very heart of human experience. It is the center that gives understanding to the whole. . . . Once found, life is altered because the very root of human identity has been deepened . . . LSD appears to facilitate the discovery of this apparently ancient and universal experience (15).

Echoing this is the statement from other researchers in the same field.

> This central experience, apparently of all who penetrate deeply in their explorations, is that behind the apparent multiplicity of things in a world of science and common sense there is a single reality, in speaking of which it seems appropriate to use such words as infinite and eternal. . . . The perception of this in the psychedelic experiences is an immediate one. . . . It is not inconsistent with rational examination of our more usual ex-

> periences, but it does not arise from such rational examination. . . . After such an experience the person is never the same: in a sense he is born anew . . . since never can he completely forget the knowledge of the underlying reality which he has glimpsed (16).

However uneasy we may be over the various conceptualizations which have been associated over the centuries with this third process of personality change, it appears to be a fact of human experience which can hardly be ignored when considering the nature of the highest human potentiality.

WHERE DO WE SEEK?

With this much as a background, let us return to the question of how a "human potentialities" seminar might be set up. From a logical standpoint, an obvious place to start would seem to be with some sort of picture of what the highest potentiality of the individual human being appears to be. But because this must be discovered anew by each person, and because he simultaneously wants and resists such discovery, this is not such a straightforward matter as it might seem. I know of no better guideline for the search than the following: "Truth is not that which is demonstrable. Truth is that which is ineluctable" (17). Inescapable, discoverable—yet elusive because of the ambivalence toward it which is the universal condition of man.

A reasonably good beginning is provided by asking: Where in the vast realms of human knowledge are we likely to find useful guidance in our search for the nature of and the means for actualization of man's potentialities? Science, of course, and particularly the sciences which have most directly to do with man's mind and its development seem the first places to explore. But the contemporary scientific world view, with its positivistic-physicalistic prejudice, reflects within it the resistance and denying of our highest potentialities which is part of the psychic economy of the individuals who make up the culture. Thus it is useful to examine critiques of the limited view of man which is implied in many scientific presentations (18). Students find it a valuable mind-opening exercise to suspend premature judgment and to examine sympathetically the data of such scientifically offbeat areas as extrasensory perception (19), faith healing (20), teleportation and other psychokinetic effects (21), occultism (22), mysticism (23), etc.

Thus, scientific knowledge is, to use a phrase common in mathematical disciplines, "necessary but not sufficient" as a guide (24). "The self-directed development of the faculties of the inner life has been almost entirely neglected in the modern study of psychology" (25). We need also to look to the humanities and to ponder the meaning of such statements as the following: "The areas of experience with which only literature and the other arts can successfully deal are those which involve the consciousness rather than either mere behavior on the one hand, or on the other, the impersonal forces which are supposed by science to determine that behavior. The phenomena of this area can be successfully presented only when they are organized in terms of concepts which recognize the validity of value judgments" (26). "Poetry is a form of knowledge. . . . The disciplines of poetry may be expected first to teach the evocative power of words, to introduce the student, if we may so put it, to the mighty power of symbolism, and then to show him that there are ways of feeling about things which are not provincial either in space or time" (27). "One of the principal functions of all art is . . . to bring the individual to himself to transcendence . . . to lead him to the timeless radiant dynamic that is at the heart of the world. In this sense the greatest art is learning to see in the way described by Rabbi Nachman of Bratislava: 'Just as a hand held before the eyes conceals from view the vast lights and mysteries of which the world is full, and he who can withdraw it from his eyes, as one withdraws a hand, will behold the great light of the innermost world'" (28). "All art exists to communicate states of consciousness which are higher synthetic wholes than those of ordinary experience" (29).

And then, what of religion? Not as a social institution serving to promote morality, nor as a neurotic escape from the harshness of life, nor as a highly intellectualized abstract theology, but as a living, vibrant, empirical record of man's inner experience and a guide to the most profound levels of self-discovery. What is the difference between the scientific search for truth and that in the

Indian *Vedas,* the Egyptian *Book of the Dead,* the Hebrew prophets, Plato's *Dialogues* and St. John of the Cross?

SEMINAR PROCEDURES

Space allows only the merest mention of topics which may with profit be read about and discussed in the progress of such a seminar—creativity, love, freedom, acceptance, nonattachment, transcendence of opposites such as good and evil. I have found useful the technique of presenting as discussion-openers a few provocative statements such as the following.

On Knowledge

Truth is within ourselves . . . and to know, rather consists in opening out a way whence the imprisoned splendour may escape, than in effecting entry for a light supposed to be without (30).

It is only when a man has shed his egotistical self and with it his needs that he is open to a truth not specially moulded by himself nor determined by his needs. If the truth which comes to us when we are detached from ourselves is the same as is perceived by others vastly different from us in race and creed and separated from us in time, then we are as near as we can ever be to absolute truth, even considered by the most rigid standards of science (31).

On the Paradoxical Nature of Wisdom

True words always seem paradoxical, but no other form of teaching can take its place (Lao-tse).

The recognition of the direction of fulfillment is the death of the self, and the death of the self is the beginning of selfhood (32).

Die and Become.
Till thou hast learned this
Thou art but a dull guest
On this dark planet (33).

Having realized his own self as the Self, a man becomes selfless; and in virtue of selflessness he is to be conceived as unconditioned. This is the highest mystery, betokening emancipation (Upanishads).

Hold well in your mind this brief word: Forsake all things

and you will find all things. . . . Print well in your mind that what I have said, for when you have fulfilled it, you will know well that it is true. . . . This lesson is not one day's work, or play for children—in it is contained the full perfection of all religion (34).

On Other Levels of Consciousness

To me the occurrence of mystical experience at all times and places, and the similarities between the statements of so many mystics all the world over, seem to be a significant fact. *Prima facie* it suggests that there is an aspect of reality with which those persons came in contact in their mystical experiences, and which they afterward strive and largely fail to describe in the language of daily life (35).

The important thing is to see and admit . . . that there does exist a real and recognizable fact (that is, a state of consciousness in some sense), which has been experienced over and over again, and which to those who have experienced it in ever so slight a degree has appeared worthy of lifelong pursuit and devotion. . . . The question really is not to define the fact—for we cannot do that—but to get at and experience it (36).

There are certain root experiences a man never forgets. . . . The first time he breaks the chrysalis of being to emerge as a conscious spiritual unit . . . is the greatest of all. . . . The Overself makes no demand of man other than he open his inner eyes and perceive its existence. . . . Once we push the gate of the mind slightly ajar and let the light stream in, the meaning of life becomes silently revealed to us. . . . Man as a spiritual being possesses a capacity for wisdom which is infinite, a resource of happiness which is startling. He contains a divine infinitude within himself, yet he is content to go on and potter about a petty stretch of life as though he were a mere human insect (37).

Particularly in the earlier meetings of the group, participants are asked to consider such personally relevant questions as:

What is the most significant and moving experience you have ever had? (What does your answer tell you about what you value?)

What is the worst (most unpleasant, humiliating, painful, horrible, etc.) experience? What, in essence, made it so bad?

What meaning does life hold for you?

What "makes" you anxious, fearful, irritated, frustrated, angry? How?

What seems to you to be the fundamental existential (contrasted with situational) problem in your life?

To whatever extent he is willing, the participant is encouraged to share the results of these ponderings. In these and various other ways he is made aware that he is being asked to set aside well-entrenched preconceptions and to approach afresh the question: "What can I be?" to see how feelings enter into thinking and communication and to deepen the level of communication with other group members.

As the seminar progresses, individuals gain trust in the group and become more and more willing to share personally significant material. At the same time they become more aware of their own feelings and of the way in which they create them through their attitudes, but also of the value of these as signposts leading to further self-discovery. They may carry on experiments, in the group or outside, along lines of meditative introspection, active imagination, self-acceptance and affirmation, exercises in awareness (38) and so on.

At the end, each person is asked to formulate in writing his own individual progress report or tentative conclusions and to share orally with the rest of the group as much of this as he feels is appropriate. The following sample comments are representative.

The idea of tearing down the defenses and narrowmindedness carefully built up over most of my life has not been an easy one to accept. . . . I have altered what I originally believed to be the structure of my life: a well-ordered collection of selected experiences set and evaluated against an unchangeable list of criteria, wherein man's only defense against the environmental control which held him by the scruff of the neck was organization and the avoidance of unfamiliar experience. . . . At this point I feel as Wendy in Peter Pan must have felt when she screamed delightedly, "I can fly!"

The mere fact that I feel a change in myself to be necessary shows the importance with which I view this working for self-knowledge. I know the emptiness, the incompleteness I have

> felt for life in the past. Searching inside myself, knowing myself better, no matter how painful such knowledge may be, seems to hold an answer. . . . For me it's an amazing beginning.
>
> It is as if I have come upon a new religion, capable of originating within myself.
>
> How can I convince anyone that after twenty years of search a few short classroom discussions and a little reading could produce any significant improvement or alteration or gain in insight—I must record that I think I have glimpsed something that causes me to meditate in awe. . . . I do not presume that what I have seen is either all, or even a significant part of reality. I do say that it is a little more than I have ever seen before, and this fills me with both comfort and wonder.

I confess to feeling a pleasurable sense of gratification when I read such reports. They indicate that, clumsy as our efforts may be, it is yet possible to provide such a situation that there may take place a bit of what might well be called the true "higher education"—in the sense that the highest to which man can attain is knowledge of himself.

REFERENCES

1. Rogers, C. R.: *On Becoming a Person.* Cambridge, Massachusetts, Riverside Press, 1961, p. 276.
2. Maslow, A. H.: *Toward a Psychology of Being.* Princeton, New Jersey, Van Nostrand, 1962, p. 58.
3. Rokeach, M.: *The Open and Closed Mind.* New York, Basic Books, 1960.
4. Proverbs 23:7.
5. See Part IV, Chapter 3 of this volume and references therein.
6. A somewhat similar listing of unwholesome beliefs is given in Chapter 3 of Ellis, A.: *Reason and Emotion in Psychotherapy.* New York, Lyle Stuart, 1962.
7. See Fingarette, H.: *The Self in Transformation,* Chapter 1, for an analysis of psychoanalytically oriented therapy as a process of "meaning reorganization" (New York, Basic Books, 1963). Particular emphasis on the healing capabilities of reinterpretation of experience is given by Frankl, V. E.: *In Man's Search for Meaning.* New York, Washington Square, 1963.
8. Maltz, M.: *Psycho-Cybernetics.* Englewood Cliffs, New Jersey, Prentice-Hall, 1960.

9. See Part V, Chapter 5 of this volume.
10. ASSAGIOLI, R.: *Psychosynthesis: A Manual of Principles and Techniques.* New York, Hobbs, Dorman, 1965.
11. MARTIN, P. W.: *Experiment in Depth.* New York, Pantheon, 1955, p. 115.
12. PROGOFF, I.: *The Symbolic and the Real.* New York, Julian Press, 1963, p. 167.
13. UNGER, S.: Mescaline, LSD, psilocybin, and personality change: A review. *Psychiatry, 26*:111-125, 1963. See also HARMAN, W. W.: Some aspects of the psychedelic drug controversy. *J. Human Psychol.*, 93-107 (Fall), 1963.
14. JAMES, W.: *Varieties of Religious Experience.* New York, Modern Library, 1929.
15. VAN DUSEN, W.: LSD and the enlightenment of Zen. *Psychologia, 4*:11-16, 1961.
16. SHERWOOD, J. N., STOLAROFF, M. J., and HARMAN, W. W.: The psychedelic experience: A new concept in psychotherapy. *J. Neuropsychiat.*, *4*:69-80, 1962.
17. ST. EXUPERY, A.: *Wind, Sand and Stars.* New York, Harcourt Brace, 1940.
18. One of the most scholarly is MICHAEL POLANYI's *Personal Knowledge* (Univ. of Chicago Press, 1958) with, as a sequel, *The Broken Image* by FLOYD MATSON (Brasillier, 1964). Others from varying points of view include the later books of the biologist E. W. SINNOTT (particularly *Matter, Mind and Man*), P. A. SOROKIN's *The Ways and Power of Love* in sociology, CARL ROGERS and ABRAHAM MASLOW, in psychology. Still more critical writers are JACQUES BARZUN in *Science: The Glorious Entertainment,* JOSEPH WOOD KRUTCH in *The Measure of Man* and JOHN LANGDON-DAVIES in the paperback *On the Nature of Man.*
19. Especially recommended is RAYNOR JOHNSON's *The Imprisoned Splendour* (Harper, 1963). Also ROSALINE HEYWOOD, *Beyond the Reach of Sense* and J. B. RHINE, *New World of the Mind.*
20. RUTH CRANSTON, *The Miracle of Lourdes* (McGraw-Hill, 1955) is reliable and easy-reading. The story of Edgar Cayce, *There Is a River* by THOMAS SUGRUE, is interesting in connection with a related phenomenon.
21. Two particularly good references are *Parapsychology,* by RENE SUDRE (Evergreen Paperback) and *Mind Over Space,* by YANDOR FODOR.
22. Try *Living Time,* by MAURICE NICOLL (London, Vincent Stuart, 1952).
23. One of the best, in paperback form, is *The Teachings of the Mystics,* by W. T. STACE.
24. HARMAN, W. W.: The humanities in an age of science. *Main Currents in Modern Thought, 18*:75-83, 1962.

25. Progoff, I.: In the Introductory Commentary to *The Cloud of Unknowing*. New York, Julian Press, 1957.
26. Krutch, J. W.: *The Measure of Man*. New York, Universal Library, 1953.
27. Weaver, R. M.: *Ideas Have Consequences*. Chicago, Phoenix Books, 1958.
28. Neumann, E.: *Art and the Creative Unconscious*. New York, Pantheon, 1959.
29. Sullivan, J. W. W.: *Beethoven, His Spiritual Development*. New York, New American Library, 1949.
30. Robert Browning: "Paracelsus."
31. Guirdham, A.: *Christ and Freud*. New York, Collier, 1962. See also Aldous Huxley's *The Perennial Philosophy*.
32. Warren, R. P.: *Brother to Dragons*. New York, Random House, 1953.
33. von Goethe, J. W.: Spiritual Longing, Book I of *West-Eastern Divan*.
34. Kempis, Thomas A.: *The Imitation of Christ*.
35. Broad, C. D.: *Religion, Philosophy, and Psychical Research*. New York, Harcourt Brace, 1953.
36. Carpenter, Edward: *From Adam's Peak to Elephanta*.
37. Brunton, P.: *The Secret Path*. New York, Dutton, 1935.
38. Some good suggestions will be found in Perls, F., Hefferline, R., and Goodman, P.: *Gestalt Therapy*. New York, Julian Press, 1951.

Chapter 29

THE PSYCHEDELIC DRUGS AND HUMAN POTENTIALITIES

ROBERT E. MOGAR

THE CONTEMPORARY SCENE

OVER fifty years of intensive research has provided convincing evidence that almost all human abilities, aptitudes and special talents represent an unanalyzable mixture of inborn potential and educational experience. It is also axiomatic that human beings possess far greater latent potential than they are able to realize in the course of their lives. Understandably, a concerted effort to cultivate man's vast personal resources has rarely been attempted in the course of human history. Until recently the motive power of civilization, particularly Western cultures, has necessarily focused on survival and environmental mastery. In Maslow's terms, the organismic equilibrium made possible by satiated bodily needs, physical safety and some measure of psychological security is prerequisite to more uniquely human pursuits. This hierarchical conception of man's strivings depicts him as a self-directed creature with impulses toward growth and self-enhancement as well as homeostatic maintenance (23). If the image of man that emerges from this view meshes with the modern temper, the realization of human potentialities should reach unprecedented heights in the present era. For we have at our command a technology capable of making the lives of men healthy, safe and reasonably secure for the first time in history.

The image of man and optimistic predictions stemming from a humanistic frame of reference contrast sharply with the more scientistic—though not necessarily more scientific—positions of behaviorism and psychoanalysis. Each of these theories is a vision of the world and its value depends on how much it sees and how clearly (28). In this connection, recent developments in the philosophy and sociology of science point up clearly the transactional interplay between theory and actuality. Rather than laws of nature, scientific theories are more accurately viewed as working fictions or convenient myths and reflect the belief system of a given time and place (27, 30). From this perspective, the equipotent theories currently prevalent in American psychology—reflecting and in turn effecting social values and individual conduct—are representative of the preoccupations and uncertainties of our time. The fact that three divergent orientations occupy the same stage simultaneously attests to our ambivalence concerning man's foreseeable possibilities.

Behaviorism and psychoanalysis have frequently been criticized for reducing man to a fragmented creature, passively pushed and pulled by forces outside his conscious control. Although the intent and objectives of these theories are misinterpreted by such criticism, it must be conceded that neither behaviorism nor psychoanalysis recognize emergent human potentialities. The capacity to transcend a rather narrowly conceived bio-social heritage is especially precluded in both disciplines. To the degree that a viable theory tends to become a self-fulfilling prophecy, this omission is indeed a serious one.

Recently there has been some indication that these theories of man no longer have what Bruner describes as "an immediate resonance with the dialectic of experience" (5). Yet their continuing impact on our self- and world-view is clearly substantial. Many writers, impressed with the progressive subordination of personal identity to the "technological superidentity" (11), do not foresee any greater actualizing of human potentialities in the immediate future. Particular attention has been called to our ultrarational commitment to structured, controlled forms of experience, that is, the restricted range of experience sanctioned by public consensus. Narrowing the scope of human awareness to manageable proportions has no doubt permitted man's remarkable technical progress and made his existence far less precarious. But the toll exacted in sensibilities and imaginative thought has been excessive and may be irreversible. The danger of making life perhaps too predictable has been well summarized by Seidenberg, who warns that contemporary man may lose his freedom along with his anxiety, his personal consciousness along with his insecurity (39).

In order to counteract those aspects of modern culture which tend to destroy consciousness rather than heighten it, N. O. Brown would cultivate a "Dionysian Ego" (4). Similarly, the antidote suggested by Marcuse included "libidinal rationality" (22). While prescriptions differ, there seems to be essential agreement on the nature of our current dilemma. W. Barrett has said that the most formidable problem of man in the twentieth century is the conciliation of opposites (1). More recently, this theme was underscored by Maslow who called attention to the artificial polarity "between Apollonian and Dionysian, classical and romantic, scientific and poetic, between reason and impulse, work and play, verbal and preverbal, maturity and childlikeness, masculine and feminine, growth and regression" (23, p. 151). Needless to say, the problem of fusing these apparent contradictions confronts the individual as well as the larger society. In either case, a well-ordered existence untempered by poetic vision becomes stagnant and meaningless. Similarly, diversity and complexity seem to work against man unless shaped and enriched by an organic unity.

Western man has traditionally failed to grasp the difference between tension as a negative force and tension as a basic condition of all growth processes. This is tantamount to confusing death with life itself. The result has been a profound sense of alienation rather than optimal development. Better ways need to be found of resolving this human paradox, whether the issue concerns cultural or personal evolution, collective- or self-identity, common or unique potentialities.

Viewed against this background of more pervasive trends in our culture, the growing interest in the potential value of psychedelic experiences (i.e., experiences of expanded consciousness or awareness) becomes more understandable. Within this broader context, it is not surprising that the major application of LSD-25, mescaline, psilocybin and similar agents has shifted recently from *producing* mental illness to *treating* it. Beyond this shift in emphasis, the psychedelics have been found to facilitate "growth-fostering" self-discovery as well as therapeutic insight or symptom-relief. Both as a clinical and as an educative device, the psychedelic drugs seem to hold considerable promise as one means of ameliorating modern discontent and cultivating unrealized potentialities.

THERAPEUTIC VALUE OF THE PSYCHEDELICS

Since over three hundred studies on the use of LSD-25 as a therapeutic agent have been reported, only the most salient and consistent findings will be summarized. Despite great diversity in the conduct of these studies, impressive improvement rates have been almost uniformly reported with both adults and children (3) and in group as well as individual psychotherapy (41).* Used in conjunction with traditional psychotherapy (29), or as a primary vehicle for inducing rapid personality change (40), LSD has been found to facilitate improvement in patients representing the complete spectrum of neurotic, psychosomatic and character disorders. Particularly noteworthy are the positive results obtained with cases highly resistant to conventional forms of therapy. High remission rates among alcoholics, for example, have frequently been reported following a single, large dose LSD session. Based on their findings with over one thousand alcoholics, Hoffer and his coworkers concluded that LSD was twice as effective as any other treatment program (21). Other researchers working with alcoholics also have found LSD highly effective, although no controlled double-blind study testing the effectiveness of LSD in the treatment of alcoholism has as yet (January, 1965) been reported. Other chronic conditions carrying a poor prognosis which have been reported to respond favorably to psychedelic therapy include sexual deviations (19), criminal psychopathy (8, 18), autism in children (3) and adolescent behavior disorders (8).

When employed as an adjunct to psychotherapy, most investigators have associated the beneficial effects of LSD with reduced defensiveness, the reliving of early childhood experiences, in-

* Representative and recent studies are cited. Unger (42) and Schmiege (36) have reported more extensive bibliographies on the therapeutic use of LSD.

creased awareness of unconscious material and greater emotional expression (44). In contrast, when used as a primary vehicle for rapid personality change, emphasis is usually placed on the transcendental quality of the experience, the resynthesis of basic values and beliefs and major changes in the relationship between self and environment (13, 25).

Since most reports on the therapeutic effectiveness of LSD consist of clinical evaluations lacking in objectivity, it is worth noting that comparable results have been obtained by investigators in many other countries (26). The likelihood of a significant positive bias is further lessened by the widely divergent theoretical persuasions represented. These include Freudian (8), Jungian (9), behavioristic (7), existentialist (16) and a variety of eclectic orientations (19, 37). It seems safe to conclude from the breadth and consistency of the clinical evidence that LSD can produce far-reaching beneficial effects in some people, under some conditions. However, controlled studies of the process variables involved have yet to be conducted. Specifically, in what ways do various kinds of people respond to LSD, both during the experience and afterward? What are the optimal conditions of administration for given objectives? How can we account for the various kinds and extent of change which follow an LSD experience?

Beyond these initial questions lies a host of unknowns directly relevant to the problem of investigating and developing human potentialities. For example, is the psychedelic experience akin to the creative process? Is it related to similar altered states of consciousness, such as hypnosis, transcendental experiences, identity crises, dream states or religious conversions? Can LSD facilitate the cultivation of special talents and abilities? Although careful study of such questions has barely begun, the data currently available are at least suggestive of the ways in which these powerful agents might be employed to explore and enhance human resources.

THE PSYCHEDELIC EXPERIENCE AND SELF-DISCOVERY

An almost invariant effect of the psychedelics, cutting across the wide range of individual reactions, is an extraordinary alteration in perception. This usually takes the form of intensified sensory experience in all modalities and a blurring of self-nonself boundaries. Whether expanded awareness or increased insight accompany these unhabitual perceptions and altered frames of reference is not a function of the chemical agent. In contrast to the earlier search for "drug-specific" effects of LSD, it is now generally recognized that the nature, intensity and content of the experience are the resultant of complex transactions between the subject's past history and personality, the set and expectancies of both subject and administrator and the physical and psychological environment in which the experience takes place (34). Importantly, most of these determinants can be intentionally arranged and manipulated so as to foster either a propitious or a stressful experience. Based on data obtained from over three hundred cases, Harman noted that when the context of the experience is optimized, the subject "is able to re-examine his relationships with others, his attitudes and values, his beliefs about his own nature and that of the world he lives in—all with unusual nonattachment and freedom from threat" (13, p. 95). Similarly, in a careful study of 690 administrations of LSD, Chandler and Hartman concluded that:

> . . . the drug does not appear to produce any serious or marked impairment in the major ego functions. . . . The patient remains oriented for person, place, and time. He does not appear to lose contact with everyday reality but, rather, seems to gain contact with other levels of his own psyche . . . he can withdraw his awareness from the physical reality of the moment and allow his attention to become completely absorbed by the phenomena at the deeper psychic levels, but he retains the ability to focus his awareness back on to external objective reality whenever he chooses . . . (6, p. 290).

The striking similarity between this state and certain phases of the creative process has been described by Barron (2) and demonstrated in a study of thirty artists given LSD (17). In psychoanalytic terms the psychedelic experience resembles a "regression in the service of the ego" or a merging of impulse and realistic thinking. In the light of the cultural trends noted earlier, it is noteworthy that this capacity to blend primary and secondary processes has been recognized recently as a condition of superior functioning or positive mental health (14, 35). Importantly, there is some indication that individuals tend to display more of this ability following an LSD session as well as during the psychedelic experience itself. If conditions are favorable, the experience and its aftermath has much in common with a self-actualizing "peak experience" (23). The process of transformation operative in such cases seems highly similar to Erikson's penetrating analysis of the "identity crisis" as a catalyst for rapid personal growth (10).

The nature, extent and stability of changes following a large dose LSD session has been a major focus of study in the psychedelic research program conducted at the International Foundation for Advanced Study, Menlo Park, California. Over a three-year period, extensive assessments were obtained on almost four hundred subjects before, during and at various points following a single psychedelic experience. Following the procedure described in detail by Sherwood and his coworkers (40), a series of preparatory interviews designed to accustom the subject to altered states of consciousness preceded the LSD experience. Although trained staff members were present during the session itself, primarily for emotional support and human contact, the subject was urged to explore himself and his universe without external guidance or intrusion. The physical setting was made as comfortable and aesthetically pleasing as possible.

The battery of assessment procedures selected for this project was based on the assumption that significant changes following the psychedelic experience would occur along three main dimensions: values and beliefs; personality; and actual behavior in major life areas. Specifically, the research design permitted a comprehensive test of the hypothesis that a profound LSD experience tends to be followed by a major resynthesis of one's personal values and life outlook, which in turn is followed by slower alterations in personality structure and characteristic behavior patterns. The findings reported thus far provide considerable support for the general hypothesis concerning parallel changes in values, personality and conduct (26, 32, 33). Briefly, the results indicate that almost all subjects derive some benefit along the lines indicated, although the nature, extent and stability of changes vary considerably. Specific sources or correlates of this variability included diagnosis, pre-LSD personality structure, the type of presenting problem and variations in the psychedelic experience itself. Further analysis of these variables and their relationship to subsequent changes revealed that subjects tended to cluster into two groups: the emotionally-disturbed; and the relatively well adjusted. Of particular relevance here are the findings with this latter group.

Approximately one third of the total sample did not present complaints of a psychiatric nature and revealed minimal neurotic symptomology according to both diagnostic evaluation and psychological test data. Consistent with the independent assessment, the interest expressed by these subjects in the psychedelic experience seemed to be "growth-motivated" rather than "deficiency-motivated" (23). Some were dimly aware of potentialities or personal aptitudes which they hoped to activate and develop more fully. Others expressed a feeling of emptiness and lack of meaningful purpose while adequately meeting the exigencies of life. Still others sought a deeper understanding or more satisfying resolutions to problems of an existential nature.

Being relatively free of psychological disturbance, these subjects were more likely to grapple with ultimate problems during the LSD experience. In addition to self-identity and personal worth, questions of love, death, creation and the conciliation of opposites received frequent attention. Unlike other subject groups, childhood memories, intrapsychic conflicts and specific interpersonal relations were explored minimally during the session. While seemingly more receptive to universal or "cosmic" concerns as a result of their psychological health and stable life circumstances, it should be emphasized that their particular set toward the experience and the response of the clinical staff to individuals of this character also played a role. In any event, both the content and affective tone of the session contrasted sharply with that of the modal neurotic subject. For example, significantly higher ratings were obtained by this group on both intensity and duration of positive affect. This finding was consistent with personal accounts of the experience written shortly afterward. Healthy subjects were less likely to view the psychedelic state as fantastic or totally discontinuous with past experience.

Follow-up interviews, clinical ratings and subjective reports indicated that these subjects benefited considerably from the psychedelic experience along the lines of self-actualization, richer creative experience and enhancement of specific abilities and aptitudes. Unfortunately, the original battery of objective assessment procedures were relatively insensitive to these changes since they were designed for a clinical population. Recently, the assessment battery was revised to include measures more appropriate for a normal sample. Thus it will be possible to compare individuals, differing in personality and presenting problems, with regard to health-growth dimensions as well as decreases in pathology.

The interest in altered states of consciousness and the response of adequately functioning persons to psychedelic drugs seem consistent with the cultural climate described earlier. More specifically, the nature of human discontent in a modern technological (and affluent) society has been undergoing rapid and profound change. Artists and scholars representing a wide range of disciplines and fields of interest have flooded the various media of communication with discussions of the quest for identity and meaning, the decline of traditional values and religion, modern man's deep sense of alienation and the advent of science as a way of life (24). The current interest in humanistic psychology, oriental philosophy, existential psychiatry and self-realization represent reactions to these trends and offer solace to the "encapsulated man" (31) living in an age of spiritual poverty. Similarly, the traditional neuroses and character disorders are in decline, being replaced by what one writer termed the "philosophical neurosis" (38). It may well be as some critics suggest that conventional therapy with its emphasis on early childhood conflicts and social adjustment is already obsolete (12, 20). Many individuals who understand all too well the antecedents of their behavior still feel unfulfilled and find their lives lacking in significance and purpose. These pervasive features of modern society suggest that the age-old question: Who am I? is once more in vogue.

Since psychedelic substances have been known and ingested throughout man's history (43), the current fascination with the states of consciousness they produce seems less than a coincidence. Holt recently observed that, after fifty years of ostracism, altered states of consciousness and novel perceptual experiences have once more become a legitimate area of study within the mainstream of American psychology (15). Some altered states of consciousness are also produced by certain so-called psychoactive drugs, although the promise of these drugs in relation to the human potential has not as yet been fully ascertained and awaits more detailed investigation. As might be expected, the *zeitgeist* in the social sciences shares a common direction with major trends in the larger culture. Despite this apparent convergence, the present is clearly a period of transition characterized by strong ambivalence toward psychedelic phenomena. As Holt noted, we live "in a factually oriented, skeptical, anti-intraceptive, brass-tacks culture. . . . We live in an age of literalism, an era that distrusts the imagination." Yet the paradox or dilemma of western man has never before been in sharper focus; ". . . must we choose between abstract thought and richness of fancy, between reality testing and the capacity to regress in the service of the ego? I have enough faith in man's flexibility to believe that if we plan for it properly, we can preserve the simultaneous capacities for scientific and mythopoetic thought" (15, p. 262).

REFERENCES

1. Barrett, W.: *Irrational Man.* New York, Doubleday, 1958.
2. Barron, F.: *Creativity and Psychological Health.* Princeton, Van Nostrand, 1963.
3. Bender, L., Faretra, G., and Cobrink, L.: LSD and UML treatment of hospitalized disturbed children. *Recent Advances Biol. Psychiat.,* 5:84, 1963.
4. Brown, N. O.: *Life Against Death.* New York, Random House, 1959.
5. Bruner, J. S.: *On Knowing.* Cambridge, Harvard Press, 1962.
6. Chandler, A. L., and Hartman, M. A.: LSD as a facilitating agent in psychotherapy. *Arch. Gen. Psychiat.,* 2:286, 1960.
7. Costello, C. G.: LSD as an adjunct to behavior therapy. Unpublished paper, Ottawa, Canada, 1963.
8. Crockett, R. A., Sandison, R., and Walk, A.: *Hallucinogenic Drugs and Their Psychotherapeutic Use.* Springfield, Thomas, 1963.
9. Cutner, M.: Analytic work with LSD-25. *Psychiat. Quart.,* 33:715, 1959.
10. Erikson, E.: Identity and the life cycle. *Psychol. Issues, 1*:1, 1959.

11. Erikson, E.: Youth: Fidelity and diversity. *Daedalus, 91*:5, 1962.
12. Frankl, V.: Logotherapy and the challenge of suffering. *Exist. Psychol. Psychiat., 1*:3, 1961.
13. Harman, W. W.: Some aspects of the psychedelic-drug controversy. *J. Hum. Psychol., 3*:93, 1963.
14. Hilgard, E. R.: Impulsive vs. realistic thinking. *Psych. Bull.,* 59:477, 1962.
15. Holt, R. R.: Imagery: The return of the ostracized. *Amer. Psychol., 19*:254, 1964.
16. Holzinger, R.: Analytic and integrative therapy with the help of LSD-25. *J. Exist. Psychiat., 4*:225, 1964.
17. Janiger, O.: The use of hallucinogenic agents in psychiatry. *Calif. Clin.,* 55:251, 1959.
18. Leary, T.: How to change behavior. In Nielsen, G. H. (ed.): *Clinical Psychology*. Copenhagen, 1962.
19. Ling, T. M., and Buckman, J.: *Lysergic Acid (LSD-25) and Ritalin in the treatment of neurosis*. London, Lambarde Press, 1963.
20. London, P.: *The Modes and Morals of Psychotherapy*. New York, Holt, Rinehart, and Winston, 1964.
21. MacLean, J. R., MacDonald, D. C., Bryne, U. P., and Hubbard, A. M.: The use of LSD-25 in the treatment of alcoholism and other psychiatric problems. *Quart. J. Stud. Alcohol,* 22:34, 1961.
22. Marcuse, H.: *Eros and Civilization*. Boston, Beacon, 1955.
23. Maslow, A. H.: *Toward a Psychology of Being*. Princeton, Van Nostrand, 1962.
24. Mogar, R. E.: Value orientations of college students. *Psychol. Rep., 15*:739, 1964.
25. Mogar, R. E.: Current status and future trends in psychedelic research. *J. Hum. Psychol.,* 1965, in press.
26. Mogar, R. E., and Savage, C.: Personality change associated with psychedelic (LSD) therapy. *Psychotherapy, 1*:154, 1964.
27. Murray, H. A.: Myth and mythmaking. *Daedalus, 88*:211, 1959.
28. Restle, F.: Review of "Uncertainty and structure as psychological concepts." *Amer. Scient.,* 52:306A, 1964.
29. Robinson, J., Davies, L., and Sack, E.: A controlled trial of abreactions with LSD-25. *Brit. J. Psychiat., 109*:46, 1963.
30. Rosenthal, R.: On the social psychology of the psychological experiment. *Amer. Scient., 51*:269, 1963.
31. Royce, J. R.: *The Encapsulated Man*. Princeton, Van Nostrand, 1964.
32. Savage, C., Hughes, M. A., and Mogar, R. E.: The effectiveness of psychedelic (LSD) therapy. *Int. J. Soc. Psychiat.,* 1964, in press.
33. Savage, C., Savage, E., Harman, W. W. and Fadiman, J.: Therapeutic effects of the psychedelic experience. *Psychol. Rep., 14*:111, 1964.

34. Savage, C., Terrill, J., and Jackson, D. D.: LSD, transcendence, and the new beginning. *J. Nerv. Ment. Dis., 135*:425, 1962.
35. Schachtel, E.: *Metamorphosis*. New York, Basic Books, 1959.
36. Schmiege, G. R.: The current status of LSD as a therapeutic tool. *New Jersey Med. Soc. J., 60*:203, 1963.
37. Schoen, S.: LSD in psychotherapy. *Amer. J. Psychother., 12*:35, 1964.
38. Schofield, W.: *Psychotherapy: The Purchase of Friendship*. New York, Prentice-Hall, 1964.
39. Seidenberg, R.: *Posthistoric Man*. Chapel Hill, Univ. of North Carolina, 1960.
40. Sherwood, J. N., Stolaroff, M. J., and Harman, W. W.: The psychedelic experience—a new concept in psychotherapy. *J. Neuropsychiat., 4*:69, 1962.
41. Spencer, A. M.: Permissive group therapy with LSD. *Brit. J. Psychiat., 109*:37, 1963.
42. Unger, S. M.: Mescaline, LSD, psilocybin, and personality change. *Psychiatry, 26*:111, 1963.
43. Wasson, R. G.: The hallucinogenic fungi of Mexico. *Psychedelic Rev., 1*:27, 1963.
44. Whitaker, L. H.: LSD in psychotherapy. *Med. J. Australia, 21*:4, 1964.

Chapter 30

A PSYCHOEDUCATIONAL TREATMENT PROGRAM: IMPLICATIONS FOR THE DEVELOPMENT OF POTENTIALITIES IN CHILDREN

GASTON E. BLOM, MARK RUDNICK and EDWARD WEIMAN

A PSYCHOEDUCATIONAL treatment program for emotionally handicapped elementary school age children at the University of Colorado Medical Center makes it possible to view the problem of developing human potentialities. Although this is a special setting and deals with handicapped children, some of the definitions, assessments and treatment approaches have applicability to a wider range of children and to other treatment and educational settings dealing with children.

The Day Care Center in the Department of Psychiatry of the University of Colorado Medical Center was initiated in September, 1962, and is considered a laboratory school in special education and treatment modes with demonstration, training and research aims. Its staff is multi-discipline, consisting of teachers, psychologists, psychiatrists, social workers and pediatricians, with trainees in all these diciplines. The Center is employed as a field placement for the School of Education and other interested academic and clinical departments of the University. Attending are approximately sixteen children of elementary school age who have serious emotional problems which interfere with social and academic adjustment.

The purpose of our program is to emphasize a wide range of human potentialities. From our experiences as teacher, psychologist and psychoanalyst, this point of view is often neglected in the institutions of our society. Such neglect contributes to disturbances in the psychic, social and body spheres of the personality as well as to skewed and limited personality functioning. These results can be considered indicators of failure in potential realization. The dimensions of human potentialities, particularly in children, are often considered within a restricted range of behavior, namely, academic or intellectual activities. While academic learning is significant in a child's life, there is more to school life than the development of academic competence and intellectual potential. The school can also be considered a social laboratory for experimentation, experience and teaching in human relationships with peers, older and younger children, the same and opposite sex, adults other than family members and authority figures. Particularly at the present time teachers can capitalize on these opportunities and enhance the socialization process by communicating the moralistic and realistic expectations of our society. Other nonacademic experiences and skills should receive emphasis in the child's life. The enrichment activities after school need not be limited to those which are called "cultural." Children develop the skill of getting along with others outside of the classroom structure and in exploring their world with peers and by themselves.

Our focus is on the elementary school age child, and a psychoanalytic development frame of reference to potentialities is used (1, 2, 3, 4, 5). In psychoanalytic language the elementary school years are referred to as the latency stage of psychosexual development. During this time the sexual interests of the child are supposedly dormant (6). In part, it was the energies from the sexual drive which Freud used to explain the tremendous effort put forth by the child during this age to learn and master what society expected of him. As others have commented (7, 8), and has been observed of many normal children, sexual interests are not necessarily dormant. At the same time that the child's parents disapprove of his sexual interests, his world is greatly expanded in the process of going to school. Being a part of a group which concerns itself with learning becomes of primary importance.

In Harris' study of normal children and their families (7), the observation was made that children in whom there was no physical aggressiveness and curiosity about sex in thought and behavior had a difficult time adjusting to the full impact of increased sexual prowess and physical strength during the teen years. Those children who were more "lively" appeared to be better able to find more adaptive channels for both drives as teenagers. The latency years appear to provide children with the time to work in miniature and experiment with channels of discharge so that they will not be so overwhelmed by these urges in adolescence as to be unable to find proper avenues of expression.

Erikson (3) refers to this age period as a stage of the life cycle called industry *versus* inferiority. At this time a child develops a sense of usefulness and a drive of initiative. He wants to make and do things out of a desire to learn and to work. Recognition by others and self-esteem are obtained through successful achievement. Reality and practicality have a greater attraction over play and fantasy. Play now has rules and requires the exercise of body and mental skills. The child begins to deal with the complicated social reality of the real world. Education may be seen as offering the child substitute gratification, socialization, habits and patterns of behavior, control over impulses and increasing reality testing and awareness (1, 2).

While recognizing the importance of assessing the development of the child in depth, breadth and balance as emphasized by Anna Freud (4, 9) and others, the focus of this presentation will be on manifest behavior and reality adaptation. The many manifest behaviors in the latency age child's life can be grouped under developmental areas such as learning, socialization, world view and body-motor skill. We shall consider a series of manifest behaviors as dimensions of potentialities. This is a pragmatic approach to defining potentialities, and it is arbitrary since other manifest behaviors could be listed as well. The series of manifest behaviors include: (a) proficiency in learning within the child's range of endowment; (b) the use of body and motor skills; (c) the development of idiosyncratic individual skills and hobbies; (d) participation in group situations; (e) the acquirement of accepted social skills in dealing with others; (f) the development of friendship with peers; (g) the age-appropriate opportunities of play; (h) participation in age-appropriate interests for himself and others; (i) a comfortable position of the child in relation to adults; and (j) an age-appropriate proficiency in dealing with the world.

Potential realization will be influenced by a number of factors that both facilitate and impede its achievement. The factors may reinforce each other negatively or positively. Their adequate assessment is crucial for the synthesis that determines the resultant potentiality. In Erikson's terms (3), potential realization can be seen as a function of and synthesis of (a) endowment, (b) realistic opportunities and (c) basic drives. Endowment may be viewed as including innate factors and acquired stable personality characteristics. Realistic opportunities include family circumstances, socioeconomic and environmental possibilities and past experiences. Basic drives from our viewpoint would consist of the control of drives as well as their strength. There are instinctual drives and those which originate from the ego, independent of instinct. The latter are referred to in ego psychoanalytic terms as autonomous (10, 11).

While Erikson (3) considers that successful accomplishment of earlier stages of the life cycle are crucial for later stage development, Bruner (12) also sees early problems of mastery and stresses to be overcome as preconditions of attaining human potentiality. Bland impoverishment of early experience, however, may be too great an obstacle to overcome in later life. Clinical experiences with children would support both concepts.

It is imperative for those who work with children that the evaluation of endowment, opportunities and basic drives be adequate and realistic within the limitations of assessment methods that are currently available. Furthermore, a developmental and broad frame of reference to human potentialities is also crucial. Such viewpoints make it possible to anticipate and provide favorable circumstances for the development of human potentialities. Helping agents and the child himself, however, are limited in their endowments and in their abilities to predict fate and to deal with it effectively. Freud, in his paper "Analysis Terminable and Interminable" (6), emphasized the realistic limitations to individuals in terms of conflict resolution and of predicting fate and coping with it.

FACTORS IN POTENTIAL REALIZATION

What are considered potentialities is an arbitrary decision. Huxley (13) says that they are based on feeling and faith and not on reason. They are also influenced by historical and cultural situations which may prevent or actualize desirable and undesirable potentialities. Nevertheless, he defines potentialities within a stable and elastic society as improving intelligence, deepening and extending feelings of love and friendliness and diminishing violence and aggression.

There are other frames of reference to human potentialities. Otto (14) uses the concepts of individual and family strengths and, while not establishing criteria for strengths, emphasizes imagination, spontaneity, self-confidence and emotional freedom. Group methods are employed to facilitate and foster them. Murphy emphasizes that "affection and trust, belief in unrealized potentialities of other human beings, call into existence not only what is waiting to bud but what never could otherwise be" (15, p. 313).

As previously mentioned, potential realization is viewed as a function and synthesis of (a) endowment, (b) realistic opportunities and (c) basic drives. Each of these might be expanded to include various subfactors, any of which can be most influential in forwarding or impeding the realizing of potential in a child.

In working with the constitutionally limited child, one attempts to help him cope and adapt better to the restrictions that were placed upon him by the limitations. Working with this child one accents compensation; this can take the form of substituting one activity or approach for another. The child who cannot draw an angle might be taught to draw one line, lift his pencil and draw another line down to the first line. He is never drawing angles, he is drawing straight lines. Yet the final product is a drawing *with* angles.

SKILLS WHICH FULFILL THE LATENCY AGE POTENTIAL

For the latency age child the realization of motor, intellectual and social potentials within the scope of the child's endowment and acquired abilities is, in our society, a necessity. Only to the extent that the child has realized his latency age potential in these areas will he be able to further develop and realize his adolescent and adult potentials. The emotionally disturbed child is often crippled in his development in at least two if not all three areas to some extent.

The development of potential in motor activity is of importance to the six- to ten-year-old child. The degree of competence in this area is not only the vehicle by which many friendships are formed and rules of fairness are learned but it is taken as a concrete reflection by the child of his adequacy in many other areas of functioning.

In our society and particularly at the present time in our history, intellectual achievement and academic excellence are of central importance. Immense pressures are brought upon the child to achieve, if not by the parents, then by peers, school personnel and other authorities. This area of development at this age is particularly vulnerable to the disrupting effects of emotional disturbance. Emotional problems can manifest themselves in the learning process in as many ways as there are children. For healthy children learning symbolizes the gradual attainment of the tools to cope and master an ever-growing complex environment. For other children learning may symbolize their aggressive feelings and must be avoided. For still other children, learning is avoided since it symbolizes growing up and the loss of love and protection of their mothers. A preoccupation of some kind for a child, for example, the constant fear of a loss of an important person in his life, will not allow him to turn his attention to what is to be learned or to have the energy to learn the material.

A continual state of anxiety also seriously disrupts the child's ability to attend and to concentrate on materials long enough so they can be learned. The child's problems can color the way he perceives learning material and how he conceptualizes and forms responses to it to such an extent that the final product by the child bears no relationship to the original material.

Betty is a child of average intellectual ability who failed the first grade three times before entering treatment. She was a very shy and withdrawn child who had no relationship with age mates or adults outside of her immediate environment. Her learning difficulties in school appeared to be directly related to a problem around emotion and its expression. Words in and of themselves had symbolic emotional meaning as well as literal meaning for Betty. A refusal to read a page in a book, not an infrequent occurrence in school, was related to her fear of what the words on the page might mean. Much of what she had learned in school in the past was relatively unavailable to help her learn new material because of massive repression. Adding to the problem of learning was her inability to muster the aggressiveness necessary for learning, because any form of aggressiveness for Betty was taboo.

Betty spent two years in the psychoeducational treatment program at the Day Care Center. Probably because all phases of her problems, that is, emotional, academic and social, could be treated in an integrated fashion, she gradually began to fulfill expected potentials in many areas at once. By the time she left the Center, she was comfortable enough with her peers to be considered an important member of her group and to be sought after by the preteenage boys. She was achieving at the fifth grade level in most academic areas. Most important was the change in her attitudes about herself and others. She initially experienced herself as an inadequate, lost little waif and then later perceived herself as being realistically capable in some areas, needing to improve in others. When she first came to the Center she was extremely narcissistic. Her orientation toward people was only in terms of what they might do for or to her. Two years later, she was able to think about how she affected others, as well as how others affected her.

PSYCHOEDUCATIONAL APPROACH

Some psychoeducational principles and practices of the program have been reviewed in detail elsewhere (16, 17). The concept "psychoeducational" indicates an integration of clinical and educational viewpoints in the operation of the Day Care Center. Maladaptive behavior is understood but not condoned, while appropriate and adaptive behaviors are taught and reinforced. The program consists of schooling, therapy of children and their parents, and activities, comprising a full day. Sufficient time is taken to program for individual children through as many aspects of the total program as possible. Individual programming requires careful assessment of behaviors using the extensive observational data that are available from the child and his family obtained from the classroom, lunch period, activities, individual therapy sessions and casework interviews with parents.

In order for psychoeducational treatment to operate successfully, a system of behavioral control needs to exist. This system has many facets and will be dealt with in greater detail elsewhere (11). Classroom management, individual programming, program structure, psychotherapy, the communication of expectations and the existence of rules and expectations are some of these many facets. One particular aspect will be mentioned herein, *standby*. Standby is the name given to a special experience in control and discipline. It is operated by a single individual who functions as the principal of the day. He is immediately available to a child or children whose behavior cannot be contained and handled in the situation where the child is located. The standby officer takes the child away from the situation to his office to reestablish control and to avoid disrupting the psychoeducational experience of others not involved in the difficulty. Based on his assessment of the behavior the standby officer deals with the child in a number of ways similar to but different from the life-space interview (18). Silence and cooling off may be the most beneficial approach. Discussion of the situational psychodynamics involved may be considered helpful. The goal of returning the child to the program as soon as feasible is kept in mind.

Therapy of the child and his parents is viewed as one aspect of the total milieu. Therapy and milieu are seen as mutually reinforcing one another, by the staff and the children as well. The child is able to refer comfortably to "his going to therapy" or to "his therapist" and to discuss this with his classmates and teachers. To have therapy and school in one place provides the stamp of acceptance and indicates that these two things work together.

While the staff assists the child in developing mastery and gratifications, they also help the child control and direct his impulses and affects. In addition, the child is influenced by the support, pressure, understanding, intolerance and teaching from his schoolmates. Staff direction and attention to the influence of other children on a given child are an important aspect of program operation. Capitalizing on other children as an educational resource has been emphasized by Lippett and Lohman (19). The influence of peers on a child follows the principles of positive and negative reinforcement. In a similar but more planned manner the staff acts as reinforcers. The more spontaneous responses of children may not always support the behavioral change one is seeking. In such instances interference by the staff is crucial.

Medication may be used to accomplish purposes not easily achievable through environmental manipulation and therapy alone and indeed may result in a child's becoming more responsive to psychological and social approaches. Reduction of anxiety with a tranquilizing drug, the use of a sedative to provide sleep and minimize nightmares and the employment of amphetamines to produce more organization in behavior are examples of specific individual application of medication.

There are some particular aspects of the program which have been more fully appreciated as we observed their influence on the children. One of them is the large number and variety of staff, trainees and volunteers who are in contact with the children, particularly in the activity part of the program. New people frequently come while others are leaving. The core staff, however, has offered stability and continuity in the structure. The variety of others has produced a kind of elasticity. Some of these people are much more strongly reality-oriented and less clinically sophisticated, differences that are perceived and appreciated by the children. In some instances they offer more neutral relationships that become welcome relief from more intense involvements. The children test themselves with such people in ways different from the regular clinical staff. They also have the chance to prove themselves to these different people; and if they fail or have a difficult experience, they can try again. They tend not to be shy with these persons and, in fact, are curious about them. The latency age child more typically has contact with many adults, and such adults offer enrichments of variety, difference, comparison and newness. Such experiences make it possible for the child to respond to the external world differently when he returns to regular school and his own environment.

Another aspect of the program which now receives considerable emphasis is desensitization. Desensitization is the gradual diminution of unpleasant feelings and associations connected with tasks, experiences and situations. These may involve people such as teachers, doctors, therapists, authority figures and other children. They may consist of the school as a whole, classroom, physical education, tests, lunch or eating, music and the outside world beyond the classroom. Sensitive areas represent fixations or arrests which do not allow for growth, mastery and change, particularly so when they are defended against.

Many methods are used in desensitization. Dosing and timing of experiences are carefully considered, since too much and too fast confrontation to the sensitive area can overwhelm certain children. Corrective reality experiences may modify previously unassimilated past painful events or repetitive neurotic interactions. Nonverbal behavior from the adult can often provide such a correction. On some occasions a lack of response to a piece of behavior may be effective in reducing its repetition.

Discussion of fears in therapy and elsewhere is also a desensitization method. Clarification and interpretation can make the mysterious known and understood. In play therapy, particularly, the fearful macrocosm of the world can be brought into the microcosm of toys and small objects which can be mastered and controlled.

Another guiding principle in the program is the French proverb: "Nothing succeeds like success.*" Success is used as a motivating factor toward greater potential realization and self fulfillment. Not only do the children need to experience success but

---

* *Rien ne reussit comme le succes* (anonymous) (20).

realize and accept it as well. This provides an improved self-concept with greater confidence and self-esteem. *It is to be seen as one of the most important therapeutic events that can happen to a child.*

In the structured environment of day care it is possible to program experiences for children so as to attain mastery and achievement. For most of the children academic tasks need to be designed that offer interest, challenge and the realistic possibility of succeeding. In some instances an adequate learning style or capacity such as a short attention span or a nonconformance behavior pattern can be exploited. That is, one can program for a short attention span and gradually increase the span as success is repeatedly experienced. With success a child may be able to look at his deficiencies, gain insight and have a desire to change old patterns and develop new, more adaptive ones.

An important variant of the success-failure issue is met in academic situations with most of the children. In order to acquire new information or a new skill a child must be willing to accept the position of not knowing, i.e., "I don't know." "I don't know" has different individual meanings to children but generally includes self-reference concepts and how others view them. All children have been called stupid, idiot and moron, derogatory names referring to not knowing. In many children this may assume a narcissistic hurt which creates vulnerability or resignation. Defenses may be set up against this hurt such as denial, bravado, anger and avoidance. One child might read rapidly so that his mistakes cannot be identified. A mistake means degradation. Not to know may mean being bad or no good or to be defective, weak and injured.

Another child links early rejection by his mother with not knowing, i.e., being no good and rejected. Teachers who pointed out his mistakes or made incorrect marks on his papers were viewed as rejecting too. There may be shame associated with not knowing. Not to know may represent a position that a child takes with others or characterizes his object relations. It can be stubbornness where there is a refusal to give and an attempt to control others. Some children maintain not knowing as a way to remain helpless and infantile and to make others care for them; therefore, it is a form of pseudostupidity.

> Louise, for example, evidenced a fear of depending on and trusting others and hence experienced difficulty in acknowledging lack of information. She expressed extreme convictions and refuted strongly that she was in error when confronted by an adult.

The antonym of "I don't know," "I know," similarly has conflicted meanings and associations. To know may mean to have secrets, usually sexual in nature. In contrast to "I don't know" it represents being grown up, independent, worthy and lovable. For one child, "to know" meant to be assertive and masculine, and following such assertions he would frequently withdraw into passivity and inertness. To know can also signify the end of infancy. For example, Sheldon became silly to avoid learning and even went to tears. Defenses against knowing can run a gamut of reactions such as dozing, sleepiness and verbal combat.

> Nelson wished to remain helpless and not know, but there was some conflict, for he also wished to be independent and know. Furthermore, the conflict of knowing *versus* not knowing in Nelson's case represented a sexual identification struggle between being like father—i.e., knowing, masculine, powerful, independent, depriving and cruel and being like mother—i.e., not knowing, feminine, weak, dependent, giving and loving.

This variant of the success-failure issue represents a stumbling block to learning progress and defeats instructional approaches. While the meanings, defenses and conflicts need clarification in therapy, they appear so constantly in the classroom, gym and activities that they cannot be ignored by the staff who is teaching. Once a child has obtained success it is more possible for him to view his patterns of knowing and not knowing. Careful identification and clarification of them can be used significantly by teachers. Anticipating the patterns of expression and defense can gradually diminish their constant repetition. *It is possible to present right and wrong as information rather than as indicators of love and rejection.* Teachers can encourage some expression of the negative meanings to know and not know and also present positive attitudes that can take their place such as "to know is to be" grown up, smart, masculine or feminine as the case might be, acceptable and strong; while to not know is: acceptable, a way to find out and shared by all children and adults. Teachers can blunt their own discouragement toward a child who is not learning through understanding its basis. Empathic understanding of the child's feelings and reasons can offer support and diminish the necessity to repeat behaviors which interfere with learning.

In activities other than academic, the staff can program for various achievements, both individually and in groups. Immediate, tangible results in crafts and shopwork provide a sense of accomplishment. The use of cutting tools and the careful glazing of vases can provide experiences in self-control. In contrast, an inhibited boy could eventually saw a board, use a hammer and kick a ball in a game, which achievements were seen as aggressive and masculine. Another child's eyes were opened to more potential gratifications in the world through hunting for ants and a field trip to the airport which she had never visited before.

One girl was gradually able to use a greater variety of colors in her paintings than subdued blue, green and purple. When the children are able to come to the Day Care Center by public transportation they feel more masterful and comfortable in the larger world. To experience how rules and instructions can be beneficial and lead to gratifications may lead to an important shift in attitude. Activities provide opportunities to develop leadership as well as capacities to follow. One can also observe in these children the pleasure derived from the exercise of a newly developed function or skill. White (21) states that intrinsic pleasure or self-reward in gaining competence feeds upon itself in the sense that the development of taste leads to increasing development of taste.

While methods of instruction are often first based and dependent on an extrinsic reward system from the environment of good-bad, success-failure, and reward-punishment, one tries to shift to intrinsic rewards of self-discovery and self-achievement as advocated by Bruner (12). It takes considerable time for the children, and some do not make it, to experience success and failure not as reward and punishment but as information. The desire for competence then controls behavior.

SUMMARY

The frame of reference to potentialities in children has been defined pragmatically to include a wide range of manifest behaviors that can be grouped under developmental areas. The focus has been on the psychoanalytic development of the latency age child following the concepts of Erikson (3). Potential realization will be facilitated and impeded by the interaction of factors such as endowment, realistic opportunities and basic drives. Realization of potentials in motor, intellectual and social skills are viewed as a necessity for continued development and are followed by realizations in adolescence, adulthood and old age.

Psychoeducational treatment represents an integrated and comprehensive approach to the child to modify maladaptive patterns of behavior, free up fixated and arrested areas of the personality and foster potential realization. A large number of its elements have been presented: (a) individual programming based on adequate and repetitive assessment of the child; (b) an overall system of behavior control; (c) therapy of the child and parents; (d) adult and peer reinforcement; (e) the appropriate use of medication; (f) desensitization; (g) capitalizing on spontaneous occurrences and intuitive approaches; (h) nothing succeeds like success; (i) dealing with the meanings of and defenses against knowing and not knowing; and (j) the development of competence.

REFERENCES

1. BORENSTEIN, B.: On latency. *Psychoanal. Stud. Child, 6*:279, 1951.
2. BUXBAUM, E.: A contribution to the psychoanalytic knowledge of the latency period. *Amer. J. Orthopsychiat., 21*:182, 1951.
3. ERIKSON, E. H.: Growth and crises of the healthy personality. *Psychol. Issues, 1*:50, 1959.
4. FREUD, A.: The concept of developmental lines. *Psychoanal. Stud. Child, 18*:245, 1963.
5. NAGERA, H.: The developmental profile: Notes on some practical considerations regarding its use. *Psychoanal. Stud. Child, 18*:511, 1963.
6. FREUD, S.: Analysis terminable and interminable. *Collected Papers*, Vol. V. London, Hogarth, 1950.

7. HARRIS, I. D.: *Normal Children and Mothers.* Glencoe, Free Press, 1959.
8. THOMPSON, C.: *Psychoanalysis: Evolution and Development.* New York, Grove, 1957.
9. FREUD, A.: The assessment of childhood disturbances. *Psychoanal. Stud. Child, 17*:149, 1962.
10. HARTMANN, H.: Comments on the psychoanalytic theory of the ego. *Psychoanal. Stud. Child, 5*:74, 1950.
11. HARTMANN, H.: Notes on the theory of sublimation. *Psychoanal. Stud. Child, 10*:9, 1955.
12. BRUNER, J. S.: *The Process of Education.* Cambridge, Belknap, 1963.
13. HUXLEY, A.: Human potentialities. In FABER, S. M., and WILSON, R. H. L. (eds.): *Control of the Mind.* New York, McGraw-Hill, 1961.
14. OTTO, H. A.: Personal and family strength research and spontaneity training. *Group Psychother., 17*:143, 1964.
15. MURPHY, G.: *Human Potentialities.* New York, Basic Books, 1958.
16. BLOM, G. E.: Psychoeducational aspects of classroom management. *Except. Child.,* in press.
17. BLOM, G. E., RUDNICK, M., and SEARLES, J.: Some principles and practices in the psychoeducational treatment of emotionally disturbed children. *Psychol. in the Schools,* in press.
18. REDL, F.: Strategy and techniques of the life-space interview. *Amer. J. Orthopsychiat., 29*:1, 1959.
19. LIPPITT, P., and LOHMAN, J. E.: Cross-age relationships—an educational resource. *Children, 12*:113, 1965.
20. BARTLETT, J.: *Bartlett's Familiar Quotations.* Boston, Little, Brown, 1955.
21. WHITE, R.: Motivation reconsidered: The concept of competence. *Psychol. Rev., 66*:297, 1959.

PART VI

MEANS AND METHODS DESIGNED TO ACTUATE HUMAN POTENTIAL

Chapter 31

MULTIPLE STRENGTH PERCEPTION METHOD, MINERVA EXPERIENCE AND OTHERS

HERBERT A. OTTO

ONE of the goals of the Human Potentialities Research Project has been the development of methods designed to help individuals make better use of their personality resources, strengths and assets and to help them to actualize their potentialities. Beginning in 1960 a number of methods have been developed and field-tested, both in laboratory groups conducted at the University of Utah as well as in various social agency and institutional settings. In the latter case use of the methods was with patient groups. The most effective of these methods are the Multiple Strength Perception Method (1, 2), Action Programs (2), use of Your Strengths forms and Strength Role Assignment (3). Application of these methods will be described in detail and some of the major findings and conclusions based on their use briefly summarized. A brief initial report of a recently discovered method (1964) which shows great promise, the Minerva Experience, will also be presented. All methods are essentially for use in groups, although Action Programs, These Are Your Strengths forms, Strength Role Assignment and the Minerva Experience have been used with good effect in individual therapy, counseling and casework.

It must be stressed that these methods should be used with patient and counseling groups or in an institutional or therapeutic setting *only after there has been a considerable working through of the basic problems and pathology of the group members and when in the therapist's judgment participants are ready to profit optimally from an ego-supportive type of experience.* Experience indicates that this is usually sometime beyond the midpoint in the treatment process. If used with nonpatient populations for the purpose of actualizing potential, these methods are best employed: (a) only after the group has developed a considerable degree of interpersonal closeness; (b) after members are able to communicate spontaneously and freely about their real concerns; (c) after they are able to share of the depth of their feelings; and (d) after they can use confrontation productively.

THE MULTIPLE STRENGTH PERCEPTION METHOD

The M.S.P. Method is designed for use in groups which focus on the mobilization of human potential and can also be used in group therapy, group counseling and group work, as well as in educational programs which focus on helping a person to "get to know himself better." The method can be of particular value (a) in helping group members gain a clearer understanding and overview of their strengths, personal resources, capacities and potentialities and (b) in providing an ego-supportive type of experience for members. The following are detailed procedures for use of the method.

1. The M.S.P. Method should be used with nonpatient groups only after group members have reached a point where they "really know each other" and after most of any underlying present hostilities which might be present have been worked through.

2. It is of value if the M.S.P. Method is described in detail to the group and *the choice left to them whether they wish to use the method or not.* This avoids the onus of members feeling that the method was "imposed on them." While describing the method the voluntary nature of participation is stressed. A blackboard can be used to outline the essential steps of the M.S.P. Method and to write out the key questions.

3. It is essential that prior to the use of the method the group work through and recognize *on a feeling level that the facing of problems, unrecognized aspects of the self or blocks to the actualization of unused or latent resources* is a prerequisite to helping a person identify and develop strengths and potentialities. The group should also be helped to face the fact that sometimes a (seeming) strength may be symptomatic of a problem or create an impediment to the optimum functioning of a person. Group members should therefore be encouraged to feel free also

to contribute their perceptions and insight as to what is *preventing* an individual from making better use of his strengths or resources. However, the group should be helped to recognize that the focus is essentially strength-centered. Emphasis is on the use of perceptions and insights as a means of helping the target person make fuller use of his potentialities.

4. All those wishing to participate in the use of the method are asked to write their names on a slip of paper and to fold this slip. These slips are then placed in a receptacle and the name of the *target person* is drawn so that selection is essentially random.

5. The target person begins the process by *enumerating and sharing aloud what he sees as his strengths.* While he is doing this, the group normally does not interrupt or question.

6. When the target person has finished listing what he sees as his strengths, he then turns to the group and asks the group the *key question* in the following or similar words: "What other strengths do you see me as having, and what (factors or problems) do you see as keeping me from using these strengths?" It should be noted that the group *must not begin* sharing their perceptions of the target person's strengths (or factors which keep him from making better use of these personality resources) unless the target person first asks the key question. By voicing the key question, the target person in effect issues an invitation and takes responsibility for what transpires during the experience. In addition, there appears to be a greater ego involvement and readiness to accept the perceptions of the group if the target person asks the group for help by addressing to them the key question.

7. The group now "bombards" the target person with its perceptions of his strengths and factors or forces which keep him from utilizing these strengths. Group members may also address questions to the target person designed to solicit clues about strengths or potentialities or questions designed to explore or clarify possible blocks or impediments to the use of personality resources.

8. The group interaction around the target person usually lasts about forty minutes. When the group leader senses that the

group's perceptions of the target person's strengths are running out, he asks the following question: "Are there any other strengths that you see in John (or Mary)?"

9. If no further perceptions are forthcoming, the group leader or therapist asks the following key question: "Now that we have seen the range of some of the strengths and potentialities in John (or Mary), what sort of group fantasy or dream do we have about him (or her); that is, if he (or she) uses all these strengths —*how would we see John (or Mary) functioning five years from now?* The group then shares their fantasies and dreams about the target person. Although this is not done routinely, the target person can be asked to share the dream or fantasy he has for himself by using the following or a similar question: "Now John (or Mary), if you used your strengths and potentialities and *could do anything you wanted to do,* what is your deepest dream or fantasy about yourself?" Finally, and as a means of closure, the following question can be addressed to the target person: "What sort of feeling did you have when Strength Bombardment was going on?"

Since all laboratory group sessions are tape-recorded, it has been possible to analyze the interaction which occurs during the Multiple Strength Perception Process. The Strength Bombardment interactions of three groups were subjected to analysis in a recent study (4). It was found that duplication of strength perceptions (group members repeating to the target person his own verbal listing of strengths) accounted for only 1.5 per cent of all strength perceptions addressed by the groups to the target person. Another finding was that if the target person's own listing of his strengths is placed side by side with the strength perceptions of the group and the strength block perceptions (what group members see as keeping the target person from using his strengths), a clear-cut *strength perception profile* emerges. This profile has implications for a fuller understanding of the person and how he may be helped to make more optimal use of his potentialities. (For the psychotherapist using this method in a treatment setting, the profile which emerges can have both diagnostic and treatment implications.)

Analysis of the group fantasies revealed that they are largely a product of the personality profile which emerges as a result of the Multiple Strength Perception Method. Group fantasies are thus realistically related to the pattern of the group's strength perceptions and strength block perceptions. Further studies of the Multiple Strength Perception Method are underway. It is of interest that a follow-up interview type study (5) of two laboratory groups conducted one year after termination of the group experience revealed that *76 per cent of those interviewed identified the Multiple Strength Perception Method as the most effective of the methods used.*

A number of additional conclusions and findings emerge from use of the Multiple Strength Perception Method during a period of over four and a half years.

1. Within a comparatively short period of time the average participant in the group experience is able to develop significantly increased sensitivity or perceptivity of strengths, resources or potentialities in other persons. For example, it became evident during the first experimental groups that group participants used a wide range of nonverbal clues. Remarks such as: "I noticed your voice changed when you said this during our last meeting," and "There was a sparkle in your eye when you talked about this three sessions ago" were frequent. It has for years been a byword in clinical circles that the more severely emotionally disturbed or psychotic the individual, the more sensitive is he to emotional pathology in the therapist or others. This research indicates the correlative, namely *the more healthy an individual, the more able is he to develop a perceptiveness and sensitivity for strengths, resources and potentialities in others.*

2. The process of being the center of intensive interaction was consistently reported by the target person as being a highly significant emotional experience. Remarks such as: "It really shakes you up," and "I could feel myself sweating, but it felt good," were commonplace. There is also some evidence that for many group participants who volunteered to become target persons, integration and assimilation of the experience does not fully take place until some later point in time. This was indicated by comments such as the following: "I will have a lot to think about in the next weeks," and "It is going to take time to let it all soak in."

3. Use of the M.S.P. Method seems to have contributed to a strengthening of the self-image of participants as well as enhancing self-confidence. In many instances a marked change in the direction of a more positive self-concept was noted. Group members reported feeling "more capable," "more competent," "more ready to try out new ideas or activities," and "more able to relax and enjoy myself after work." Participants also pointed out that prior to this experience they did not have a clear idea of the range of their personality assets and potentialities whereas they had a fairly good grasp of their weaknesses and problems. They stated that the use of the method has contributed to a clearer understanding of the "topography of their strengths" leading to a more realistic self-appraisal. This was evident from recurrent statements of the following or similar nature: "This has given me a much more balanced picture of myself," and "I am much clearer about my personality assets and liabilities–this helps me select goals I can achieve and stick to them because I know I have the resources to carry through."

4. Use of the M.S.P. Method appears to be related to changes in the productivity and professional functioning of participants. For example, businessmen reported increased productivity and increased use of creative thinking. A persistent pattern was evident which can be summarized by the remarks of one businessman: "I find that I suddenly have the energy to do things that I have put off for months and years. Most of these are things that seem to make an extra emotional demand on you, and it is like taking that extra step which you know you ought to take but never get around to doing. It is a nagging sort of feeling, and you don't know what a relief it is to finally do these things which you have put off." Examples of changes in professional functioning were also reported by graduate students of the School of Social Work as well as secretaries and other office personnel. These group members reported that relations with fellow workers improved as they began to recognize strengths and potentialities in their associates. Graduate students of social work noted that in their agencies and in the course of the casework treatment process they began to place greatly increased emphasis on the

strengths and potentialities of clients and that the clients responded positively to this.

5. The shared group fantasy often corresponded surprisingly with the deepest wish-dreams of the individual. The fantasies of the group coincided in most instances with 60 per cent or more of some of the deepest wishes and dreams the target person had about himself. This was a profoundly ego-supportive and ego-building experience for the target person as revealed by the following or similar remarks: "You don't know what it means to me that you can see these things in me which I have dreamed and wished I could do all my life. It means that what I have dreamed I could do, others see in me and I can accomplish them."

THE MINERVA EXPERIENCE

This method is named after the Roman goddess, Minerva, goddess of health and wisdom who sprang fully armored from the head of Jupiter. It will be recalled that one of the contributions from psychoanalysis, and traceable to the early works of Freud, is the hypothesis that every person in the process of growing up undergoes a series of traumatic experiences which are repressed or "forgotten" and which become part of the unconscious. It is one of the tasks of the therapist to help the patient explore his unconscious and to discover and work through these traumatic incidents so that they can be more successfully integrated into the life experience. Psychic energy is thus made available which has formerly been invested in the repression of traumatic material.

In a similar manner, it is our hypothesis that *there are in the background of every person, especially during childhood and also throughout life, a web of highly formative positive experiences. This web-work of creative, positive incidents consists of experiences charged with deep emotional meanings called Minerva experiences. These experiences have a great deal to do with the way an individual grows and develops and the network of his strengths and potentialities and are believed to be as important, if not more important, than traumatic incidents.* The uncovering and recall of Minerva experiences can make psychic energy available through increased self-understanding and by providing clues to strengths and potentialities, some of which may be latent or hidden. Although there are some similarities, the Minerva experience concept differs from Maslow's concept of *peak experiences* which he defines as follows: "The word peak experience is a generalization for the best moments of the human being, for the happiest moments of life, for experiences of ecstasy, rapture, bliss, of the greatest joy" (6). The essential difference is that Minerva experiences are defined as *a network of highly formative and growthful experiences having strongly positive affective components and which play a dominant role in the genesis of personality resources thus significantly affecting personality development.* It is our finding that the preponderance of these experiences are not readily accessible to recall; however, uncovering of *Minerva experiences provides clues to personality assets and the unfolding of the individual's potentialities.* Maslow's research and findings from peak experiences add to and deepen our understanding of Minerva experiences, a more inclusive construct.

The following are examples of Minerva experiences taken from tape recordings of laboratory groups:

> I finally thought of some experiences. We lived on a farm, and it was not too far from town, but we didn't go into town very often. Mother and Dad usually went in on Saturdays and got their groceries and we were hoping that they would bring us home something good; so while they were gone, we rushed and rushed and rushed to get Sunday's cleaning done just in time for Mother so that she would be so surprised. They would come home, and they would have a small bag of candy for nine kids; but that candy was *really* treasured. Maybe that is why today that I like candy so much. I just eat tons of it.

* * *

> This incident I remembered of the teacher opening the window, and we sang to the birds—I still have a good feeling toward birds, and I, of course, am not a member of the Audubon Society, but there is a fellow at work that is, and I like to go talk to him about the birds; and if I see a certain bird, I like to go and ask him what type it is. If I go to the farm at Mirror Lake, I observe some hill cranes; and I reported them to this fellow, and every year I report when I return—and so forth. I

have always had a good feeling, since then, toward birds and outdoor birds.

There is another incident that I can recall that has made me, what would you say, unafraid to tackle mechanical jobs—repairing, for instance, my refrigerator or washer at home or at work. I was the engineer on testing a big rock mill, and everybody seemed to be afraid to touch it; but I wasn't afraid to make a modification on it—and I could see it work. I believe that stems back to when I was seven or eight and I bought a bicycle, and I took the brake apart. I believe it was a Morrow Brake, and if you remember those brakes—all the parts that used to be in there . . . I was sitting on the cellar steps trying to fix this brake, and I was washing it—and my father came along and looked at it, and saw all those parts and said "Do you think you can get it back together?" And I said, "Yeah." I worked on it for a while, and then I wrecked it—and it sat there for a couple of days; and my father asked me what I was going to do with it. And I said, "Well I didn't know." And he got a can and gathered up all of the parts and put them in the can. He didn't say a word. He just took them all downtown and had it put back together. He didn't bawl me out or anything. He could have set a pattern there where I would have been afraid to tackle mechanical things, but he left a good feeling in my mind—even though I failed. Now I am not too afraid to tackle any mechanical thing, although that is not particularly my line, I remember I redesigned a part—so it doesn't bother me to try.

Based on the preliminary analysis of data, there are indications that in most instances participants identify as Minerva experiences incidents which characteristically have strong emotional affect associated with them. Participants are, however, not usually aware of the part played by the experience in relation to their personality development. Although there is recognition that the experience is important and has had a lasting impact on the personality, the causative ramifications of a particular experience often appear difficult to trace. The following is illustrative of this category of incident:

I had the measles one year when I was about six years old, and someone was reading me the Wizard of Oz, it seems to me, and one of the witches had some silver shoes—and I wanted some silver shoes in the worst way. I think the little girl, Doro-

> thy, got them when the witch was killed; so on Easter morning, when I woke up and there was just a little bit of light coming through the window, and it looked like silver shoes on the floor. . . . I lay there wondering for quite a while. It seemed like hours, finally the sun came up—and I could see they were silver. My mother the night before had gotten an old pair of my patent leather shoes and had painted them silver, and that was such a thrilling experience that I just went out and played with those silver shoes on. We had a huge yard, quite private.

The person reporting the above experience was noted by group members as having outstanding grooming and taste in wearing apparel and was always meticulously and strikingly dressed. It is, of course, a moot question whether this facet of her personality functioning had its genesis in that particular incident. There is an excellent likelihood that this experience may be one, if not the first, of a series of similar experiences which were of deeply formative nature and which left a lasting impact on the personality.

On the basis of experience with laboratory groups the writer has increasingly come to the conclusion that self-understanding (in the sense of *analyzing personality components as traceable to childhood experiences and relationships* or acquiring awareness of the causative roots of one's actions) is a *learned* frame of reference, an acquired skill. Many normally functioning individuals have not been exposed to this frame of reference and have not acquired this skill. On the other hand, many individuals with a background of college training, which usually seems to provide some rudiments of an analytical frame of reference, utilize this framework *defensively*. They rationalize or trace the onset of a condition to explain why it is the way it is now, but *do not utilize their understanding to bring about change and growth. This type of self-understanding is used by them mostly to maintain the status quo and is inimical to the development of individual potential.*

Minerva experiences have been largely used as a group method, although this concept has direct application to individual therapeutic and treatment programs. To initiate use of the method, Minerva experiences are defined and the method described in detail to the group. The decision whether to use Minerva experience is then made by the total group. When the group reaches a decision to use this method, an assignment is made asking all group members to think about and "go back into their childhood" to uncover such Minerva experiences. It has been found that if an assignment is given to recall these experiences, most group members will in the interim period between sessions make an effort to recall such experiences. This considerably facilitates use of the method.

During the session following the assignment, a layer removal or "onionskin procedure" is used to foster recall of Minerva experiences. A chart is placed on the blackboard with the top item reading "Age 15 to 18," under that are placed the words "Age 10 to 15," then "Age 6 to 10," "Age 3 to 6" and "Below 3 years." This chart has been found to be helpful and fosters the process of recall. Participants are urged to let their "mind and memory wander freely and to free-associate if needed," and to begin by recalling Minerva experiences at the top of the chart, between ages fifteen to eighteen. They are asked to hold off voicing out loud experiences which they recall from an earlier period. Whenever a participant finishes sharing an experience, the person directing Minerva experiences asks the following questions: "About what age would you place this experience—can you recall anything else about the experience?" and "What other experiences do you recall during this period of your life?" Oftentimes a "trigger phenomenon" can be observed as the sharing of an experience triggers the recall of forgotten incidents in other group members. The group moves down the chart but not rigidly since to maintain spontaneity of sharing it is often best to have a group member share an especially vivid memory even though it falls outside of the age range which the group is exploring.

When there is a marked decline in the recall of Minerva experiences, or when the group has reached the bottom of the chart, the person conducting the group experience states that he will now describe some odors (or experiences with smell), as this has been found to greatly facilitate the recall of early memories often leading to the uncovering of Minerva experiences. He then recites (using his own free flow of associations) in a similar manner as follows: "The smell of the hot sun on sand, of a wet dog coming in from the rain, of the seashore and seaweeds, of bread (cookies) baking, of freshly mown hay, etc." Participants usually interrupt with exclamations indicating recall, which is then shared and explored with relation to possible Minerva experiences. It is always well to ask the participant to try to pinpoint the age at which a particular experience took place, as this seems to help place the experience in perspective and provide structure for more recall.

The description of odors (an appeal to one of the most primitive and basic senses) at times produces an unprecedented flow of memories and associations and can be used a number of times in succession. As a final step in the use of the method, the following question is raised: What clues to your strengths and potentialities do you now have, and what are the implications of this experience? The group then spends some time on integrating material which has been uncovered, on deepening insights and on relating their discoveries to the aims and goals which they wish to achieve within the framework of the group.

The use of Minerva experiences is a fairly recent development and has been field-tested in only four groups to date. Although a detailed analysis and evaluation of data has not as yet been completed, preliminary findings can be summarized as follows.

1. There is evidence of considerable "amnesia" or inability to recall much of significance which has transpired during the childhood of so-called healthy and normal persons. This difficulty of recall seems to be in part responsible for the relatively low number of Minerva experiences (two to three) identified per person.
2. Minerva experiences are often related to specific places, smells, holidays and people as well as specific statements which are remembered verbatim.
3. Although experiences with mother and father were important, in one group there was an identification of as many Minerva experiences with grandparents as with parents.
4. Other members of the group could usually see the lasting effects of the Minerva experience in relation to the per-

sonality and life course of an individual before the member relating it could. Oftentimes the impact of a particular Minerva experience on the whole future course of life of a person appeared in dramatic relief.

5. Some group members reported "a tremendous upsurge in energy" following Minerva experiences as well as "very positive feelings about life and living."
6. There are indications that the uncovering and working through of trauma could lead to easier recovery and recall of Minerva experiences. (One almost gets the impression that the trauma rests as a heavier strata on top of and keeps the Minerva experiences from emerging.)
7. There have been several instances of a dramatic change in attitude toward parents as a result of the Minerva experience. Some group members who had had comparatively little contact with their parents or who had felt emotionally isolated from them re-established warm and vital relationships following the Minerva experience.
8. Group response and evaluation reveals that this method holds considerable promise for the identification of latent strengths and the development of potentialities.

ASSIGNED STRENGTH ROLES

This method is another comparatively recent addition. It is essentially a group method (7) but has also been used in individual treatment programs. The method offers an opportunity to live a defined role selected by the participant and to engage in specific behavior over a period of time which he believes would strengthen him or which could lead to better utilization of his potential. A precursor of this method is Kelly's (8) fixed-role therapy. There are, however, some significant differences in these methods. In fixed-role therapy the client is asked to act out a fictitious person over a period of time on the basis of a "fixed role sketch" furnished by the clinician. Assigned Strength Roles, primarily used in a group setting, encourages the participant to select and define his own role using the group as a resource.

In group use the method is first described, and choice whether to use the method is left to the group members. A set of four by five cards is passed around with each card having one strength role typed on it. It is pointed out that the strength roles on the cards are only illustrative and that the group would need to make up a strength role for the person selected. those wishing to participate then write their names on a piece of paper, and selection is made by random drawing.

Before beginning the process, the person in charge again carefully stresses that the purpose of strength role assignment is not to correct a person's shortcomings, weaknesses or problems by asking him to do something he may not wish to do. *The purpose of the method is for everyone to help the person whose name has been drawn to work out a strength role which he will enjoy carrying out, which will strengthen him and which he feels will enable him to make better use of his potential.* To initiate the process of strength role assignment, the person whose name has been drawn should turn to the group and ask members the key question in words similar to the following: "What is the role which you think would strengthen me most or do most by helping me to mobilize my potentialities?" It is only after the key question has been asked that everyone should begin by contributing their ideas.

The following is a list of possible strength roles.

1. You are a person who has definite latent leadership qualities. You seek opportunities to exercise these qualities. At meetings and other events you "let your voice be heard" and your influence be felt.
2. You are a person with a good sense of humor who likes to tell jokes and entertain people.
3. You are a creative (artistic) person, and you express your creativity through painting, drawing, writing, or you think up new and novel ways of doing things. You can, for example, lend touches of beauty to the home for the time the family has together.
4. You are a person with considerable "stick-to-itiveness" or perseverance. You use this quality to tackle specific things you have put off doing, you stick with it and persist in your efforts until there has been change or accomplishment.

5. You are a very friendly and outgoing person. You like to share your ideas and thoughts with others and to take the initiative.
6. You are a very honest person who never holds back the truth as you see it. You are completely honest with people.
7. You are a very observant and sensitive person who pays special attention to the feelings and needs of others. You give of yourself and your understanding.

Strengths roles should be made up and tailored to the specific needs of the person who chooses to participate in strength role assignment, with his wishes a fundamental consideration in the role assignment. He should want to enter into the strength role assignment of his own accord and should be able to enjoy the role. Coercion or forcing a strength role on a person through group pressure should very rarely be attempted and only under special circumstances as, for example, when a person "wants to be persuaded" by the group into accepting a role. Assignment of strength role is on the basis of group discussion and consensus. Immediately following the assignment, specific behaviors associated with the role are spelled out by the group. Notes of these suggestions concerning specific behavior are taken either by or for the person selected. Approximately a week later the person then shares with the group his experience with strength role assignment. The effect of the strength role on those associated with him is examined as well as any growth or change which is taking place in him.

Strength role assignment appears to be of particular value by providing an individual with a broad framework of behavior and actions for "trying out" and developing latent abilities and capacities. There is evidence of a noticeable "carry-over effect" in that both specific behaviors as well as attitudes associated with the behavior continue beyond the period of assignment and into the life experience of the individual. In many instances family and associates will recognize changes in behavior and make such comments as: "You are much more creative than you have ever been," and "You are so much more outgoing." Such comments and observations appear to reinforce the behavior and contribute to positive change and increased utilization of potential.

Other methods including Action Programs (2), the Supportive Environment Approach (2), use of These Are Your Strengths forms (3) and Sensory Awareness Experiences (9) have been described in detail elsewhere. A number of new methods are presently in the process of being field-tested. Among the most promising of these are the Life Goals Inquiry and the Ideal-Self Utilization Method. A need exists for the development of means and methods specifically designed to help the healthy and well-functioning individual make fuller use of his powers and capacities. The development and evaluation of such methods represent a comparatively neglected area of inquiry. It is hoped that this report will stimulate increased interest and productivity in method development.

REFERENCES

1. Otto, H. A.: The personal resource development research—The multiple strength perception effect. *The Proceedings of the Utah Academy of Science, Arts and Letters, 38*:182-186, 1961-62.
2. Otto, H. A.: The personal and family strength research projects—Some implications for the therapist. *Ment. Hyg., 48*:439-450, 1964.
3. Otto, H. A.: *Toward a Holistic Treatment Program—Some Concepts and Methods.* Unpublished manuscript.
4. Hansen, K. W.: *Multiple Strength Perception Analysis.* Unpublished master's thesis, Salt Lake City, Utah, Univ. of Utah, 1964.
5. Dover, W. B.: *Personal Strengths Research—A Follow-Up Study.* Unpublished master's thesis, Salt Lake City, Utah, University of Utah, 1965.
6. Maslow, A. H.: Fusions of facts and values. *Amer. J. Psychoanaly., 23*:117-131, 1963.
7. Otto, H. A.: Personal and family strength research and spontaneity training. *Group Psychother. J., 17*:143-149 (June, Sept.) 1964.
8. Kelly, George A.: *The Psychology of Personal Constructs.* W. W. Norton & Company, Inc., New York, 1955, pp. 360-451.
9. Otto, H. A., Murphy, M. (ed.): Sensory unfoldment through smell, touch, and taste. *Ways of Growth* (in preparation).

Chapter 32

REPORT ON WORK IN SENSORY AWARENESS AND TOTAL FUNCTIONING

CHARLOTTE SELVER

In conjunction with CHARLES V. W. BROOKS

AGAIN and again in the course of practical work in sensory awareness my students have recognized that many of their difficulties go far back into earliest childhood. Not only have the conscious beliefs and attitudes acquired in growing up often stood in the way of a fuller functioning, but the tissues themselves have been learning responses—and often what will later be inappropriate responses—since the beginning of life. It is as though the very fact of civilization, with all its potential for help and for hindering, must be confronted in the first experiences of the infant, before consciousness as we usually think of it exists at all.

The capacity of learning, which extends so much farther in us than in other creatures, is, it seems to me, the noblest gift man has at his disposal; but while his greatest asset, it is also his greatest danger. The marvelous process by which we come to stand and speak, to form shapes and rhythms, to analyze, calculate and organize, is in its very flexibility and versatility peculiarly liable to deformation. This is why education has such importance for everyone: It is the same pruning shear with which the gardener thins out the fruit tree for healthier living and richer bearing and with which also, year after year, he cuts back the spring shoots of the shrub to form a hedge.

These two activities call for different virtues. For the one, what is needed is merely a geometrical sense of form; for the other, a feeling for the organism in its environment. One who has the latter will have studied and loved the tree since it first sprang from seed and will understand the principles of its growth.

The nature of growth, which may be considered as identical

with the learning process, is directly revealed in the developing child, who, when left to himself, lives in a state of incessant exploration which tends to bring him in contact, in one way or another, with all the elements in his environment. It is his drive to explore, his curiosity, his fascination (1), which from babyhood on leads to all physical and mental development. Unconditioned, healthy children have a strong drive to do things by themselves and to find out by themselves, even when they go out in groups; and the milieu which confronts the child with selective challenges, giving him not answers but opportunities for exploration, leads to full branching and to sturdy roots.

But it is between the active process of learning and the largely passive process of being educated that the child actually develops. The purposive impact of the environment on the growing child, which in its formal aspects we call education, begins with the first reactions of the mother to the infant at her nipple, whenever she indicates her own preferences or what *she thinks* is good for the baby, instead of *feeling out* the momentary relationship that best permits mutual functioning. This directive rather than permissive attitude, insisting on how to do it, may be encountered by the child as the basic element in most of his education throughout life. He will not be given the occasion to learn by experience but will be told in advance. In our education, in contrast to that prevalent among animals and primitive peoples which is by *example in context* and not by *abstract precept*, the analytical, evaluative, directive tendency is paramount. A "loving" mother asks herself "what is best" for the baby, a "selfish" mother how it is for herself. A mother of integrity would simply sense the total functioning.

In the work I am going to present here, which is based on that originated and developed over the past fifty years by Elsa Gindler in Berlin and Heinrich Jacoby in Zurich (2), and which I have been teaching for the last twenty-five years in the United States, the latter attitude is cultivated. I would say Elsa Gindler was a natural scientist and one of extraordinary quality. She made it her life work to explore to what degree we human beings develop our sensitive and perceptive power and to what degree we cooperate with the forces of nature, e.g., with the spontaneous development of energy within a given activity, with the processes of life and regeneration as they occur through us, with the dynamics of activity and rest, with the ever-present pull of gravity and so on.

She found out that in the process of this exploration one can discover through sensing how hindering tendencies come about. As the individual becomes more sensitized and learns to make friends with the potentials he gradually uncovers, the way slowly opens to a fuller experiencing and deeper relating to himself, his fellows and all activities of daily living.

The work of Heinrich Jacoby, which was so closely related to Elsa Gindler's that both considered it one, was directed mainly to freeing creative energies and exploring our potentials of self-expression—whether in our daily tasks and activities or in the arts. He found that the way we are conditioned to approach tasks tends to inhibit our vital powers, while in contrast an attitude of awareness and readiness of the total self in contact with our activity and obedient to its dynamics releases them. The core of his work lay in bringing about an attitude of receptivity and permissiveness, rather than the customary alternatives of "trying hard," "making efforts" and "doing," on the one hand, or "taking it easy," "letting go" and "relaxing," on the other.

Both Gindler and Jacoby came to the same conclusions: (a) that the full range of our potentials has never been discovered by us but can be gradually unfolded; and (b) that what we do use we often use to disadvantage with regard to our energy expenditure (and subsequently to our functioning) as well as to the quality of our actions; and (c) that there are no ungifted people (3). If we believe we are ungifted, we will find on closer examination that we are only hindered and that hindrances can gradually be shed when we see deeper and give ourselves new chances.

It is interesting that the findings of my teachers, based on empirical experimentation, coincide with the discoveries of modern neurological research (4), as well as with the age-old knowledge and practices of Zen and Taoism (5). They all recognize that if we would allow the giving up of the effects of previous conditioning and become able again to experience and develop our untapped potentials, then and only then, as Elsa Gindler used to say, would we live *normally,* i.e., according to our actual human design.

What is it—this something which some people seem to have? Those who have it, and to whom we always feel strangely attracted, seem to live out of a great inner richness. I saw this quality at work once when I watched a friend, a delicate, fragile woman of over eighty, giving a treatment to a patient for almost two hours. After she had finished, the patient, wonderfully relieved, exclaimed, "Where do you get this strength and this marvelous sensitivity?" My friend smiled at her and answered, "Everybody has it, only *we don't know about it!*"

This is basically the same answer that my teachers have given; and the practical work towards "knowing that we have it" or, more to the point, gradually discovering and cultivating it, is the substance of our classes (6).

The conditioning which we gradually begin to give up is as complex as it is deeply ingrained. What is involved is not the mass of information, whether true or false, which we have acquired at home and in school, but the *value* which we place on this information, just as it is not the manifold skills we may have learned but the *techniques* which take the place of skill. A glance at the actual training of young children, which, except in its grossest aspects, is still so generally overlooked, reveals the problem. The parent invades every aspect of the child's development. The child is taught when and how much it is *good* for him to eat, when and how long he *ought* to sleep, what parts of him are *bad* or *dirty,* what is *good* social behavior (smiling), etc., etc. When he falls and cries he is taught not to allow the pain and shock to go their way but to seek instant distraction from them and to expect fuss and anxiety from the parent rather than quiet sympathy: "You *good* boy, that *bad* banana peel!" A little later he will be taught that exposure to cold or getting wet in the rain is *unpleasant* and *dangerous,* as it will actually become after the lesson has been thoroughly learned.

This evaluative education is the earliest and deepest, and of course it confuses the child's capacity for judgment. From that point on, the evidence of his own senses cannot simply be trusted (7), and he tends to judge at second hand and generally. The living context, on which all real value depends, becomes obscured.

Consider the efforts of the parents to influence the baby's very way of perceiving: exaggerated looking and listening; sniffing at flowers; smacking lips over food to make him taste it; and in speaking to him the artificiality and distortions of "baby-talk," implying that verbal communication cannot be peaceful and simple. These almost universal practices create the impression from the very beginning that something *extra* is necessary, that a *technique* of some sort is inseparable from living, so that the grown woman applies lipstick, not as a part of *dressing up*, but because she feels "naked" without it, and nobody can find employment in radio or television for just speaking naturally. The lily is not to be simply watered but must be gilded.

Close to this necessity for the something extra is the education towards *making efforts,* which is so common in our competitive society. It is not enough that the anxious mother urges her baby to make efforts to move his bowels. Think of the ambition of so many parents for their baby to sit, to stand, to walk as early as possible—*earlier than other children.* The natural processes of energy development are not enough: *They must be coaxed.* "This can't be right," said a student in an experiment through which she had previously forced herself. "It feels so easy!" And another: "All week I have tried very hard to undo my overdoing." It is the same in the child's intellectual development: it is not enough that he learns words as his ever-widening experience requires them; he must be taught a vocabulary, whether he experiences what he says or not.

Finally, among the factors in the young child's development, I must note the widespread practice of interrupting his play as though it were of no importance and impressing on him, often as not, that a "good" child always comes when mother calls him. Through this he comes to feel that there is no natural rhythm in things and that it is right for activities to be cut off in mid-air and for others to be begun, as though magically, without preparation—an impression that will be totally confirmed by what he sees on television, where presentations are violently interrupted by the ones that follow and the only preparations are shouts or blares.

When the child has been interrupted often enough, his innate sense of rhythm becomes confused; and his sense of the social value of his own experience becomes so too.

What comes to replace the real world of perception—the living context—is a world of ideas and images created not by the child's own discoveries but, consciously to him or unconsciously, by our whole history and culture. These images guide and mold him as he grows—angel and devil, good baby and bad baby, nice girl and tramp, he-man and sissy—and as they are static, he tends to stasis too, slowly exchanging the dynamism of life for the rigidity of "character," so that eventually he fits into one of the pigeonholes which society presents. This is the growing old without growing up which fills our time with octogenarian "boys" and "girls" who may at the same time have been executives or congressmen, matrons or old maids.

In this process of conforming to the demands of the images within him, the growing child begins to find himself accompanied by one particular image which is a composite of all the others, tempered unevenly by real perceptions and memories. This is the image of himself which, for better or worse, interposes itself in his functioning, urging here, restraining there; and which in any case is as a film that has grown between him and reality. The notion that it is in character for us to do this and not to do that or to feel this and not to feel that compels or censors our activities and diminishes or distorts our experience. Only in moments of true connection is the self-image absent, permitting us just to be as we really are.

In the work in sensory awareness we gradually and patiently sort out what is perception and what is image. We build upon sensations, and particularly on our proprioceptive sensations, the cultivation of which has been neglected in our education so that they no longer come easily. Except for sensations of pain and very general feelings of comfort or discomfort, the sensations from within are like the stars, which only appear when the artificial lights are turned off. When there is quiet enough, they can be very precise.

But even then, when genuine sensations seem to occur, in the sensations themselves there is very often an extraneous component (8). For the organ which provides sensory perception, the sensory cortex in our brain, not only registers sensations where and when they occur but is also the storeroom of past impressions. When a new sensory stimulus reaches the cortex, it may reactivate related impressions that had been stored away in the past. The consequence is that a sensation rises into consciousness which is not purely of the moment but is charged with a relation to something perhaps altogether remote. This is the basis of neurotic behavior, and so we sometimes see a person protect himself from a friendly touch or a dog recoil from a friendly greeting. This is a reaction, not to the actual sensation, but to the memory of a cruel experience in the past. So in our work the mere invitation to quiet is often not enough, and we must devise simple means of inviting sensations in a context of peace and security where the actual perception may be recognized and distinguised from the irrelevant or neurotic component.

In general the work may be described as the gradual unfolding and cultivation of sensibility, of greater range and delicacy of feeling, which brings about concurrently the awakening and freeing of our innate energies. This we practice through the *activity of sensing*. Sensing alone is an astonishing and rich experience. Many people, hungry for more depth and immediacy in living, want it for its own sake. Others come to become keener and more differentiated in their perceptions. Others, again, come to free themselves from habits and blocks—often from aches and pains. Whatever the entrance gate may be, whether general inclination or very acute need, the paths are soon all interwoven. We may start just for the delight of going deeper and presently collide with heretofore unknown blocks which must gradually dissolve for fuller living and more availability for our daily tasks and circumstances. Or, on the other hand, we may start with specific symptoms and in the course of working discover the scope and richness, the many-dimensionality of simple functioning. In sensing the person will meet consciously for the first time the creative, *self-directive* powers of his own nature, finding that he can orient himself where he formerly used to seek advice and that his most reliable sources of information and guidance lie within him.

In our classes I give occasion to the students to feel more clearly what is happening in their own organisms. To experience this, as I have said, we need quiet and peace. No urging can bring anyone to faster sensations; on the contrary, it would only block experiencing. At first, lying on the floor may help bring quiet, for nearly everybody likes to lie down and with that gains a feeling of comfort which facilitates sensory awakening. Of course, some people who are particularly restless may feel this is indulgence and become uneasy. Others who have always equated consciousness with activity will become drowsy. But gradually they recognize that peace can bring gradual clearing of the head rather than drowsiness and that giving time as needed is essential for the development of quiet alertness.

Soon the first discoveries come: Here one lies comfortably, here it presses. "The floor presses," a person may announce, sure of his discovery—only to recognize later that the "pressing" comes from *him;* here one feels free, while somewhere else constricted. One person may feel light in lying, another heavy. One may get fresh, another tired. At some point the insight comes that all these sensations are simply personal reactions which can be accepted without evaluation and labeling and explored for new and fuller understanding, and that "right" and "wrong" are inappropriate here. The receiving and accepting of messages from inside and outside, without feeling pangs of bad conscience or a sense of failure when they are not as expected, contributes greatly to one's sense of independence and, of course, leads to further and clearer sensing and to surer discoveries. Little by little the tendency to *expect* diminishes and vanishes, so that sensations can arrive just as they are; and gradually the general tendency to notice only in terms of what feels pleasant or unpleasant diminishes too.

Concurrently with these first attempts goes a reorientation of the head. Is it possible to give up *watching,* a kind of looking into what happens even when the eyes are closed? Is it possible to give up associative, compulsive *thinking*—the internal gossip, the talking to oneself?

The student begins to become aware of changes which happen all by themselves—the effects of the *self-directive processes* within the organism. At this stage he only feels the effects, not yet how they come about. He may become warmer or cooler, or his lying which felt heavy may become lighter. Or the floor which formerly "pressed" now "feels so soft," or where he felt tense before he may feel resting now. He may feel an urge to yawn and gradually dare to let a yawn break through. He may become conscious of his breathing as it changes from slower to faster or faster to slower or stops and picks up again. Occasional questioning by the teacher may make him more conscious of this or that; and it is the part of the teacher to sense how much time is needed for exploration and when to stimulate or indicate directions that may bear fruit. But though such questions are often felt in the beginning to be suggestive, it is in the nature of the work that the student's discoveries are his own. The suggestiveness is only his own suggestibility (or his wish to please the teacher), and this also diminishes as his independence grows.

The basic human activities of *lying, sitting, standing and walking,* which in a culture more attuned to the significance of these activities were called "the four dignities of man," offer the easiest opportunity of discovering our attitudes to our environment and the extent to which we are conscious of what we are doing. It is obvious that many people stand as little as possible because it tires them, sleep on mattresses that are carefully designed to give to them and "sit" in overstuffed or contoured chairs, thereby to a great extent avoiding full contact with the environment. Rather than accept an environment which requires vitality and giving on their part, they seek one which permits them to maintain their "tensions" and flaccidities intact while actually supposing that this "easy life" brings "relaxation." Of course, the insulation from contact which all this "comfort" represents leads, like any insulation, to a degree of starvation and merely encourages the tensions to grow and actual rest to become ever more elusive.

When confronted with a genuine opportunity to permit change and renewal, such as a hard floor or a stool where there is nothing to lean against, many new students suppose a considerable task has been set them; and on the stool they will either collapse or hold themselves erect, imagining this is sitting. Much time is needed before these complementary attitudes, between which their sitting experiences have been divided, begin to yield to a relationship and connection in which the sensation of the outer realities of the chair and the pull of gravity and the inner reality of life processes in tissues and structural coordination blend together into living functioning. Each of the processes involved—really *experiencing* the pull of gravity, not only *thinking about it,* and the becoming conscious of growing aliveness and more changeability—is an unexpected and delightful finding in itself, encouraging more exploration. Likewise, in lying on the floor many pertinent sensations may come to consciousness, raising ever clearer questions. Are we *in contact* with what we touch or acting as though we were in a vacuum? Do we accept the support of the floor or the chair, or do we pull away from it? Or do we press on it or close ourselves against it, or push into it? This is psychosomatic language, which tells us so much more than our usual intellectual language: These are not just "tensions" which need to be "relaxed" or "limberness" which is "right." Innumerable indications in this language of the tissues express the attitudes we have acquired—often through very painful experiences. But in coming to sense them we can also begin to *allow their resolution,* which had heretofore been blocked by their repression from memory and consciousness. By sensing the *here and now* we come to recognize that there is no reason any more to resist or close ourselves to the situation at hand. As one becomes more attuned to a given activity, hindering tendencies gradually disappear, for otherwise a deep connection cannot come about. At the same time a heightened sense of being occurs which is, in fact, how real contact can be recognized.

Standing also offers rich possibilities for sensing experiments. Alone the restoration to fuller functioning of the bare foot (which in flexibility and sensitivity is far nearer to the hand than we usually realize) offers great rewards. Standing is the starting point of greatest potential for physical activity, from which walking, running, fighting, dancing and all sports begin and to which they return. It is the specifically human activity, which is exploited by all the less civilized peoples and by children who have not yet abandoned its uses and pleasures for the chimera of "relaxation." Easy and balanced standing, in which our inner reactiveness mobilizes precisely the energy needed to counterbalance the pull of the earth, permits a full sensing of the total organism. The student may discover that he follows mental pictures or former instruction instead of messages of his organismic needs—that he pulls himself up or makes himself broad, that he stands before an imagined mirror—and that it is not very easy for him to give it up. The length of limbs and torso upward and downward, their interconnection with the head, our width and depth, the coordination of our skeletal structure and our tissue masses—all these indications of our extent and character are there to be explored, as are those more or less subtle but ever-present signs of life in the organic functioning which our habits and responses so often impede.

Work on *balancing* is begun only when a considerable degree of inner awakeness is reached already. We have to be able to give up the use of the eyes to orient ourselves in this and entirely rely on sensing. Distinguishing what is habit (which often feels good because we are so used to it) from what are new necessities in coordination and being comes slowly. Daring to give up positions and postures is already a great step forward. We begin to notice that finest changes in weight distribution often make a world of difference in sensations of effort or ease in muscle tissues. Together with the gradual approach to the center comes a feeling of lightness, freedom and peace incomparable with any other experience. One begins to discover that one is in constant flux—nothing is static (9)—for if one wants to "keep" a moment of balance which has this exquisite quality it is lost. We realize that it has to be allowed from moment to moment anew. This calls for keenest awareness. In fact, balancing creates this kind of awareness in which one wakes up not only inside but for everything which exists and happens around one. Students comment on approaching difficult tasks much more sensibly, on feeling warmer towards others, seeing, hearing, perceiving more fully (10) and having new and deeper thoughts and ideas. "It simply happens this way," they discover with astonishment. "I don't have to try—it comes by itself!"

Lying, sitting and standing to a great extent involve coming, being and staying in touch with the floor, with the seat on which one takes a place and sits, with the surface on which one lies.

Also, the more awake one becomes inside and the more sensitive skin and breathing become, the more one becomes conscious of the air around one and of the constant interaction between the environment and oneself.

We often approach the change from sitting to standing, or from lying to standing, from the point of view of awakening to the air and to the space through which we move and of feeling what we approach or leave with our totality and not just with the immediate region of contact. This "being open" for what we do, as we sometimes call it, does not mean making a special effort such as stretching or "concentration," but just that we become awake and adjustable to the constant changes which such simple actions necessitate. This awakening may have surprising effects: "This is the first time that I became conscious of the floor under my feet!" There may be very powerful consequences: "When I left, every blade of grass reached out toward me and the earth was alive and supported me" (11).

This is particularly true in an experiment we often practice: shifting our weight while standing and sensing the process of walking very slowly backwards and forwards. Leaving the base of support and returning to it, including the space traveled in between, can be the occasion for an intense sense of connection between the whole person and what is beneath him. Simultaneously, the sense of connection extends to the whole environment, both animate and inanimate.

The Buddhist practice of meditative walking, as described in Shattuck's *An Experiment in Mindfulness* (12), shows how such very simple activities, when fully felt, can lead to the highest states of consciousness and are at the opposite pole from the "physical" exercises of calisthenics.

It must seem astonishing, in a culture in which what we call "mind" and what we call "body" are still so separate (13), that experiences which at first glance seem purely "physical" can have such far-reaching consequences in personal life. In balancing, for example, a student who found himself either not coming close enough to where balance happens or going beyond it suddenly realized that this was how he acted in life: "I either hold back or go too far. I am either not interested or too much involved." When a state of higher awakeness is reached throughout the organism, people experience, often for the first time, a true feeling of self, a vivid sense of existing. A constant rapport with daily life is fostered. After discovering contractions around the eyes and a consistent tension in the area of the inner ears and at the base of the skull, with the consequent release which such awareness makes possible, a mother reported: "This week I could be more sensitive with my children. I was not as demanding as usually." It became clear to her that her attitude to the children and the condition which she could sense inside her head were two sides of the same coin.

After work on sitting, a student stated: "For the first time I really *sat* at the dinner table, and I tasted the food so much more." After experiencing more space and freedom in his organism, a student reported: I had to rearrange my room and throw a number of things out. I need more space to move in!" Many reports from those working in the arts speak of the immense effects on their work when the capacities for the nuances of tasting and feeling are enlarged.

Experiencing becomes deeper and more differentiated by our work in perception: the attuning of our sense organs and the recovery of their innate automatic reactiveness. We work on allowing more quiet in and around the eyes, on giving up the effort in looking and on "letting come" rather than "doing," so that what comes through vision can be received not by the eyes alone but by our totality, and one can truly say: "*I* see," or "*I* hear." We allow our eyes and ears, mouth, nose, hands, feet—our whole sensitized surface, antenna-like—just to be the entrance doors through which impressions, sensations, odors, tastes and sounds enter us, there to be received, absorbed and digested by our whole self. We practice sitting quietly, with eyes closed and becoming receptive to whatever sounds may reach us (slight stirrings, voices, wind or rain, music next door, street noises, etc.) *without trying to identify and label them immediately*, but letting them freely enter us and be experienced. Quietly allowing our eyes to open, without "looking," we receive impressions: the people in the room whose presence speaks to us in many ways; objects and plants; the play of color; light and shadow; the garden downstairs and people moving through it; the city traffic. In stillness and openness, striking changes occur in our ability to perceive; our voice also is influenced; so are our movements, our being with people and all our creative activities.

People work together. One person helps the other to new discoveries. In this atmosphere of peace many more shutters can be opened. Seeing a person, one senses more of what is going on in him. The fine movements of breathing, his expression, the whole language of his body begins to speak. In this nonverbal communication, the coming more in touch without actual touching is the first fruit of growing quiet and sensitive.

Touch itself helps greatly to mobilize or soothe a person so that sensing is made easier, emotional reactiveness is increased, and inner changes can more easily come about. One student may place his hands on both sides of another student's head or around the top or back of his head, and both may sense what the presence of the hands brings about in the receiver. Or the touch is given on the other's shoulders or chest, or at the small of the back, knees, feet, the abdominal wall—anywhere. Or when one is lying or sitting, another may slowly and delicately move his limbs or his head to try out whether he can yield and let himself be moved or carried or whether he interferes by resisting or by doing the moving himself. "It's just as it is in the taxi: I always help the driver drive." Of course, so much depends on one's approach: The quality of the touch instantly influences the other. It is hard to believe, even when people have spent much of their lives thinking about sensitivity, how little they have at their disposal when it comes to practice. I remember a fine writer, in a session, suddenly raising his hands to his head and exclaiming: "I have written about this—I have never experienced it!" He was sensitive enough to have this recognition, but most people are not. Few of us are sufficiently awake to feel how far away we are from real contact and how much of what we live is just following ideas and images. Absent-mindedness, shyness, agressiveness, lingering taboos, meaningless manipulation, restlessness, all become manifest in a touch. Most people immediately want to *do something* to or for their partner, instead of just *being there* for him. No wonder there are many negative reactions. It takes time to develop the inner preparation needed for full presence in approaching or leaving another, and the sense of the creative pause in which the after-effects are allowed to take their course.

But even when the approach is sensitive, some of us shy away from such personal contact with a "stranger." I remember one student who resisted violently when another was asked to move his arm and called it an "assault on his privacy." Quiet, patient work is necessary before such needs for isolation can gradually give way to an admitting of relationship. But for those who do not hold themselves on guard or translate our attempts into "techniques" which they want to learn and employ (another means of evading the really human, intuitive connection), reactions may be unexpected and deeply moving. In a class a student said, weeping, "Nobody has ever touched me so kindly!" And another, when her partner thanked her for her help, which "felt so good," said with tears in her eyes, "How could I have known what to do?" This is the beginning of trust in oneself—a first indication that we *do* know but never have tapped these deep layers in ourselves. New avenues are slowly being opened, for when it can happen once, *it is possible* and needs now only time and occasion to happen more and more often.

There are many ways in which people work together. One which we often use to awake and refresh ourselves is *slapping*—either ourselves or one another. We may tap the head, or a small area of the chest or shoulder girdle to get more alerted in our breathing and then cease the tapping so that the reactions thus created may continue and go their way spontaneously. Tapping or slapping can be very stimulating; it can also be so boring that it puts one to sleep. It all depends on the quality of the tap. Is it mechanical? Is one's mind somewhere else while one is tapping? Is it just something one is told to do—or is one ready for it, really staying with it from moment to moment and giving what is needed? Full participation is necessary, both in receiving and in giving. Here one must tap lighter, here stronger to penetrate to the depth; here more time is needed, here more yet, now it may be already too much. How do I know? *I can sense it.* Our inner indicator is at work. The intuitive connection with the situation can more and more unfold by being cultivated. It merely requires giving the situation one's respect and care, allowing the quiet to feel out both one's own part and the other's. Each one, the "giver" and the "receiver," can be tuned in for what is needed and for what happens. Respect for life and living tissue fosters more life and refinement. The quality of the tap or slap is constantly explored; punitive associations or elements are recognized; callousness, apathy, timidity, impatience, aggressiveness—all the "character traits" may be discovered and gradually relinquished in favor of what is appropriate to the here and now. What is appropriate is immediately felt as satisfying.

Of course, what is true of slapping is true of all other contacts—of how one plays the piano, or speaks in a conversation or washes dishes. It becomes particularly clear in the classes when, for example, one student is invited to place his hand on another's forehead. Some people at first, in their unrelated and restless way, just push at the other and create disturbance. "The first set of hands felt cold and aggressive; the second soothed me and made me feel easier."

Here are two people without connection to each other. The first toucher is "cold and aggressive," but the recipient himself is one who thinks of a person as a "set of hands." Such a tendency to the disconnected and superficial only slowly gives way to a growing sense of communion. When it does give way our attitudes in daily life will change, for the quality of contact is acute in all our relationships. After such experiences a woman reported that she had become conscious of habitually interrupting her husband when he hesitated in conversation to say the word she felt he was looking for. "This time," she said, "I had the patience to wait for him. At the end of the evening he said that this was the first real conversation he had had with me in a long, long time. He thanked me, and since then our relationship has been much better."

Hand in hand with the awakening of the proprioceptive sense and the sense of touch, which, compared with seeing and hearing, have been so neglected in our upbringing—when not tabooed or, at the least, stigmatized as "indulgence" and "sensuality"—a new depth and vitality arise in all other senses. Elsa Gindler once expressed it: "It tastes, it smells, it hears, it sees, it feels through us."

In this phase of the work we turn again and again to the cultivation of inner quiet, so that in a true sense one can become *all eyes*, as one sometimes calls a heightened receptivity. "Do you see with your feet? Do you hear with your belly?" Suzuki reports the Zen master asking. These questions do not call for a mystical explanation, as so many people think; they are merely a vivid way of describing total functioning, a being there for it throughout. As long as the head is still busy, full sensory receptivity is impossible; while with increasing stillness in the head, all perception, traveling unimpeded through the organism, automatically becomes sharper and more in context. In this new stage of more awareness and permissiveness the self-directive powers of the organism reveal themselves ever clearer, and we experience on a deeper level the unexpected transformations we can undergo.

When the rigidities and muscular activities in the head that attend unnecessary effort, insistence or anxiety are gradually replaced by sensations of life-processes of weight and changes in weight distribution until one reaches a state of relative balance, simultaneous changes happen throughout the whole person. The closer we come to such a state of greater balance in the head, the quieter we become, the more our head "clears," the lighter and more potent we feel. Energy formerly *bound* is now more and more at our disposal. Pressure and hurry change into freedom for speed. We find ourselves being more one with the world where we formerly had to cross barriers. Thoughts and ideas "come" in lucidity instead of being produced. We don't have to try to express ourselves (as the word so vividly depicts), but utterances become just part of natural functioning. Experiences can be allowed to be more fully received and to mature in us. As Heinrich Jacoby once remarked: "Through becoming conscious we have been driven out of paradise, through consciousness we can come back to paradise."

REFERENCES

1. Schachtel, Ernest: *On memory and childhood amnesia.* In Mullahy, Patrick (ed.): *Part I, A Study of Interpersonal Relations.* New York, Hermitage Press, 1949.
2. Although Gindler and Jacoby assembled a great deal of material, almost none of it has been published. Most of Gindler's was destroyed

during the bombing of Berlin. At this writing, Jacoby's is being posthumously edited by Dr. Ruth Matter, Zurich.

3. Jacoby, Heinrich: *Muss es Unmusikalische geben?* Zurich, 1925. Obtainable from Dr. Ruth Matter, Toblerstrasse 94, Zurich.
4. Goldstein, Kurt: *The Organism.* New York, American Book Co., 1939.
5. Suzuki, D. T.: *Zen Buddhism.* New York, Doubleday, 1956.
6. Selver, Charlotte: Sensory awareness and total functioning. *Gen. Semantics Bull.* pp. 21-22, 1957.
7. Selver, Charlotte, *op. cit.*, p. 10.
8. Schilder, Paul: *The Image and Appearance of the Human Body.* New York, International Universities Press, 1950.
9. *Cf.* Watts, Alan: *The Wisdom of Insecurity.* New York, Pantheon, 1951.
10. Compare also Fromm, Erich: *The Art of Loving.* New York, Harper, 1956.
11. Experiences like this, which are not uncommon in the work and which may lead to basic reorientations of the individual, may be compared with the satori of Zen Buddhism and with the frequently reported "religious" or "cosmic" experiences induced by LSD.
12. Shattuck, E. H.: *An Experiment in Mindfulness.* New York, Dutton, 1960.
13. *Cf.* Whyte, L. L.: *The Next Development in Man.* New York, Mentor, 1950.

Chapter 33

RECENT PROGRAMS IN BUSINESS AND GOVERNMENT DESIGNED TO DEVELOP HUMAN POTENTIALITIES

ROBERT T. GOLEMBIEWSKI

LARGE-SCALE organizations exist to increase man's mastery over his environment, but this goal has a breathtaking price-tag. From one point of view, large-scale organizations require that man become more the master of himself, of the capabilities that he possesses and of those that he can come to develop and enlarge. This is a task difficult enough, but the nature of large organizations complicates it severely. Large organizations imply acute problems in all of these crucial areas: identifying capabilities that individuals possess; training individuals to exploit and to expand their capabilities; allowing individuals to use their "old" and newly augmented capabilities; and determining the degree to which individuals do in fact utilize their capabilities. Inferior efforts can be hidden in the labyrinthine recesses of large organizations, and capabilities that exist in untapped abundance can be overlooked.

Both business and government organizations increasingly accept the challenge of developing human capabilities. The mood of acceptance does vary over this wide range: occasional joy over the promise of a new freedom for organization man; a common grim realization that there is no reasonable alternative; and frequent idealism-realism that what often is practically unavoidable also ought to be done on ethical grounds alone. The intensity of acceptance also varies widely. But, on the whole, both business and public organizations are increasingly acting in terms of that "imaginative policy" recommended by the Rockefeller Report on Education: To identify talented people of all ages in organizations and to institute an ongoing program to rescue able people "from situations which stifle individual potentialities." That Report concluded: "Such talent development should become a settled policy of every organization. Every corporation, union, government agency, military service and professional group should—in its own best interest as well as that of its personnel—conduct a never-ending search for talent within its own staff" (1).

THREE SPECTRA IN DEVELOPING HUMAN CAPABILITIES: DIVERSE PROGRAMS; VARYING DEPTHS; AND DIFFERENTIAL COMMITMENTS

The enormity of the problem of developing human capabilities in organizations is matched by the kaleidoscopic diversity of programs, of levels of capabilities which programs attempt to tap and of commitments to them. Thus, an IBM can spend scores of millions of dollars yearly on development programs for many purposes at all levels, and other firms can remain more or less blissfully unconcerned. And high-ranking military men can average some 15 per cent of their working lives in one kind of training or another, while some government agencies spend far less on training than that modest percentage of budget authorized by 1958 legislation. Moreover, some programs develop only "surface" capabilities; others provide intense technical or mathematical instruction, while still others are behaviorally oriented and seek "a deeper self" which can be got at only by digging "through surface layers."

Since there is no easy cataloguing of programs for developing human capabilities in organizations, attention below will be selective. That attention will be basically dual: on approaches to developing human capabilities that are established and burgeoning; and on approaches to developing human capabilities that are more or less "gleams in the eyes" of many students of organizational phenomena. The former category includes: executive development; the stress on "creativity"; and sensitivity training. The latter focus of attention includes a variety of efforts aimed at fundamentally reorganizing work in ways that will at once require more of man while they permit man to self-actualize. This latter focus encompasses such existing programs as job enlargement and decentralization, and it implies nothing less than a revolution in ways of thinking about organized effort.

Although such distinctions are only conveniences, they usefully illustrate the fullness of the underlying range of programs. Thus, executive development can be taken to represent a macro-program approach to developing broad capabilities for general roles. In the same terms, creativity training illustrates the variety of programs which have a micro-focus and are basically intrapersonal; and sensitivity training illustrates a micro-program that takes an interpersonal approach to extending human capabilities. These illustrations merely suggest the fullness of the range of existing programs; and, as will become manifest, they are not watertight categories.

There is a unity underlying the diversity of programs in business and government agencies designed to develop human capabilities, however. Thus, few would argue with the general position of the Committee for Economic Development that the effort encompasses nothing less than that "complex process of accumulating the skills, attitudes, knowledge, and experience essential to produce performance of the highest order" (2). More specifically, although disagreement does exist about whose formulation best reflects the underlying unity, the general core of agreement has it that structural forms and managerial techniques usually considered as "axiomatically good" differ radically from those that are "normatively good" and often differ from those arrangements and techniques that are "practically good" (3). Or, to put it otherwise, traditional notions about organizing generate arrangements of men at work and techniques for monitoring their work that often are ill designed to achieve high output, let alone to achieve a broad range of other valued ends such as maximizing the probability of the mental health of organization members. Specifically, maximizing this latter probability would require organizations structured in such ways that members would be more likely to (4):

1. Experience the wholeness of the organization;
2. Act because of self-motivation and within the limits of self-responsibility;
3. Aspire to excellence in problem solving;
4. Strive to decrease compulsive and defensive behavior, while increasing the degree to which organization members can

control their own environment;

5. Utilize a wide range of abilities, particularly of cognitive and interpersonal kinds; and
6. Increase their time perspective.

As perceptive students have subtly shown, traditional notions about organizing tend to decrease such probabilities. The effect is particularly marked at lower organizational levels (5), but it is felt everywhere.

The Emphasis on Executive Development: General Managerial Macro-Programs

Considerable attention has recently been lavished on developing the human capabilities of executives. This is no mere evidence of an elite serving its own interests, however. Indeed the most massive training program of the kind dealt with lower-level supervisors during World War II, and firms such as Mobil Oil Company and states such as Illinois have exerted substantial training efforts at lower levels. But firms and government agencies increasingly have felt pressures for developing their executives and upper-middle management. The vogue of executive development programs has various motivations, but major among them is the desire to "broaden the perspective" of individuals who are (or soon may be) exercising policy initiative. For traditional patterns of organizing work are such that an individual's early organizational roles are likely to be those of the "narrow specialist" rather than of the "integrative manager" who must develop a balanced program of the often-conflicting demands of several specialties. Organization reality at higher levels ill suits this bias of early organizational experiences. The details are beyond the scope of this piece, but patterns of growth in many industries and in virtually all governments have been such within the last few decades that "managerial qualities" are increasingly necessary in today's enterprises and often at relatively modest levels of organization (6).

The various approaches to executive development have genetic similarities, as it were, in that they have come late, they have come strong, and they show promise of far greater growth. For example, the first such program given by a major educational institution took place at MIT in the 1930's. Today at least thirty-five major educational institutions count organizations for executive development among their extramural services to business and government. In 1963 these thirty-five centers processed something less than four thousand executives. And at least one dean of one major school sees executive development as *the* single most important function of the schools of business and public administration in the 1980's (7). In addition, several thousand individual consultants and consulting firms provide similar services outside of educational contexts. Many, many companies also field their own "house" programs and provide some of their own staff "training officers" for manning them, as does Mobil Oil Company for both its senior and junior managerial personnel. A host of trade associations and professional groups do their part in similar efforts, further, as in the massive programs of the American Management Association.

The trend toward executive development in government agencies started later but has been no less bullish. Over the last decade or so a number of appropriate institutions for fielding such programs have developed; and more are in sight at federal, state, and local levels. The University of Wisconsin's respected Summer Institute in Executive Development for Federal Administrators sets the pace for programs outside of existing agencies; the Internal Revenue Service fields an extensive set of within-agency programs. Literally hundreds of agency-sponsored programs also exist, the most ambitious being in the military agencies. More recently the U. S. Civil Service Commission has embarked upon an executive development program that probably will involve setting up several regional training centers in addition to the existing facility at King's Point, New York. The size of this mission is suggested by two data. Thus there are over 100,000 employees of the federal government classified at or above GS-13 or its equivalent (8). These officers comprise the upper-middle management of the federal service, and projections call for increasingly more of them. Moreover, the eventual goal at the federal level is to have executives spend some 10 per cent of their work-life in training, a figure which most agencies do not begin to approach at present.

Further, approaches to executive development tend to be alike in their common emphasis upon "simulation," and recent developments promise exciting breakthroughs in executive training. Simulation, broadly defined here, refers to the induction and analysis of real-life analogues for training purposes. The goal is a degree of realism sufficient to motivate and engage learning processes but which also admits analysis often impossible in the "real world." Early simulations used "human relations cases" or "policy cases" to provide concrete (and usually simplified) situations for analysis. Of late, far more sophisticated simulations have been employed. Some create organizational analogues or communication systems within which action occurs and is analyzed; other simulations employ the power of computers to provide quasi-realistic and changing conditions of a firm's operations, etc. Such new tools promise intense and profitable training experiences in appropriate areas.

Executive development programs are also alike in their diversity. The content of programs is widely variable; the art of developing and giving them is unevenly developed, and much remains to be learned about which executives will profit most from which programs at what specific points in their careers. For example, at the extremes, programs might be organized around: general managerial processes, such as motivating, communicating and so on; and specific organization functions, such as personnel or production or the like or specific and narrow managerial problem-situations. Similarly, the base-content can vary from introductions to esoteric mathematics through the more conventional human relations materials.

Justice permits no blanket evaluation of this diversity-within-similarity. Suffice it to note four points. First, much remains unknown, but the need for developing the capabilities of executives is so great that this datum is lilliputian in comparison. Second, only the surface has been scratched by existing efforts. Third, a considerable body of research and experience has been accumulated, a degree of professionalization has been achieved, and various regularized organs for sharing knowledge in this area have been developed. Fourth, we are witnessing the evolution of a corps of trained executive development administrators who will be increasingly significant actors in contemporary organizations. The recognition of the executive development function in high corporate offices testifies to this fact, as does the recent recommendation of the CED that a similar recognition be accorded the function in the several major federal agencies and in the President's immediate staff (9).

Creativity as a Learnable Capability: An Intrapersonal Micro-Program

It may seem ironic that the country which prides itself on its common sense also has been most active in attempting to teach uncommon ways of making sense. The formal history of the effort is brief. Indeed, the movement to "teach creativity" traces many of its modern roots to Alex F. Osborn's *Applied Imagination* (10), and Osborn is a contemporary. But there is no gainsaying the importance of the field envisioned for improvement, usually by zealous missionaries of the new gospel. "Creativity" may be defined broadly for our purposes as the organization of existing knowledge in new ways that yield novel results.

The stress on creativity as a learnable (or improvable) capability proved attractive. Industry was quick to see its implications, although government agencies have reacted much more slowly. Thus, leading creativity programs may be found in such organizations: General Electric; Ford Motor Company; Corning Glass; and the AC Spark Plug Division of General Motors. Nor is the approach some businessman's fad. For example, a number of universities—including the range from established Harvard to relative latecomer Buffalo—have developed creativity programs of one kind or another; substantial scholarly research has been accumulated on various aspects of the topic (11), although much of the literature has an evangelistic and inspirational tone; and some of the work on creativity implies a revolution of techniques and approaches in a field as wide as that of all education (12).

Basically, creativity programs have as their objective the elimination of barriers to problem solving that do not inhere in the problem. The nonproblem barriers to problem solving may be found in: the techniques utilized; the person utilizing them; or the environment in which the application takes place. All creativity programs stress the first barrier, and many deal more or less directly with the second and third.

Creativity programs do not run to a common mold, but distinguishing two basic varieties helps illustrate the ways in which the several barriers to problem solving are hurdled. Thus, one variety of program basically serves to increase the capacity for insightful grappling with problem situations by substantial doses of suitable conceptual materials and by extended opportunities to put the conceptual tools into operation in more or less narrow areas of interest. General Electric's "Creative Courses" illustrate the genre (13). They extend over two full years, the first of which deals basically with the conception of ideas and the second with the reduction of these ideas to practice. Appropriate texts have been developed for both emphases, which implies the permanency of the effort. Moreover, the courses are taken seriously; formal classes are held four hours each week, on company time, and an estimated average of twenty hours per week is spent on homework. Various prestigeful audiences to whom the trainees report their results serve to heighten the motivation.

General Electric's Creativity Courses heavily emphasize techniques and specific applications, but they also attempt to minimize personal and organizational barriers to problem solving. For example, the courses reflect in several ways the training liabilities endemic in large, specialized organizations. Basically, the GE trainee actually performs—or oversees the performance of—the full range of activities from conceiving a project, through development, on to economy costing of one or more designs. This experience directly exposes a few—and they are a very few—trainees to a range of considerations and specialties that are normally organized out of the operating area of younger organization members. The point of the program is to give trainees a fullness of experience without waiting on the fullness of years.

A second, less comprehensive, variety of creativity program stresses technique to the virtual exclusion of organizationally relevant applications. The specifics differ widely, but the "principle of deferred judgment" is usually fundamental. That is, the various sets of techniques or procedures argue that ideation and the evaluation of ideas are separate phases of problem solving.

Hence, techniques—like deferred judgment—attempt to free ideation from evaluation; and proponents argue essentially and sometimes explicitly that "quantity breeds quality" and stress the loss of "good ideas" due to premature closure or exclusion of apparently unusual ideas. Rigidities in large organizations often are faulted as causing premature cloture, as (for example) in pleasing a superior by developing an idea that is acceptable to him rather than seeking ideas of all varieties. The gospel of proponents may be popularized as: There is no best way to do a job; there are only better ways. "Group brainstorming" is the variant of this approach which has received the most popular attention (and criticism), but the techniques are applicable to individual ideation and/or evalution (14).

The claims and counter-claims in this area urge caution. At base, however, the results indicate that there are learnable or improvable component skills in creative problem solving, and some of the techniques which sharpen such skills have been isolated and can be transmitted. Practice also shows that even valuable insights can be perverted, as in some applications of "group brainstorming" that abort in avoiding responsibility for stupid ideas rather than in developing creative ones, but this is hardly novel. Finally, the cultivation of creativity certainly has been neglected in our several institutions for training, if, indeed, they do not discourage creative effort.

Sensitivity as a Learnable Capability: An Interpersonal Micro-Program

Like creativity training, sensitivity training stresses the understanding and elimination of nonproblem barriers to problem solving. And adherents of both types of training do constitute a movement in the classical sense. Beyond these points the similarities become increasingly attenuated. Thus, if nothing else, sensitivity training is a bigger movement. More relevantly, sensitivity training rests on a very substantial theoretical base of techniques and concepts that constitute some of the major products of behavioral research of the past few decades. Further, the focus in sensitivity training is on interpersonal barriers in self and others to problem solving or simply to living. The guiding notions include trust, feedback, awareness of feelings and helping relations. Basically, a relatively unstructured environment becomes the laboratory within which members of a T (for training) Group develop their own data, analyze them and experiment with new patterns of interaction (15). Sensitivity training is not therapy as conventionally understood, then; and it defines its clientele as those without incapacitating emotional difficulties.

Sensitivity training *qua* movement is a relatively new approach to increasing human capabilities, but it has its legions of advocates. The movement has an immediate history going back only to the late 1940's, but it is an object of interest in many areas (including productive organizations). The 1964 brochure of the National Training Laboratories—which is the major institutional embodiment of the movement—reveals some interesting dimensions: It indicates the nineteen major laboratory programs were scheduled for summer-fall in five locations across the country; it acknowledges cooperative relations with a number of regional training associations; and it lists some 160 member-trainers, while announcing that various intern programs for would-be trainers also are in operation. Although NTL is the orthodox association in sensitivity training, its "network" includes but a small fraction of the individuals involved in sensitivity training, and its programs process but a small fraction of the participants. Many thousands of persons have a "laboratory experience" each year, and not a small percentage return for advanced exposures. These participants include many individuals having substantial responsibilities in business and public organizations, and they often attend "house" programs staffed by outside consultants for particular firms or agencies. Increasingly, many firms are coming to have what amounts to trainers-in-residence, as in units concerned with training which are relatively common in both business and government. More generally, T Group participants tend to be "elite groups" of various descriptions, such as leaders of student government in college populations. Any estimate of the impact of sensitivity training must take this datum seriously.

The relevance of the "laboratory experience" to life in organizations has been stressed of late (16), and policymakers in many organizations have been predisposed to assess its value fully. Again, much of the effort is directed at dealing with some common consequences of traditional thought about organizing work. For example, usual formulations deal with feelings by exclusion, in the main.

Sensitivity training helps develop the subtle relations of cognition and emotion in a living situation and often highlights the penalties of an undue emphasis upon either "knowing" or "feeling." Business concerns again have been the leaders in exploiting this new avenue to enhanced capabilities of their employees, but public agencies such as the Port of New York Authority and the Internal Revenue Service have supported laboratory training as a part of their total training effort.

Sensitivity training has found a place in the battery of programs to improve human capabilities in organizations, even though there are dissenting voices (17). At best, the T Group helps expose the participant to a range of experience that he often neglected; it further sensitizes him to those influences that he perceived in diluted ways, and the experience often encourages the modification of behavior patterns that are seen by the participant as nonfunctional for him in his T Group experience. Critics give sensitivity training much more the worst of it and particularly on the issues of the misuse by clientele of laboratory training as a substitute for therapy and of the improbability of behavioral change under conditions of the normal two-week exposure. At least many of the major difficulties stressed by the critics relate to badly run laboratory programs fielded by inexperienced staff. A very minor residuum is due to lack of knowledge in crucial areas, particularly in the matter of who should be admitted to sensitivity training. Well-run laboratory programs include staff with capabilities for coping with any gross errors in admission. It is fair to note, in the critics' defense, that it is not yet altogether clear what are the full ranges of either the usefulness or the dangers of sensitivity training. As a "deeper technique" than creativity training—albeit less "deep" than the various clinical therapies—one can reasonably expect that both ranges are relatively extensive.

STRUCTURAL CHANGE AS A CATALYST FOR DEVELOPING AND REINFORCING CAPABILITIES

A growing opinion maintains that any programs for developing human capabilities in organizations, however locally successful, will remain mere palliatives in the absence of the fundamental rethinking of ways of organizing work. For example, an individual who returns from a trusting T Group to a paranoid and hostile work environment may not be able to act safely on whatever learnings he has accumulated. Indeed, he may only be frustrated by his inability to do so. It is an improvement (for example) to encourage "family groups" who work together to have their laboratory experiences together, but this is no substitute for basic structural change at the work site.

The full argument for developing the inappropriateness of orthodox structural relations and managerial techniques for developing human capabilities cannot be developed here. Fortunately, the job has been done elsewhere, both in the global sense (18) and in terms of the impact of orthodox arrangements on micro-topics such as creativity (19). For illustrative purposes here notice only that orthodox jobs are organized around routinized tasks and that narrow functions or processes are prescribed as the bases for departmentation at high and low levels, respectively. The major practical consequence is that delegation must be severely hedged. Consequently, the integration of the several particularistic operations must take place at relatively high organization levels. Lower-level supervisors, in turn, will be under pressure to produce while they lack control over the immediate work environment. The all-too-probable supervisory adaptations include a directive style and a punitive atmosphere. Under general—but hardly universal—conditions, these adaptations are likely to be associated with low output and low satisfaction of operatives (20). Moreover, operatives will be rewarded for performing a narrow job. Resistance to change and lack of motivation to develop broader abilities are probable outcomes. As a further consequence, supervisory jobs at many levels will lack training opportunities at work. Even ambitious programs for developing human capabilities are likely to have spotty success in the face of such dismal probabilities. The consequences are similar in business and government organizations (21).

A variety of programs have been developed to avoid these probabilities (22). For example, enlargement of the jobs of both operatives and supervisors has been resorted to in many cases. Such changes permit greater delegation further down the organizational hierarchy, increase supervisory control of the work environment and permit supervision in terms of meaningful measures of performance on a managerially relevant set of operations rather than on particularistic functions or processes (23). At higher levels of organization, decentralizing around independent profit centers has been employed in order to moderate the problems of measurement and motivation inherent in traditional approaches to organizing. The consequences have proven happy, on balance (24).

Such outcomes do not flow freely, of course. They are paid for (in part) by greater training of operatives and supervisors. The increased possibilities for delegation to lower levels, that is, at once encourage, require and depend upon the development of human capabilities. Appropriate structural changes can help develop and reinforce human learning and probably are necessary to make best use of whatever training programs are employed.

These unorthodox structural arrangements are not universally applicable, nor are their effects universally favorable (25). If existing research does make these arrangements seem a good bet, we still lack explicit demonstrations that (for example) creative problem solving in organizations is more likely where the unorthodox structural arrangements are approached. And we certainly lack detailed knowledge of the specific conditions under which specific consequences are probable. These jobs remain to be done, basically, although we have available a volume of descriptive and experimental research which permits some optimism that the jobs can be done without changing the broad outlines of what is presently known.

DENOUEMENT

There are, in sum, a wide variety of programs in business and government designed to develop human capabilities. It is trite to note that much more could be done, for that is almost always the case in matters human. Perhaps more relevant, more and more is being done. This datum permits some optimism that organizations need not thrive upon, nor help create, the kind of developmentally crippled persons so often cited as the products of our organizational society. At one stage of our economic development, deep pessimism was perhaps as applicable a generalization as any. Increasingly, however, organizations cannot afford the awful convenience of stunted capabilities. Increasingly, organizations will grow as their employees do and, perhaps for the first time in history, this generalization applies with some force at both high organizational levels and low.

REFERENCES

1. Rockefeller report of education: *The Pursuit of Excellence.* New York, Doubleday, 1958, p. 1.
2. Committee for economic development: *Improving Executive Management in the Federal Government* (July), 1964, p. 35.
3. Golembiewski, R. T.: *Men, Management, and Morality.* McGraw-Hill, 1965.
4. Argyris, C.: The integration of the individual and the organization. In Strother, G. W. (ed): *Social Science Approaches to Business Behavior.* Homewood, Irwin-Dorsey, 1962, p. 76.
5. Argyris, C.: *Personality and Organization.* New York, Harper, 1957.
6. Chandler, A. D., Jr.: *Strategy and Structure.* Cambridge, MIT Press, 1962, esp. pp. 19-51.
7. Sheriff, D. R., and West, J. P.: University sponsored executive development programs. *The Pers. Administrator,* 9:1, 1964.
8. CED, *op. cit.,* p. 67.
9. *Ibid.,* p. 26-27.
10. Osborn, A. F.: *Applied Imagination,* rev. ed. New York, Scribner's, 1957.
11. Parnes, S. J., and Harding, H. F.: *A Source Book for Creative Thinking.* New York, Scribner's, 1962, pp. 345-371.
12. Getzels, J. W., and Jackson, P. W.: *Creativity and Intelligence.* New York, Wiley, 1962.
13. Samstad, G. I.: General Electric's creativity courses. In Parnes and Harding, *op. cit.,* pp. 333-389.
14. Parnes, S. J.: Do you really understand brainstorming? In Parnes and Harding, *op. cit.,* pp. 283-290.
15. Bradford, L. P., Gibb, J. R., and Benne, K. D.: *T-Group Theory and Laboratory Method.* New York, Wiley, 1964.

16. ARGYRIS, C.: *Interpersonal Competence and Organizational Effectiveness.* Homewood, Irwin-Dorsey, 1962.
17. A number of common charges against the laboratory method are raised and discussed by C. Argyris: T-groups for organizational effectiveness. *Harvard Bus. Rev., 42*:68-70, 1964.
18. ARGYRIS: *Personality and Organization.*
19. GOLEMBIEWSKI, R. T.: Innovation and organization structure. *Pers. Adm., 27*:3-5, 17-21 ,1964.
20. LIKERT, R.: *New Patterns of Management.* New York, McGraw-Hill, 1961.
21. GOLEMBIEWSKI, R. T.: Civil service and managing work. *Amer. Pol. Sci. Rev., 56*:961-973, 1962.
22. This analysis neglects programs like the Scanlon Plan which—although they stop short of structural redesign of work—do significantly alter patterns of employee-management relations via the motivation of a cost-saving plan.
23. WORTHY, J. C.: *Big Business and Free Men.* New York, Harper, 1959, esp. pp. 90-99.
24. CHANDLER, *op. cit.* Problems do remain, of course. See WHINSTON, A.: Price guides in decentralized organizations. In COOPER, W. W., LEAVITT, H. J., and SHELLY, M. W., II (eds.): *New Perspectives in Organization Research.* New York, Wiley, 1964, pp. 405-448.
25. A large number of "boundary conditions" for successful applications are detailed in Golembiewski: *Men, Management, and Morality.*

Chapter 34

MOTIVATION OF POTENTIALITIES OBSERVED IN HYPNOTICALLY HALLUCINATED UNCONSCIOUS BODY IMAGES

FREDERICKA F. FREYTAG

THREE years ago at Colgate University at a symposium fathered by Dr. George H. Estabrooks, Aldous Huxley presented an address entitled "Human Potentialities." The central theme of this presentation he expressed in the question: What can we do in order to help individuals to actualize a greater number of their desirable potentialities? He quotes Ophelia: "We know what we are, but we know not what we may be" and continues with the profound observation: "We certainly don't know what our potentialities, both for good and for evil, may be." He concludes that the "problem must be attacked on many fronts: chemical, psychological, social, sexual, linguistic, etc., and that we need to educate ourselves and our children in such a way that we and they shall be able to realize more of our potentialities for intelligence, for love and compassion, for creativity and for enjoyment."

The purpose of this presentation is to demonstrate one approach to the motivation of potentialities. For the benefit of those who are not familiar with the hypnotic modality employed in this approach I wish to offer a brief description of the technique used.

It is generally well known to psychiatrists as well as to psychologists that the projective personality tests enable the examiner to deduce and to describe the unconscious self or the unconscious body image of the subject. The deductions made on the basis of these findings are valuable to the therapist but are meaningless to the subject, even though the subject is able to comprehend them intellectually. It has been learned, however, that in the hypnotic state, a subject is able to visually hallucinate the unconscious body image of the self and that, *in the unconscious mind, there exists a multiplicity of body images which are in a constant state of flux in response to changes in the perceptive state.* These hallucinated unconscious body images are symbolic representations of unconscious wishes, urges, strivings, impulses and emotional conflicts present in the unconscious mind. In the visual hallucination of the unconscious body images the subject uses ideo-sensory and ideo-motor experiences through which he objectifies his emotional state. As an example, excessive unconscious hostility may be symbolically represented by a wild animal with large claws or huge protruding teeth, by an image of a snake with protruding tongue or by an image of the devil or by certain changes in the human figure, such as exceedingly broad shoulders, large clenched fists, an excessively muscular figure, etc.

As the subject describes what he sees and *Feels*, and as he associates to the hallucinated body image, he makes his own interpretations, obtains feeling insights, new understandings, new ideas and new feelings. He notes that with every significant feeling, insight changes take place in the appearance of the body image, which he again interprets. He learns the needs underlying the motivation of his behavior, and he becomes more aware of his potentialities.

At the termination of the hallucinatory experience, thoughts, associations and feelings verbalized by the subject during the hallucinatory experience are discussed on a conscious level. The subject is also asked to draw the hallucinated unconscious body images as soon as possible after leaving the office. As well as possible he is to draw only what he sees to the best of his ability. He is never to try to make a good drawing. The subject is further requested to study each drawing carefully and to write out all the associations and feelings he recalls from his trance experience as well as any additional associations and feelings he may have experienced while making and studying the drawings. Thus, the constructive effects of the hallucinatory experience usually become markedly enhanced.

While the material presented in this paper is clinical and deals with personality disturbances and neurotic behavior, *it serves as an example of how the objectification of the unconscious body image may be equally effective in those who are relatively normal by enhancing the awareness of the self and its potentialities.*

CASE I

The patient was a woman who entered into psychotherapy because of obsessional thinking and compulsive behavior which reached pathological intensity after the death of her father. She was obsessed by the thought that she was somehow responsible for her father's death, and several years later felt responsible for her mother's death. During her entire life she felt excessively responsible for the sorrows, the disappointments or the traumatic events in her family as well as for all and sundry with whom she was in contact. Her compulsive behavior was an unconscious attempt to compensate for the past and to avert future disaster to others as well as to herself.

In her many hallucinatory experiences in which she objectified her unconscious body image, the body image never had any feet; and this body image was always in a location from which it was imperative that she escape. As she became able to correlate the feelings in the body image with her own emotional pathology, the body image gradually developed feet and one day was able to walk down from the top of the mountain (the perfectionistic goal) on which she saw herself, into the valley where all was calm and pleasant. True, she had to hold on to bushes, rocks and trees in her descent. (These represented her compulsive attitudes and defenses.) The feet developed in the body image during her descent though she did not know exactly when this happened.

In one of the most clinically significant hallucinatory experiences she saw her unconscious body image wrapped in a cocoon (Fig. 1) (Note the absence of feet). She struggled to extricate herself, and following are a few of her comments in reference to Figure 1, "I feel wrapped up tight—my hands were at my sides feeling for freedom. I feel tall and straight like a stick. I feel taut, like I feel when I am afraid or scared, just like when I am afraid I have caused or may cause some suffering to others. I want to move my hands and run—run for freedom away from myself or my fears—but it does no good to run—I must face life—face reality—so I fight and start rationalizing—did I do that, or am I to blame for this—or could I have caused that or such—someone's death—am I or am I not just wavering back and forth—could I or could I not—did I or did I not do it—feeling so responsible and more and more guilty—and still waving my hands and trying to find a way out. I'm just looking in front of me—thinking just to get out—not knowing I could back out or look around and maybe there would be other means to help myself—because there isn't any reason for me to be in the cocoon or jail—I only put myself in that position—no one else is around to see or criticize or blame me—just myself. Now I look in back of me (Fig. 2) and feel not so straight (not so rigid)—but I am getting more rounded—I have rounded hips and rounded buttocks—I feel more in proportion and feel I can move around with freedom—the cocoon was bigger than I thought, and the walls were not so close—there is no cocoon in the back and there is a round, big opening (notice the development of feet) where I can feel free to move around and go—no one can look at me, no one can stop me or keep me in the jail. There is a courtyard which goes out to the road and the road goes out to the living—to humanity—to persons—to life. I am free, I don't feel like a stick, rigid and taut or guilty; I feel good, free to go and come like others—the cocoon seems far away and I can hardly see it. I feel like a human being."

With every hallucinatory experience this patient became more and more aware that she possessed the potential for recovery and reported corresponding clinical progress.

CASE II

In the phobic individual the need to avoid harm, the dependency need, is so intense that other motivational needs are overshadowed; and it becomes extremely difficult for them to recognize their potentialities for the mastery of fear.

Among the numerous phobic situations identified by this forty-year-old woman (married and the mother of two children) that of driving the car loomed largest; not so much actually driving the car as preparation for driving from home, taking a bath, dressing, etc. The real fear was the fear of leaving the home, which represented to her the area of maximum security.

She related the following hallucinatory experience, "I see two of me—we are in the bathroom bathing—the one is going away, singing and happy—she is dressing now—the other asks where are you going and do you really want to go—are you not afraid to go—the happy me says 'no—why should I be?'—I am like two people—the one gay and happy, the other dark and like a doubting Thomas—the singing, happy woman wants to go and has no doubt of her ability to drive alone, and now she is making fun of the doubting one—there is no question about the happy one going—she told the doubting one she was going; and if she (the doubting one) wanted to stay home and be gloomy, all right—the happy one got into the car and drove away—she just backed the car out and went—that is me—I am in the heart of the city all alone

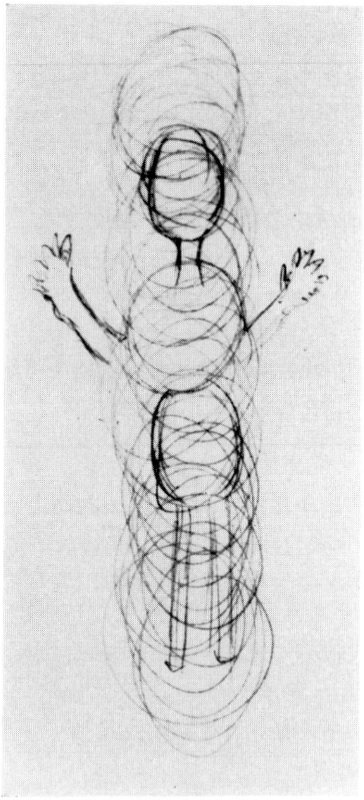

Figure 1

Figure 2

in the car, and I am not two people anymore—I am one person.

Hallucinatory experiences such as this allow constructive motivational needs to bring into the individual's awareness his abilities and potentialities. We see illustrated in this experience the need for ego integration and the identification of the self.

CASE III

Mr. R. M. is a twenty-four-year-old married male, the father of one child, and sought psychiatric help because he has always had "academic difficulties." He failed at one university and was on the brink of failure at another college. He stated that he is lacking in energy, has no initiative, is unable to remember what he studies and is also unable to concentrate.

This type of complaint is encountered only too frequently in students at all levels of school attendance but becomes more incapacitating at the high school and college level.

The psychometric evaluation revealed that he functioned at a bright average level with a mental endowment adequate for college work. The projective test data revealed "a tremendous sense of inferiority and that he views other people as strong and overpowering as well as hostile and brutal. He tends to overintellectualize and is inclined to be pedantic as a defense against his feelings of inferiority. As a result he habitually overlooks the relevant and important facets in a situation and becomes involved with the unimportant and nonessential. Thus, he creates the impression of brilliance and is spared the threat of defeat in dealing with the real issues in the situation. He cannot commit himself to a course of action, as he is convinced he will fail. To fail when you try is ever so much more devastating to the ego than to fail when you do not really try or make a commitment. When confronted by emotional stress and the necessity to make a commitment and take a risk as to the outcome of his behavior, the patient becomes immobile and assumes a pattern of avoidance, rationalization and denial. In his effort to overcome feelings of inferiority he sets up high goals and standards of achievement and when these are not reached, he rationalizes by saying, 'I am unable to concentrate and stick to things. If I could, I would succeed.' Thus he is spared the responsibility for his failure."

Figures 3 and 4 are the Draw-A-Person figures of a man and a woman made in the projective personality tests. The male figure represents the patient's idealized self and the high goals and standards of achievement which he had set up for himself. When asked to see his unconscious body image in reference to his unconscious self-evaluation, he sees numerous images such as the upper part of the body seen in Figure 5, and a body without arms or legs as seen in Figure 6. From unconscious body images such as these he brought into his awareness the lack of feelings of inner worth, his feelings of inadequacy and inferiority and his inability to approve of and love himself. When he was told that his unconscious mind would present experiences which would enable him to build up feelings of inner worth and resolve feelings of inadequacy, he participated in a feeling way in many ex-

Figure 3

periences, one of which may be seen in Figure 7, in which he is performing adequately in a baseball game.

Some of his comments following these experiences are very interesting. "The past several weeks have been rather meaningful weeks. I make mention of a two-week period separately because each week seemed different in many respects. The first week my mind was very rapidly organizing and planning. This was not only obvious to me; but it was also obvious to my wife. In the morning I would rise, organize and perform. I caught myself consolidating time and effort in performing the daily tasks of life. When I read or studied, I was better organized, for I read and studied looking for the main ideas; note taking was more

Figure 4

analytic and less wordy." Here we note that he was looking for the relevant and important facets in a situation and becoming less involved with the nonessential material; he was becoming less pedantic.

Continuing with the patient's comments, "The second week I saw how my feelings of inferiority were being projected onto the job and onto my wife, and I was determined to guard against this and not accept my projected interpretations. From these experiences I learned to do some concrete planning and to narrow the scope of my activities, labeling in my mind those things which are important, necessary and vital, and those ambitions that can be done away with because I no longer have a need for them."

Anxiety always accompanies a lack of adequate unconscious self-evaluation. Experiences designed to allay anxiety were objectified in many unconscious body images such as that seen in Figure 8. The patient comments, "The picture of me lying on the bed is a meaningful representation of me in a deep state of anxiety. I have experienced these same identical feelings this week, and I have dealt with them much more effectively. As I lie here across the bed, my mind is being bombarded by two or more stimuli both demanding my immediate attention. Somehow I find myself unable to respond to either of the stimuli; so I respond to a third, that of masturbation, which helps to ease the pangs of anxiety and lead me to a relaxing sleep. But afterwards

Figure 5

Figure 6

Figure 7

I have feelings of depression, guilt and listlessness or lethargy." The patient then continues a lengthy dissertation on how this type of experience had been operative in his past life and in his pathology. He then concludes, "As I lie here, I feel moved to get up and to study my textbook, for I'm feeling frustrated because I'm already behind with my reading and assignments. I get up and begin to dress."

Figure 9 reveals one of the long series of conflicts in which he was trying to experience feelings of inner worth. Unfortunately space does not permit the patient's comments, but I quote from a letter he received from the dean of the college at this time: "You will recall that you were on academic probation—I am pleased to tell you that as a result of your grades for the past semester, and by recommendation of the Scholastic Standards Committee, you have been released from academic probation. The past semester has seen considerable improvement in your academic work; it is my hope that these improved skills and disciplines will form the foundation for still higher academic achievement in the future." As he gained in unconscious self-esteem, his anxiety decreased; and he was able to increase his learning ability.

That this man had deep emotional conflicts will be apparent to all. The inability to identify the self may clearly be seen in such unconscious body images as Figure 10. Figure 11, which is one of many unconscious body images, both clothed and nude, seen only from the waist up, was always associated with sexual conflicts referable to his voyeuristic drives and voyeuristic behavior and latent homosexuality. Figure 12 is one of the unconscious body images in which he resolved the latent homosexuality.

As the patient began to understand the needs and to feel the needs motivating his pathologic behavior, he became able to recognize his potentialities for integrating the ego and actualizing his potentialities.

CASE IV

Shirley is a seventeen-year-old girl who sought psychiatric help because she felt unable to attend school any longer. She was in her senior year, and it was only ten weeks until graduation.

Figure 8

Figure 9

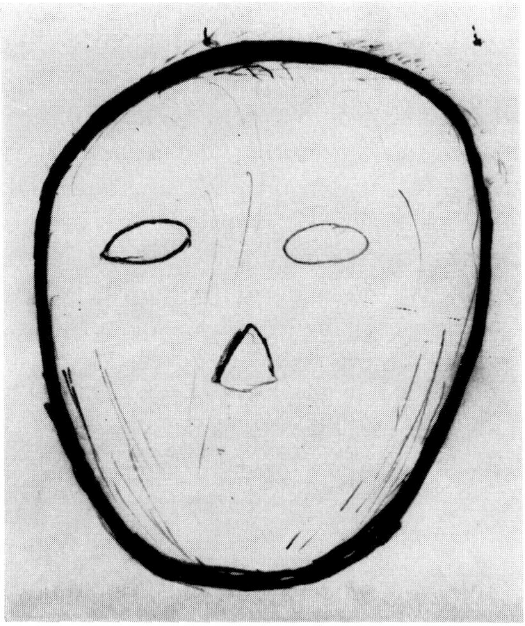

Figure 10

She rated superior in intelligence and had been accepted at a university for her college work.

Both parents recognized the emotional basis for Shirley's behavior and wisely the father brought no pressure to bear on her directly; and the mother denied critical attitudes toward Shirley, though one received the impression that she was covering up her true feelings. This was later substantiated by Shirley. There was, however, a difference in the parental religions which indirectly produced additional conflict in Shirley. As a result Shirley is excessively religious, though her scrupulousness is also associated with her compulsive pattern.

At the first therapeutic interview Shirley was adamant in her contention that she could never return to school. She said, "I don't want to go to school, because I don't want to see anyone; and I don't want anyone to see me—I get the grades but can't study as I should—I feel under criticism and then I cry—I even turn things into criticism—I have to try to prove my inferiority—I feel I'm trying to hurt myself somehow—I'm bothered by religious obligations which I am unable to filfill."

During psychiatric interview Shirley was friendly, spontaneous and cooperative. She displayed considerable anxiety and apparently always anticipated rejection and a lack of understanding from others. She felt threatened by life situations and used denial and withdrawal as defensive mechanisms. Her idealized self-image is impossible of attainment because her severe feelings of inferiority permit her to see herself only as a failure. In general she deals with her problems in a schizoid manner; and her defenses include denial, repression, withdrawal and phobias.

Figure 13—"I see a red bird with a yellow beak and a sort of black mask on its face—its mouth is open, its tongue is moving, and it seems to be making a great deal of noise—it seems rather angry—its feet are wrapped very tightly around the branch on

Figure 11

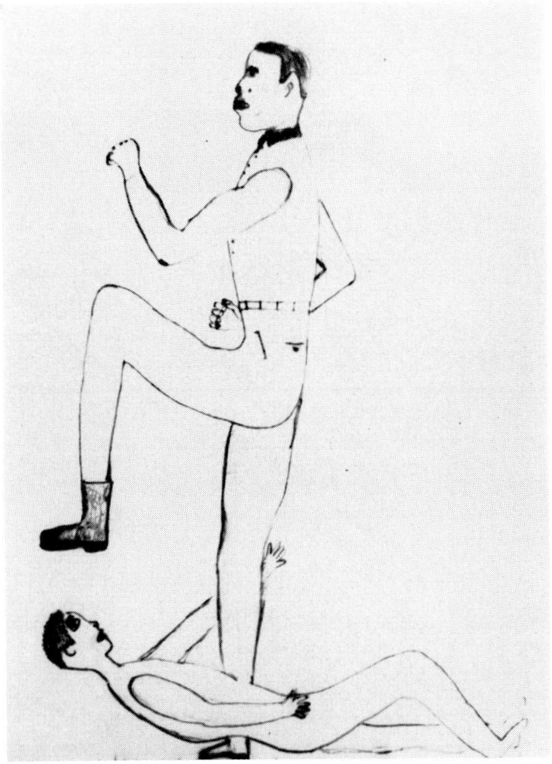

Figure 12

which it is sitting. As it stood there it seemed to dart its head around in different directions. The bird seemed rather distasteful to me—it was making too much noise and moving too fast and jerkily—its actions suggested fanatiscism to me. It seemed to personify the way I feel inside when I'm talking to people. Maybe the tightly clenched feet are a symbol of the trapped feeling I get when I talk to people about the things they want to talk about. Maybe I want to violently disagree with the person I'm conversing with just as the bird is disagreeing with its surroundings—or maybe it just has its mouth open because it is hungry for something. That reminds me of myself because I eat a lot but never feel satisfied—I guess I expect the food to give me a kind of emotional satisfaction."

The need for love and dependency is symbolized by the open

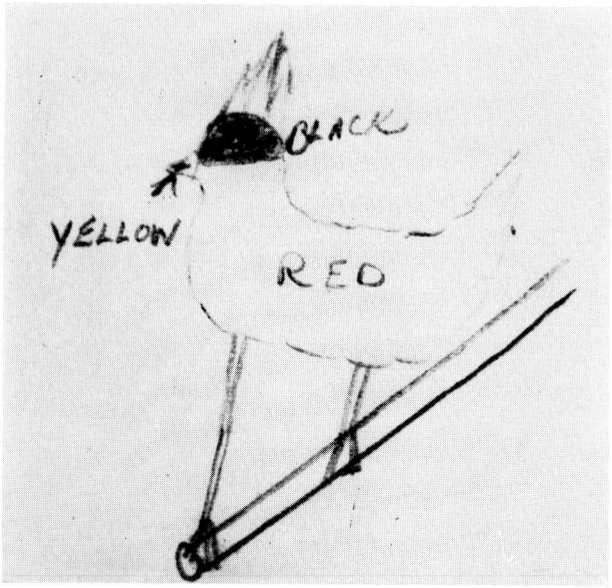

Figure 13

mouth; the moving tongue and the accompanying noise reveal the need for autonomy or ego integration. The anger arises from the anxiety which has been provoked. The darting of the head from side to side indicates the beginning motivation to find a solution to her conflict. The motivation becomes increasingly strong, as she relates her need for a good relationship with people even though she disagrees with them. The first recognition that she possesses potentialities of which she had not been aware is encountered in her statement: "I eat a lot but I never feel satisfied. I guess I expect the food to give me a kind of emotional satisfaction."

Figure 14—"The changes occurred in the bird after I said that people do not evaluate people by the right criteria. The bird then appeared to close its mouth and be more quiet. (As the bird closes its mouth, dependency needs are undergoing favorable resolution; anxiety is allayed, and the anger decreased.) It had a quizzical look on its face, however; and it seemed to be looking at its surroundings more intently. Its eyes seemed very shiny and black and perceptive. Perhaps the bird quieted down because the

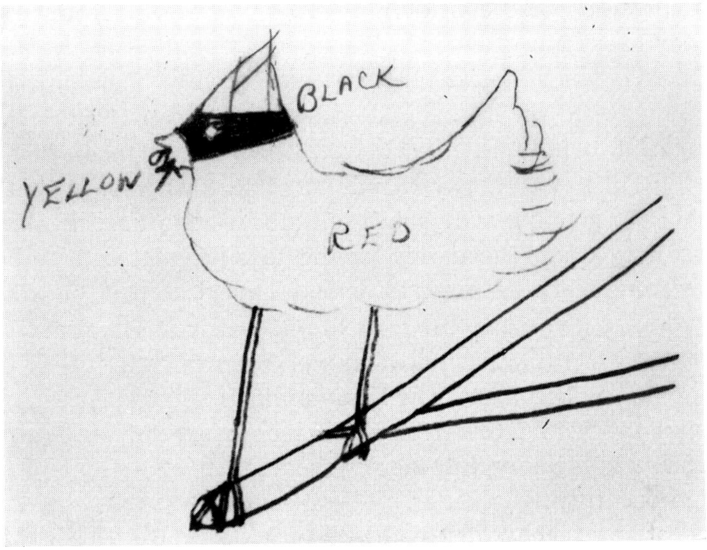

Figure 14

statement I made about people was bothering me a great deal. (She had commented that none of the people talked about worthwhile things. She said all they think about is looks, clothes, money, etc.) Perhaps I see myself as knowing more about the real essence of things than most people do."

Figure 15—"I see a horse—the horse is wearing a bit and bridle—someone is sitting on its back and tugging at the reins. This is

Figure 15

annoying the horse considerably—it is a horse that pulls people in wagons—it is a carriage horse. It is showing its teeth in a sort of snarl. It has yellow teeth. It is plainly very uncomfortable at having anyone on its back. Perhaps this means that I feel as though I'm being pushed or driven—it could also mean that I am rebelling at the authority that others held over me, in that they are able to give me orders and tell me what to do. I have never consciously experienced this feeling to any great extent. I have never minded being given orders; I have just been afraid that I would not be able to carry them out satisfactorily. Once again, the horse was rather repellent to me."

The person tugging at the horse's rein is becoming much more strongly motivated. She is on the horse's back, but she is also the horse and is bringing into her awareness her anger and rebellion at authoritative figures. She will not return to school at the command of any teacher or truant officer. Consciously she has never resented orders and used the mechanism of denial as a defense against their emergence into the conscious. This augmented the hostility.

At the next therapeutic interview Shirley quickly announced that she had returned to school. She was making up the work lost

Figure 16

in ten weeks of absence. She had had three therapeutic interviews.

Figure 16—"Now the person is off the horse's back—the horse no longer looks annoyed and is just standing looking at its feet and all around as though it doesn't know what to do. This probably means that if I had no authority over me that I wouldn't be any more satisfied than I am now, chafing under authority, as it were. The horse looks better now."

Figure 17—Shirley's comments were as follows: "I see a bird. The bird is a very bright pretty blue. It has a white stripe down the back and white circles around its eyes. It has black legs and feet. It is much more pleasing to me than were the other images. It is located in a more pleasant place too—a tree with grey branches and pink and white flowers. I rather think it is a magnolia tree. The bird is neither unhappy nor excited. It seems

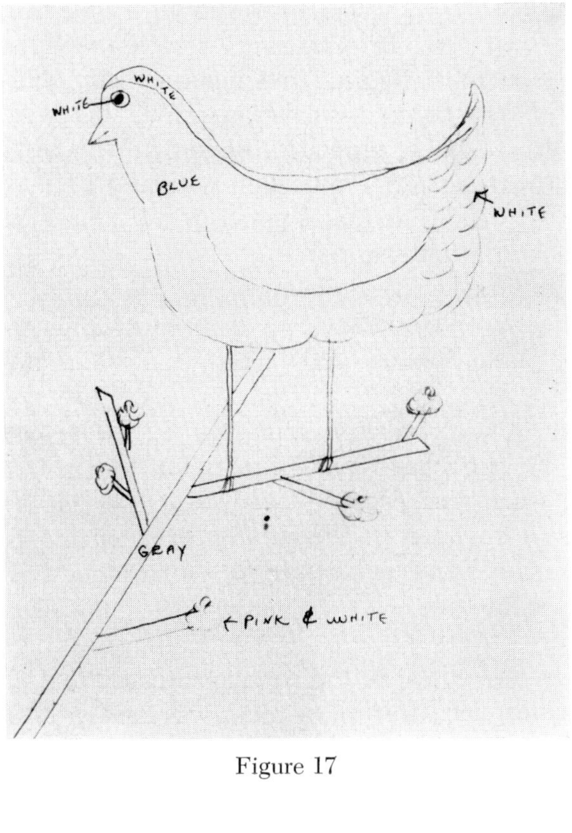

Figure 17

rather calm. It is swinging on the branch as though it's playing a game. The bird is thinking that perhaps it would like to get off the branch and go somewhere else, but it does not know exactly how. I think it knows it can fly, but it is just refusing to think about it. Finally it gets tired of pretending it can't fly and flies away. This is like me because I want to do things and go places, but I usually do not because I tell myself I won't be a success at whatever I'm going to do. Somewhere back in my mind I know that there are things that I can do and do well, but I don't have any feelings to back up my thought. Sometimes I actually see proof (as in the tests, etc.) that I have done better than anyone else, but I still don't feel as though I have."

Shirley has recognized the favorable change in her hallucinated unconscious body image. She feels an increase in self-worth, which in turn is a motivating force. This is needed at this point to resolve the schizoid trends expressed in her verbalization of a flat affect. The need to overcome obstacles and the need for achievement motivate her to strive toward a goal. The same goal-directed behavior accounts for her return to school. How beautifully she expresses the growing recognition of her potentialities when she says—"Somewhere back in my mind I know that there are things that I can do and do well, but I don't have any feelings to back up my thought."

The four cases described illustrate only a few of the underlying needs which motivate behavior and make possible the development of potentialities both in the intellectual and in the emotional areas.

The therapeutic modality employing the hallucination of unconscious body images rapidly brings into the patient's awareness the pathological psychodynamic material and is almost invariably well tolerated by the patient. Probing into the past becomes minimal and overshadowed by the awareness of emotional needs which in turn serve as motivations for a change in behavior. In all the cases presented the ideo-sensory and ideo-motor experiences made possible the conscious recognition of pathological motivations, and thus the patient was enabled to resolve the pathology and to utilize his psychic energy in creative and constructive responses.

Even the relatively healthy and relatively normal personality is hampered in the actualization of constructive and creative potentialities by energy spent in defense against id forces as well as by the demands of a rigid superego. The sensitivity of the perceptive apparatus is markedly increased in the hypnotic state; the subject becomes more or less oblivious to external stimuli. Thus, he becomes so involved in himself that he is able to explore his subjective experiences in a more meaningful manner. These then become part of his awareness.

Awareness has an intrinsic and absolute value and, in employing the hypnotic hallucination of the unconscious body images, the relatively healthy and relatively normal individual can also experience motivations for the recognition of and the development of hitherto unknown potentialities.

REFERENCES

1. Freytag, Fredericka F.: *Hypnosis and the Body Image*. New York, The Julian Press, 1961.
2. Freytag, Fredericka F.: The hallucinated unconscious body image. *The American Journal of Clinical Hypnosis, VII*:3 (Jan.), 1965.

Chapter 35

GESTALT THERAPY AND HUMAN POTENTIALITIES

FREDERICK S. PERLS

GESTALT therapy is one of the rebellious, humanistic, existential forces in psychology which seeks to stem the avalanche of self-defeating, self-destructive forces among some members of our society. It is "existential" in a broad sense. All schools of existentialism emphasize direct experience, but most of them have some conceptual framework: Kierkegaard had his Protestant theology; Buber his Judaism; Sartre his communism; and Binswanger his psychoanalysis. Gestalt therapy is fully ontological in that it recognizes both conceptual activity and the biological formation of *Gestalten.* It is thus self-supporting and truly experiential.

Our aim as therapists is to increase human potential through the process of integration. We do this by supporting the individual's genuine interests, desires and needs.

Many of the individual's needs contend with those of society. Competitiveness, need for control, demands for perfection and immaturity are characteristic of our current culture. Out of this background emerge both the curse and the cause of our neurotic social behavior. In such a context no psychotherapy can be successful; no unsatisfactory marriage can be improved. But, more importantly, the individual is unable to dissolve his own inner conflicts and to achieve integration.

Conflicts extend to the external as well. In demanding identification and submission to a self-image, society's neurotic expectations further dissociate the individual from his own nature. The first and last problem for the individual is to integrate within and yet be accepted by society.

Society demands conformity through education; it emphasizes and rewards development of the individual's intellect. In my language I call the intellect a "built-in computer." Each culture and the individuals composing it have created certain concepts and images of ideal social behavior, or how the individual "should" function within its framework of reference. In order to be accepted by society, the individual responds with a sum of fixed responses. He arrives at these responses by "computing" what he considers to be the appropriate reaction. In order to comply with the "should" demands of society, the individual learns to disregard his own feelings, desires and emotions. He, too, then dissociates himself from being a part of nature.

Paradoxically, the more society demands that the individual live up to its concepts and ideas, the less efficiently can the individual function. This basic conflict between the demands of society and one's inner nature results in tremendous expenditures of energy. It is well known that the individual ordinarily uses only 10 to 25 per cent of his potential. However, in times of emergency, it is possible for the conditioned responses to collapse. Integration becomes spontaneous. In such situations the individual is able to cope directly with obstacles and, at times, achieve heroic results. Gestalt therapy seeks to bring about integration without the urgency of emergency situations.

The more the character relies on ready-made concepts, fixed forms of behavior and "computing," the less able is he to use his senses and intuition. When the individual attempts to live according to preconceived ideas of what the world "should" be like, he brackets off his own feelings and needs. The result of this alienation from one's senses is the blocking off of his potential and the distortion of his perspective.

The critical point during any development, both collectively and individually, is the ability to differentiate between *self*-actualization and the actualization of a *concept*. Expectations are products of our fantasy. The greater the discrepancy between what one can be through one's inborn potential and the superimposed, idealistic concepts, the greater the strain and the likelihood of failure. I give a ridiculously exaggerated example. An elephant wants to be a rose bush; a rose bush wants to be an elephant. Until each resigns to being what they are, both will lead unhappy lives of inferiority. The self-actualizer expects the possible.

The one who wants to actualize a concept attempts the impossible.

In responding to "should" demands, the individual plays a role not supported by genuine needs. He becomes both phony and phobic. He shies away from seeing his limitations and plays roles unsupported by his potential. By seeking cues for behavior from the outside, he "computes" and responds with reactions not basically his own. He constructs an imaginary ideal of how he "should" be and not how he actually is.

The concept of perfection is such an ideal. In responding, the individual develops a phony facade to impress others what a good boy he is. Demands for perfection limit the individual's ability to function within himself, in the therapeutic situation, in marriage as well as other social situations.

One can observe in marital difficulties that either one or both of the marriage partners are not in love with the spouse but with an image of perfection. Inevitably, the partner falls short of those expectations. The mutual frustration of not finding perfection results in tension, increased hostility which results in a permanent status quo, an impasse or, at best, a useless divorce. The same condition applies to the therapeutic situation. Either a status quo of many years or a change of therapists occurs, but *never* a cure.

By turning his perfectionistic demands toward himself, the neurotic tears himself to pieces in order to live up to his unrealistic ideal. Though perfection is generally labeled an "ideal," it is actually a cheap curse which punishes and tortures both the self and others for not living up to an impossible goal.

At least two more phenomena interfere with the development of man's genuine potential. One is the formation of character. The individual then can act only with a limited, fixed set of responses. The other is the phobic attitude which is far more widespread than psychiatry has been willing to recognize thus far.

Freud was the genius of half-truths. His investigations of repression, blocks and inhibitions reveal his own phobic attitude concerning phobias. Once an impulse becomes dangerous, we turn, according to Freud, actively against it and put a *cordon sanitaire* around it. Wilhelm Reich made this attitude still more explicit in his armor theory. But danger is not always aggressively neutralized. More often we avoid and flee from it. Thus, by avoiding the means and ways of avoidance, we miss half the tools for a cure.

The organism avoids actual pains. The neurotic avoids imaginary hurts such as unpleasant emotions. He also avoids taking reasonable risks. Both interfere with any chance of maturation.

Consequently, in Gestalt therapy we draw the patient's attention to his avoidance of any unpleasantness. We work through the subtle machinations of phobic behavior in addition to working through the blocks, inhibitions and other protective attitudes.

To work through imaginary pains and unpleasant emotions we need a fine balance of frustration and support. Once the patient feels the essence of the "here and Now" and "i and Thou," he begins to understand his phobic behavior.

At first the patient will do anything to keep his attention from his actual experiences. He will take flight into memory and expectation (past and future); into the flight of ideas (free associations); intellectualizations or "making a case" of right and wrong. Finally, he encounters the holes in his personality with an awareness of nothing (no-thing-ness), emptiness, void and the impasse.

At last the patient comes to realize the hallucinatory character of his suffering. He discovers that "he does not have to" torture himself. He acquires a greater tolerance for frustration and imaginary pain. At this point he begins to mature.

I define maturity as the transition from environmental support to self-support. In Gestalt therapy maturity is achieved by developing the individual's own potential through decreasing environmental support, increasing his frustration tolerance and by debunking his phony *playing* of infantile and adult roles.

Resistance is great because the patient has been conditioned to manipulate his environment for support. He does this by acting helpless and stupid; he wheedles, bribes and flatters. He *is not* infantile but plays an infantile and dependent role expecting to control the situation by submissive behavior. He also plays the roles of an infantile adult. It is difficult for him to realize the difference between mature behavior and "playing an adult." With maturation the patient is increasingly able to mobilize spontaneously his own resources in order to deal with the environment. He learns to stand on his own feet, thus becoming able to cope with his own problems as well as the exigencies of life.

Human potential is decreased both by inappropriate demands of society and by the inner conflict. Freud's parable of the two servants quarrelling, with the resultant inefficiency, is again, in my opinion, but a half-truth. Actually, it is the masters who quarrel. In this case the opposing masters are what Freud named *superego* and *id*. The *id* in Freud's concept is a conglomeration of instincts and repressed memories. In actuality we observe in each and every case that the *superego* is opposed by a personalized entity which might be called *infraego*. In my language I call the opposing masters Top Dog and Under Dog. The struggle between the two is both internal and external.

Top Dog can be described as righteous, bullying, punishing, authoritarian and primitive. Top Dog commands continually with such statements as, "You should," "You ought to" and "Why don't you?" Oddly enough, we all so strongly identify with our inner Top Dog that we no longer question its authority. We take its righteousness for granted.

Under Dog develops great skill in evading Top Dog's commands. Only half-heartedly intending to comply with the demands, Under Dog answers: "Yes, but . . . ," "I try so hard but next time I'll do better," and "Mañana." Under Dog usually gets the better of the conflict.

In other words, Top and Under Dogs are actually two clowns performing their weird and unnecessary plays on the stage of the tolerant and mute self. Integration, or cure, can be achieved only when the need for mutual control between Top and Under Dogs ceases. Only then will the two masters mutually listen. Once they come to their senses (in this case listening to each other) does the door to integration and unification open. The chance of making a whole person out of a split becomes a certainty. The impasse of the status quo or the eternal conflict of the nonending therapy can be overcome.

A Gestaltist integration technique is dream work. We do not play psychoanalytical interpretation games. I have the suspicion that the dream is neither a fulfilled wish nor a prophecy of the future. To me it is an existential message. It tells the patient what his situation in life is and especially how to change the nightmare of his existence into becoming aware of and taking his historical place in life. In a successful cure the neurotic awakens from his trance of delusions. In Zen Buddhism the moment is called the great awakening *(satori)*. During Gestalt therapy the patient experiences a number of lesser awakenings. In coming to his senses he frequently sees the world brightly and clearly.

In actual practice I let the patient act out all the details of his dream. As therapists we do not imagine we know more than the patient does himself. We assume each part of the dream is a projection. Each fragment of the dream, be it person, prop or mood, is a portion of the patient's *alienated* self. Parts of the self are made to encounter other parts. The primary encounter, of course, is between Top Dog and Under Dog.

To illustrate the method of integrating Top and Under Dogs by working through a dream, I relate a case of a patient who impressed everybody with his psychotic eccentricities. During one of my group sessions he related a dream in which he saw a young man enter a library, throw books about, shout and scream. When the librarian, an elderly spinster, rebuked him, he reacted with continued erratic behavior. In desperation the librarian summoned the police.

I directed my patient to act out and experience the encounter between the boy (Under Dog) and the librarian and police (Top Dogs). In the beginning the confrontation was belligerent and uselessly consuming of time and energy. After participating in the hostile encounter for two hours, the different parts of my patient were able to stop fighting and listen to each other. True listening *is* understanding. He came to recognize that by playing "crazy" he could outwit his Top Dog, because the irresponsible person is not punished. Following this successful integration the patient no longer needed to act crazy in order to be spontaneous. As a result he is now a freer and more amenable person.

When Top Dog feeds Under Dog expectations of success, results, improvements and changes, Under Dog generally responds with pseudo-compliance or sabotage. The result is inefficiency and spite. If the Under Dog sincerely tries to comply, he has the choice between an obsessional neurosis, flight into illness or "nervous breakdown." *The road to Hell is paved with good intentions.*

Externally, Top and Under Dogs struggle for control as well. Husband and wife, therapist and patient, employer and employees play out roles of mutual manipulation.

The basic philosophy of Gestalt therapy is that of nature—differentiation and integration. Differentiation by itself leads to polarities. As dualities these polarities will easily fight and paralyze one another. By integrating opposite traits we make the person whole again. For instance, weakness and bullying integrate as silent firmness.

Such a person will have the perspective to see the total situation (a *gestalt*) without losing the details. With this improved orientation he is in a better position to cope with the situation by *mobilizing his own resources.* He no longer reacts with fixed responses (character) and preconceived ideas. He doesn't cry for environmental support, because he can do for himself. He no longer lives motivated by fears of impending catastrophes. He can now assess reality by *experimenting with possibilities.* He will *give up* control-madness and let the *situation* dictate his actions.

The ability to resign, to let go of obsolete responses, of exhausted relationships and of tasks beyond one's potential is an essential part of the wisdom of living.

REFERENCES

1. Perls, Frederick S.: *Ego, Hunger and Aggression.* London, Allen and Unwin, 5-273, 1947.
2. Perls, Frederick S., Hefferline, Ralph F., and Goodman, Paul: *Gestalt Therapy.* New York, The Julian Press, 1951.
3. Perls, Frederick S.: Theory and technique of personality integration. *Amer. J. Psychother., II*:565-586, 1948.
4. Perls, Laura P.: In Barron, J., and Harper, R. A. (ed.): The Gestalt Approach. *Ann. Psychother., 1* and *2*, 1961.
5. Perls, Laura P.: Notes on the psychology of give and take. *Complex, 9*: 24-30, 1953.
6. Perls, Frederick S.: Morality, ego-boundary and aggression. *Complex,* 9:42, 51, 1955.

INDEX

C

D

M

N

O

P

R